"The Most
   Segregated
   City in
   America"

Charles E. Connerly

"The Most Segregated City in America"

City Planning and Civil Rights in Birmingham, 1920–1980

University of Virginia Press
Charlottesville and London

University of Virginia Press
© 2005 by the Rector and Visitors of the University of Virginia
All rights reserved
Printed in the United States of America on acid-free paper
First published 2005

9 8 7 6 5 4 3 2 1

Library of Congress Cataloging-in-Publication Data

Connerly, Charles E., 1946–
    "The most segregated city in America" : city planning and civil rights in
Birmingham, 1920–1980 / Charles E. Connerly.
        p.   cm.
    Includes bibliographical references and index.
    ISBN 0-8139-2334-4 (cloth : alk. paper)
    1. Segregation—Alabama—Birmingham—History—20th century. 2. City
planning—Alabama—Birmingham—History—20th century. 3. African
Americans—Civil rights—Alabama—Birmingham—History—20th century.
4. Civil rights movements—Alabama—Birmingham—History—20th century.
5. Birmingham (Ala.)—Race relations—History—20th century. I. Title.
    F334.B69N428 2005
    307.1'216'089960730761781—dc22

                                                                    2004023112

This book is published in association with the Center for American Places,
Santa Fe, New Mexico, and Staunton, Virginia (www.americanplaces.org).

For Steve Lembesis,
who showed me the way
to Birmingham

Contents

Illustrations

Tables

Acknowledgments

This book owes its origins to several times, places, and people. In some respects, it began in Birmingham's pivotal year, 1963, when the civil rights revolution came into my white, suburban Chicago life courtesy of the Huntley-Brinkley nightly news. The images of Birmingham and other civil rights battlegrounds that year were planted firmly in my mind. Out of this sprang what has become a lifelong interest in the civil rights movement as a shining example of disenfranchised individuals and groups using their power as a people to achieve social change and justice. Five years later, as a senior at Grinnell College, I had the privilege of participating in an urban history seminar with Grinnell history professor Al Jones. In 1968, urban history was just emerging as an identifiable academic field, and I was fortunate that Professor Jones decided he wanted to share this new field with the students in his senior American history seminar.

Four years later, I began graduate study in American history at the University of Connecticut. By that time, urban history had taken off as a field, and I was privileged to study that subject under Bruce Stave. After I wrote a history of urban renewal in Hartford, Connecticut, he encouraged me to pursue doctoral study in urban history. Given the history job market at that time, I decided to instead pursue graduate study in urban and regional planning at the University of Michigan. As I rushed to become a social scientist, I left my urban history interests behind, or so I thought, and began a focus on housing and community development, particularly in industrial cities, such as Detroit, under the able supervision of Al Feldt and Bob Marans.

In 1981, I arrived as a brand-new assistant professor of urban and regional planning at Florida State University. Just as Dorothy of the *Wizard of Oz* famously realized that she was not in Kansas anymore, I discovered that in moving to the Sunbelt, I was no longer in Michigan or any other place that featured older, industrial cities that had attracted my interest in graduate school. I was also living in the South, a place that I only knew from twenty-year-old images on the nightly news. Preferring to work and live in the same region, I struggled with how I would incorporate my new residence with my research interests.

Steve Lembesis, a native of Birmingham, provided the answer, and that is why this book is dedicated to him. Prior to entering Florida State's master's program in 1982, Steve had worked as a community resource officer in Birmingham's Citizen Participation Program. As Steve was my research assistant and student, I had the opportunity to talk to him about the changes that had taken place in Birmingham since 1963 that would result in a city as notoriously unjust as Birmingham adopting a program for empowering all its neighborhoods in city planning and community development. In 1984, Steve convinced me to take a group of students on a field trip to Birmingham, an opportunity that also enabled me to begin to meet public officials and neighborhood leaders in that city. Over the course of four additional field trips, my interest in that city and how it has dealt with issues of civil rights and city planning grew to the point that I knew I needed to do more than visit the city for two days each year. Sadly, Steve passed away in 1993 and so is not able to enjoy the completion of the project that he inspired me to begin.

What finally got me going on this book was the birth of another field of history, the history of city planning. In 1986, Larry Gerckens organized the first meeting of the Society for American City and Regional Planning History (SACRPH) in Columbus, Ohio, and I was among the first to join that organization. Within that context, I soon recognized that the best way to get a handle on Birmingham was to write a history of city planning there. After I began the project, I also recognized that the most compelling lens through which to examine Birmingham's city planning history was through its relationship with the city's race issues and with the civil rights movement. As my work progressed, I soon realized the very significant role that city planning has played in Birmingham's racial and civil rights history as well as the impact that the city's racial history has had on the practice of city planning in Birmingham. This recognition came from collaborative work and many fruitful conversations with friend and colleague Bobby Wilson, formerly a faculty member at the University of Alabama at Birmingham and more recently professor of geography at the University of Alabama at Tuscaloosa. The interaction between city planning and civil rights and its implications for the practice of city planning in Birmingham and elsewhere is the story that I try to tell in this book.

There are many others who have played important roles in supporting my research in Birmingham. In Birmingham, Betty Bock, Mike Dobbins, Ed LaMonte, Chuck Lewis, Charles Moore, David Sink, and Odessa Woolfolk have given freely of their time and insights. Ed LaMonte very generously made it possible for me to stay on the campus of Birmingham-Southern College on a number of my trips and continues to send Florida State top-quality urban and regional planning students from Birmingham-Southern. Charles Moore and his family welcomed me into their home as an overnight guest. Chuck Lewis and his family also had me as a guest in their home for dinner, and I had the opportunity to interview Chuck about his experiences in the creation of Birmingham's Citizen Participation Program. While working in Birmingham, I met Glenn Eskew when he was completing his doctoral dissertation on Birmingham, and I enjoyed his enthusiastic support for my research as I enjoyed the fine book, *But for Birmingham,* that emerged from his work.

Most of my time in Birmingham was spent searching the archives and holdings of the Birmingham Public Library. Birmingham and the Public Library have done a wonderful job of archiving the city's rich history, and many historians have benefited greatly. Marvin Whiting, who founded the Archives, has always been tremendously helpful and supportive, as has Jim Baggett, the current city archivist. Assisting them and greatly helping me have been Don Veasey, Jim Murray, Beth Willauer, and Yolanda Valentin. In the Southern History Department of the Birmingham Public Library, Yvonne Crumpler and Francine Cooper have been immensely helpful. All of these people not only provided superb service but also taught me about southern grace and manners, something that any guy from Chicago can stand to learn. I also benefited greatly from the staff and records at the National Archives in College Park, Maryland, and the assistance the staff gave me at the Alabama Department of Archives and History and the Alabama Highway Department, both in Montgomery. Finally, the University of Alabama at Birmingham Mervyn Sterne Library and their staff have been very helpful and hospitable.

My colleagues and friends in the Society of American City and Regional Planning History were the first people I approached about my plans to write a book on Birmingham, and they have always been supportive. In particular, June Manning Thomas and Chris Silver have offered much support, insight, and friendship. I've also benefited greatly from the comments, interest, and enthusiasm of other SACRPH scholars: Bob Fairbanks, Marsha Ritzdorf, FSU planning colleague Greg Thompson, Carl Abbott, Genie Birch, Daphne Spain, Mary Corbin Sies, Patricia Burgess, Ray Mohl, Ronald Bayor, Mark Rose, Marc Weiss, Bruce Stephenson, Alison, Isenberg, and David Schuyler. Heywood Sanders was especially generous with an excerpt from his dissertation that described how the Ensley Urban Renewal project used the construction of the interstate as a racial barrier. Outside of SACRPH, planning colleagues Charles Hoch and Dennis Gale have been supportive as well.

Closer to home, I've benefited greatly from the support of family, friends, colleagues, and graduate students. Neighbor, fellow planner, and friend Howard Pardue has followed this book project for a long time and fortunately, early on, helped me locate his relative in Birmingham, Chuck Lewis. Graduate students in urban and regional planning providing very helpful support and assistance include Joseph Addae-Mensa, John Bunn, David Alvarez, Carlos Carrero, Nancy Muller, Ramona Creel, Charles Warnken, Corianne Scally, Blair Kirtley, Jerry Anthony, Sue Trone, Karen Merritt, LaRhonda Odom, Santanu Roy, Dawn Jourdan, Ayana Perez Shepherd, and Birmingham natives Suzanne Schmith and Frank Duke. History graduate student Lynn Feldman did her master's thesis on the Smithfield neighborhood (later published as a fine book, *A Sense of Place*) and, along with her husband, John Ingham, have been very supportive and helpful over the years.

Florida State University has always been very supportive of this project. The university, along with the National Endowment for the Humanities, have provided financial support for travel to archives. Three College of Social Sciences deans, Chuck Cnudde, Marie Cowart, and David Rasmussen, have provided support, as have my colleagues in the Florida State Department of Urban and Regional Planning, who permitted me to take a sabbatical and patiently waited for me to finish this project. In particular, Bruce Stiftel, who was my department chair and journal co-editor in the early years of this project, has always made it possible for me to balance my other responsibilities with the completion of this book. Retired urban and regional planning professor Jim Frank has always been very supportive and encouraging as well. I also appreciate the interest and encouragement given to me by my History Department colleagues, especially Peter Garretson, Rodney Anderson, Neil Betten, Maxine Jones, and Jim Jones.

The staff of the Department of Urban and Regional Planning, Kathy Dispennette, Cynthia Brown, Mackie Knight, and Shawn Lewers, have also made it much easier to finish this project, especially in the past six years that I have served as department chair. Both Kathy Dispennette and Cavell Kyser have provided much valuable assistance in the preparation of the final manuscript, with Kathy seeing the project through to the very end and Cavell preparing the initial manuscript and the index. Shawn Lewers has done a fine job of preparing maps for the book. The staff of the Florida State University Library, especially the head of the documents division, Judy DePew, and her staff, including Anne Gomez and Marcia Gorin, as well as the interlibrary loan staff, have been very helpful in meeting my requests.

The staff at the Center for American Places—George Thompson, director, and Randy Jones—have been very supportive of this project. The staff of the University of Virginia Press, led by director Penelope Kaiserlian, have been very enthusiastic, prompt, and flexible. They include Ellen Satrom, Martha Farlow, Mary MacNeil, and Emily Grandstaff. Copy editor Susan Brady has done a terrific job of screening and preparing the manuscript.

I wish to also thank my family for supporting me in this project throughout the years, even as it meant frequent trips to Birmingham. My daughter and son, Beth and Robert, have understood and patiently accepted the time away from home this book has required. My wife, Martha Ann Crawford, has always been very supportive of my academic interests, encouraging me to get a Ph.D. when I had other ideas and never begrudging me the time spent three hundred miles away in Birmingham. As a native Texan, I think she also delighted in my growing appreciation for the South and the people who live there that this book has taught me. Finally, I want to thank my parents, Jim and Muriel Connerly, for instilling in me the values of hard work and loyalty that have enabled me to finish this project.

I wish to acknowledge Johns Hopkins University Press for granting permission to republish revised portions of work that originally appeared in "Federal Urban Policy and the Birth of Democratic Planning in Birmingham, Alabama: 1949–1974," published in *Planning the Twentieth-Century American City,* 1996, edited by Mary Corbin Sies and Christopher Silver. That material appears in chapters 6 and 7 of this book. I also wish to acknowledge Sage Publications for granting permission to republish the following: "'One Great City' or Colonial Economy? Explaining Birmingham's Annexation Struggles, 1945–1990," *Journal of Urban History* (November 1999): 44–73, which now appears in altered form in chapter 6 and the epilogue; "From Racial Zoning to Community Empowerment: The Interstate Highway System and the African-American Community in Birmingham, Alabama," *Journal of Planning Education and Research* (December 2002): 99–114, which now appears in altered form in chapters 5 and 8; and "The Roots and Origins of African-American Planning in Birmingham, Alabama" (coauthored with Bobby Wilson), in *In the Shadows: Historical Notes on Planning and the African-American Community,* edited by June Thomas and Marsha Ritzdorf, 201–19 (Sage, 1997), which now appears in revised form in chapter 7.

In Birmingham, you would be living in a community where the white man's long-lived tyranny had cowed your people, led them to abandon hope, and developed in them a false sense of inferiority. You would be living in a city where the representatives of economic and political power refused to even discuss social justice with the leaders of your people.

You would be living in the largest city of a police state, presided over by a governor—George Wallace—whose inauguration vow had been a pledge of "segregation now, segregation tomorrow, segregation forever!" You would be living, in fact, in the most segregated city in America.

—Martin Luther King Jr., *Why We Can't Wait*

Introduction

City planning and civil rights have had a profound influence on each other. Birmingham, a city well known for its civil rights history, is less well known for its city planning history and the connection between city planning and civil rights. Formal city planning in Birmingham began in 1920 with the publication a year earlier of the city's first plan and the passage several years later of the city's first zoning ordinance. Because the zoning ordinance institutionalized racial zoning—the practice of separating whites from blacks through land use zoning—it also marked the beginning of city planning's impact on civil rights in Birmingham. This impact lasted through the 1970s as the city and its black community adapted planning to their particular needs. By the end of the 1970s, Birmingham's civil rights era had ended. No longer was the city controlled by white politicians who sought to limit the rights of the city's black residents. By 1980, Birmingham's black population was in the majority. The city had elected its first black mayor, Richard Arrington, in the fall of 1979. This is not to say that race and racism were not issues after 1980, but rather that the city's government no longer consciously and systematically practiced racism in its city planning functions.

Although race has been an important topic of planning research, planning's place in the history of civil rights and the civil rights movement in the United States has not been a major area of focus. Many accounts of the civil rights movement barely mention urban planning and its effect on civil rights.[1] But urban planning—particularly through zoning, urban renewal, and public housing—has had a significant impact on where blacks could live and therefore on their freedom to live in decent neighborhoods with good public services.[2] Although the civil rights movement of the 1960s, particularly in the South, was often fought over Jim Crow laws requiring segregation in schools, parks, buses, and other public accommodations, these battles were fought within the context of racially divided cities whose social geography had been shaped, at least in part, by city planning.

At its roots, city planning is about controlling the land—most directly about what uses land is put to—but also, at least indirectly, about who gets to live on the land and where. From its earliest days, city planning and its primary regulatory tool, zoning, have been used not only to determine land use but also to protect property values and keep out or restrict groups of people whose presence was not desired by those in power.[3] The latter purposes also lie at the heart of the white establishment's efforts to erect and maintain racial segregation in Birmingham. Fundamentally, the battle for civil rights in Birmingham, as well as in other cities, was fought over who controls the land, with whites attempting to limit where and under what circumstances blacks could live. Moreover, the tension this battle created was heightened by the fact that for the entire twentieth century, African Americans constituted at least 38 percent of the city's residents. Therefore, the struggle for land that lay at the root of Birmingham's civil rights conflicts was, at least in the eyes of the white establishment, a struggle for control of the city. Because city planning lay at the heart of the city's civil rights battle, it provides a key lens through which to view Birmingham's civil rights history as well as the civil rights experience of other cities where planning was racially motivated.

By examining Birmingham, where civil rights history of national significance was made, we can more clearly observe the impact that planning had on civil rights and that civil rights had on planning. The spring 1963 "children's crusade" of black civil rights protests, led by Fred Shuttlesworth and Martin Luther King Jr., who called Birmingham "the most segregated city in America," set the stage for the 1964 Civil Rights Act and the beginning steps by the federal government to end racial discrimination in the U.S.[4] "But for Birmingham," Fred Shuttlesworth recalled President John Kennedy saying in June 1963 when the president invited black leaders to meet with him, "we would not be here today."[5]

But city planning heavily influenced Birmingham's civil rights history. In the 1920s, Birmingham used city planning as a rationale for adopting a racial zoning law, even though the U.S. Supreme Court, in its 1917 *Buchanan v. Warley* decision, had struck down racial zoning.

Comprehensive planning and zoning, popularized in the 1920s, offered southern cities what appeared to be a legal means by which they could separate white and black neighborhoods and thereby sidestep *Buchanan v. Warley*. The result was the South's longest-standing racial zoning law, lasting from 1926 until 1951, when it was declared unconstitutional by the U.S. Supreme Court.

In the 1930s, Birmingham implemented the federal public housing program in a racially segregated context. In the 1940s, Birmingham's black citizens rebelled against the city's racial zoning law and challenged it both in court and in practice by purchasing homes in neighborhoods designated for whites. Because the racial zoning law was rooted in the adoption of city planning in the 1920s, the black community's efforts to challenge the law was a challenge to city planning and its role as a determinant of who lived where. The white community responded, as it did often throughout Birmingham's civil rights history, by using government and the courts to block black entry into white neighborhoods and by using bombings and other vigilante tactics to frighten blacks who dared move into neighborhoods zoned for whites. The fifty bombings that took place in Birmingham between 1947 and 1966—which grabbed the nation's attention in 1963 when four black girls were killed in the bombing of the Sixteenth Street Baptist Church—began in response to black efforts to nullify the zoning law that separated by race as well as by land use. They did so by moving into the white North Smithfield neighborhood that forever after would be known as Dynamite Hill. City planning did not bomb the Sixteenth Street Baptist Church, but it was used to codify the segregation that those who bombed Dynamite Hill were attempting to preserve.

In the 1950s and 1960s, city planning continued to influence civil rights as Birmingham used the federal urban renewal and highway programs to segregate and relocate its black residents. These programs were used for the same purposes as racial zoning, thereby enabling the city to segregate even though the U.S. Supreme Court had declared racial zoning in Birmingham unconstitutional in 1951. Despite the loss of racial zoning that year, Birmingham was able to continue to segregate a major land use in the city: its parks. And when, in 1961, the city shut down its parks rather than integrate them, the business community that supported parks and planning as keys to economic development began to realize that segregation might be bad for the city. In the 1960s, in response to the civil rights revolution, the city also began to reform itself, but it was nevertheless very slow to open up opportunities for blacks to participate in decisions that affected the planning of their neighborhoods. Instead, the city was primarily guided by its business leaders into using planning to revitalize the downtown area. Also, in the 1960s, white fears of the city becoming majority black helped drive efforts to annex Birmingham's most affluent, white suburbs. At the same time, suburban fears of racial integration in the schools kept their residents from voting to merge with Birmingham.

In contrast to other southern cities that were able to maintain a racial balance through annexation, Birmingham's inability to annex new population meant that it would become an increasingly black and poor city as its white middle class moved to the suburbs and voted to stay independent of Birmingham. Finally, in the 1970s, black residents of Birmingham asserted increasing power and began to reform the planning process so that they were no longer its victims and could finally begin to enjoy the fruits of urban planning. In so doing, they relied on indigenous black neighborhood organizations, some formed in the 1920s and 1930s, to set the framework for what would become a citywide network of neighborhood-based organizations that would be incorporated into the city planning process. Birmingham's black citizens were assisted by increased federal attention to the equity impacts of planning decisions. Moreover, in the 1970s, a new form of planning, advocacy planning, was instrumental in obtaining increased rights for blacks to participate in the planning process.

Some might argue that Birmingham's distinctiveness as a civil rights battleground makes it a poor choice in which to study the connection between civil rights and city planning. Headlines such as "America's Johannesburg," "Bombingham," "Fear and Hatred Grip Birmingham," or "Birmingham: Integration's Hottest Crucible," have helped to create the perception that Birmingham stands apart from other southern cities and other cities in the nation as being more racist and more violent than the American norm.[6] But Birmingham's distinctiveness may not be as great as some might like to believe. As historian Henry M. McKiven Jr. has written: "Historians have repeatedly written about the failure of Birmingham and the South to enter the American mainstream. They typically cite the city's chronic racial troubles as a primary reason for the city's and region's distinctiveness. But in a perverse way Birmingham has always epitomized the national experience."[7]

While racial struggles have been vividly dramatic in Birmingham, leading in large part to passage of the Civil Rights Act of 1964, when viewed up close the city's past shares many characteristics with the rest of the United States. Racism has been endemic in other American cities, as has violence in defense of racism. Moreover, like Birmingham, other cities have used city planning to limit the rights of blacks to live where they wish. Birmingham was one of a number of southern cities that adopted racial zoning statutes, many of which, like Birmingham's, had been written by northern planning consultants.[8] Birmingham was not the only city that greeted blacks with bombs and other forms of violence as they moved into white neighborhoods. As Raymond Mohl has written, in the early 1950s other cities in which blacks were greeted with "mob violence, arson, and bomb throwing" include Chicago, Atlanta, Dallas, Kansas City, East St. Louis, Louisville, Cleveland, Philadelphia, Indianapolis, Los Angeles, and Tampa.[9] Birmingham's urban renewal program, which was basically a Negro clearance program, was not dissimilar in its impact on blacks than such programs in other cities (such as Chicago, Baltimore, Detroit, Kansas City, Cincinnati, Cleveland, Philadelphia, Norfolk, and Washington, D.C.), in which over 90 percent of the residents forced to relocate were black.[10]

Birmingham's experience with racism and city planning was one that was shared with other cities in the nation. That experience points to the very important role that housing and neighborhood played in shaping the civil rights movement of the 1950s and 1960s. Participants at a 1952 meeting in Birmingham of southern regional representatives of the National Urban League, the NAACP, the National Council of the Churches of Christ, the American Friends Service Committee, the Southern Regional Council, the American Missionary Association, the Anti-Defamation League, the Catholic Committee of the South, and the National Council of Negro Women reflected on the more than forty bombings that had taken place in the South in the prior sixteen months. The participants saw the roots of the violence stemming from the black struggle in the South for better housing and neighborhoods as well as white resistance to that struggle: "Those roots go deep into the everyday conditions under which our people live—and in no case more than in housing. The wretched slum dwellings of our Southern cities—nearly three-fourths of them occupied by Negroes—do us incalculable harm, morally as well as materially. Distrust, fear, rumor, and ultimately open violence are the fearful price we pay for the failure to provide long-range, constructive remedies for this problem."[11] In the 1950s, when blacks struggled to find better housing, and cities like Birmingham were using urban renewal and slum clearance to reduce the housing stock available to them, blacks were forced to look in white neighborhoods for housing. The resulting conflict between blacks and whites over housing, and the violence that ensued, helped set the stage for the more nationally visible civil rights struggles of the 1960s.

Moreover, because Birmingham's civil rights history is so vivid and sharp and so intertwined with the history of planning in that city, it is possible to clearly see the moral ambiguity—that is, the tendency of planning to appeal to both high and low moral values—that is endemic in planning, but that was highlighted in Birmingham. At least since Ebenezer Howard's Garden City proposal at the turn of the twentieth century, planning has concerned itself with high ideals and visions for the city.[12] But planning's lofty visions can also accommodate social injustice. Zoning was devised as a way to protect city residents from the "negative externalities" that urban living could impose on them. Zoning was a means by which cities could arrange their land uses so that people did not have to live near polluting industries or busy commercial districts. But zoning was also a means to protect not only the quality of life but also the value of property, and this was a concept that could be easily translated into racial zoning. With widespread acceptance of the notion that race mixing would reduce the value of property, it was relatively easy to transform zoning into racial zoning, using it not only to classify land by use but also by race.

Similarly, the visionary planning of John Charles and Frederick Law Olmsted Jr.—whose 1925 Birmingham park plan painted images of converting Birmingham's Village Creek to a linear park similar to Boston's Riverway and Chicago's Washington Park—was stymied by the hard reality of racial zoning. In a city where less desirable land was zoned for blacks, the land along the creek, which flooded often, was zoned for black occupancy. In addition to missing an opportunity to build a fine park system, the city's actions condemned many black neighborhoods to decades of flooding problems. It was not until the end of the twentieth century that the city, with assistance from the federal government, began to undo the mistakes of the 1920s and convert substandard neighborhoods along Village Creek to park land.

Perhaps the Southside Medical Center best illustrates the moral ambivalence of planning. Today, the University of Alabama at Birmingham (UAB) is the city's leading employer. Nearly the entire university, with its renowned medical center, is built on land obtained through the federal urban renewal program. Pound for pound, it is arguably the most successful urban renewal project in the nation. It enabled a city whose economy was foundering in the 1950s and 1960s to convert from a dying iron- and steel-based economy to an economy focused on the dynamic health care field. Without UAB, Birmingham would have been an economic basket case.

But UAB came at the high price of destroying an entire neighborhood and forcing its black residents to find housing in a city with very little housing for black citizens. While planners could orchestrate the economic transformation of the city, they could simultaneously ignore the relocation needs of its black citizenry and pretend that they could find decent homes in which to live. In fact, they knew they could not.

Planning's moral ambiguity is summarized by its inability to clearly and consistently answer the question: What is land for? Does land serve the needs of the residents who live on that land, providing them with sustenance and domicile? Or is it primarily a resource to be exploited by investors seeking profits? As the Birmingham case makes apparent, planning's inability to clearly answer this question has resulted in the city's land being used for narrow racist and materialistic purposes, as well as for broad humanitarian values.

Even though racial zoning has been declared unconstitutional, the moral issues emerging from racial zoning and other racist planning tools continue to be relevant to planning and zoning. Today, while zoning continues to be used to protect and enhance the quality of the land that people occupy, it is also used to exclude certain groups from enjoying certain lands. Exclusionary zoning, through the employment of, for example, minimum lot sizes and limits to multifamily housing, operates in the same way and for the same purpose as racial zoning—to limit the access to property of groups who are considered undesirable. Although exclusionary zoning is economic and not racial in its content, its impact is still racial as it exploits the differences in income between whites, blacks, and other minority groups to limit minority occupancy in "exclusive" neighborhoods.[13]

Birmingham also illustrates how, even though white institutions and individuals dominated planning for much of the city's history, an African American tradition of planning also emerged in the city's black neighborhoods. This tradition helped to shape the city's nationally recognized Citizen Participation Program in the 1970s.

From the city's founding in 1871 to the 1970s, Birmingham's planning depended on economically privileged white institutions, both public and private. Ten investors, all white, incorporated Birmingham in 1871, after purchasing 4,457 acres of farmland where the South and North Alabama Railroad was expected to cross an existing railroad, the Alabama and Chattanooga.[14] In planning for the entire Birmingham area, one of the nation's early city plans, Warren H. Manning's 1919 *City Plan of Birmingham,* focused on the physical environment, but made no mention of the housing and sanitary issues that affected the lives of both black and white residents in Birmingham.[15] Only a few years earlier, *The Survey* had published a major study of Birmingham, with close attention paid to the housing and sanitation problems found in that city's poorer neighborhoods, particularly the black ones.[16]

In 1925, when the Olmsted Brothers' firm prepared their plan for parks and playgrounds in Birmingham, blacks were unable to use any city-owned parks.[17] The following year, Birmingham instituted its racial zoning ordinance.[18] In the 1930s, the city's first public housing development, Smithfield Court, was located in an area designated for blacks, who were the only people who could live there.[19] The city's premier urban renewal project in the 1950s and 1960s, which resulted in the establishment of the University of Alabama at Birmingham, wiped out most of the city's largest black neighborhood.[20]

At first glance it appears that the planning tradition in Birmingham was dominated by white-controlled institutions, leaving no room for a black planning tradition. But at the same time that whites controlled the city's formal planning mechanisms, indigenous organizations operating in the city's black neighborhoods attempted to lobby for, or directly provide, the public services that were often lacking. Out of these roots emerged the city's 1974 citizen participation plan, which has gained national recognition for its inclusion of citizens in the city's planning and community development process. At a time when the city attempted to once again impose a top-down approach to citizen participation, the black community's long tradition of grassroots organizing transformed the city's citizen participation program into one whose foundation rested in the city's neighborhoods.

In one sense, part of the African American tradition of planning is really an anti-planning tradition. Going back to the 1920s and even earlier, blacks in Birmingham organized to protest what planning was doing to them. When the city first considered a racial zoning law in 1914, blacks met with city commissioners to persuade them to reject such an ordinance. In the 1920s, when the city debated a racial zoning law, black newspaper editor Oscar W. Adams led an effort to prevent the law from being enacted. In the 1930s, black homeowners protested the loss of their homes to the Smithfield Court public housing development. They were particularly concerned that the racial zoning law limited their choices in finding a suitable replacement home. Their protest to the federal government forced the city to redraw the racial zoning line so that these homeowners could have their homes moved to lots just west of their former location. In the 1940s, blacks protested racial zoning both in the courts and by moving into white neighborhoods; and in the 1950s, Birmingham blacks protested removal of a large black neighborhood in the city's Southside community by again taking their protest to the federal government. In the 1950s and 1960s, Birmingham blacks, under the leadership of Reverend Fred Shuttlesworth, created a grassroots-based organization, the Alabama Christian Movement for Human Rights (ACMHR), that challenged racial segregation in various venues, including public transportation and city parks. Also, in the 1960s, black residents of the Ensley community protested the city's Model Cities application, citing lack of resident participation in the preparation of the application. Finally, in the 1970s, black and white residents of the Central City public housing development successfully protested the proposed route of the Red Mountain Expressway that would have taken more than two hundred of their homes.

But the African American planning tradition in Birmingham was more than an anti-planning movement. It also attempted to work positively to gain improvements for black neighborhoods. Beginning in the 1920s and 1930s, black neighborhoods formed civic leagues whose primary purpose was to improve the basic public services that city government so often denied to Birmingham's blacks. Planning and zoning had relegated Birmingham's black residents to the least desirable neighborhoods, and public services were often inferior to those found in white neighborhoods. Civic leagues responded to these conditions by petitioning city government for better services and by launching self-help projects such as neighborhood cleanups and fund raising for community centers or street improvements. Although the civic leagues worked within Jim Crow, they established the experience of black residents coming together to address the problems of their neighborhood. This tradition would bear fruit in 1974 when the black community responded to a mayor-dominated citizen participation proposal by supporting a grassroots-oriented proposal that built on the black tradition of neighborhood organizations taking responsibility for the welfare of their neighborhoods.

An African American planning tradition therefore developed in reaction to the white-dominated planning institutions of Birmingham. This tradition was one of both reaction and action, with the former being a response to various plans to zone or relocate blacks in that city. At the same time, black residents formed themselves into civic leagues so that they could be in a better position to petition for public improvements and to directly improve their neighborhoods themselves.

Chapter 1 describes the housing and neighborhood conditions that Birmingham's blacks found themselves in during the first half of the twentieth century and the differences in quality between black and white neighborhoods. Birmingham was planned not only as an industrial city but also as a city that relied heavily on black labor. But by forcing black labor to live in the city's "vacant spaces," near creeks and railroads where whites did not wish to live, Birmingham's leaders set the stage for the black community's mid-twentieth-century struggle to escape these inferior spaces and move into the better neighborhoods enjoyed by whites. The struggle by blacks for better housing, and the violent white reaction, helped set the stage in the late 1940s and early 1950s for the civil rights battles that would grab the nation's attention in the early 1960s. Chapter 1 therefore establishes the framework in which civil rights and city planning influenced each other in Birmingham.

Chapter 2 describes the impact that the promise of comprehensive planning and zoning had on Birmingham's decision to adopt racial zoning in the 1920s and the black protest against that legislation. It also describes the city's first public housing project, built for blacks, and how black protest responded to the project's relocation plans and to the actual design and management of the development. Chapter 3 details the black reaction to racial zoning and ultimately to city planning, both in the courts and in the white neighborhoods where blacks attempted to move into homes they had purchased. Chapter 3 also describes how Birmingham's racial bombings began in response to black movement into white neighborhoods. Chapters 4 and 5 detail how Birmingham officials used the federal urban renewal and interstate highway programs to relocate the city's black residents and to redevelop black neighborhoods primarily to the advantage of the city's white community. Chapter 5 also describes the impact that the federal interstate highway program had on the city's black neighborhoods and how the dislocation of the city's black population through urban renewal and the interstate highway programs ignited neighborhood racial change in the city. Chapter 6 describes the beginning of change that took place in the intensive civil rights era of the 1960s, while also noting that the business-dominated city government still sought to keep blacks outside of the planning process. At the same time, white leaders attempted to merge the city with its white, affluent suburbs. The failure of this campaign along with white flight to the suburbs meant that the city was increasingly likely to be a majority black city.

Chapter 7 describes the rich history of the civic leagues and describes the role played by the black community in reshaping the city's approach to involving citizens in planning decisions. Chapter 8 completes the 1970s, describing how black neighborhoods were finally able to obtain a degree of power in influencing key planning decisions regarding the Red Mountain Expressway, the 1977 bond issue, and the federal Community Development Block Grant Program.

The epilogue examines the 1979 election of the city's first black mayor, Richard Arrington, and the challenges that he and the black community faced in his twenty-year tenure in building upon the enfranchisement of the black community in the city's planning process. With the election of Arrington, the black community played a greater role in the city's planning process, but the concentrated poverty found in many of the city's black neighborhoods makes it very diffcult for black residents to enjoy the economic fruits of increased sovereignty.

Moreover, the turn of the twenty-first-century controversy over the future of the Metropolitan Gardens public housing project reveals that the critical question of who controls the land still remains an unresolved issue in city planning. Business and political leaders, white and black, moved to tear down the public housing project, located near the city's downtown, and replace it with mixed-income housing. Black progress in obtaining influence in the city's planning process, therefore, has not resulted in a diminution of black poverty nor an increase in the impoverished black community's ability to control the use of the land it occupies. Progress in enabling equal access to the planning process has been great in twentieth-century Birmingham, but the persistent poverty in the city's black neighborhoods challenges both the black community's economic sovereignty as well as planning's ability to serve the city's "truly disadvantaged."[21]

1 Big Mules and Bottom Rails in the Magic City

As an industrial city built on its rich deposits of iron and coal, Birmingham has the distinction of being a city whose very name identifies it as a planned city. Named after the industrial city of Birmingham, England, Birmingham was incorporated in 1871 by the Elyton Land Company, which consisted of ten investors. The company purchased nearly 4,500 acres of Jones Valley farmland in Jefferson County, Alabama, where the South and North Alabama Railroad was expected to cross an existing railroad, the Alabama and Chattanooga. The investors were well aware of the area's rich deposits of coal and iron as the Alabama state geologist had systematically recorded the state's mineral deposits beginning in the late 1840s.[1] So confident were they of the city's future that at the 1873 annual meeting of the Elyton Land Company, one of the investors, Colonel James R. Powell, described Birmingham as "this magic little city of ours."[2] Birmingham's enduring if often ironic nickname, the Magic City, was born.

The investors were joined in this knowledge by the South and North's chief executive, Frank Gilmer, and chief engineer, John Milner. They had ridden over Red Mountain and through Jones Valley before the Civil War and had seen the mineral deposits and imagined the industrial development that would take place there. Milner had been appointed in 1858 as chief engineer to survey the feasibility of building a railroad through the hill country of North Alabama, where the state's iron and coal deposits were concentrated. His 1859 report to the governor outlined the costs, possible routes, and benefits of building a railroad through Alabama's mineral region. By demonstrating the feasibility of laying a rail line through North Alabama's hilly but mineral-rich terrain, Milner's report caused among railroad promoters a sensation that would last the next twenty years, culminating in the birth and growth of Birmingham in the 1870s.[3]

Milner's report made clear that Birmingham would not only be a source of raw materials but would become an important manufacturing center as well. To this end, Milner predicted that mills in the Birmingham area could successfully depend on black workers to perform the arduous tasks of making pig iron and rails. Writing just before the Civil War, Milner saw slavery as compatible with the industrial development of the South and that cheap black labor would be a key contributor to Alabama's competitiveness in manufacturing.

> I am clearly of opinion, that negro labor can be made exceedingly profitable in manufacturing iron, and in rolling mills. The want of skillful labor, has hitherto been the grand objection to the manufacture of rails in the South. This is compensated for by the freedom of the Southern States, from that curse of Northern works, "strikes among their workmen." Making Railroad bars is a monotonous process. Each bar is the facsimile of the other, and the great labor consists in the heavy lifting, and managing the heated masses in the machines or rolls. It requires no great mechanical skill, even, for every part is done by machinery, which simply requires to be fed. A negro who can set a saw, or run a grist mill, or work in a blacksmith shop, can do work as cheaply in a rolling mill, even now; as white men do in the North, provided he has an *overseer—a southern man,* who knows how to manage negroes. I have long since learned that negro labor is more reliable and cheaper for any business connected with the construction of a railroad, than white. It is said that there are five thousand pieces in a locomotive, each requiring the nicest adjustment. To make such machinery as this, skilled mechanics are required, and such is the case in erecting fine buildings of lumber, but the lumber can be sawed into boards by ordinary hands, and such is the case in the manufacture of iron into bars.[4]

Even before the Civil War, Alabama's rich supply of cheap black labor was seen as instrumental to its industrial development. Horace Ware, a pioneer ironmaker in Shelby County, just south of where Birmingham would be established, had already employed slaves in operating the Shelby Furnace in the 1840s and 1850s.[5] Ware was not alone, as blacks were employed in mills, furnaces, tobacco factories, textile mills, mines, steamboats, wharves, and railroads throughout the South before and during the Civil War.[6]

After the war and the founding of Birmingham, Birmingham's industrialists were quick to employ black labor in mines and mills. An 1886 account of Birmingham's industrial development reports that "about 40 percent of the total population of Birmingham is negro. About 90 percent of the labor employed by all the furnaces, near Birmingham, is negro. . . . Besides the negro furnace labor, much of the labor employed by the city manufacturing industries in iron, such as the rolling mill, foundries, etc., is negro."[7] Just as northern employers preferred European immigrants, southern employers preferred blacks for the difficult, hot, and dangerous work of the mines and mills, believing African Americans to be better suited to such labor than whites.[8] James Sloss, who established the Sloss Furnace Company in Birmingham in 1881, told U.S. Senate investigators in 1883 that he would not hire white labor over black: "Well, as a matter of business, I don't think it would be an improvement to substitute white labor." In response to a follow-up question, he explained: "Yes; we have got no white labor on our place, though, except skilled labor. The balance of the iron men, the coke men, the yard men, the furnace men, and some of the helpers and stock men are all colored, and that colored labor is as good labor as I want if I could just keep it at work."[9] Birmingham employers also preferred largely black workforces because they feared the social friction that might result from mixing white and black laborers on an equal basis.[10] By relying on black workers to do the most unpleasant, physically demanding jobs, Birmingham industrialists believed they also made their white workers more manageable:

The manifest result of the presence of the negro labor here is that we have a more intelligent and orderly white laboring population, than otherwise might be anticipated. The negro here is satisfied and contented; the low whites elsewhere are dissatisfied and turbulent. The white laboring classes here are separated from the negroes, working all day side by side with them, by an innate consciousness of race superiority. This sentiment dignifies the character of white labor. It excites a sentiment of sympathy and equality on their part with the classes above them, and in this way becomes a wholesome social leaven.[11]

As a consequence of Birmingham's hiring practices, the city's black population grew rapidly as former sharecroppers left the cotton fields of the rural South for the opportunity to earn a wage in Birmingham.[12] By 1890, when Birmingham's population had grown to 26,178 from 3,086 in 1880, 43 percent of the population was black.[13] As the city's population grew to a peak of 340,887 in 1960, the black population remained at around 40 percent of the total (see table 1.1). In 1910 and 1920, Birmingham had a higher percentage of blacks in its population than any other U.S. city with 100,000 or more population, and in 1920 Birmingham was the eighth-largest city in the nation in terms of black population. In 1920, only one southern city, New Orleans, had a larger black population than Birmingham.[14] From its very beginnings, Birmingham was planned not only as an industrial city but also as a substantially black city.

Overseeing Birmingham's black population were the city's industrialists, bankers, and utilities, commonly known as the city's (and the state's) "Big Mules."[15] The biggest and most powerful Big Mule firm was Tennessee Coal and Iron (TCI), which in 1907 was purchased by U.S. Steel. TCI had bought its way into Birmingham and by 1892 had become the largest iron producer in the South.[16] After TCI's Ensley plant, located just west of Birmingham, began producing open-hearth steel rails in the late 1890s, it gained the attention of the steel-making world when in 1907 the Union Pacific and Southern Pacific railroads placed an order for 157,000 tons of steel rails.[17] Facing increased competition for the steel rail market, gigantic U.S. Steel, formed in 1901, bought out TCI in November 1907, placing Birmingham's largest firm into the hands of the New York financier J. Pierpont Morgan.[18]

Big Mules such as TCI–U.S. Steel exercised control over both the city's economy and its politics. Refraining from running for political office, the Big Mules preferred to rely on middle-class politicians to run the city, making sure all the time that the city kept its taxes and expenses low and maintained the separation of the races in all forms.[19] According to longtime Birmingham reporter and observer Irving Beiman, "The city's industrial and financial interests have always insisted on 'cheap government' for Birmingham."[20] As a result, whenever Bir-

Table 1.1. Total and black population in Birmingham

Year	Total	Black	% Black
1870	—	—	—
1880	3,086	—	—
1890	26,178	11,254	43.0
1900	38,415	16,575	43.1
1910	132,685	52,305	39.4
1920	178,806	70,230	39.3
1930	259,678	99,077	38.2
1940	267,583	108,938	40.7
1950	326,037	130,025	39.9
1960	340,887	135,113	39.6
1970	300,910	126,388	42.0
1980	284,413	158,224	55.6
1990	265,968	168,277	63.3
2000	242,820	178,372	73.5

Source: U.S. Census data as reported at http://www.bplonline.org/locations/central/gov/HistoricalCensus.asp.

mingham's per capita expenditures were compared to those of other cities, Birmingham's were invariably the lowest. In 1939, for example, the *Louisville Courier-Journal* compared Birmingham to seven other southern cities and found that Birmingham's per capita cost of government was the lowest of the eight cities. At $20.15 per capita, it was one-third lower than the next lowest city, Memphis.[21]

The Big Mules also had a stake in maintaining racial segregation. Building on racial antagonism between whites and blacks, Big Mule industrialists could keep unionization in check by making sure that whites had no desire to join with blacks to fight for higher wages and better working conditions. Even when unionization did come to the steel industry in 1937, TCI–U.S. Steel's settlement with the local Steel Workers Organizing Committee called for using seniority to enforce sharp occupational and wage distinctions between whites and blacks. By maintaining racial segregation in Birmingham, the Big Mules discouraged interracial solidarity in local labor unions, thereby enabling the city's industrialists to maintain a dual wage system.[22]

For maintaining the racial status quo, the Big Mules relied on

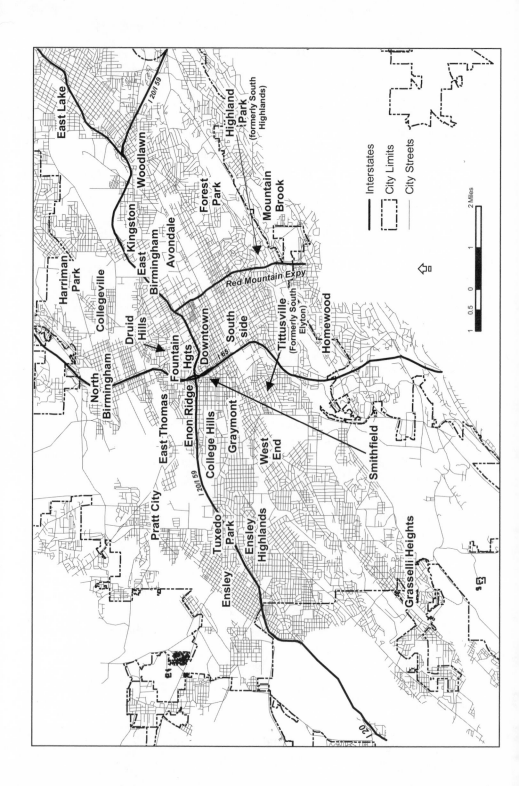

East Lake

I 20/I 59

Woodlawn

Kingston

East
Birmingham

Avondale

Forest
Park

Highland
Park
(formerly South
Highlands)

Mountain
Brook

Red Mountain Expy

Harriman
Park

Collegeville

Druid
Hills

Downtown

South
side

Tittusville
(Formerly South
Elyton)

Homewood

North
Birmingham

Fountain
Hgts

I 65

East Thomas

Enon Ridge

College Hills

Graymont

West
End

Smithfield

Pratt City

I 20/I 59

Tuxedo
Park

Ensley
Highlands

Ensley

Grasselli Heights

I 20

Interstates

City Limits

City Streets

2 Miles

1   0.5   0   1

T. Eugene "Bull" Connor, who served as one of the city's three elected city commissioners from 1937 to 1953 and from 1957 to 1963. Connor was a radio sportscaster who gained fame for announcing the Birmingham Barons minor league baseball games. His popularity as an announcer provided the support he needed to be elected to the state legislature in 1934. In 1937, encouraged by state senator James Simpson, Connor was elected to the Birmingham city commission as chief of public safety.[23] Throughout his career, Connor's folksy glibness, along with his strong support for segregation, endeared him to the white working classes in Birmingham.[24]

Connor's connection to the Big Mules went through corporate attorney James Simpson. Simpson set up his corporate law practice in Birmingham in 1919 and proceeded to become the Big Mules' principal spokesman, serving as counsel to TCI–U.S. Steel and the *Birmingham News,* among others. Elected to the state senate the same year that Connor was elected to the state house, Simpson served three terms as Birmingham's sole representative in the state's upper chamber. After two unsuccessful races for the U.S. Senate in 1944 and 1946, he focused on his Birmingham law practice and on advising Bull Connor.[25] According to James T. "Jabo" Waggoner, who served on Birmingham's city commission with Connor from 1957 to 1963, Connor called Simpson "every day of his life," and when Connor suggested to his fellow commissioners, "Let's hold off on this till next week," he meant, "I've got to ask Jim." Longtime *Birmingham News* writer Irving Beiman recalled that "Bull was close to the corporate interests, and would carry out what they wanted, but he stayed on the good side of the union people as well. He was shrewd. He received support from both groups."[26]

Connor's electoral support came primarily from the white working-class communities in Birmingham, such as West End and Ensley, located in the western part of the city, and Woodlawn and East Lake, located to the east of downtown (see map 1.1).[27] These working-class areas had been developed as suburbs beginning in the latter part of the nineteenth century.[28] In contrast, the city's Big Mule executives lived in the city's affluent Southside neighborhoods—South Highlands and Forest Park. After the 1920s, they increasingly lived in the suburbs

Map 1.1 (*opposite*). Birmingham neighborhoods

of Homewood and Mountain Brook, south of Birmingham and Red Mountain, which separated them from the mills and working-class neighborhoods of Birmingham.[29]

By the 1920s, the city's black residents were firmly ensconced in the spaces that working-class and upper-class whites conceded to them, and generally these were the less desirable neighborhoods in the city. According to Blaine Brownell's description of Birmingham in the 1920s: "It was in the city's 'vacant spaces'—areas of undeveloped land bypassed for more pleasant sites by industry and white neighborhoods—that the majority of Birmingham's Negroes settled. These black neighborhoods were generally situated along creekbeds, railroad lines, or alleys, and they suffered from a lack of street lights, paved streets, sewers, and other city services."[30] Emory Jackson, the longtime editor of the city's black newspaper, the *Birmingham World,* wrote in 1949, "Negroes in Birmingham are zoned near the railroad tracks, near the over-flowing creeks, near the shops."[31]

In the 1870s, when the city was first settled, much of the population lived in grim circumstances, with "marshes and mud roads everywhere and yellow pine shacks and a box car for a depot."[32] Although nineteenth-century Birmingham was concentrated along a twenty-block-long, six-block-wide swath that ran east-west, straddling the railroad tracks that ran through the center of the city, blacks tended to live on different blocks from whites. Blacks did live in the city's alleys, particularly on the south side, but other blacks were concentrated adjacent to the Alice Furnace on the west side and the Sloss Furnaces on the east side.[33] In general, Birmingham would continue, along with Atlanta and Memphis, to display a "new southern" racial pattern in which blacks lived on different blocks from whites, while older southern cities such as Charleston, New Orleans, Washington, D.C., and Baltimore displayed blacks living in alleys adjacent to white residents. This meant that by 1960 Birmingham's index of segregation of 92.8 was as high, if not higher, than the very high indices found in northern cities such as Chicago.[34] Birmingham had become a city of highly segregated neighborhoods.

Many of the blacks, as well as the whites, who lived near industrial operations such as Sloss Furnaces or coal or iron mines lived in "quarters," or company-built towns or camps. The Sloss Furnace Company, established in 1881, built worker quarters at its Sloss City Furnaces around 1900 just east of downtown Birmingham, as well as at its Sloss-Sheffield Furnace in North Birmingham. Sloss Quarters at Sloss City Furnaces primarily housed blacks, who lived in wooden houses, painted red, with no indoor plumbing or running water. Shortly before the quarters were torn down in the late 1950s, indoor toilets and running water were finally installed to meet the city's 1957 housing code. The few whites who lived in the quarters lived in houses that were separated from the black workers. The quality of the houses varied.[35] Will Prather recalled Sloss Quarters: "Some of the houses was pretty good, some of them. But some of them you could stand in the house and look outdoors. I have set in my house many times and see folk pass by. See, they had these six-inch thick boards and you put a strip across it. You didn't have no walls. See, heap of times the wind got so bad you had to stop up the cracks."[36] Nevertheless, residents in the 1930s and 1940s reported that Sloss was good about providing carpenters and plumbers to make repairs.[37] Several miles north of Sloss Quarters, Fannie Brown lived with her husband in the Louisville and Nashville (L and N) Railroad's company housing until the late 1950s. They had no plumbing or water in the house, using a hydrant in the yard. They also lacked electricity and gas, heating with a coal stove and using kerosene lamps for light.[38]

In 1912, *Birmingham News* reporter Ethel Armes visited Sloss Quarters and spoke to the black families who lived there. She found families living in poorly constructed and unsanitary houses: "These shacks, unpainted, rotting away, with broken windows, split doors, and ashy surroundings, look as if they too were made out of slag . . . the shacks were put all in a heap together, without sewerage, or any sanitary provisions whatsoever, without fences—just sort of makeshift shelters. None of the shacks is plastered, few have ceilings. Very few were even provided with toilets until two or three weeks ago."[39]

Earlier in 1912, the progressive magazine *The Survey* toured Birmingham with an eye to sanitation and housing. John Fitch, a member of *The Survey* staff, wrote that Sloss Quarters had "a slag dump for a rear view, blast furnaces and bee-hive coke ovens for a front view, railroad tracks in the street, and indecently built toilets in the back yards, in an abomination of desolation. The houses are unpainted, fences are tumbling down, a board is occasionally missing from the side of a house. Colonel Maben, president of the company, told me that he didn't believe in 'coddling workmen.'"[40]

More generally, *The Survey's* authors found housing in Birmingham's neighborhoods, especially its black areas, to be unsanitary and unsound. Fitch and engineer Morris Knowles reported that in the mining camps, "Sanitary equipment is generally poor. Water supply in most of the camps is inadequate. Dry closets in the back yards are often in bad condition."[41] An example of the latter was found in the Porter mining camp, whose population of six hundred was about 60 percent black. In 1911, the camp experienced a series of typhoid cases attributable to "the transmission of the germs from open privies by flies and also to the contamination of certain springs from which the people occasionally obtained their drinking water."[42] U.S. Senate investigators, visiting Birmingham in 1910, reported: "As a general rule the company houses of the mining villages are the more cheaply constructed, while around the steel plants there is usually a variety of grades for the different classes of workmen, the smallest and poorest being usually occupied by negroes. In the ore-mining camps the houses are well built and well kept, as a general rule, although occupied chiefly by negroes."[43]

Investigators also found poor housing conditions in black neighborhoods outside the company towns. Morris Knowles, who would prepare Birmingham's first zoning ordinance in the 1920s (see chapter 2), also found dry closets, or privies, in unsanitary condition in Ensley, the industrial neighborhood where TCI–U.S. Steel located its first open-hearth steel manufacturing plant in Birmingham. According to Knowles:

> The community near and west of the steel works at Ensley consists mostly of colored people. Drinking water is supplied by the Birmingham Water Works Company, one tap to every four or five houses. Each house has a trash barrel. The privies are unsatisfactory and exposed, presenting opportunity for fly and other contamination. Many are located over ditches or gutters, which are the natural run-off courses for the surface drainage from the side hills. Several of these channels lead to sewers, so that the filth is occasionally washed away—a simple but unsatisfactory method, as the care-

takers tend to delay cleaning them, in the hope of rains that will relieve them of their dirty work.[44]

U.S. Senate investigators visiting Ensley at nearly the same time as Knowles took a more positive view, finding that the housing situation in Ensley was better than other iron and steel plants in Birmingham. The investigators noted, however, that the better conditions in Ensley were found primarily in areas occupied by whites and European immigrants: "In the section of the company quarters occupied by the negroes, the houses are smaller and less substantial in construction. Many are finished on the exterior with rough lumber, to which a coat of white wash is applied. Only dry closets are provided, and there is no public bath, as in the other section."[45]

W. M. McGrath, an engineer and secretary of the Birmingham Associated Charities, focused his attention on the city's "Negro 'Quarters,'" which, judged by the photographs accompanying his article, were the black-occupied streets and alleys located south of downtown Birmingham. Forty years later, this neighborhood would be the focus of the city's first major urban renewal project (see chapter 4). In 1912, McGrath wrote:

> The Negro "quarters" are particularly nests of infection, and an investigation of living conditions affords cause for wonderment that any in them escape. Block after block will contain from fifty to sixty houses. . . . A recent survey of one of these "black blocks" showed that the fifty or more houses, almost without exception, were in need of repair, while in some instances it seemed only by some magic that the walls supported the so-called roofs. The toilet and water facilities in some instances were horrible, six, eight, and ten families using the same closet and twice that number the same hydrant—this in the face of the ordinance that not more than three families shall use the same closet. Nor are these conditions confined alone to the Negro quarters. Conditions equally deplorable exist in the homes of many of the white laborers throughout the city.[46]

McGrath's comment on the number of families served by water closets and hydrants was reflective of the city's failure to enforce sanitation codes in the black and poor neighborhoods. Since 1901,

Birmingham had a building code that regulated the construction of new buildings, but despite occasional outbursts of concern, it was generally not enforced in black neighborhoods. The city's real estate interests, led by the Real Estate Exchange, opposed efforts to regulate construction and maintenance of housing in poor areas, and it was not until 1957 that the city, at the behest of the federal government's Workable Program requirement, adopted a housing code (see chapter 5).[47]

Likewise, the city's sanitation code was also ignored in its black neighborhoods. Continuous outbreaks of typhoid fever called attention to the fact that the city still had eight thousand dry toilets by 1916, and public-minded citizens and health officials periodically called for "immediate action" to address the city's "greatest menace."[48] In 1920, Jefferson County health officer J. D. Dowling caused considerable consternation among the city's real estate interests when his department brought 150 cases against realtors, "practically all of them being for violation of the ordinance requiring a separate water closet for each tenement house." Realtors objected to the high cost this would impose on the construction of single-room-wide "shotgun" houses (fig. 1.1) that would "entail an expenditure of money almost equal to the cost of the houses themselves." As a compromise, realtors asked that the law be changed so that a water closet would be required only for every two houses. In defense of this position, one realtor contended, "we are not fighting any sanitary regulations that are necessary, nor are we opposing Dr. Dowling's programme for sanitation but there are many cases in congested colored settlements where one toilet can easily suffice for two families."[49]

In response, Dowling invited members of the Birmingham City Commission to visit the city's black slums, contending that in some cases one sanitary closet was serving as many as twelve families. Dowling explained:

> I am very anxious for every member of the City Commission to see conditions as they actually are in the negro alleys and other congested places of Birmingham. Because real estate interests are making money out of filth is no reason why they should jeopardize the health of the people of Birmingham. Inadequate sanitary connections have developed in Birmingham some of the most dangerous disease breeding agencies ever seen anywhere and when the com-

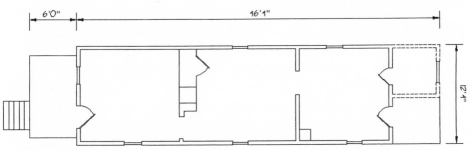

Figure 1.1. Plan for a typical shotgun house in Birmingham. (New South Associates and John Milner Associates, *"More Than What We Had": An Architectural and Historical Documentation of the Village Creek Project Neighborhoods, Birmingham, Alabama,* U.S. Army Corps of Engineers Technical Report, November 27, 1989)

mission sees conditions for itself its members will be of the same opinion that I am. In the meantime the health department will vigorously enforce the ordinances requiring sanitary sewage connections wherever needed.[50]

After several months of debate, a compromise was reached whereby realtors had to provide sanitary sewer connections to every house within two hundred feet of a sanitary sewer. They were given two years to comply with the new law.[51]

Builders had resisted providing sanitary sewerage because the city required developers to provide such facilities through special assessment of the property owners to be served, thereby rendering the development of cheap housing uneconomical. As much as progressive-minded residents called for better sanitation, the city itself was unwilling to foot the cost of the sewers, thereby leaving it to developers and property owners to pay an assessment. The same was true for paved streets. The cheapest areas of the city, where the city's blacks were housed, had few paved streets and sanitary sewers.[52]

Beyond attempting to improve the sanitary conditions of the city's slums, the other significant housing reform of the early twentieth century centered on the development of model industrial communities. The best known of these in Birmingham was Corey. In 1910, U.S. Steel contracted with a real estate development company headed by Birmingham developer Robert Jemison Jr. to construct the industrial new town that would later be known as Fairfield. Two years later, Graham Taylor wrote in *The Survey*, "it is doubtful if in America there may be found a better planned industrial community."[53] But Jemison's plan did not include housing for low-income workers, many of whom were black.[54] After the 1907 takeover by U.S. Steel, TCI–U.S. Steel, under the leadership of George Gordon Crawford, endeavored to improve housing, health, and education for its employees and their families. This effort included company-owned mining villages such as Docena, Bayview, and Edgewater, each of which was built with housing provided separately for blacks and whites.[55] *The Survey's* 1912 assessment of the newly built Edgewater described it as the "best and the most up-to-date mining camp in the district." A water tap was available in each yard, but *The Survey* expressed regret about the "lack of facilities in the houses." Nevertheless, "The privies, located some distance from the houses, are substantially built with waterproof roof covering and hinged rear doors to facilitate cleaning and prevent exposure to flies. They are well taken care of, being cleaned out regularly and limed, and are altogether a marked step in advance of the conditions in the older camps."[56] In the early twentieth century, the American Cast Iron Pipe Company (ACIPCO) also upgraded its company housing and provided indoor plumbing, electricity, and hot water to both blacks and whites.[57] TCI–U.S. Steel's experiment in "welfare capitalism" contrasted with the Sloss Furnace Company's fear of "coddling workmen" and lasted until the unionization of the steel industry. By 1950, TCI–U.S. Steel had sold off its company towns.[58]

Despite *The Survey's* pioneering research, no systematic assessment of Birmingham's housing and neighborhood conditions was published until 1937, when the Jefferson County Board of Health released a report on Birmingham's blighted neighborhoods. The report surveyed twenty-two blighted neighborhoods, of which thirteen were predominantly black, and found that blacks bore a large share of the burden of substandard housing and neighborhoods in Birmingham. At a time when blacks constituted 38 percent of Birmingham's population, 70 percent of the dwelling units located in the twenty-two blighted neighborhoods were found in predominantly black neighborhoods. Black neighborhoods contained two-thirds of community toilets where more than one family used the same toilet facilities; 72 percent of dwelling units lacking running water; 74 percent of dwelling units

Table 1.2. Distribution of neighborhood deficiencies by predominant race in blighted Birmingham neighborhoods, 1933 (in percentages)

	Black	White	Total
Number of dwelling units (DUs)	70.3	29.7	100.0
Number of DUs w/out bathing facilities	73.6	26.4	100.0
Number of DUs w/out running water	72.5	27.5	100.0
Number of DUs using kerosene for lighting	83.9	16.1	100.0
Number of community toilets	66.8	33.2	100.0

Source: J. D. Dowling and F. A. Bean, *Final Statistical Report of Surveys of the Blighted Areas, Birmingham, Alabama, Showing Some Comparative Figures for the Years 1933 and 1935,* Jefferson County, Alabama, Board of Health, 1937, 5–6.

lacking bathing facilities; and over 80 percent of dwelling units using kerosene for lighting among Birmingham's blighted neighborhoods (see table 1.2). The absence of basic public services, such as running water and electricity, was concentrated in the city's black neighborhoods.[59] Several years later, the Housing Authority of the Birmingham District, which was established in 1935, surveyed housing conditions in Birmingham and found "at least 40 percent of the housing in every district (except East Lake) was reported as substandard. In most cities these conditions are concentrated in a few fairly large areas, but in Birmingham they are spread over the city in a number of smaller pockets, some of which are found in almost every district."[60] Despite the efforts of TCI–U.S. Steel and ACIPCO, substandard housing still permeated the city, especially its black neighborhoods. The housing authority's study reported that the highest percentages of substandard housing were found in areas with the highest concentration of African American residents.[61]

Despite the higher incidence of substandard housing in Birmingham's black community, the quality of housing and neighborhoods consumed by the city's African American residents varied. Two neighborhoods, Smithfield and Enon Ridge (see map 1.1), housed the city's middle-class black population. In Smithfield in the early twentieth century, black architect Wallace A. Rayfield designed houses for some of the leading black professionals of the city, including Arthur H. Parker, principal for thirty-nine years of the city's first black high school, and Edward A. Brown, one of the few black attorneys at that time in Birmingham.[62] Enon Ridge, a fashionable neighborhood for black professionals since the 1890s, was home to the Tuggle School, which Carrie Tuggle founded in 1903 as an orphanage and private school. Among its most famous students were A. G. Gaston, who eventually became one of Birmingham's most affluent businessmen, and Angela Davis, a nationally known radical of the 1960s who, as a member of the Communist Party, displayed a very different attitude toward capitalism than did Gaston.[63] With Birmingham's black middle-class population contained in these two neighborhoods, eventually these middle-class households would seek new housing opportunities in neighborhoods claimed by the city's whites. Consequently, as discussed in chapters 2 and 3, black middle-class residents were pioneers in testing the barriers, legal and otherwise, to their movement out of Smithfield and Enon Ridge.

Improved housing conditions were available to working-class blacks as well. Beginning in the decade before World War I, blacks moved into neighborhoods such as Tuxedo Park and Moro Park in the Ensley community and into East Birmingham. Blacks in East Birmingham moved into neighborhoods adjacent to Village Creek, where they were able to live close to employers such as Stockham Valves. They could either own their homes or rent from private landlords rather than from private companies for which they worked.[64] While the housing was fairly plain, consisting primarily of single and double shotguns and bungalows, Georgia Scott remembers moving there in the 1940s and comparing it to the mining camp where she had formerly lived with her family: "We thought we were in heaven . . . we love this house . . . you know when you lived in a mining camp so long and when you get something that's better, you love it. And we had never had a house with stairs. When we moved up here we had to buy a gas stove . . . we had never had a gas stove before . . . we just liked it cause it was more than what we had before in the mining camp."[65]

Despite the better housing, many of the dwellings in East Birmingham lacked plumbing until the 1940s.[66] Moreover, because of the proximity to Village Creek, flooding was a major problem in both East Birmingham and Moro Park. Ann McCray Penick, who grew up in Moro Park in Ensley in a house built by her father and uncle, recalls the flooding in her neighborhood: "As long as I can remember, we always had floods. We always had what I called high water. And that creek, when it would rain. . . . Our house was on the higher end because the water never got into our house or it never got in the lady across the street's house or up this way further. And a lot of the people who the water would get into their houses would come up to our house and they would spend the night and stuff and come up here."[67]

By 1950, a pattern of inferior housing and neighborhoods for most of Birmingham's black residents was firmly in place—housing occupied by blacks was much more likely to be substandard and much more likely to be located in neighborhoods with inferior public services. Overall, Birmingham's housing stock was inferior to that of most American cities in 1950. With slightly less than half of its housing stock having hot running water and a private toilet and bath and not being dilapidated, the Birmingham area trailed all metropolitan areas of one hundred thousand or more dwelling units in the incidence of standard quality housing; only a few metropolitan areas had lower percentages than Birmingham's.[68] In Birmingham in 1950, only 54.8 percent of all dwelling units were of standard quality. For the city's black residents, however, the percentage was much lower—only 15.5 percent of dwelling units occupied by black households were of standard quality. Constituting 40 percent of the city's population, Birmingham's black households occupied two-thirds of the city's substandard housing—27,530 of the city's 41,528 substandard units were occupied by black households that year. Birmingham led the nation in substandard housing, in great part because of the housing occupied by its black residents. Of these 27,530 substandard units, only about one-third—36 percent—were dilapidated. Instead, the most common problem was the absence of complete plumbing, usually because of the lack of an indoor toilet—83.5 percent of nondilapidated substandard dwellings occupied by blacks lacked a private toilet or bath or lacked running water altogether.[69] Thirty-five years after the city's high incidence of dry toilets, especially in its black neighborhoods, was labeled as Birmingham's "greatest menace," which required "immediate action," the basic sanitation needs of the city's black residents were still not being met.

In 1950, Birmingham's blacks were also more likely to live in overcrowded dwellings. Using the census measure of overcrowding as 1.01 or more persons per room, of the 19,491 overcrowded dwelling units in the city, 12,843, or nearly 66 percent, were occupied by African American households.[70] Many of Birmingham's black residents lived in three-room shotgun houses, which consisted of three connected rooms, front to back, with no hallway (see fig. 1.1).[71] In houses of this size, overcrowding was quite likely. Dorothy Inman-Johnson, who grew up in Ensley in the 1950s, recalls living in three-room shotgun houses in which there were beds in every room: "We could look in the front door and see right out the back door. Little three-room houses where you didn't have a living room. They called it the front room because all of your rooms had beds in them, even the kitchen, so that you had sleeping room for everybody."[72]

In the 1950s, city services as well were not distributed evenly among the city's white and black neighborhoods. This is documented in an urban renewal survey commissioned by the city in 1958 and carried out by the Chicago consulting engineer firm, De Leuw, Cather and Company. Although the consultant reported the blighted conditions found in the Ensley and Pratt City communities, it inadvertently provided information on the differences between white and black neighborhoods in the availability of adequate public services. The study area consisted of 390 blocks, almost evenly divided between predominantly white and predominantly black blocks. Overall, of the 6,319 households in the study area, two-thirds were black.[73] Given that the entire Ensley–Pratt City neighborhood consisted of households in which men worked primarily in the area's mills (including TCI–U.S. Steel's steel plant) and mines, an analysis of the area provides an opportunity to directly compare the neighborhood characteristics and availability of public services of the city's white and black working-class populations.

Table 1.3 shows a comparison of the white and black blocks in the Ensley–Pratt City neighborhood that was obtained from the inventory maps prepared for the De Leuw, Cather study. While the study area was primarily residential, the De Leuw, Cather study found that black blocks were slightly more likely to be located next to industrial areas as well as next to areas zoned for industrial use. As described in chapter 2, the city's zoning law, adopted in 1926, resulted in black neighborhoods frequently being zoned for occupancy near industrial areas of the city.

The De Leuw, Cather study also found a dramatic difference in the incidence of paved streets. Nearly all of the black blocks were adjacent

Table 1.3. Comparison of white and black neighborhoods in the Ensley–Pratt City communities

	White	Black
Adjacent to industrial area	8%	13%
Adjacent to area zoned industrial	13%	20%
Bordering unpaved streets	48%	89%
Unpaved on one side	30%	27%
Unpaved on two sides	12%	26%
Unpaved on three sides	5%	23%
Unpaved on four sides	1%	13%
Lacking sewer-connected toilets[a]	2%	14%
Presence of open drainage ditches	19%	42%
Occasional flooding from creek overflow	1%	8%
Regular flooding from storm runoff	2%	9%
Number of blocks	191	192

Source: De Leuw, Cather and Company, *Ensley–Pratt City Urban Renewal Study,* prepared for the Housing Authority of the Birmingham District, August 1958.
[a] For at least a portion of the block

to at least one unpaved street, compared to only about one-half of the white blocks. Moreover, about one-third of all black blocks had unpaved streets on three or four sides compared to only 6 percent of the white blocks.

Although by the 1950s much of the Ensley–Pratt City study area had been connected to sewage lines, 14 percent of the black blocks lacked sewer connections for at least a portion of the block, compared to only 2 percent of the white blocks. The De Leuw, Cather study also reported on the flooding problems that characterized portions of Ensley–Pratt City. Nearly half (42 percent) of black blocks had open ditches for drainage, compared to 19 percent of white blocks. Seventeen percent of the black blocks experienced occasional or regular flooding problems, compared to only 3 percent of the white blocks. The higher incidence of flooding problems in black areas was accounted for by the closer proximity of black neighborhoods, such as the Moro Park neighborhood, to Village Creek. The incidence of open ditches contributed not only to flooding but also to sanitation problems and to increased chances of injury or death. The De Leuw, Cather study reported that "in several locations houses straddle the ditches, and some of the ditches which run beneath houses appear to carry sanitary sewage as well as storm runoff."[74] While the De Leuw, Cather report did not address the safety hazards associated with open ditches, especially during flash floods, the *Birmingham Post-Herald* later lamented the "mile after mile of open ditches which are an offense to the eye and the nostril and, when brimming with sudden downpours, often a threat to life itself."[75]

Finally, blacks living in the Ensley–Pratt City area found that they had fewer recreational opportunities than did whites. In 1958, although the Reverend Fred Shuttlesworth had filed suit to desegregate the city's parks that year (see chapter 6), they were still segregated. Blacks living in the area primarily had access to a very small Tuxedo Park and several other parks that were primarily playgrounds for black schools. The largest park in the area, Ensley Park, was designated for whites only.[76] Black residents of Ensley were also limited in their moviegoing. While the downtown Ensley area nearby featured a movie theater, blacks were required to enter on the side and sit in the balcony.[77]

Ensley's black community was able to make the best of the lack of recreation opportunities available to them. Dorothy Inman-Johnson recalls the fun and adventure of being able to jump from one house roof to another in her neighborhood of narrow-lot, shotgun houses with roofs within a few feet of each other (see fig. 1.2): "I can remember my younger sister, who was a tomboy, and my brothers and their friends . . . they would play this game where they would go down and climb up on top of the end house and they would jump from roof to roof all the way down—playing this tag game."[78] While growing up in Ensley in the 1950s, Dorothy Inman-Johnson did not have access to the same parks as whites did. Nevertheless, she and her family and neighbors enjoyed playing baseball in the dirt street in front of their houses with the mothers and daughters playing the fathers and sons: "Everybody knew everybody. We would get out in these dirt streets in the evening when Mom was home and after we had dinner and Dad was home from work. The grownups and the children would get out in the dirt streets and play ball—stickball. And parents would divvy up the teams. Like the moms would get on the girls' team and the daddies would get on the boys' team."[79] Also growing up in Ensley in the

1950s, Ann McCray Penick recalled roller skating on Twelfth Place in her Moro Park neighborhood, located several blocks from where Dorothy Inman-Johnson grew up:

> Yeah. One big thing. And that was every year, and I was fortunate to live in the neighborhood. This is 12th Street here. They blocked it off—the city. From this end and all the way up to 13th Street here we skated the whole week of Christmas—the week before Christmas and the week after until we went back to school after New Years. In this street, no cars were allowed to come down this street and we skated. Roller skated. And everybody was here from all over the city would come here to 12th Place to skate. . . . From seven in the morning until dark, this street was filled with kids skating. This was a fun time for me. . . . Like I said, they had skating rinks. But, then blacks wasn't allowed—we couldn't go in them. So, for these kids to go skate once a year was really something for them.[80]

Figure 1.2. Row of double shotgun houses in Ensley, 1958. The double shotgun had two dwelling units under one roof. (De Leuw, Cather and Company, *Ensley– Pratt City Urban Renewal Study*, prepared for the Housing Authority of the Birmingham District, August 1958)

In these and other examples, Birmingham's black community was able to creatively respond to the discrimination and segregation that they faced. Dating back to at least the 1930s, black residents also formed neighborhood associations, called civic leagues, which lobbied for better public services or attempted to provide these services on their own (see chapter 7). Nevertheless, the fact was that although Birmingham was established with the intent of using black labor to do the heavy lifting required in an industrial city, its black residents were treated as second-class citizens, and consequently their homes and neighborhoods were inferior to those enjoyed by the city's white residents.

Residents of other black neighborhoods found similar problems to those of Ensley. Rosa Kent described her Collegeville neighborhood located in North Birmingham: "Our community was a rejected community when it came down to the city. Every three or four houses didn't have any running water. The streets were so dirty, they weren't paved. Women had to hang out their clothes at night because if a car came through you couldn't see anything for the dust."[81]

In his Harriman Park neighborhood where he moved in 1948, Benjamin Greene found that there was one water meter that served all the residents on his street. The woman who owned the property served by the water meter charged all the other residents for use of her water. Because the street is located on a hill, residents at the top of the hill had diffculty getting the water they needed. In addition, none of the roads in the neighborhood were paved and there were no sanitary sewers.[82] Similar circumstances existed in the Grasselli Heights neighborhood, located in Southwest Birmingham. John Culpepper reports that in the 1950s, when he moved into that neighborhood, the dust from the unpaved streets meant that a person could not sit in front of his house and the neighborhood had no fire hydrants.[83] Drainage was also a problem in black neighborhoods, with open ditches creating flooding problems when rains were heavy. According to Simmie Lavender, in his Jones Valley neighborhood, which borders Valley Creek, "they didn't have ditches, they had rivers."[84] Fannie Brown had similar recollections of flooding from nearby Village Creek in her East Birmingham neighborhood: "That creek came all the way across the street into the yard and looked like a river."[85]

In sum, Birmingham was a city shaped by planning. Its earliest visionaries saw it as an industrial city in which the abundant black labor of the South would provide a lower-cost alternative to the white labor employed in the industrializing North. But the low cost of black labor came at a cost that was borne by Birmingham's black residents themselves in the inferior houses and neighborhoods most were forced to occupy. By 1920, as the Blaine Brownell quote reminds us, most of Birmingham's blacks lived in the city's "vacant spaces," a pattern that would last well into midcentury. After 1920, Birmingham, the planned industrial city, began to look to comprehensive planning as a means for further organizing the city. But in so doing, Birmingham would employ planning as a tool that would not only regulate land use but also would help to maintain the inequality of housing and neighborhood opportunity that had already developed.

2 Planning and Jim Crow

Two significant movements of the early twentieth century, one southern and the other national, influenced the development of planning in Birmingham and planning's most visible manifestation in Birmingham, racial zoning. In the South, Birmingham, like other southern cities and states, adopted Jim Crow laws that were used to segregate blacks and whites in various public and commercial places. Nationally, planning—particularly zoning—was adopted by many cities during the early part of the twentieth century as a means to use separation of land uses to protect property values. Together, these movements encouraged Birmingham and other southern cities to develop racial zoning ordinances that would supplement existing Jim Crow laws by also regulating where whites and blacks could live.

Throughout the South, municipalities adopted Jim Crow laws in the first two decades of the twentieth century to segregate whites and blacks in public places.[1] During this period, the City of Birmingham constructed a complex set of laws that were designed to completely separate whites from blacks. Whites were particularly concerned about sharing city parks with blacks and periodically complained to the board of aldermen that parks should be segregated. In 1910, the Birmingham board of aldermen responded by adopting legislation that denied blacks the opportunity to use city-owned parks.[2] At the same time, the city provided no city parks for blacks and allocated only a small amount of funds for black playgrounds.[3] Not until May 31, 1942, did Birmingham create the first city-owned park for use by blacks, Memorial Park in the South Elyton neighborhood located immediately southwest of downtown.[4]

The board of aldermen also adopted a law in 1910 requiring segregation of races on public transportation.[5] During this period, the Hillman Hospital and Louisville and Nashville railroad station were segregated, and the city zoo and library were closed to blacks.[6] By 1930, Birmingham had adopted ordinances preventing the mixing of races in dice, dominoes, or checker games, as well as in restaurants, pool rooms, railroads and street rail facilities, street cars, or toilet facilities. Just in case this list was not sufficiently exhaustive, Birmingham also prescribed segregation in "any room, hall, theatre, picture house, auditorium, yard, court, ball park, public park, or other indoor or outdoor place."[7] These ordinances left no doubt about the city's total commitment to racial segregation.

Within this broad movement to exercise Jim Crow in every aspect of urban life, by 1910 efforts emerged to legislate where whites and blacks could live. By 1913, a number of southern cities, including Baltimore, Richmond, Louisville, and Atlanta, as well as some smaller cities, had adopted residential segregation ordinances.[8] Baltimore's 1910 law, adopted in response to a black attorney moving into a white neighborhood, prohibited blacks from moving into all-white blocks and whites from moving into all-black blocks.[9] On the heels of Baltimore's law, Richmond's 1911 racial zoning law prohibited residential integration and expanded the Baltimore definition of all-black and all-white blocks to include blocks where a majority was black or white. The Richmond ordinance was upheld by the Virginia Supreme Court in 1915.[10] Atlanta's 1913 racial zoning ordinance, modeled after the Baltimore ordinance, also adopted the Richmond model of using the majority race on a block to determine the designation of racially mixed blocks. The Atlanta ordinance failed its initial court test, but a revision was sustained by the Georgia Supreme Court in 1917.[11]

A 1914 Louisville racial zoning ordinance was adopted in response to white residents' concerns about the effect of integrated neighborhoods on property values.[12] At the same time, Louisville's ordinance attracted the attention of the National Association for the Advancement of Colored People (NAACP) central office, which sent its attorney, J. Chapin Brinsmade, to Louisville to mount a case against the city's racial zoning law. In cooperation with the local branch of the NAACP, a test case was arranged whereby William Warley, president of the local NAACP branch, offered in October 1914 to buy a lot located in a designated white block from Charles Buchanan, a white realtor.[13] Warley's offer included a stipulation stating, "It is understood that I am purchasing the above property for the purpose of having erected thereon a house which I propose to make my residence, and it is a distinct part of this agreement that I shall not be required to accept a deed to the above property or to pay for said property unless I have the right under the laws of the State of Kentucky and the City of Louisville to occupy said property."[14] After Buchanan accepted Warley's offer, Warley refused to pay for the lot, citing the racial zoning law as preventing him from occupying the land. Buchanan then sued for breach of contract.[15]

With the lower courts affirming Louisville's racial zoning ordinance, the NAACP brought the case to the U.S. Supreme Court.[16] In its November 5, 1917, decision striking down Louisville's racial zoning ordinance, Justice Day, writing for a unanimous court, focused attention on the fact that Buchanan, the white property owner, was prevented by the racial zoning law from selling his property to Warley, a black man. Distinguishing this case from the Supreme Court's previous decisions upholding racial segregation laws, *Plessy v. Ferguson* and *Berea College v. Kentucky*, Justice Day wrote: "The case presented does not deal with an attempt to prohibit the amalgamation of the races. The right which the ordinance annulled was the civil right of a white man to dispose of his property if he saw fit to do so to a person of color and of a colored person to make such disposition to a white person."[17] Writing that the Louisville ordinance was thereby a violation of the Fourteenth Amendment's prohibition of the taking of property rights without due process, the Supreme Court ruled that racial zoning was unconstitutional.[18]

In the period prior to the *Buchanan* decision, Birmingham had also considered racial zoning. In January 1911, soon after Baltimore's segregation law was adopted, a race zoning law was proposed by Birmingham board of aldermen member George Huddleston.[19] Two years later, after Birmingham had converted to a commission form of government, Birmingham commissioner James Weatherly revived the issue and proposed a racial zoning law, citing the benefits of racial zoning to the protection of property values. He stated, "We have had several complaints that a man building a nice home has had its usefulness and value partially destroyed by negro dwellings near there."[20] Supporters of the law also argued that racial zoning would help the city deal with its sanitation problems.[21] The city commission approved this law, but one day before its enactment in July 1914, the commission referred the law back to the city attorney. E. A. Brown, a respected black attorney who lived in the Smithfield neighborhood, led a committee of blacks that met with the city commission that day. After the meeting, the city commission, noting that the law was based on the Louisville and Richmond racial zoning ordinances, asked the city attorney to investigate court rulings regarding these two ordinances.[22]

Two years later in 1916, the Birmingham city commissioners were still sitting on their nearly adopted racial zoning law, waiting to see what happened to the other racial zoning laws in the courts. In 1915, Virginia's highest court had upheld Richmond's racial zoning law, but Louisville's 1914 law was being challenged in the *Buchanan* case, and by late 1915 the NAACP had already filed an appeal with the U.S. Supreme Court.[23] This meant that Birmingham would still have to wait for a resolution on this issue.

Nevertheless, pressure from white neighborhoods to adopt a racial zoning law persisted. In March 1916, newly elected Birmingham commissioner Arlie Barber reported to his fellow commissioners that several houses were being constructed in the Ensley neighborhood, in the city's northwest, some of which had been leased to blacks, "to the great objection of white people who lived adjacent." Commissioner James Weatherly explained to Barber "that there was a city ordinance already drafted and ready for a vote the moment the U.S. Supreme Court handed down a decision that the using of the police powers of a municipality to segregate negroes in certain parts of a city was not in conflict with the Fourteenth Amendment of the federal constitution."[24] Despite receiving "several complaints of white people that negroes are encroaching upon their property, moving near to the white section of the city, and making the property less valuable," the city commission continued to postpone adoption while waiting for a U.S. Supreme Court decision on the constitutionality of the 1914 Louisville racial zoning statute.[25] With the 1917 *Buchanan v. Warley* decision, however, it seemed that efforts to achieve official designation of black and white residential areas had come to an end.

Despite the Supreme Court's 1917 decision, Birmingham and other southern cities persisted in their attempts to obtain legally sanctioned residential segregation.[26] In contrast to the period prior to 1917, however, many of these cities conceived of racial zoning as but one part of a *comprehensive* effort to zone their cities' land areas. After 1917, racial zoning initiatives were frequently prepared by planners and included a variety of land use classifications, based not only on race but also on the comprehensive zoning categories of land use, density, height, bulk, and setback.[27]

In the nation, support for comprehensive zoning came primarily from business and class interests seeking to protect property values. Although the nation's early zoning and planning movement had been motivated by a concern for the eradication of congestion and slum housing, the primary concern that motivated the adoption of zoning ordinances was the protection of property values. Reformers of the Progressive era, such as Benjamin Marsh, were inspired by the example of German zoning, which they saw as instrumental in reducing the unhealthy and unsafe congestion that characterized the nation's largest cities. Although Progressive-era reformers trumpeted the value of zoning for solving the problems of the cities, adoption of the first comprehensive zoning ordinance in the United States was accomplished in New York City at the behest of Fifth Avenue merchants concerned about the encroachment of the garment industry into their previously exclusive territory. Zoning had begun as a reform movement to make the city a better place for its poorer inhabitants but had been converted by business and class interests into an effort to maintain property values and keep out unwanted land uses and population groups.[28]

Not surprisingly, business leaders in the South also appreciated the value of zoning as a protector of property values.[29] The property value protection rationale could also be used to market planning and zoning as the means by which cities could legally segregate whites and blacks.[30] As indicated by Birmingham commissioner Weatherly's comments on the efficacy of racial zoning for protecting property values, southern whites were certainly sympathetic with the belief that racial mixing affected property values. They believed, or hoped, that comprehensive planning and zoning could be used to provide a new legal defense for legislating racial segregation.

Birmingham had flirted with the idea of comprehensive planning in 1914, but it was not until comprehensive zoning had gained legitimacy that the city would seriously pursue planning land uses. In 1914, the city contracted with Boston landscape designer Warren H. Manning to prepare a city plan.[31] The plan, published by private subscription in 1919, made recommendations on transportation, natural resources, parks, land use, and a downtown civic center.[32] Manning's plan called for the creation of zoning districts, and he made some general land use recommendations.[33] Of these, only the civic center concept was ever implemented, resulting in a civic square surrounding the city's Capitol Park.[34] Other recommendations, such as Manning's proposal for acquisition of land for parks and recreation areas, were generally ignored, even after a 1925 Olmsted Brothers plan for the Birmingham Park and Recreation Board elaborated on Manning's concepts.[35]

Twenty years later, in a letter to one of the men who helped publish his Birmingham plan, Manning reflected on why his suggestions were never carried out: "I have come to feel from my experience with town planning projects and the experiences of others that a plan must be the plan of the people guided by experienced planners and not the plan of an expert who is supposed to 'know it all.' I now feel that if we had called in the aid of many people in Birmingham in securing data and in giving advise [sic] that we could have made a plan that would have been largely realized in a few years."[36]

In contrast to the community's tepid response to Manning's plan, Birmingham's business community and white neighborhoods reacted quickly and favorably to the concept of land use zoning. One year after the publication of Manning's plan, in June 1920, the Alabama chapter of the American Institute of Architects wrote the Birmingham City Commission urging the adoption of zoning that would prevent the encroachment of commercial and industrial activities into residential areas. As was the case with New York City's pioneering zoning ordinance, the immediate threat that propelled interest in zoning came from the incursion of unwanted land uses in an exclusive area. In this case, the target was the Highland Avenue area, on the city's south side, that was home to many of Birmingham's most affluent families.[37] Soon thereafter, the Birmingham Real Estate Exchange, representing the city's realtors, called for adoption of a comprehensive zoning plan, emphasizing the importance of zoning for the protection of property values.[38] Three years before, the Real Estate Exchange had bragged about its defeat of "several drastic and unreasonable housing 'reforms.'" These earlier reforms had been aimed at establishing minimum housing standards in Birmingham's black neighborhoods.[39] Clearly the push for zoning was not coming from any social reform tradition, such as provided the original impetus for zoning in New York

City, but rather from business interests that saw zoning as a mechanism for protecting property values.

In quick response to these sentiments and to a request made by a group of residents, the city commission, in November 1920, passed its first zoning ordinance, declaring a neighborhood in the Ensley area as "strictly residential."[40] Soon other neighborhoods in Birmingham began asking for similar treatment, but at the same time property owners sought to enjoin the city from limiting their ability to use their property as they saw fit. By the spring of 1921, a property owner had obtained a temporary injunction restraining the city from interfering with his right to construct a retail store in an area that had been declared residential.[41] In response, the city's realtors and commissioners urged passage of a state enabling law that would permit Birmingham to regulate land use through zoning.[42]

In late 1920, during this brief flurry of zoning actions, Birmingham's city commissioners heard, as they had in 1916, complaints from whites about blacks moving into their neighborhoods. In one incident, the city commission responded by convincing a black home buyer to sell his house to the white residents of the neighborhood, while reminding the white residents that the U.S. Supreme Court had declared racial zoning to be unconstitutional.[43] Within two years, however, the Birmingham city government saw the possibility of using comprehensive zoning as a means by which a racial zoning ordinance could be adopted. By the end of 1922, with the counsel of the Birmingham Real Estate Exchange, the city commissioners and the city attorney fashioned a state zoning enabling statute that included the following passage: "For the promotion of the public peace, order, safety, and general welfare, such municipal corporations may, within residence districts established pursuant to this act, further regulate as to the housing or residence therein of the different classes of inhabitants, *but such regulations are not hereby authorized as will discriminate in favor of or against any class of inhabitants*" (emphasis added).[44]

By invoking a "separate but equal" clause in the proposed enabling statute, Birmingham was attempting to take advantage of the fact that the Supreme Court had not yet renounced the separate but equal doctrine of its 1896 landmark *Plessy v. Ferguson* decision. Birmingham city attorney W. J. Wynn believed that the proposed state enabling act might not be constitutional, but because "the federal constitution prohibits discrimination, not segregation," and because the proposed statute did not discriminate against whites or blacks, it stood a chance of being declared constitutional.[45] Soon thereafter, responding to concern that the use of zoning to promote racial segregation would be found unconstitutional, Wynn responded that "racial separation ought to be possible of accomplishment under the same interpretation as the so-called 'Jim Crow' law, namely, that separation is not discrimination, but operates to the advantage of both races."[46]

City Attorney Wynn's initial comment was in response to a *Birmingham News* editorial supporting the zoning enabling legislation but criticizing the racial zoning element of the proposed enabling act. While supporting the zoning law's purpose of protecting residential areas from invasion by nonresidential uses, the *News* questioned the constitutionality of the use of zoning for enforcing residential segregation, citing the U.S. Supreme Court's decision on this matter. The *News* also questioned the practicality of enforced residential segregation, noting that "white neighborhoods change" and that the creation of white and black zones would prevent blacks from improving their housing conditions, while making it harder for white property owners to dispose of their property when white demand diminished. The *News* also expressed concern that the segregation of black neighborhoods would result in the lack of "consideration in the way of paving, lights, sanitation, policing" and predicted that proximity to white neighborhoods would encourage "better citizenship on the part of the majority of these colored people."[47]

In contrast, the *Birmingham Age-Herald* supported the state enabling act, stating that "it would help to preserve harmony of the races and protect property values." Weaving together racial separatist and property value arguments, the *Age-Herald* editors wrote, "There is little stimulus to investment when the investor cannot count upon the permanent character of the neighborhood where he has placed his money or founded his rooftree." This was followed by a statement that whites and blacks should live separately because each group wants to be with its own race.[48]

Leaders of Birmingham's black community came forward to protest racial zoning. A committee of black professionals and clergy included its chairman, Oscar W. Adams, editor of the *Birmingham Reporter;* Reverend Charles L. Fisher, pastor of the Sixteenth Street Baptist Church, whose congregation consisted of many black professionals; and Reverend H. N. Newsome of St. John African Methodist Episcopal (AME) Church, the oldest and largest AME church in the city. The committee met with city officials and wrote a letter of protest that was published in the *Birmingham Reporter*. The *Reporter* wrote that the committee's presentation to the Birmingham City Commission on January 15, 1923, stressed that while blacks "would prefer to live to themselves," areas of the city that are completely black "are without the necessary sanitary arrangements, street improvements, lights, police protection and the necessary comforts given other peoples in the municipality."[49]

These leaders recognized the deficiency of public services in black neighborhoods and saw it as being exacerbated by racial zoning. In an editorial published prior to the meeting with the city commission, the *Birmingham Reporter* wrote: "Some might get the impression that the Negro would oppose the bill because they desire to live with or near white people. Nothing is further from the truth. They oppose the measure because Negroes are unprotected when they are not near white people. They don't have police supervision, lights are not given, streets are not kept up and a general lack of interest is exercised in any absolute Negro community."[50]

The Adams committee also attempted to appeal to the white community's economic self-interest. Reflecting on the outmigration of blacks from Alabama to the North, the committee's letter to the city commission contended that black workers were less likely to stay in Birmingham if they had to contend with confinement to neighborhoods with inferior services. Calling attention to the issue of labor turnover, the committee wrote "laborers in the industries are frequently changing" and that "whatever will further arouse or increase such restless state would be destructive and should be avoided."[51]

Finally, citing the *Buchanan v. Warley* decision, the Adams committee wrote that racial zoning in Birmingham was likely to be declared unconstitutional by the courts.[52] The *Birmingham Reporter* had previously attributed Wynn's willingness to advocate a law of questionable constitutional validity to his statement that even if the racial zoning provision is unconstitutional, the "psychology" of the ordinance would be helpful and that it might be "some time" before the ordinance is challenged in the courts.[53]

Since it was not until 1946 that the racial zoning law was challenged in the courts, Birmingham's backup defense turned out to be its most effective rationale for a racial zoning statute. At the time that Birmingham was formulating its zoning plan, white power in Birmingham was reinforced by the intimidating strength of the Ku Klux Klan, the organizational weakness of the Birmingham branch of the NAACP, and the absence of black voting power. According to Kenneth Jackson, the Birmingham Klan was "perhaps the most powerful klavern in the Southeast" and had an estimated 10,000 to 14,000 members, including many local business leaders and public officials.[54] In addition to the Klan's activities, the Birmingham Police Department was a source of violence against blacks during the 1920s.[55]

The NAACP branch in Louisville, with assistance from the national NAACP office, had been instrumental in organizing the *Buchanan v. Warley* lawsuit that tested that city's racial zoning law.[56] In contrast, the Birmingham branch of the NAACP was nearly dormant. Founded in 1919, the Birmingham branch had soon succumbed to fear of white violence and to apathy and by the 1920s had become inactive. In January 1931, the branch had six paid members. The branch was not reorganized until 1932.[57]

Finally, Alabama's voting laws, including the white primary, the poll tax, and property and literacy requirements resulted in the disenfranchisement of Birmingham's blacks. In the 1880s, blacks had constituted 45 to 48 percent of all registered voters in that city, but the 1901 Alabama constitution had used these devices to greatly diminish the number of black voters. By 1928, only an estimated 352 blacks were registered to vote in Birmingham, rising to only about 712 ten years later.[58] As a result, Birmingham blacks had no power to challenge the city's elected leaders at the polls and hold them accountable for their actions.

Given this context, City Attorney Wynn's statement that racial zoning might not be challenged in the near future appears to explain why Birmingham was willing to adopt an ordinance that was seen, even in the white community, as unlikely to be upheld by the courts. Cast in the cloak of comprehensive planning and zoning, which was sweeping the nation, racial zoning could now be sold as simply protecting private property values. But in case this reasoning failed to impress the courts, Birmingham was also counting on the power imbalance between its white and black populations to keep racial zoning out of the courts.

Consequently, the Birmingham city commissioners and real estate interests persisted in preserving racial zoning in their proposed state zoning enabling act. As a result, in September 1923, the Alabama legislature passed a zoning enabling act that contained the same language permitting racial segregation as had been proposed by the Birmingham city commissioners and realtors.[59]

Soon after passage of the state enabling act, Birmingham's city commissioners urged quick adoption of a zoning ordinance. The commissioners' attention was sparked by an application for a building permit to construct housing for blacks in an area adjacent to the homes of white residents. City commission president D. E. McLendon noted that if a zoning law was in place, the city could prevent dwellings for blacks from being constructed in this neighborhood. McLendon promised that a local zoning law would be adopted in 1924.[60]

Progress in preparing a zoning law, however, did not come easily. Standing in the way of adoption was an estimated twenty-thousand-dollar expense for mapping the city, as well as delays in appointing zoning commissioners to draw up a zoning ordinance.[61] Half of this amount was finally authorized by the city commissioners in October 1924, but the zoning commission did not begin active work until February 1925.[62] Soon thereafter, the zoning commission began a national search for a city planning consultant. After considering Robert H. Whitten, a nationally recognized zoning consultant, the zoning commissioners selected planning consultant Morris Knowles, who was chairman of Pittsburgh's city planning commission and who contributed to *The Survey*'s 1912 analysis of Birmingham's housing conditions. The zoning commissioners had prepared for their job by visiting Pittsburgh, Cleveland, New York City, and Washington, D.C., and they concluded that the Pittsburgh zoning scheme was most relevant to Birmingham.[63]

The consideration of Whitten and Knowles and the selection of the latter are significant for two reasons. First, both Whitten and Knowles were national leaders in the zoning movement. Whitten had been instrumental in creating the New York City zoning ordinance and had prepared zoning ordinances in several Cleveland suburbs; Providence, Rhode Island; Dallas; and Atlanta.[64] Knowles had been named by Commerce Secretary Herbert Hoover in 1921 to the advisory committee that drafted the Commerce Department's 1924 model zoning enabling act, *A Standard State Zoning Enabling Act*.[65]

Second, both Whitten and Knowles were involved in the creation of racial zoning statutes in other cities. In 1922, Whitten had written a zoning plan for Atlanta that included de jure racial segregation. Knowles, in 1931, developed a general plan for Charleston, South Carolina, that included the designation of areas for blacks and whites.[66] In considering Whitten and Knowles and in hiring Knowles, Birmingham was operating in the national mainstream of American planning and zoning. That both Whitten and Knowles were capable of preparing comprehensive zoning ordinances that contained racial zoning provisions indicates the ease with which the U.S. planning and zoning movement could accommodate itself to race-based planning.[67]

After hiring Knowles, the Birmingham zoning commission lost no time in asserting the importance of racial segregation. One day after announcing the selection of Knowles, and before any extensive field-work and mapping could be done, the zoning commission approved the establishment of a racial boundary between the white Graymont neighborhood and the black Smithfield neighborhood, located about one and one-half miles west of Birmingham's central business district. The zoning commission's racial boundary corresponded to a line drawn by the Graymont Civic Association in 1923. Except for some slight shifting to the west, the boundary would remain intact until racial zoning was invalidated by the U.S. Supreme Court in 1951. The speed of this action demonstrates that despite the rhetoric of comprehensive zoning employed by Birmingham in the 1920s, and used later when Birmingham was attempting to defend racial zoning in the federal courts, the actual delineation of racial boundaries began strictly in response to white neighborhood demands for racial segregation. While the city planning and zoning movement of the 1920s provided a protective cover for racial zoning, the motivation to use comprehensive zoning to enforce racial segregation was rooted in the same white opposition to racial integration that prompted the near-adoption of a racial zoning law in 1914.[68]

After sixteen months of preparation, Birmingham's zoning commission completed its zoning plan and submitted it to the city commission for approval. On July 13, 1926, the city commission approved its first zoning ordinance, effective August 4, 1926.[69] Under Sections 9 and 10 of Article II of the ordinance, occupancy by blacks and whites was restricted. Under Section 9, "in 'A-1' [single-family dwellings] and

'B-1' [multifamily dwellings] Residence Districts, no building or part thereof shall be occupied or used by a person or persons of the negro race." Whites were similarly restricted from living in A-2 and B-2 Residence Districts.[70]

Three months after adoption of Birmingham's first zoning ordinance, the U.S. Supreme Court, in *Euclid v. Ambler,* upheld the constitutionality of zoning. Birmingham's city attorney, W. J. Wynn, wrote city commission president Jimmy Jones that the Supreme Court decision meant that Birmingham's new zoning law was not only likely to withstand legal challenge, but it might even be able to avoid a court challenge. He wrote: "The effect of the decision is to sustain the validity of a typical zoning ordinance on all of its essential features. This decision is so clearly in point as to very greatly increase the chances of Birmingham's zoning laws being upheld; it is so strong and so clearly in point that it may even have the effect of deterring anyone from testing the validity of our law."[71] In reviewing the Supreme Court's specific holdings, however, Wynn did not mention whether he thought the decision had any direct implications for racial zoning. Consequently, it is not possible to determine whether Wynn's optimistic statement about the city's zoning law included a belief that the Supreme Court's decision in *Euclid* had opened a path for racial zoning.

Others in the South believed that the Supreme Court's *Euclid* decision did offer the prospect for reconsidering racial zoning. In 1927, in the *West Virginia Law Quarterly,* George Hott wrote, "If a municipality can prevent the establishment of a 'Piggly-Wiggly' store in a residential section, without violating any of the constitutional prohibitions, it should follow that an ordinance, excluding negroes from a 'white' zone and vice versa, should, in the absence of infringement of existing property rights, be constitutional."[72] Hott hoped that popular support for racial segregation would eventually persuade the Supreme Court to change its mind on racial zoning; and with the *Euclid* decision in place, the City of Birmingham, as well as other southern city governments, hoped that comprehensive zoning was large enough to include the segregation of races as well as the segregation of land uses. In addition to Birmingham's zoning ordinance, Atlanta; Dallas; Dade County, Florida; Norfolk; Richmond; Oklahoma City; Miami; New Orleans; and Winston-Salem each adopted comprehensive racial zoning ordinances or plans after the *Buchanan v. Warley* decision.[73] In many instances, these zoning ordinances and plans were prepared by nationally recognized planning experts such as Whitten in Atlanta in 1922; Knowles in Birmingham in 1925 and Charleston in 1931; and Harland Bartholomew in New Orleans in 1927. As Christopher Silver has noted, racial zoning after the *Buchanan* decision was a southernwide movement in that region's larger cities, fed by the national planning movement's embrace of zoning as a tool to protect property values and assisted by nationally recognized leaders of the planning and zoning movement in the 1920s.[74]

Although Birmingham's racial zoning ordinance was part of a southern post-*Buchanan* movement using comprehensive planning to reinforce racial segregation, Birmingham's ordinance stands out because it remained unchallenged until struck down by the U.S. Supreme Court in 1951. In Norfolk and New Orleans, local NAACP branches were able to challenge racial zoning ordinances, with the U.S. Supreme Court ruling the New Orleans law unconstitutional in 1927.[75] Atlanta's 1922 racial zoning ordinance was struck down by a lower federal court in 1926 as was Richmond's 1924 ordinance in 1930.[76] In contrast, Birmingham's racial zoning ordinance remained on the city's statute books for twenty-five years. Consequently, it had a significant impact on that city's neighborhoods during the second quarter of the twentieth century, both in terms of fixing in time land uses in developed areas as well as setting future land uses in less-developed areas of the city.

Map 2.1 shows the actual distribution of neighborhoods zoned for black occupancy in 1926. In many cases, the zoning map was *retrospective;* its boundaries recorded land uses that had already been determined prior to government intervention. The Smithfield neighborhood, for example, located just west of the city's center and the intersection of Interstates 65 and 59, was by 1910 an established black neighborhood.[77] In the East Birmingham neighborhood located about two miles east of the I-65 and I-59 intersection on I-59, Tenth Avenue had by World War I become a dividing line between the black neighborhood to the north and the white neighborhood to the south.[78] The 1926 racial zoning map recognized this distinction and zoned the two areas accordingly.[79]

Of course, by setting the boundaries of black neighborhoods in the city's zoning ordinance, Birmingham was assigning them a per-

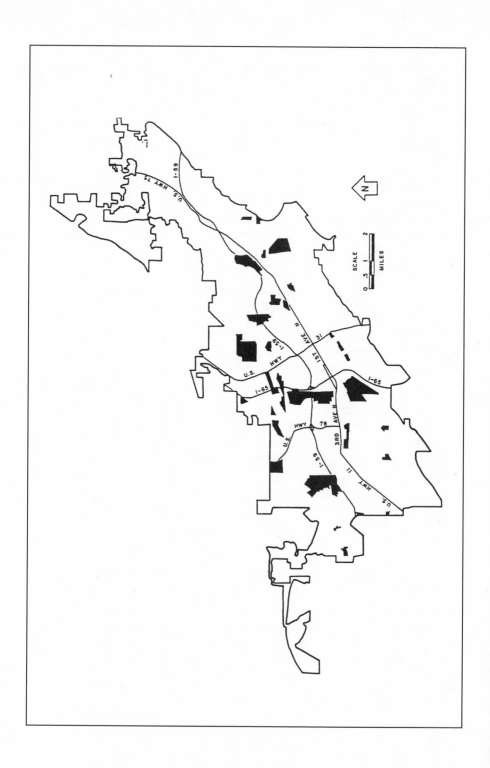

manency that they may not otherwise have had. In implementing the zoning ordinance, Birmingham saw to it that the racial boundaries remained fixed. According to the city's longtime zoning board of adjustment chairman John H. Adams, 360 applications for converting property from white to black occupancy were denied by the board between 1926 and 1935. According to Adams, if these application had not been blocked, the white zones "would now have negro tenants therein . . . which would have brought about a very much larger invasion of white zones by colored during the past years of the depression."[80] The city's leading black journalist, Emory Jackson of the *Birmingham World,* confirmed that the city was not willing to relinquish land zoned for whites. He said that petitions to change white land use designations to black were usually denied by the city.[81]

But the racial zoning map was also *prospective* and reflected a fundamental choice made by the city in determining its future. As noted, the 1919 Manning plan and the 1925 Olmsted Brothers plan called for a substantial increase in park and recreation space in Birmingham. Both plans proposed the building of a water-based park along Village Creek, which runs east-west through the northern half of Birmingham. Village Creek's waters had initially been used by many of Birmingham's early iron industries who located along its banks in the mill towns of East Birmingham, North Birmingham, Thomas, and Ensley, each of which the city annexed in the Greater Birmingham annexation of 1910. After 1910, Birmingham's industries used alternative sources of industrial water, but the future of Village Creek remained in question. The Olmsted firm was aware that the creek had become a "storm-water drainage channel" that was prone to periodic flooding and predicted that this problem would only get worse as development continued. They saw that the best use for Village Creek was as a linear park, whose natural features could provide recreational opportunities for city dwellers while also providing natural flood control.[82] By the time of their report in 1925, however, residential development along the banks of Village Creek in East Birmingham had been taking place

Map 2.1 (*opposite*). Areas zoned for black households in Birmingham in 1926. (Bobby Wilson, "Black Housing Opportunities in Birmingham, Alabama," *Southeastern Geographer* 17 [1977]; courtesy of *Southeastern Geographer*)

since World War I, with black laborers buying the lots closest to the creek.[83] The Olmsted firm proposed only a fairly narrow park for this portion of Village Creek (see map 2.2, in which East Birmingham is the area surrounding Coosa Street and Tenth Avenue).

But farther west, in the portion of Village Creek bounded by Ensley to the south and Pratt City to the north, the Olmsteds proposed a much broader water-based park (see map 2.2). In contrast to East Birmingham, this area around the creek had not been fully developed and consequently there was still opportunity to preserve the area as a park without having to buy out existing residents. The City of Birmingham did not heed the Olmsteds' advice, however, and in the 1926 zoning map, the areas along Village Creek lying along the banks of the Ensley and Pratt City neighborhoods were zoned for occupancy by black residents.[84] In fact, the zoning map did not even include a recreational land use category. While delineating existing parks, it did not use its powers to set aside any future areas for park development, either along Village Creek or anywhere else in Birmingham.

Overall, with the exception of a two-mile stretch in the easternmost portion of Birmingham (the East Lake area in map 2.2), the neighborhoods bordering Village Creek were zoned for either heavy industry or occupancy by black households.[85] Not only did this result in the loss of a major park system, but the worsening flooding problems associated with Village Creek were thereby disproportionately inflicted on the city's black residents. Although flooding would worsen after construction of the Birmingham Municipal Airport in 1931 and shopping centers after World War II, both the Olmsted firm and the Birmingham City Commission had identified Village Creek's flooding problem by 1926.[86] By zoning the Village Creek neighborhoods for black occupancy, the city was knowingly taking steps that would exacerbate flooding problems while assuring that those problems would be experienced most directly by the many black residents living in the creek's vicinity.

By the 1970s, the floods had worsened significantly such that the Army Corps of Engineers estimated annual property losses at $2.5 million.[87] Since then, with federal and local funds, four hundred households have been relocated, with plans to relocate more. In place of the black households in East Birmingham, the city has constructed a public park, which is the first completed project of the Village Creek

Greenway.[88] Seventy years after the Olmsted plan proposed such a greenway, it is finally being implemented.

In addition to assigning Birmingham's black residents to flood-prone neighborhoods, the 1926 racial zoning map reinforced existing patterns in which blacks tended to live in or near industrial or commercial areas. Map 2.3 is a 1940 census map of Birmingham, showing the city's fifty-two census tracts.[89] Fifteen of the tracts were 75 percent or more black, and, as table 2.1 shows, seven of these tracts (6, 7, 9, 14, 26, 42, and 46) also included land that was zoned for heavy industry. In contrast, table 2.2 shows that of twenty-five census tracts with a 75 percent or more white population, only three (tracts 3, 23, 35) also included areas with heavy-industry designations. Predominantly black census tracts were about four times more likely than white tracts to contain land designated for heavy-industry land use.

Moreover, four tracts (43 through 46) located in the area south of downtown (tract 27) housed nearly seventeen thousand persons but contained only small areas that were zoned black residential. Instead, the bulk of these neighborhoods were zoned for commercial and light industrial uses, but under these land use categories these neighborhoods could be occupied by blacks or whites, although it is clear in this case these neighborhoods were occupied primarily by blacks. Consequently, racial zoning in Birmingham extended beyond the designation of residential areas for blacks; it also included the zoning of black residential areas for nonresidential uses.

Yale Rabin has identified this practice in a number of cities throughout the South and placed it in a special category of racial zoning that he calls *expulsive zoning,* the designation of black neighborhoods within commercial or industrial zones. Expulsive zoning is actually effected when these nonresidential uses so diminish the residential quality of a neighborhood that its residents are displaced by industrial or commercial uses.[90] In this case, much of the black population in tract 44 was relocated as the area was redeveloped as the University of Alabama at Birmingham (see chapter 5). But even before construction of UAB in the 1950s, blacks living in commercial areas were vulnerable to redesignation of their residences to white residential occupancy.[91]

At the same time, only one black neighborhood in Birmingham was designated for predominantly single-family occupancy: the Enon

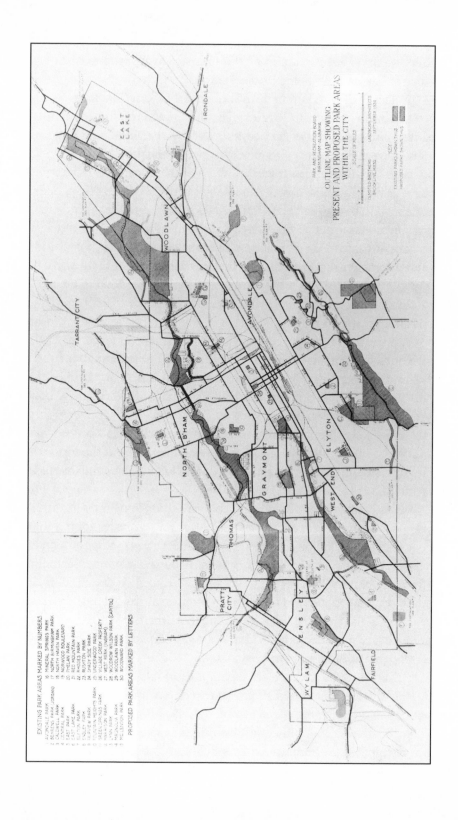

EXISTING PARK AREAS MARKED BY NUMBERS

1. AVONDALE PARK
2. BELVIEW PARK (URBAN)
3. CALDWELL PARK
4. CENTRAL PARK
5. NORWOOD BOULEVARD
6. EAST PARK
7. EAST LAKE PARK
8. ELYTON PARK
9. ENSLEY PARK
10. FAIRVIEW PARK
11. FEDERAL HEIGHTS PARK
12. GREEN SPRINGS PARK
13. HIGHLAND PARK
14. INGRAM PARK
15. MANILLA PARK
16. MCLENDON PARK
17. MINERAL SPRINGS PARK
18. NORTH BIRMINGHAM PARK
19. NORTH HAVEN PARK
20. PHELAN PARK
21. RED MOUNTAIN PARK
22. RHODES PARK
23. RUSHTON PARK
24. SHADY SIDE PARK
25. UNDERWOOD PARK
26. VILLAGE CREEK PROPERTY
27. WEST PARK (INGRAM)
28. WOODROW WILSON PARK (CAPITOL)
29. WOODLAWN PARK
30. WOODWARD PARK

PROPOSED PARK AREAS MARKED BY LETTERS

PARK AND RECREATION BOARD
BIRMINGHAM, ALABAMA

OUTLINE MAP SHOWING
PRESENT AND PROPOSED PARK AREAS
WITHIN THE CITY

OLMSTED BROTHERS   LANDSCAPE ARCHITECTS
BROOKLINE, MASS.   SEPTEMBER 1924

SCALE OF MILES

KEY
EXISTING PARKS SHOWN THUS
PROPOSED PARKS SHOWN THUS

Ridge neighborhood located in census tract 14 (see map 2.3).[92] All other neighborhoods zoned for black occupancy could also house multifamily dwellings, as well as hotels and other group living facilities.[93]

Overall, the 1926 racial zoning ordinance meant that predominantly black neighborhoods in Birmingham were much more likely than white neighborhoods to be located near areas zoned for heavy industrial uses. These neighborhoods were also less likely, as in the case of tracts 43 through 46, to be protected by a residential zoning classification. They were also much less likely to be zoned exclusively for single-family occupancy.

With these outcomes the divergence between the promise and reality of planning was made clear. Nationally, planning advocates had portrayed planning and zoning as the means by which property values could be protected from unwanted industrial and commercial uses. As planning and zoning came to Birmingham, as well as to other southern cities in the 1920s, zoning would also be used as the subterfuge by

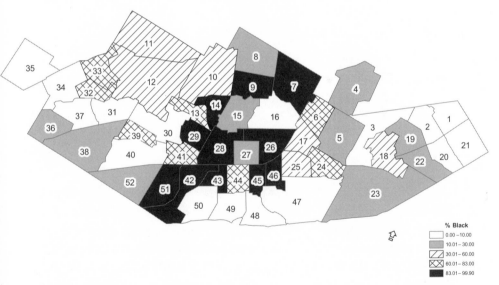

Map 2.3. Birmingham, Alabama, 1940 census tract map. (Source: 1940 U.S. Census)

Map 2.2 (*opposite*). Olmsted Brothers plan for Birmingham's parks. (Olmsted Brothers, *A System of Parks and Playgrounds for Birmingham*, Park and Recreation Board of Birmingham, 1925)

Table 2.1. Zoning characteristics of predominantly black tracts in Birmingham (75% or more black)

Tract	1940 black population	Tract zoning characteristics
6	3,235	Black residential, heavy industry
7	4,845	Black residential, heavy industry
9	6,276	Black residential, heavy industry, light industry
13	2,045	Black residential
14	3,622	Black residential, heavy industry
26	4,577	Commercial, heavy industry
28	9,661	Commercial, light industry
29	7,403	Black residential
32	5,939	Black residential
42	4,673	Black residential, heavy industry
43	4,384	Commercial, light industry, small black residential area
44	4,467	Commercial, light industry, small black residential area
45	5,197	Commercial, light industry, small black residential area
46	2,843	Commercial, light industry, heavy industry
51	2,134	Black residential, small commercial, undeveloped land
Total	71,301	

65.5% Total percentage of city's black population

Sources: U.S. Bureau of the Census, *Population and Housing, Statistics for Census, Tracts, Birmingham, Alabama*. Washington, D.C.: U.S. Government Printing Office, 1942; 1926 Birmingham Zoning Map.

which these cities could adopt racial zoning laws that had been struck down by the U.S. Supreme Court in 1917. The logic of property value protection that propelled the zoning movement's progress could be applied to the legal separation of the races.

Moreover, given that both nonresidential land uses and black residential land uses were seen by Birmingham's political and business leaders as threatening property values in white neighborhoods, it made sense for the 1926 zoning law to draw lines that resulted in black neighborhoods being placed near the many heavy industries that had located in that city. But in doing so, the 1926 zoning law showed that the promise of zoning applied to white neighborhoods and the reality

Table 2.2. Zoning characteristics of predominantly white tracts in Birmingham (75% or more white)

Tract	1940 white population	Tract zoning characteristics
1	2,783	White residential
2	1,767	White residential
3	3,776	White residential, commercial, heavy industry
4	4,144	White residential, black residential
8	6,279	White residential, black residential, commercial
15	6,779	White residential, black residential, commercial
16	8,423	White residential, black residential
19	2,619	White residential, black residential
20	2,155	White residential
21	3,933	White residential
22	2,378	White residential, black residential
23	3,964	White residential, black residential, heavy industry
27	3,333	White residential, commercial
30	6,131	White residential, commercial
31	5,214	White residential
34	5,618	White residential, commercial
35	3,754	White residential, commercial, black residential, heavy industry
36	2,334	White residential, black residential
37	4,032	White residential
38	5,302	White residential, black residential
40	9,387	White residential, commercial, black residential
47	10,508	White residential
48	4,707	White residential
49	9,118	White residential, commercial
50	4,245	White residential
52	2,200	White residential, black residential
Total	124,883	
	78.7%	Total percentage of city's white population

Sources: U.S. Bureau of the Census, Population and Housing, Statistics for Census, Tracts, Birmingham, Alabama. Washington, D.C.: U.S. Government Printing Office, 1942; 1926 Birmingham Zoning Map.

of zoning for black residents reinforced occupancy patterns that re-sulted in their occupancy of the city's less desirable areas.

The reality of zoning also meant that while predominantly white neighborhoods were zoned for white residential land use, in areas to the south of downtown Birmingham, black neighborhoods were pre-dominantly zoned for light industry and commercial land uses, not for residential land uses. Such a pattern, which Rabin indicates was repeated throughout the South, created conditions that latter genera-tions of planners would categorize as "slum and blighted," thus en-abling the expulsion of blacks from these neighborhoods.

Finally, the divergence between the promise and reality of planning is seen in what happened to the Manning and Olmsted plans' rec-ommendations for parks, particularly in the Village Creek watershed. The promise of planning for Birmingham was created by the natural beauty of a creek running through the city and the opportunity to cre-ate a water-based park such as the Riverway in Boston or Washington Park in Chicago, both of which were cited in the Olmsted report. But the reality of planning in Birmingham was the rejection of this future in exchange for the zoning of the Village Creek areas in East Birming-ham and Ensley as black neighborhoods. The irony of planning in Bir-mingham is that seventy years after the zoning of these neighbor-hoods for black residents, the City of Birmingham, along with the federal government, is spending millions of dollars to relocate these residents to higher ground while slowly transforming Village Creek into the river parkway that Manning and the Olmsteds had advocated.

Challenging Racial Zoning: Smithfield Court

Although the Birmingham racial zoning law was not challenged in the courts during the twenty years following the ordinance's passage, on several occasions the law was threatened with the possibility of a court challenge. The most significant of these instances took place in con-junction with the development of Birmingham's first federally assisted housing project, Smithfield Court, completed in 1937.[94]

Although the federal government had made a limited foray into the development of housing during World War I when the government built housing for war workers, the first significant sustained federal in-tervention in the housing market began in 1933 with the creation of the

Public Works Administration's (PWA) Housing Division. Between 1933 and 1937, the PWA Housing Division provided direct support for fifty-eight housing developments.[95]

In the spring of 1934, soon after the PWA had announced that it would begin direct development of low-cost housing, Dr. J. D. Dowling, health officer for the Jefferson County Board of Health, organized the Birmingham Housing Committee to develop a plan for applying for PWA funds. The committee was established because the City of Birmingham lacked authority to borrow money from the federal government to engage in slum clearance and construct replacement housing.[96] Under such circumstances, the PWA encouraged local communities to create a sponsoring committee that would invite the PWA Housing Division to implement a slum clearance project. In choosing cities for such development, the PWA examined the degree of support in the city for the project.[97]

The Birmingham committee consisted of J. C. deHoll, a member of the Birmingham Board of Education; Reverend Graham Lacy, pastor of Second Presbyterian Church and chair of the housing committee of the Interracial Relations Committee; Mrs. Paul Lanier, representing the Alabama Federation of Women's Clubs; Margaret Beddow, representing the Jefferson County Anti-Tuberculosis Association; Charles Feidelson, editorial writer for the *Birmingham Age-Herald;* James E. Mills Jr., editor of the *Birmingham Post;* Mrs. M. E. Morland, social worker; Rabbi Morris Newfield of Temple Emanuel; General J. C. Persons, banker; and Guy Snavely, president of Birmingham-Southern College.[98] No black Birmingham residents were invited to serve on the committee; instead, in October 1934, a group of black citizens were organized at the request of Dr. J. D. Dowling to serve as the Auxiliary Committee to the Birmingham Housing Committee. The auxiliary committee included B. G. Shaw, bishop of the African Methodist Episcopal Zion Church, Fourth District, as chairman; Mrs. H. C. Bryant, chairwoman of the YWCA; Mrs. R. M. Nelly; Dr. B. J. Anderson; Dr. E. W. Taggart, president of the NAACP Birmingham branch; and Arthur Parker, principal of Industrial High School for Negro Children, reputed to be the largest black high school in the world, with an enrollment in 1935 of 3,221 students.[99] In February 1935, Birmingham Housing Committee member Graham Lacy wrote a PWA official requesting that at least two members of the auxiliary committee be included on the housing committee.[100] Lacy was unsuccessful, however, and according to a 1938 statement of the Inter-Denominational Ministers Alliance, the auxiliary committee "worked diligently with the [Birmingham Housing] committee in all things when permitted to do so, but in major matters were left out entirely."[101]

The housing committee focused its attention on two potential projects, one in a white neighborhood and one in a black neighborhood. Both of these projects were in "slum areas" and would entail slum clearance as well as development of new low-cost housing. Although the PWA housing program was not targeted exclusively to slum clearance, Interior Secretary Harold Ickes, who oversaw the PWA's programs, believed slum clearance was a central focus of the housing division's efforts. Moreover, under the standard operating procedures of the PWA Housing Division, housing was to be segregated based on the racial characteristics of the neighborhood. Consequently, nearly all PWA housing developments were occupied exclusively either by blacks or by whites. Moreover, in most cities where there were two PWA housing projects, the PWA developed one for blacks and one for whites.[102]

Birmingham would be no exception. The housing committee focused its efforts on developing a white project in the white neighborhood and a project for blacks in the black neighborhood.[103] The white project area, located in the Avondale neighborhood about one and one-half miles east of downtown, consisted of 130 houses and stores, classified as "mill village type" duplex buildings, constructed close together, with little light and air space. The area was conveniently located to a large number of manufacturing plants.[104]

The Birmingham Housing Committee selected a site in Smithfield for the black housing project. Although the original site consisted of twenty-two blocks, Talbot Wegg, of the PWA Housing Division, requested that the site be reduced, which it was, to seven and one-half, plus an additional one and one-half blocks. In the nine-block area, the committee found 436 families living in 524 dwelling units, including 356 duplexes. Nearly all of the houses were shotgun houses, and according to the committee's research, "in a bad state of repair." The area had higher than normal rates of "crime, delinquencies, disease, bad sanitary conditions, general filth, as well as, general poverty." Despite the poverty, the report noted that 19 percent of the families were members of the black middle class, including "school teachers, railway employees, and nurses."[105]

Consequently, although Smithfield had significant problems with poverty and substandard housing, it also had a black middle-class component, thereby presenting a mixed economic community.[106] In terms of pure economic need, Smithfield was better off than many other neighborhoods in Birmingham that were labeled as slums. In a survey of twenty-two slum areas in Birmingham, Dr. J. D. Dowling and F. A. Bean of the Jefferson County Board of Health reported that sixteen neighborhoods contained more blight than Smithfield. Of twenty-six indicators of blight, Smithfield ranked in the upper quartile of the twenty-two slum areas on only three indicators: population density, incidence of substandard housing, and number of illegitimate births. Thirteen of the twenty-two slum areas were predominantly black, and of these Smithfield displayed less blight than nine other African American neighborhoods.[107]

Thus, although the Smithfield neighborhood was selected for a PWA housing project partly on the basis of need, it is apparent that other factors entered into its selection as well. In its assessment of the nine-block area in which the Smithfield project would go, the Birmingham Housing Committee noted that Eighth Avenue, which lay adjacent to the project area, was one of the major streets connecting the center city to the west side of Birmingham. The neighborhood also had good streetcar service. Moreover, the nine-block site was located just west of Industrial High School. Also, several black churches were within walking distance of the site, and nine small stores served the area. Consequently, the project site was accessible to key community services.[108]

Unlike nearby Atlanta or Nashville, however, the PWA would build only one housing development in Birmingham, and it would be the Smithfield Court development for blacks. On October 17, 1934, the Birmingham Housing Committee formally selected the Avondale and Smithfield sites for PWA slum clearance and redevelopment as low-cost housing. Their recommendation was forwarded to the PWA Housing Division. Also at this meeting the housing committee "conferred" with the auxiliary committee members, as well as other black leaders, including former *Birmingham Reporter* editor Oscar W. Adams.[109]

By 1935, the PWA had approved only the Smithfield site. Responding to an inquiry from Alabama Senator Hugo Black about the white housing project, Horatio Hackett, director of the PWA Housing Division, explained the PWA's decision to go ahead with a housing project for blacks: "At the time our investigators visited Birmingham it was felt that the need of a slum clearance project for negroes was much more acute and for that reason the colored project was advanced first. A white project in the city will require further study of existing conditions before our recommendations can be made."[110] The PWA's choice of Smithfield was consistent with the wishes of the Birmingham Housing Committee. According to its chairman, J. C. deHoll, because housing need was greatest in the black community, the housing committee recommended to the PWA that the entire amount of Birmingham's housing allotment of $2,500,000 be spent on the Smithfield project.[111]

In September 1935, Smithfield became the only PWA housing project, however, as the PWA rejected the Avondale site because of concern over difficulty with purchasing land and the possible encroachment of adjacent industry. Instead, the PWA recommended a white housing project site in Graymont, just west of Smithfield and south of McLendon Park. Soon after, PWA housing funds ran out and the project was not funded until 1937 after Congress had passed the U.S. Housing Act that created the modern public housing program, administered by the U.S. Housing Authority.[112]

Soon after approval of the Smithfield site, controversy began to surround the relocation of families from the six blocks that the project would actually occupy—a controversy that would eventually result in a challenge to the city's racial zoning ordinance. On May 8, 1935, Sallie B. Russell and twenty-seven other homeowner households in the six-block Smithfield site wrote PWA Housing Division director Horatio Hackett and Interior Secretary Harold Ickes to complain about their forced relocation. The protesters contended that their neighborhood was not a slum "because this district is centrally located, convenient to car lines, surrounded by schools including the Industrial High School, and having many modern homes several of which have been recently improved. It would be impossible for the Home Owners to find a suitable site as good and convenient as the one we have."[113] Consequently, the same elements of convenience that made the Smithfield site attractive to the PWA and the Birmingham Housing Committee also made it attractive to the small core of homeowners in the area who wished to remain.[114]

Later in May, Sallie Russell, on behalf of the homeowners in her neighborhood, wrote J. C. deHoll to object to being forced to sell and move. In addition to listing the concerns that had been expressed to Hackett and Ickes, Russell emphasized that "We have no place to go that is as centrally located as we have now due to the Zoning law of 1926 for Negroes."[115]

DeHoll responded to the protesting homeowners by holding a meeting with them and the members of the Birmingham Housing Committee on May 29, 1935. J. E. Bacon, land appraiser for the PWA Housing Division, was told by deHoll that no one from the federal government should be at the meeting with the residents. Later, Bacon learned that deHoll had scheduled a meeting on June 4 with the protesting homeowners and the auxiliary committee in an attempt to have the black leaders on that committee influence the homeowners to sell their properties.[116] Members of the auxiliary committee later acknowledged their role in influencing the homeowners in the area to sell their homes.[117]

Several weeks later, Sallie Russell wrote Harold Ickes that even though the housing committee had offered the homeowners "a substantial increase in the price offered and every variety of persuasion," the homeowners had not changed their opposition to selling their properties. Russell emphasized that their opposition was based on personal attachments to the area, not money, and "the fact that we *cannot* find locations in the immediate vicinity or one equally desirable."[118] Again, Russell was expressing concern about Birmingham blacks' limited housing choices permitted by the city's racial zoning law.

The City of Birmingham then responded to the homeowners' complaint by expanding the black housing zone slightly to permit at least some of the homeowners to move their homes just west of where Smithfield Court would be constructed. This was done by moving the racial dividing line 150 feet to the west of Center Street. Several of the homeowners whose houses were being purchased for Smithfield Court could then move their houses west, across Center Street, to face their old neighborhood.[119] This solution, of course, required an amendment to the city's 1926 zoning law that had established Center Street as the north-south racial dividing line between white Graymont and black Smithfield. On June 28, 1935, the Zoning Board of Adjustment adopted a resolution calling for the rezoning of nine lots just west of Center Street from white to black occupancy. The board took this action on the condition that three additional lots that separate white homes from the new black lots would be "donated to the City as a park" and "planted heavily in shrubs and trees making the dividing line between white and negro occupancy." The city's dedication of these three lots to parkland also required that they only be useable by whites.[120]

In November 1935, the Birmingham City Commission took up the June 28 Zoning Board of Adjustment resolution. In preparing Mayor Jimmy Jones for the issue, zoning board chairman John H. Adams wrote him that the Smithfield zoning case was "the most important appeal ever made to the City Commission since the adoption of the Zoning Ordinance of Birmingham, effective August 4, 1926." The appeal was important because Adams claimed that, "Certain 'legal authorities' have prepared direct application papers to the Supreme Court of the United States for an immediate ruling and enforcement of the Constitutional right of any person or persons of any race or color to buy, sell, rent or live peaceably in any part of any community, town, or city within the United States."[121]

The appeal to the June 28 zoning board decision had been filed by Walter L. McNeil, president of the Graymont Civic League, representing the residents of the white Graymont neighborhood. On November 29, 1935, more than seventy-five white residents of Graymont attended the city commission's consideration of McNeil's appeal. McNeil contended that Center Street was the logical dividing line between white Graymont and black Smithfield and that it had been established "after public hearings and interracial meetings."[122] McNeil was apparently referring to the racial boundary that the Graymont neighborhood organization had drawn in 1923 that was incorporated in the city's 1926 racial zoning law.[123] McNeil also argued that moving the line would devalue the properties owned by white residents. Other white residents argued that the decision to change the zoning from white to black would only result in future requests to move the racial boundary further west until a request would be made to take in the all-white Birmingham-Southern College, lying some eight blocks west of Center Street.[124] When the city commission voted unanimously to approve the zoning change, Graymont resident Herman J. Downey told the city commissioners, "In other words, you've sold out the white people to the Negroes."[125]

Despite such accusations, the Birmingham City Commission voted to move the racial boundary in order to keep racial zoning on the books. Even McNeil admitted as such when he was paraphrased as saying that "the destruction of the entire zoning law is threatened if the change is not made." Harold Henderson, former member of the Zoning Board of Adjustment and chairman of the appraisal board for the Smithfield Court project, testified that federal officials insisted that a place be found for blacks relocated from the Smithfield Court site, and that he had devised the plan to shift the racial boundary west as a way of satisfying federal interests while providing a "permanent barrier between the races."[126] Previously, J. E. Bacon, the PWA Housing Division's local representative, had told the city commission that the PWA was delaying the opening of construction bids until the city had changed the zoning and that it was necessary to take action before December 15, 1935.[127]

Although the Smithfield development's challenge to the city's racial zoning law had been settled, Birmingham's black community continued to press for enhancement of the Smithfield Court project and the role that blacks would play in managing it. The settlement of the Smithfield Court relocation issue represented an early sign of the ability of the black community in Birmingham to obtain outside support from the New Deal administration in Washington, D.C. The New Deal represented an unprecedented federal intervention in local policy matters that gave blacks in Birmingham and other cities at least the opportunity to lobby for change. At the same time, after a period of quiescence in the 1920s, the black community in Birmingham was becoming organized and capable of sending a message to both the city and to Washington, D.C., that it aimed to have more influence over how its neighborhoods were planned and managed. The Birmingham branch of the NAACP, after having diminished to six members in 1931, had grown to 750 members by 1937 and showed a new willingness to take strong stands on key issues.[128]

Consequently, when members of the NAACP Birmingham branch and other black leaders learned that Smithfield Court would not be built as planned, they fired off protests to both the Housing Authority of the Birmingham District (HABD) and to the federal government.[129] Specifically, the black community in Birmingham protested the decision to remove the planned community center, to furnish the apartment kitchens with coal stoves instead of gas ranges, and to not furnish the kitchens with refrigerators.[130] The protest included public statements; a petition to H. A. Gray, director of Housing for the PWA, with the signatures of "thousands of our citizens"; and several trips to Washington by Birmingham's black leaders.[131] Responding to this criticism, the PWA assured black leaders that these deficits would be remedied, and when Smithfield Court was completed, it included all these features among its 544 units.[132]

As Smithfield Court was about to open in early 1938, black leaders in Birmingham began to protest plans to hire a white manager for the project. H. D. Coke, managing editor of the *Birmingham World*, wrote U.S. Housing Authority head Nathan Straus to protest rumors that a white would be named as manager of Smithfield Court.[133] At the same time, the Inter-Denominational Ministers Alliance, along with the leaders of several other black organizations, petitioned the federal government to hire a black manager and black staff, as well as to pay black Smithfield Court employees at comparable wages to what whites earned.[134] Once again, black leaders, including Bishop B. G. Shaw, *Birmingham World* editor H. D. Coke, and NAACP Birmingham branch president E. W. Taggart, traveled to Washington, D.C., to lobby housing officials on these matters.[135]

The impact of their efforts was limited, however. The city was aware that under the PWA's housing program, black managers frequently managed black projects, but the city was nevertheless adamant that the project have a white manager. Moreover, Mayor Jimmy Jones recommended that housing authority board member J. C. deHoll be the person for this post.[136] U.S. Housing Authority staffer Donald Jones agreed that in this case it would be necessary to appoint a white manager and suggested J. C. deHoll was the right person for the job:

I talked with some of the most important men in Birmingham and it is unquestionable that the philosophy of negro control in Birmingham indicates that any other policy would be fatal and subject to grave and continuous criticism. . . . The criticism which would be launched from the negro side would not be great as would a unified

opposition from the white side which is more important. There is
no question in my mind but that a white manager is the only logical
solution of this problem.[137]

Given the city's strong stance on this issue and the New Deal's general
acquiescence to local opinion, it is not surprising that U.S. Housing
Authority administrator Nathan Straus wrote HABD chair J. C. deHoll
that "the selection of personnel for the efficient management of the
[Smithfield] project is solely the responsibility of the Authority." Moreover, Straus went on to say that the legal obligation to pay prevailing
wages did not apply to "administrative personnel such as resident
manager, bookkeeper, rental clerk, and stenographers."[138]

Despite the flexibility granted, the housing authority grudgingly
hired a black bookkeeper, as well as other black staff, even though
HABD chair deHoll found it difficult to hire an experienced black
bookkeeper who would work for what deHoll said was the prevailing
wage. DeHoll reported that two factions in the black community had
attempted to control the selection of staff, which deHoll felt made it
more difficult to find an affordable black bookkeeper. DeHoll identified
Bishop Shaw and Oscar Adams as the leaders of one faction and the
Colored Democratic Club as the other, with D. L. White, an aspirant for
the manager's position, identified as its leader. DeHoll also pledged
that the housing authority would not pay blacks less than what whites
would be paid, in spite of the fact that "to do so is customary here."[139]

Although the housing authority also named A. T. Govan, who was
black, as resident manager of Smithfield Court, Bishop Shaw reported
that Govan testified that "he never took the responsibility of deciding
anything in the connection with the management of the project without the approval of his chief Mr. deHoll," who had his office at Smithfield Court and who had resigned from the housing authority so that
he could accept a position as its secretary and executive director.[140]
Straus responded by reminding Shaw that Smithfield Court was leased
to the Housing Authority of the Birmingham District and that body
had responsibility for employee relations.[141] Although the black community had achieved its goal of getting black staff employed at Smithfield Court, control of that staff still rested firmly with the white director of the housing authority and the housing authority's white
members.

Despite the increasing strength of Birmingham's black community and newfound ability to at least influence local public policy through federal intervention, Birmingham's racial laws and customs, including the racial zoning ordinance, remained in place through the end of the New Deal and World War II. It would only be after the war when blacks in Birmingham, as well as other southern cities, sought to improve their housing circumstances that they would succeed in successfully challenging the city's racial zoning ordinance. As in other southern cities, however, black efforts to obtain better housing would be greeted by white violence. In Birmingham's case, it would also mark the beginning of the city's twenty-five-year history of racial bombings.

3 Planning, Neighborhood Change, and Civil Rights

In its 1923 editorial criticizing the racial zoning component of the proposed state zoning enabling act, the *Birmingham News* argued that racial zoning would impede the process of neighborhood change, thereby harming both whites and blacks. Specifically, the paper wrote:

> There is another feature: white neighborhoods change. People seek other surroundings—there is a vogue for a certain neighborhood, and the older portions of towns and cities are sometimes deserted for newer and more modern ones. Very often negroes fall heir to these neighborhoods, and are glad to get them; there are better houses than the average of negro rental property, paving, sewerage, lights, and so on. To adopt a race segregation zoning ordinance would cut both ways—the owners of this unfashionable property would be cut off from a market, or perhaps the only rental class available, and the negroes would find an inexorable law against their better class moving into better surroundings. It would be to cut off a possible salvage value of such property.[1]

In other words, because racial zoning failed to recognize the forces of change that underlie urban housing markets, the *News* was saying that racial zoning was bad city planning. In making this argument, the *News* was both displaying a keen understanding of neighborhood change theory as well as correctly predicting where racial zoning would lead and what would lead in the end to its demise.

Although the term had not been invented by that time, in describing the neighborhood change process, the *News* was talking about the "filtering" or "trickle down" of houses and neighborhoods from whites to blacks. As neighborhoods age, and as new neighborhoods develop, demand for living in these neighborhoods subsides. If the older neighborhoods were predominantly white, then white demand declines, and, as the *News* notes, "very often negroes fall heir to these neighborhoods." In other words, the neighborhood filters from white to black households. The filtering process has been well described in the urban theory literature, and while much of this literature was developed after World War II, the *News* understood it well and therefore was in a position to warn Birmingham that racial zoning was not only illegal but also bad policy.[2]

Moreover, the *News* also understood the outcome of racial zoning. With racial zoning, owners of properties in older neighborhoods would be deprived of a market to which they could sell. White households would be moving out, but black households would be prevented from moving in. Property owners who wanted to sell or rent their properties would not be able to do so. And blacks who could afford to buy or rent in the white neighborhood—the "better class" as the *News* called them—would not be able to move into new neighborhoods, often with better services, and would be locked into their existing neighborhoods.

By twenty years later, right after the end of World War II, the *News's* predictions were borne out in the same neighborhood that had provided impetus for the first racial zoning boundary in Birmingham. That neighborhood, the Graymont–College Hills neighborhood, which in 1940 was represented by census tract 30 (see map 2.3), lay just west of the predominantly black Smithfield neighborhood, represented by tracts 13 and 29. In 1940, tract 30 had 6,296 residents, of which 6,131 (97.4 percent) were white (see table 3.1). In the same year, tracts 13 and 29 had a combined population of 10,070, of which 9,448 (93.8 percent) were black.

The Graymont–College Hills influence on racial zoning began in March 1925, one month after Birmingham's zoning commission began its work, when the Graymont Civic Association successfully lobbied the zoning commission to establish the first racial zoning boundary in the city.[3] Testifying to the importance of racial zoning, this "emergency" boundary was the first zone of any kind established by the commission. The racial boundary for the neighborhood conformed closely to one drawn two years earlier by the civic association. The Graymont representatives claimed that they did not want to see the same encroachment of blacks into their neighborhood that they reported as having occurred in Smithfield. According to the Graymont residents, "formerly there was a good white settlement in Smithfield, which has been abandoned as a result of negro encroachments . . . a Baptist and Methodist Church had to be abandoned and . . . hundreds of homes were sacrificed."[4]

The Graymont-Smithfield racial boundary that was drawn informally in 1923 and adopted by the zoning commission in 1925 largely became the same boundary that Birmingham adopted in its 1926 zoning plan.[5] Moreover, the main north-south boundary line between the white and black neighborhoods, lying one-half block east of Center Street, did not shift in the period between 1925 and 1949 (see map 3.1). The only exception was the half-block shift westward between Eighth Avenue and Ninth Court to accommodate the Smithfield public housing project (see chapter 2).

In drawing a racial boundary between the two neighborhoods, Birmingham's zoning commissioners had attempted in 1925 to assure neighborhood stability for the white residents of Graymont–College Hills. What they failed to see was that the racial boundary was untenable because it failed to recognize the dynamics of neighborhood racial change. The 1926 zoning map shows the eastern portion of the Graymont–College Hills neighborhood bordered on its north, east, and south by neighborhoods zoned for blacks.[6] In such areas, the pressure for black housing is likely to be great, and therefore the prospect of neighborhood racial change is likely to be very high.

In fact, by 1923, the Birmingham City Commission had already acted very quickly to prevent the possible entry of blacks into the Graymont–College Hills neighborhood. That year, the city commission attempted to block black entry into the south side of Graymont by acquiring a forty-acre parcel that was reportedly being eyed as the site for a "negro amusement park." White citizens of Graymont came to the city requesting protection, and the city commission responded with the purchase of the land and establishment of whites-only McLendon Park, named for the city commission president.[7] Thus the city commission was fully aware of the prospects for neighborhood racial change in Graymont–College Hills.

But despite the establishment of the park as a buffer and the establishment of a racial boundary in the 1926 zoning code, the Graymont–College Hills neighborhood still stood at the western edge of one of the

Table 3.1. Black population by census tract, 1940–1960

Tract	1940 Number	1940 Tract Population (%)	1950 Number	1950 Tract Population (%)	1960 Number	1960 Tract Population (%)
1	9	0.3	60	1.6	1	0.0
2	29	1.6	1	0.0	0	0.0
3	159	4.0	161	3.1	174	3.9
4	738	15.1	831	15.8	1,047	16.8
5	1,636	27.4	1,859	27.6	1,700	25.2
6	3,235	81.2	3,982	87.5	4,521	92.5
7	4,845	98.1	5,907	98.8	6,788	99.3
8	1,324	17.4	2,785	32.8	3,288	40.6
9	6,276	86.0	7,195	87.4	7,636	91.6
10	1,247	51.9	2,903	73.9	3,807	81.2
11	2,820	54.0	3,888	53.8	3,593	57.2
12	3,102	47.0	3,491	45.0	4,686	53.9
13	2,045	82.6	2,264	84.9	2,803	88.5
14	3,622	96.7	4,463	98.0	5,006	99.9
15	1,366	16.8	1,374	17.0	2,219	30.1
16	715	7.8	913	9.3	771	9.1
17	906	32.8	1,037	39.9	714	38.2
18	2,816	44.0	3,300	49.9	3,404	55.1
19	655	20.0	1,348	30.5	1,630	40.5
20	174	7.5	121	3.8	176	4.8
21	48	1.2	6	0.1	1	0.0
22	435	15.5	547	16.3	813	18.9
23	792	16.7	979	18.2	1,909	16.2
24	3,968	68.7	4,159	70.8	1,532	60.7
25	1,236	47.0	1,248	50.3	814	51.9
26	4,577	84.4	4,002	71.6	3,706	77.6
27	701	17.3	456	11.1	347	12.2
28	9,661	88.7	9,298	91.6	8,870	98.4
29	7,403	97.5	7,499	97.4	7,931	99.1
30	165	2.6	184	1.8	214	2.4
31	34	0.6	22	0.4	0	0.0
32	5,939	80.1	6,478	81.7	4,756	79.9

Table 3.1 *continued*

Tract	1940 Number	1940 Tract Population (%)	1950 Number	1950 Tract Population (%)	1960 Number	1960 Tract Population (%)
33	3,809	60.9	5,587	69.8	6,082	83.2
34	479	7.9	680	10.0	657	11.7
35	330	8.1	578	13.2	1,157	25.3
36	407	14.8	434	10.9	441	7.8
37	9	0.2	13	0.3	4	0.1
38	1,075	16.9	920	8.9	848	6.5
39	1,150	65.2	1,619	49.3	1,739	42.0
40	256	2.7	209	2.0	152	1.7
41	2,233	62.2	2,661	61.9	2,929	69.8
42	4,673	95.2	4,345	91.4	4,820	79.4
43	4,384	88.8	4,352	89.8	3,604	99.7
44	4,467	75.7	3,661	76.4	614	48.5
45	5,197	92.8	5,651	94.3	4,590	96.4
46	2,843	94.2	2,700	96.0	2,439	98.5
47	1,118	9.6	908	7.8	236	2.5
48	387	7.6	410	7.0	184	3.9
49	686	7.0	703	7.0	678	9.8
50	213	4.8	128	2.8	102	2.1
51	2,134	86.2	2,772	88.6	8,724	98.5
52	410	15.7	1,003	25.8	969	16.2
53	—	—	657	20.9	866	12.8
54	—	—	11	0.3	0	0.0
55	—	—	2,947	56.2	3,445	58.3
56	—	—	168	10.6	2	0.0
57	—	—	4,145	42.8	4,899	44.7
58	—	—	2	4.7	3	5.9
59	—	—	—	—	72	0.7
Total	108,938		130,025		135,113	

Sources: U.S. Bureau of the Census, *Population and Housing, Statistics for Census, Tracts, Birmingham, Alabama.* Washington, D.C.: U.S. Government Printing Office, 1942; U.S. Bureau of the Census, *U.S. Census of Population: 1950,* vol. 3, *Census Tract Statistics,* chap. 5. Washington, D.C.: U.S. Government Printing Office, 1952; U.S. Bureau of the Census, *U.S. Censuses of Population and Housing: 1960, Census Tracts,* Final Report PHC(1)-17. Washington, D.C.: U.S. Government Printing Office, 1961.

Map 3.1. Map of North Smithfield showing racial zones. (Photographic Collections of the Birmingham Public Library; Birmingham, Alabama, Police Surveillance Files)

city's largest concentrations of black neighborhoods. Map 3.2 shows that the Graymont–College Hills neighborhood, located in census tract 30, stood just west of a north-south swath of predominantly black neighborhoods located in tracts 10, 13, 14, 29, 41, and 51. In 1940, 18,684 black residents (17.2 percent of the city's 108,938 blacks) lived in these six census tracts. In 1950, the number of black residents in these six tracts had grown to 22,562 persons or 17.4 percent of the city's 130,025 black citizens (see table 3.1).

As the black population of Birmingham continued to grow and the existing areas zoned for black occupancy became increasingly inadequate, the Graymont–College Hills neighborhood stood directly in the path of the expanding black housing area. Black demand for housing in Graymont–College Hills was also fed by the fact that the adjacent black neighborhoods had a concentration of middle-class households that could afford to purchase homes in Graymont–College Hills. As the *Birmingham News* editorial noted, neighborhood racial change is likely to be led by the black middle class because they are in the best position to bid for housing in white neighborhoods.[8] Located just to the northeast of Graymont–College Hills, in 1950 the Smithfield (tracts 13 and 29) and Enon Ridge (tract 14) neighborhoods (see map 3.2), had

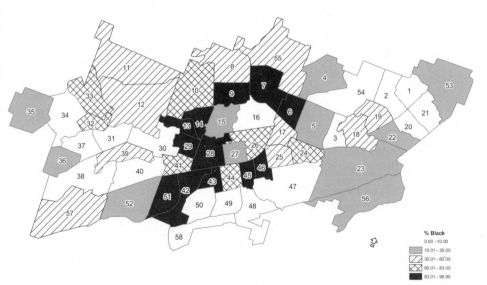

Map 3.2. Birmingham, Alabama, 1950 census tract map. (Source: 1950 U.S. Census)

the second- and third-highest median incomes of any predominantly black (75 percent or greater) census tract in Birmingham.[9] As described in chapter 1, the bulk of Birmingham's black middle class lived in these two neighborhoods.[10] Given the nearby concentration of middle-income blacks, who constituted part of a larger north-south continuum of black neighborhoods, it is not surprising that the Graymont–College Hills neighborhood, lying just to the west, became the locus of neighborhood racial change.

By the immediate post–World War II period, pressure for neighborhood racial change was also enhanced by the continued growth of the black population in Birmingham and the lack of space into which blacks could move. The city's black population had grown from 108,938 to 130,025 between 1940 and 1950, a population increase of 21,087 or nearly 20 percent (see table 3.1).[11] Thirty-eight percent of this increase was accounted for by the expansion of the city's boundaries in a major 1949 annexation that resulted in the addition of six new census tracts (tracts 53 through 58). But the remainder of the black population increase was primarily absorbed by existing census tracts that were at least 25 percent black in 1940. Only three of the twenty-six census tracts that were 75 percent or more white in 1940 (tracts 8, 19, and 52) underwent an increase in percent black of 10 percentage points or more between 1940 and 1950 (see table 3.1).

Instead, between 1940 and 1950, Birmingham's existing black neighborhoods absorbed much of the growth in the black population. The number of blacks living in census tracts that had 1940 populations 50 percent or more black increased by 8,858 between 1940 and 1950. Overall, new census tracts (53 through 59) and existing tracts in which the population was at least half black accounted for 16,788 (7,930 + 8,858) additional blacks in Birmingham, or slightly less than 80 percent of the 21,087 increase in the city's black population.

The racial zoning lines drawn in 1926 served to keep blacks confined to certain areas, and, as noted in chapter 2, the Birmingham Zoning Board of Adjustment made certain that changes to the racial zoning code were few. In 1944, when the Birmingham City Commission recodified its ordinances, it recorded all the changes made in the zoning law since 1926. Of the many zoning changes in this eighteen-year period, few entailed conversion to zones permitting black occupancy. What land was converted to black occupancy was primarily classified as "B-2" land use, indicating multifamily housing (B) that could be occupied by blacks (2). All together, eighty-nine scattered lots, parts of five different blocks, and about 1.6 acres of unsubdivided land were converted to B-2 between 1926 and 1944. In terms of conversion to "A-2," areas zoned for single-family homes occupied by blacks, Birmingham was even stingier, permitting only two whole blocks and parts of three other blocks to be rezoned to this category.

As noted in chapter 2, only one black neighborhood, Enon Ridge, had been zoned in 1926 for single-family homes. It was not surprising, therefore, that middle-class blacks living in Smithfield, which was zoned for multifamily housing, looked favorably on the Graymont–College Hills neighborhood and its single-family zoning. In the words of the *Birmingham News*, "There is literally no place for him [the Negro] to go, no district in which to buy or build that is not already closely surrounded by commercial or industrial property."[12]

In general, the City of Birmingham elected to cope with its black housing problems by retaining the same boundaries for blacks that had been prescribed in the 1926 zoning code. The resulting imbalance of black housing supply and black housing demand was exacerbated by significant demolition of housing for blacks in the immediate post–World War II period. During this time, the Jefferson County Board of Health vigorously pursued a demolition policy that resulted in the condemnation and vacation of "more than 1,200 Negro dwelling units" of which about one-half were located in census tracts 28, 43, and 44, located just west and south of downtown Birmingham. In April 1950, the Jefferson County health officer wrote that within the previous two and one-half years, "there has been very little building of new dwellings for Negroes to alleviate an increasing and acute shortage."[13] A federal observer reported that enforcement of health and sanitation laws had displaced nearly 2,500 blacks in the prior two years. Also, because the city's racial zoning laws often forced blacks to live in commercial or industrial areas, expansion of these uses was diminishing the supply of housing for blacks.[14]

Given the unequal treatment accorded black neighborhoods and the precedent set by *Buchanan v. Warley*, a legal challenge to Birmingham's racial zoning law should not be surprising, especially since such challenges had been mounted in other southern cities. As indicated, the organization most likely to pursue such a challenge, the local NAACP branch, was inactive for much of the 1920s and early 1930s. After the Birmingham branch was reorganized in 1932, it focused its attention on police brutality to blacks; lynching; discrimination against blacks in New Deal programs; defense of blacks accused of crimes, including the Scottsboro boys; and voter registration. It was not until after World War II that the Birmingham branch of the NAACP took up the racial zoning issue.[15]

By the time it began its campaign against racial zoning, the NAACP Birmingham branch had become so active that in both 1941 and 1947 the national office of the NAACP awarded the Birmingham branch its highest award, the Thalheimer Award, as the most outstanding branch in the nation. The Birmingham branch was rewarded for its rapidly growing membership, from 603 in 1938 to 8,500 members in 1946, and for its actions in combating police brutality; employment discrimination, including unequal public school teacher salaries; and voting rights.[16]

In this period of increased membership and heightened activity, the Birmingham branch in 1946 initiated a housing campaign that focused on providing more opportunities for improved housing for blacks by putting an end to racial zoning. The branch obtained authorization that year from the national NAACP office to raise five thousand dollars for a legal assault on racial zoning.[17] In August 1946, the Birmingham branch announced the beginning of its Better Housing Fund campaign and immediately reset its financial goal to $10,000.[18] September 15, 1946, was designated as Zoning Case Sunday, and black churches were asked to hold special collections for challenging racial zoning in the courts.[19] Significant individuals and organizations in the black community that pledged support to the campaign against racial zoning included the Alabama State Federation of Civic Leagues; Hosea Hudson of the Congress of Industrial Organizations (CIO); Mrs. Belzora Ward of the City Federation of Colored Women's Clubs; W. C. Patton of the American Woodmen; and Reverend J. L. Ware of Trinity Baptist Church.[20]

In launching its racial zoning challenge, the NAACP Birmingham branch relied on the legal skill of Arthur D. Shores. Shores, at that time the only practicing black attorney in Alabama, had begun arguing and winning NAACP-supported court cases in 1939 when he successfully filed suit against a white police officer for beating a black man.[21] In spite of Shores's success as an attorney, as well as the backing of the NAACP and the U.S. Supreme Court, which had been on the NAACP's side of the racial zoning issue since 1917, it would take Shores three tries before the NAACP succeeded in challenging Birmingham's racial zoning ordinances. The NAACP's initial lack of success was attributable to the city's ability to avoid a decisive and comprehensive challenge of its racial zoning law and the unwillingness of a federal judge to broadly interpret thirty years of case law that supported the NAACP's case. Only after the city forced a direct challenge to its racial zoning law did the local federal judge feel compelled to strike down racial zoning in Birmingham.

The NAACP's first try at ending racial zoning began on November 8, 1945, when Mrs. Alice P. Allen, secretary to the president of historically black Miles College, purchased a home near Eleventh Avenue North and Sixteenth Street, just northwest of downtown Birmingham and about sixteen blocks east of North Smithfield. The home was located in an area zoned commercial, which under Birmingham's zoning code meant that it was available for both black and white occupancy. Obviously, occupancy in a commercial area afforded less protection from unwanted uses nearby. In addition to these risks, blacks in Birmingham also faced the possibility that they would be zoned out of these areas. According to J. J. Green, chairman of the Birmingham branch's executive committee, "You may wake up any Wednesday after the City Commission meets on Tuesday and find that you have been re-zoned out of your home." Green cited examples in several areas in Birmingham, including Eleventh Avenue North.[22]

Mr. Green was apparently alluding to Mrs. Allen, for one week after her purchase the Birmingham City Commission voted to change the property's zone classification from commercial to B-1, multifamily housing for whites only.[23] The house was located on the north side of the street, a side that was occupied by whites. Directly south was a block occupied by blacks.[24] The real estate broker had attempted to sell the home to a white, but no buyers materialized, so the broker advertised the property to blacks. After she purchased the home, city officials told

Mrs. Allen she could not live there. Mrs. Allen persisted in preparing to occupy her new house, however, and rocks were thrown through the windows.[25]

Unable to occupy her house, Mrs. Allen retained Arthur Shores to file a federal district court suit against the city on August 6, 1946.[26] In preparing to respond to the Allen case, attorneys for Birmingham's Law Department recognized they had a weak case. Reflecting on the *Tyler v. Harmon* case, which had invalidated racial zoning in New Orleans in 1927, a law department staff member wrote in his notes that "The reversal of the decision of the State court without comment, other than 'Reversed on the authority of *Buchanan v. Warley* . . . ,' clearly indicates that the Court regarded the invalidity of ordinances segregating races with respect to residential districts was too well established to require discussion."[27]

These notes are consistent with earlier opinions expressed by Birmingham's city attorney James H. Willis. In 1941, a white property owner wished to take legal action against an adjacent property occupied by blacks in violation of the city's racial zoning ordinance.[28] Willis discouraged legal action by writing: "it would be most unfortunate if there were a court declaration of invalidity of our negro zoning regulations, for then, the situation would be completely beyond control and without benefit to your client. The chances for success of your client in litigation, if carried to the court of final resort, do not appear bright, and I would suggest that it would be better, all the way around, and even from the standpoint of your client, that litigation be avoided."[29]

Consistent with this belief that legal tests of the city's racial zoning law should be avoided, the city sought to minimize the impact of the Allen suit. On August 22, 1946, two weeks after Shores filed suit on behalf of Mrs. Allen, Birmingham's city commission repealed the November 1945 rezoning of her property. The city commission declared that the November 1945 rezoning "is and has ever been, null and void."[30] Although the commission claimed that the 1945 rezoning violated state law by providing inadequate public notice, the timing of the repeal suggests that the city was attempting to avoid a legal challenge, while conceding Mrs. Allen's right to occupy her property.

With the city attempting to limit to one house the case's impact on racial zoning, attorney Shores responded a week later by filing an amendment to Mrs. Allen's complaint that would make hers a class action suit on behalf of all blacks denied the right to use their property.[31] The city responded with a motion to dismiss, contending that the 1945 rezoning was null and void and that the city had made no effort to prevent Mrs. Allen from occupying her house.[32] The case was finally resolved when Shores's petition for dismissal was ordered by U.S. District Judge Clarence Mullins on January 9, 1947.[33] NAACP assistant special counsel Robert Carter had written Shores that the city's repeal of the rezoning meant that "I don't think we have a leg to stand on."[34]

Mrs. Allen was able to occupy her house, but racial zoning still stood in Birmingham. The city had been able to duck the racial zoning challenge because, in the end, Mrs. Allen's case had not been a good one to use against racial zoning. Just as the Birmingham City Commission could easily rezone an area from commercial to white occupancy, it could as easily undo this deed. Shores and the NAACP would have to find another test case.

Recognizing that the Allen case was not going to end racial zoning in Birmingham, the NAACP and Shores had already decided to pursue a second zoning suit. In December 1945, Samuel Matthews, a drill operator in the Ishkooda Ore Mines, and his wife, Essie Mae, had purchased two lots at 120 Eleventh Court, on the north side of the block between First and Second Streets in North Smithfield (see map 3.1 for location of the Matthewses' home in what was then a white zone). Lying one and one-half blocks west of Center Street, the lots were located in a B-1 zone reserved for white occupancy.

The Matthews family purchased the lots from William R. Coleman of the Coleman-Kendrick Real Estate Company. Coleman had purchased between thirty-five and fifty lots in the North Smithfield area, after he had learned that the city was considering rezoning the area B-2, for black occupancy, and proceeded to sell the lots to blacks such as the Matthews family.[35] Local real estate professional H. L. Farley later testified in court that the location of the lots discouraged whites from making a purchase. They were located one-half block from a predominantly black neighborhood and three blocks from the nearest white residences.[36]

The Matthews family proceeded to construct a home on the two vacant lots and on February 25, 1946, applied for and received a building permit from the city. In June 1946, however, the city denied the Matthews family a certificate of occupancy. On October 30, 1946, three months before petitioning for dismissal in the Allen case, Arthur Shores filed a petition on the Matthewses' behalf arguing that the certificate of occupancy had been denied solely on the basis of race and that the city had violated the Fourteenth Amendment of the Constitution by denying the family full use of its property. As in the Allen case, Shores argued that this was a class action suit, representing all

> Negro property owners of the City of Birmingham and tax-payers of the United States and residents and citizens of the State of Alabama and the City of Birmingham, who are denied the right to occupy and dispose of their property located in the City of Birmingham, solely on account of their race.[37]

No other plaintiffs in the class were named, however, as Shores contended that

> members of this class are so numerous as to make it impracticable to bring them all before the Court and for this reason plaintiffs prosecute this action in their own behalf and in behalf of the class without specifically naming the said members herein.[38]

In this case, where the Matthewses had built a home in an area that had been zoned white for many years, the city could not easily change the zoning as it had in the Allen case. In fact, residents of Graymont–College Hills had already made their feelings known about William Coleman's efforts to sell properties to blacks. The city had notified Graymont–College Hills residents of a possible rezoning in the neighborhood and the neighborhood association responded by calling a meeting to which Coleman was invited. Coleman tried to appease the white residents but told them if they did not want to purchase the properties to prevent black occupancy, then he was going to court. Coleman later was allegedly confronted by a white resident, J. E. Monteith, when Coleman was in the neighborhood showing properties to blacks. Coleman reported that Monteith asked him if he was going to sell more lots to blacks. When Coleman said yes, Monteith allegedly said: "We ain't going to stand for that at all. You better leave here now. You sold that lot down there to that negro knowing it was zoned for white people." When Coleman turned around, Monteith allegedly said: "You better get going. You'd better get going now. If you don't we are going to wait on you." Coleman pressed charges, but the case was thrown out for lack of evidence.[39]

Despite the fact that the Graymont–College Hills residents were not going to stand for rezoning the neighborhood to black occupancy, the city was again able to limit the impact of the NAACP's challenge to racial zoning when the federal court limited its decision to the Matthews residence. Although the city was hard-pressed to argue convincingly for the constitutionality of racial zoning, it was still able to maintain that the Matthewses' case did not present a class action suit.[40] In turn, Judge Mullins, citing the U.S. Supreme Court's 1917 decision in *Buchanan v. Warley*, ruled that the city's denial of a certificate of occupancy to the Matthewses violated the Fourteenth Amendment. He granted that the city's racial zoning law violated the rights of all blacks. With victory apparently in hand, Shores wrote NAACP special counsel Thurgood Marshall to tell him of the judge's ruling and to proclaim, "I have knocked out the Zoning Ordinance."[41]

Shores was wrong. In his written order, Judge Mullins only enjoined the city from enforcing its racial zoning law in preventing the Matthewses or any other black person from occupying the two lots on Eleventh Court North.[42] Shores had petitioned the court to declare Birmingham racial zoning law unconstitutional and void.[43] What he got instead was a decision, backed by thirty years of constitutional law beginning with *Buchanan v. Warley*, that Judge Mullins was willing to apply to only one residence in the city of Birmingham. Once again, the city, with the complicity of the federal district court, had succeeded in maintaining racial zoning in Birmingham.

Birmingham's resistance to the end of racial zoning was three-dimensional. On one plane, the legal battle against Shores and the NAACP was carried on by the city's lawyers. On a second plane, the city's elected leaders would respond, as they did in the Allen case, to the NAACP's challenge. On the third plane, an *extralegal* battle was fought in which Birmingham whites employed violence to intimidate blacks from moving in neighborhoods that had been designated white by the city's zoning code. In this respect, in the immediate post–World War II period, Birmingham was not alone. During this time blacks migrated to cities, both north and south, while whites moved to the suburbs. The result was significant neighborhood racial change and violence frequently accompanied this change. Arnold Hirsch, in his *Making the Second Ghetto,* documents the violent resistance of whites to the movement of blacks into formerly all-white neighborhoods in Chicago in the late 1940s and early 1950s. Similar acts of violence accompanied neighborhood change in at least eleven other major cities during this time period, including southern cities such as Atlanta, Dallas, Louisville, Tampa, and Birmingham.[44] A. L. Thompson, HHFA racial relations advisor, wrote of a 1952 meeting in Birmingham attended by race relations leaders from Birmingham, Atlanta, Dallas, and Rock Hill, South Carolina. As recorded by Thompson, the consensus of the group was that in the South,

> more often than not, real estate interests and fearful white home owners have joined forces to bar the development of suburban expansion areas for Negroes. Thus, hemmed in on one hand by burgeoning business districts and on the other by older white neighborhoods Negroes have had no choice but to seek a block-by-block conversion of the older housing from white to Negro occupancy. It is this desperate transition process which breeds conflict. The process has been repeated in place after place, with the inevitable climax of bombing and other measures designed to terrorize Negro homebuyers.[45]

In Birmingham, whites followed this scenario by responding with bombs to blacks moving into North Smithfield—bombs that would lead to the neighborhood's nickname of Dynamite Hill. Table 3.2 shows the ten publicized efforts made by mostly middle-class black households to move into areas zoned for whites between 1946 and 1950. In each instance, some form of violence or threat of violence took place, and in eight instances, bombs were set to intimidate blacks from moving into the neighborhood.

The first of these bombings took place on August 18, 1947, two weeks after Judge Mullins ruled in favor of the Matthews family, when an explosion blew off one side of their home and crushed the remainder of the house.[46] Although the Birmingham police investigated the bombing, no arrests were made, with the police report noting that "investigations failed to reveal sufficient evidence to make an arrest in this case."[47]

Table 3.2. Black efforts to enter white neighborhoods, 1946–1950

Name	Occupation	Date of bombing	Neighborhood
Alice Allen	Secretary to president of Miles College	No bomb, rocks thrown in 1946	11th Ave. and 16th St. (16 blocks east of North Smithfield)
Samuel & Essie Mae Matthews[a]	Drill operator, Ishkooda Ore Mines	August 18, 1947	North Smithfield
Bishop S. L. Green (two houses)	Bishop, African Meth. Episcopal Church of AL	March 25, 1949	North Smithfield
John Madison	TCI employee	March 25, 1949	North Smithfield
Willie German	Insurance salesman	Threatened, May 21, 1949, and soon moved out	North Smithfield
Rev. Milton Curry Jr. (same house that German attempted to occupy)	Pastor, New Zion Presbyterian Church	August 13, 1949	North Smithfield
Rev. E. B. DeYampert	Baptist minister	August 13, 1949	North Smithfield
J. A. Boykin	Dentist	April 13, 1950	Five blocks east of North Smithfield
B. W. Henderson (same house that Curry occupied)	Contractor	April 22, 1950	North Smithfield
Monroe & Mary Means Monk	TCI employee	December 21, 1950	North Smithfield

[a]Newspaper articles identified the Matthewses as moving into or near the East Thomas neighborhood, but the house was located in the 1886 Smithfield subdivision and was only two blocks west of Center Street, where the 1949–50 bombings took place.

The bombing may have slowed, but it did not stop, black migration into the Graymont–College Hills area west of Center Street. In 1948, four black families moved into the vicinity of Center Street and Tenth Avenue and a fifth moved in during March 1949.[48] On March 22, 1949, about twenty-five white members of the Graymont–College Hills Civic Association complained to the Birmingham city commissioners that the city's building department was issuing building permits that allowed blacks to construct homes west of Center Street and that other blacks were moving into houses west of Center Street formerly occupied by whites. Sam L. Chesnut, who moved to the neighborhood in 1908 and had lived in his home just west of Center Street since 1927, told the city commission, "we want them arrested and the zoning laws enforced" and "we've told you before that someone's going to get hurt."[49] Chesnut, as well as his neighbors John J. Gould and J. E. Monteith, each reported being approached about selling their houses. Gould had been approached by Hollins and Shores Realty Company and by the same William Coleman who had sold Samuel and Essie Mae Matthews their property. Hollins and Shores, headed by Arthur Shores, had also contacted Monteith, who refused to list his house with them.[50]

When the Graymont–College Hills citizens group reproached the city commission, fingers began to be pointed. The chairman of the city's zoning board of adjustment, George Byrum Jr., said he was aware of the zoning violations but was powerless to do anything about the situation as it was the job of the city's building inspector to enforce the law. The inspector had made no arrests, however, and his boss, public improvements commissioner Jimmy Morgan, one of Birmingham's three elected commissioners, stated, "I didn't know that we were issuing permits to Negroes to build in A-1 residential zones." Morgan equivocated, indicating that the racial zoning law should be enforced, but also stating that "our zoning laws are both weak and illegal." In contrast, Commissioner Eugene "Bull" Connor "strongly supported" the Graymont–College Hills citizens group.[51]

On the following day, the city's building inspector told the five black families living west of Center Street that they would have to move. Shortly after midnight on the following night, March 25, 1949, three black-owned houses located just west of Center Street were bombed; the houses, empty at the time, suffered significant damage.[52] Two of the homes were owned by S. L. Green, a bishop of the African Methodist Episcopal Church of Alabama. He had purchased the first of these homes at the end of 1948 and the one next door to it soon after when its owner, Mrs. W. A. Thomas, who had lived in the home for forty years, decided to sell her house because blacks were buying in the neighborhood. She told police investigators that when several real estate companies had listed her house they told her that the property

would be sold to a black household.[53] The third home had been purchased in February 1949 by Johnnie Madison, a Tennessee Coal and
Iron employee, and his wife, Emily, who worked at the Bankhead Hotel in Birmingham. They purchased the home through the Hollins and
Shores Real Estate Agency.[54]

As in the Matthews bombing, as well as subsequent bombings in
the North Smithfield area, investigations were conducted, but no arrests were ever made. One of the persons under investigation was
Robert E. Chambliss, who worked as a mechanic for the City of Birmingham garage. Chambliss was interviewed by police on May 23,
1949, two days after he allegedly threatened Willie German while the
latter was moving furniture into his new home at 1100 North Center
Street. German's new home was about one block from where the three
houses were bombed in March and just west of the Center Street racial
dividing line. According to newspaper reports, Chambliss, claiming
he was a member of the Robert E. Lee chapter of the Ku Klux Klan, told
German he should get out by midnight if he did not want his house
bombed. German moved out soon after.[55]

When interviewed by Birmingham detective Paul McMahan,
Chambliss admitted that he had spoken with German but denied he
had made any threat and claimed he was not really a member of the
Klan but had told German this in the belief that German would be
more likely to move out.[56] The city suspended Chambliss ten days for
his conversation with German; Chambliss was later fired by Mayor
Cooper Green when Chambliss broke a newsman's camera at a Klan
rally at which he was a participant.[57] Chambliss, who had been a member of the Klan since 1924, came under investigation for subsequent
bombings in North Smithfield. On April 29, 1950, Chambliss was
jailed as a "material witness" to the bombings but was released the next
day after he was questioned by police.[58]

Chambliss's niece later wrote that city commissioner and public
safety commissioner Bull Connor would not permit city detectives or
state investigators to interview Chambliss. Chambliss was a friend of
Connor's, and Connor reportedly used his office on occasion to help
Chambliss.[59] Chambliss's job with the city garage apparently was not
based on his skill as a mechanic. Connor said of Chambliss, "He could
about change a flat tire," implying that Connor had other uses for
Chambliss.[60] In 1963, Chambliss told FBI agents that Connor had

actually told him to warn Willie German away from the white side of Center Street.[61]

State investigator Ben Allen, who had been assigned by Alabama governor Jim Folsom to investigate the 1949 bombings, was told by a Klan leader that if he wanted to find out who was behind the bombings, he should "find out who Dynamite Bob's friends are" by arresting Chambliss and then waiting to see what happened. When Allen and his partner returned from lunch, they were told by the Birmingham police chief that, "he could not allow us to see our prisoner we had placed in jail because he was 'hired out'. In other words, he was tellin' us that he was under orders from 'Bull Connor' not to let us interview Robert Matthews at that time and place, which carried out the point to what the number-two Klansman had told us."[62] Neither Chambliss nor anyone else was ever charged for the North Smithfield bombings. In 1977, however, Chambliss was convicted of murder in the September 15, 1963, bombing of the Sixteenth Street Baptist Church in Birmingham that killed four black girls (see chapter 6).[63] While Connor's connections to the bombings may never be established, evidence suggests that he was very close to a prime suspect.

Although the white Graymont–College Hills Civic Association condemned the bombings, its leaders continued to press the Birmingham city commissioners to enforce and strengthen the city's racial zoning laws. Leaders of the Graymont–College Hills Civic Association advocated that a 150-foot-wide commercial buffer strip be placed on the east side of Center Street (see map 3.1). Ostensibly, this would make it easier to sell properties just west of Center Street to whites. But Arthur Shores, representing the black Birmingham Protective Property Association, countered that the creation of a commercial strip in an area previously designated for blacks would prevent black owners in this area from occupying their properties. The city commission responded by voting for a fifty-foot commercial buffer zone, which appeased neither side. Bull Connor, supporting the Graymont–College Hills residents, voted against the compromise.[64] The vote did not stand, however, as it was soon learned that over 140 black property owners had filed protests against the zoning. Representing well over one-fifth of the property owners in the proposed commercial strip, these protests meant that a unanimous city commission vote was required to pass the commercial buffer proposal.[65] Birmingham had gained no ground in resolving its zoning dispute.

In attempting to resolve the racial zoning issue, commissioners Jimmy Morgan and Bull Connor were clearly at odds. Connor adopted his characteristic approach to racial issues: no compromise. Morgan, in contrast, was apparently troubled by the unconstitutionality of the existing racial zoning law. Wondering how Birmingham's rival city, Atlanta, dealt with residential segregation, Morgan asked Birmingham's zoning board chairman, George R. Byrum Jr., to investigate. Byrum reported back that Atlanta had not had a racial zoning ordinance since 1926 and that the real estate industry, through its use of professional codes and sanctions, checked any efforts to introduce blacks into white neighborhoods, save where real estate professionals agreed that the position of white property owners is "untenable." In those instances where blacks attempt to enter an all-white neighborhood, Byrum reported that Atlanta's mayor formed an ad hoc committee of blacks and whites to forge a settlement.[66]

In fact, at the same time that Birmingham was confronted by neighborhood racial change in North Smithfield, similar events were taking place in Atlanta's Mozley Park neighborhood, located on Atlanta's west side. Blacks attempting to move into Mozley Park were greeted with threats of violence from white residents. In 1949, as some of their white neighbors started selling to black households, about one hundred white residents of the neighborhood visited city hall to petition for protection against integration. Mayor William Hartsfield formed a committee that worked out a compromise that maintained segregation but enabled blacks to move into sections of the Mozley Park neighborhood. This approach was formalized with the creation in 1954 of the West Side Mutual Development Committee, which through the early 1960s used negotiation between blacks and whites to maintain segregation while facilitating selective neighborhood racial change.[67]

Atlanta's negotiated approach to neighborhood racial change apparently reinforced Morgan's instincts, as he attempted to resolve the North Smithfield zoning controversy through the formation of a biracial committee.[68] The committee met privately during the summer of 1949 and on August 15, 1949, made its recommendations. Its letter to Commissioner Morgan, which was signed only by the white members of the committee, stipulated no commercial buffer east of Center Street; recommended that Center Street remain the racial dividing line; proposed that a thirty- to forty-acre area north of Eleventh Avenue be added to the area zoned for blacks; and recommended that the city purchase the black-owned lots west of Center Street. The committee report also noted that "Colored people are greatly in need of additional areas in which to live" and urged the city commission to see that a more equitable distribution of land be achieved.[69]

Despite Morgan's efforts to broker a compromise, the Graymont–College Hills neighborhood association and significant black leaders would have nothing of it. Black leaders felt the U.S. Supreme Court was on their side. NAACP leaders in Birmingham wrote Morgan that "it will be difficult for Negro leadership to consider discussion of any non-legal solution to this matter so long as anyone insists upon the validity of the unconstitutional racial zoning laws."[70] Emory Jackson, editor of the black newspaper *Birmingham World,* criticized the Morgan committee in July 1949 as an attempt to "overrule the United States Supreme Court" and get around the fact that the city's racial zoning laws were legally indefensible.[71] Arthur Shores, moreover, was by August 1949 pressing the legal attack on the racial zoning law by representing Mary Means Monk in her attempt to obtain occupancy of a home located on Center Street.[72]

Any possibility of compromise over racial zoning weakened in August 1949. Black leaders had their sense of rightness strengthened by two more bombings, which occurred the night of August 12, 1949. Two ministers, Reverend Milton Curry Jr., pastor of New Zion Presbyterian Church, and Reverend E. B. DeYampert, had moved into two Center Street houses. Each was bombed that night. The houses were located about one block east of the three houses bombed in March 1949. The two ministers had stayed when Commissioner Bull Connor visited them and suggested they leave. Connor reported himself as saying, "I told him I had reason to believe there may be trouble." Reverend Curry initially moved out after Connor made his remarks but moved back in the next day.[73] As before, police investigated the bombings, but no arrests were made.

Three days before the bombing, the Birmingham City Commission passed an emergency city law, introduced by Connor, that made violation of the city's racial zoning laws a misdemeanor punishable by a one-hundred-dollar fine and six months in jail. The ordinance was, according to Connor, prepared "by some of the state's best legal minds and they tell me it will hold up before the Supreme Court of the United States." Connor had bypassed the city's law department, whose attorneys knew nothing about the ordinance when it was introduced.[74] Instead, Connor had employed his political mentor, former state senator James A. Simpson, to draft the ordinance.[75] Simpson contended that the city's racial zoning law should not be labeled a zoning ordinance but instead should be grounded "on the same principle of law by which we separate our white and colored students in schools." But in approaching racial zoning, lawyer Simpson permitted his racial ideology to stand in the way of his legal reasoning: "I think this ordinance approaches the problem from a new viewpoint, and if we believe in a biracial civilization rather than amalgamation, we ought to get behind it and see if we can't convince the moderates of both races that it is in the interest of all and that it is therefore probably constitutional."[76]

The ordinance itself was premised on the grounds that racial integration was a threat to peace and safety and that the City of Birmingham and its police could not safeguard those who moved into areas zoned for another race.[77] By making violation of the city's zoning law a misdemeanor, Connor, as public safety commissioner, was also able to achieve control over enforcement of the city's racial zoning laws: "Pass this law and the first one who moves in, white or Negro, I will guarantee you, Connor's men will put him in the jug."[78]

Connor had grown impatient with what he perceived as Morgan's equivocation on racial zoning and felt that Morgan should have more vigorously punished violations of the law. In response to Morgan's statements that racial zoning was probably illegal, Connor argued that the law would stand up in court. City attorney James H. Willis, however, told Mayor Cooper Green, "Well, take it to the Supreme Court if you want to lose it."[79] On another occasion in the summer of 1949, he told the city commission that the racial zoning law was "completely untenable" and that "if we lose the case under a 'class ruling,' which is likely, we will be unable to take any restrictive action in zoning or segregation cases."[80] Willis preferred to identify an accommodation with the black community that would preserve racial zoning but keep the city out of court.[81]

In addition to going around the city's law department, Connor also succeeded in undercutting Morgan's citizens committee. An unnamed member of that committee criticized the city's actions, stating that "everything we've tried to do has been undone." Efforts to achieve a compromise with the black community were undermined by Connor's radical racist stance: "How can we trust them? We have no assurance that any Negro will keep his word on any line."[82]

Morgan said that while he favored Connor's proposal, he wondered where blacks were going to live in Birmingham: "I'm in favor of this. The only thing is, where are those negroes going to live and build? Almost 50 per cent of our people are colored. So much of our area is zoned for white. I'm not in favor of them moving in with us, but where are they going?"[83] Connor replied that the city would simply have to zone more property for blacks. But George Byrum, chairman of the zoning board of appeals, responded that "the same trouble exists all over the city" and that whites would object no matter where the city zoned land for black occupancy.[84]

As Connor moved to harden the city's stance and ignore the impact his position would have on the city's ability to assimilate a growing black population, the Birmingham branch of the NAACP responded with plans to "uncompromisingly challenge" the city's racial zoning law. On August 15, the NAACP wired the Birmingham City Commission the following statement: "The proposed zoning compromise with buffer area and 20 acres is totally unacceptable to the NAACP. It will be fought with every legal weapon the NAACP legal staff can devise. The NAACP will settle with nothing less than total abolition of all racial zoning."[85]

The NAACP supplemented its legal attack on racial zoning by cosponsoring with seven organizations an August 17, 1949, mass meeting attended by an estimated two thousand to five thousand persons on the lawn of the Smithfield Court public housing development. A bombing damage fund of about five hundred dollars was raised at the meeting, which was presided over by Reverend J. L. Ware, president of the Birmingham Baptist Ministers Conference.[86]

The *Birmingham World,* edited by Emory Jackson, executive secretary of the NAACP Birmingham branch, editorialized against the new racial zoning law, calling it a "bold, last-ditch effort to circumvent the highest courts of the land." The paper wrote that the Birmingham "City Fathers" seemed unconcerned about the bombings and the housing of blacks in Birmingham: "The fact that Negro citizens are bottled in the slums and restricted to the blighted areas does not seem to arouse them. Negroes in Birmingham are zoned near the railroad tracks, near the over-flowing creeks, near the shops. This is their lot in Birmingham as citizens of democracy on an earth God made for all, and all alike."[87]

The final lines between the city and the NAACP were drawn on September 6, 1949, when the city adopted the recommendations of the Graymont–College Hills Civic Association. The racial boundary at Center Street and about thirty acres of undeveloped land north of Eleventh Court North were rezoned for black occupancy (see map 3.1). In doing this, the city rejected recommendations of the Morgan citizens commission and the city's zoning board, both of which supported continued racial zoning but would have made more land available for black occupancy. The NAACP responded by stating that it would be testing Birmingham's racial zoning laws in federal court.[88]

The NAACP followed up on its promise on September 28, 1949, when Arthur Shores filed a class action suit in U.S. District Court to have the city's zoning laws declared unconstitutional. The plaintiffs in the case included Mary Means Monk and fifteen other individuals or entities that Shores argued had been deprived by the racial zoning law of their right to occupy property they owned.[89] By representing a group of plaintiffs, Shores and the NAACP hoped to obtain a genuine class action ruling that would apply to all of Birmingham. The lead plaintiffs were Mary Means Monk and her husband, Monroe, a twenty-nine-year employee of TCI–U.S. Steel at its wire mill in Fairfield. In 1949, the Monks purchased a lot in North Smithfield on the west side of Center Street in the area zoned for whites. The house they constructed was located about one and one-half blocks south of the DeYampert and Curry homes bombed in August 1949.[90]

Beginning on December 12, 1949, federal district judge Clarence Mullins once again heard testimony on the city's racial zoning law.[91] But as late as November 1949, city attorney James Willis was still attempting to get the Graymont–College Hills Civic Association to compromise and permit black occupancy west of the color line that had been drawn at Center Street. Willis stressed that compromise would permit the plaintiffs to occupy their property and therefore they might withdraw their case. If this was not done, Willis argued, the zoning law was likely to be declared illegal as "the group of negroes has an excellent chance to win their suit and thereby enjoin the city from enforcing the zoning ordinances all over the city." According to its president, the civic association was "one hundred percent against" changing the Center Street zoning line.[92] The city's law department had been able to dodge a definitive ruling against racial zoning in the Allen and Matthews cases, but pressure from white residents of Graymont–College Hills, coupled with commissioner Connor's unyielding racism, made it impossible for the law department to once again avoid a decisive legal defeat of racial zoning.

Shores was assisted in presenting the Monk case by NAACP attorney Thurgood Marshall, who argued that the case was about property rights and the right to occupancy that accompanied these rights. The city's case was presented by an assistant city attorney, Tom Huey, and an outside attorney, Horace Wilkinson, who was well known in Alabama as a rabid espouser of racism and as a Dixiecrat. Huey and Wilkinson attempted to introduce evidence on the impact of black occupancy on neighborhood property values and on the likelihood of violence, as evidenced by the bombings, if racial zoning was not preserved. Shores and Marshall, however, succeeded in convincing Judge Mullins that such evidence was not relevant to the case.[93] On December 14, 1949, Judge Mullins ruled that Birmingham's racial zoning ordinance was unconstitutional and the city was enjoined from enforcing the ordinance. Mullins's decision rested squarely on the 1917 *Buchanan v. Warley* decision of the U.S. Supreme Court and a long series of federal and state court decisions based on the *Buchanan* precedent.[94] In citing these cases, Judge Mullins made very clear that the courts had ruled that racial zoning laws violated property rights, which included the right to occupy as well as own land, and that laws premised on the alleged threat of black occupancy to property values or to the public peace were not justifiable if they deny basic rights provided by the federal constitution.[95]

Instead of admitting that thirty years of court decisions doomed racial zoning, the city appealed the *Monk* case to the federal court of appeals and then to the U.S. Supreme Court. Meanwhile, the North Smithfield bombings continued. On April 22, 1950, the Center Street home of B. W. Henderson, a contractor, was bombed. The home had previously belonged to Reverend Milton Curry Jr., who had moved out after the August 13, 1949, bombing. The blast occurred just nine days after a home owned by black dentist J. A. Boykin was bombed in an adjacent neighborhood five blocks from North Smithfield.[96] Finally, on December 21, 1950, one day after the U.S. Fifth Circuit Court of Appeals in New Orleans ruled in her favor, the home of Mary Means Monk and her husband Monroe was dynamited.[97] It was the eighth bombing in North Smithfield since the Matthewses' home was dynamited in August 1947. As in the other bombings, no one was ever tried or convicted.

Meanwhile, in its appeal of Judge Mullins's decision, Birmingham argued before the U.S. Court of Appeals and the U.S. Supreme Court that *Buchanan v. Warley* "was not a zoning law case." Instead, using selected quotes from that case, Birmingham's brief argued that the U.S. Supreme Court had only ruled against laws that restricted, on the basis of race, individuals from buying or selling property. In contrast, the Birmingham zoning ordinance only restricted whites and blacks from occupying property in areas that were zoned for members of the other race. In regulating the use of property, therefore, the city's attorney argued that the Birmingham ordinance fit within the doctrine of *Euclid v. Ambler Realty Company* (272 U.S. 365) in which the Supreme Court had ruled that municipalities could use their police power to place restrictions on how property was used.[98] *Buchanan v. Warley*, according to Birmingham, focused on the sale or purchase of property, while Birmingham's racial zoning law, like other comprehensive zoning laws, focused on the *use* of property.

Birmingham's argument, however, ignored the fact that the Supreme Court had also said in *Buchanan v. Warley*: "Property is more than the mere thing which a person owns. It is elementary that it includes the right to acquire, use, and dispose of it. The Constitution protects these essential attributes of property."[99] In the full context of the case, this language should have told the City of Birmingham that it could not prevail in its attempt to portray *Buchanan v. Warley* as not being a zoning law case.

Moreover, as the U.S. District and Court of Appeals noted in response to Birmingham's arguments, the U.S. Supreme Court had subsequently twice affirmed the *Buchanan v. Warley* decision in cases on racial zoning in New Orleans and Richmond. In the New Orleans case (*Harmon v. Tyler*, 273 U.S. 668), decided in 1927, the year after Birmingham had adopted its zoning ordinance, New Orleans argued that its racial zoning ordinance restricted only the use of property and not its ownership. But as the District and Court of Appeals courts noted in the *Monk* case, the Supreme Court had reversed a state court's validation of the New Orleans law by simply citing the Buchanan decision without making further comment. The Richmond racial zoning law was similarly reversed by the Supreme Court in 1930 (*City of Richmond et al. v. Deans*, 281 U.S. 704), and, as in the New Orleans case, no written opinion was supplied, reference being made simply to the Buchanan decision.[100]

Birmingham's response to previous Supreme Court racial zoning cases was that they did not apply because the Louisville and New Orleans racial zoning decisions (no mention was made of the Richmond decision) "did not involve the validity of comprehensive equitable residential segregation under an ordinance necessary to preserve the public peace and to safeguard the property and safety of the citizens of a populace [*sic*] municipality."[101] Consequently, the bulk of Birmingham's legal defense of its racial zoning statute was based on three assertions. First, Birmingham's racial zoning law fit within the Supreme Court's decisions regarding the validity of segregation statutes requiring separate but equal accommodations on private railroad cars (*Plessy v. Ferguson*, 163 U.S. 537) and schools (*Berea College v. Kentucky*, 211 U.S. 45). Second, in the context of the bombings that had taken place in the North Smithfield neighborhood, Birmingham's racial zoning ordinance was required to maintain peace between the races. Third, significant evidence existed to demonstrate that absent a racial zoning law, white property owners would suffer significant devaluation of their properties if blacks were able to move into white neighborhoods.

In the first instance, Birmingham argued that Birmingham's racial zoning statute, by providing "comprehensive equitable residential segregation" met the separate but equal test established by the *Plessy v. Ferguson*. Citing a long list of court cases that had upheld racial segregation, Birmingham's brief before the U.S. Circuit Court of Appeals asked:

If the state can separate the whites and blacks in schools, on street cars and busses and in other public places, prohibit their intermarriage and biological integration outside the marriage relation, *solely* because of the harmful effect of such conduct on society, what prevents the same state from requiring whites and blacks to live in separate but equal, residential areas in Birmingham, *solely* because of the tremendously harmful effect on society of their living side by side?[102]

As discussed in chapter 2, Birmingham was not alone in asking how and why the Supreme Court could rule that "separate but equal" racial zoning was unconstitutional while ruling that other forms of race segregation that met the separate but equal criterion were constitutional. Soon after the *Buchanan v. Warley* decision, the *Michigan Law Review*, puzzling over why the Supreme Court could approve statutes segregating blacks and whites in schools and public transportation but not in residential neighborhoods, stated: "In attempting to distinguish the residential segregation law from those allowing segregation in transportation, the court is evidently actuated by a feeling that property may be less readily subjected to restriction for the public good than liberty may be."[103]

But this defense of the logic employed in the *Buchanan v. Warley* decision would be circumscribed by later decisions that restricted property use to protect the public interest. As noted in chapter 2, Birmingham's city attorney in the 1920s, W. J. Wynn, believed that *Euclid v. Ambler* would make it very difficult to challenge Birmingham's zoning law. In a 1941 article in the *Kentucky Law Review,* Gardner noted that the Supreme Court's decision in the 1926 landmark zoning case of *Village of Euclid v. Ambler Realty Co.* demonstrated the court's willingness to curb property rights in defense of the public interest. The *Euclid* decision therefore made it difficult to believe that the employment of *Buchanan v. Warley* after 1926 to strike down racial zoning could be defended on the grounds that racial zoning restricted property rights. Gardner concludes that the Supreme Court had determined that racial zoning was not constitutional because the public interest that it protected was slight and insufficient to warrant interference with property rights.[104]

But Birmingham argued that the public interest was an important issue in this case and that it was protected by the city's racial zoning law in two ways: 1) the law was necessary in order to protect the public safety; and 2) the law helped to protect property values. Birmingham attempted to argue the former point by introducing evidence on the six houses that had been bombed in 1947 and 1949 and stating that racial violence therefore constituted a "clear and present danger" in Birmingham.[105]

In making the property value argument, Birmingham's attorneys employed the same arguments that Birmingham's real estate community and commissioners had used when zoning was adopted in the 1920s. By 1949, however, Birmingham could supplement this argument with a significant volume of contemporary real estate theory that maintained that racial integration resulted in significant declines in property values. Birmingham's brief, for example, quoted from Homer Hoyt's *One Hundred Years of Land Values* in Chicago. Hoyt's research on property values and their determinants had a significant impact on planning and real estate appraisal in the 1930s and 1940s. An extensive quote from Hoyt's book includes the following passage about the impact of black migration from the South to Chicago and the subsequent expansion of that city's black residential areas: "The significance of these racial and national movements upon Chicago land values lies in the fact that certain racial and national groups, because of their lower economic status and their lower standards of living, pay less rent themselves and cause a greater physical deterioration of property than groups higher in the social and economic scale. . . . Land values in areas occupied by such classes are therefore inevitably low."[106]

Birmingham's brief also included numerous quotes from various real estate appraisal references that emphasized the need to maintain racial homogeneity in order to preserve property values. Most notable among these sources was the Federal Housing Administration's *Underwriting Manual,* which until 1948, when the *Shelley v. Kramer* (334 U.S. 1) decision ended judicial enforcement of racial covenants in deeds, urged the use of zoning regulations and deed restrictions to guard against "adverse influences" such as "infiltration of inharmonious racial or nationality groups."[107]

In general, Birmingham's brief on the impact of racial integration on property values was grounded in the mainstream of prevailing real estate theory at that time. As Mohl has shown, in the 1930s, 1940s, and 1950s, the leading textbooks, manuals, and trade journals for real estate lenders, appraisers, and brokers all espoused "infiltration theory," according to which black occupancy of white neighborhoods was viewed as deleterious to property values.[108] Even though Birmingham's espousal of racial zoning had little chance of being accepted by the courts, the racial doctrine that black occupancy hurt property values was widely accepted in the real estate literature of that time. In this instance, as in others in the city's racial history, while Birmingham assumed a relatively extreme position on racial issues, the racial beliefs of its white citizens and leaders were never far from the American mainstream.

Despite Birmingham's effort to use conventional real estate theory, the clear and present danger argument, and the separate but equal argument, the federal courts simply looked at *Buchanan v. Warley,* and that case's reaffirmation in *Harmon v. Tyler* and *City of Richmond et al. v. Deans,* to deny Birmingham its racial zoning statute. District Court judge Clarence Mullins had denied Birmingham the opportunity to introduce evidence on how black movement into white areas constituted a clear and present danger and how property values would be diminished by the entry of blacks. Birmingham argued in its appeal that Judge Mullins erred in excluding such evidence, but the U.S. Circuit Court of Appeals responded tersely: "We find no merit in appellant's further contention that the court below erred in excluding certain evidence of a social and economic character. This evidence was irrelevant and immaterial to the issue of constitutionality."[109] On May 28, 1951, Birmingham's petition for writ of certiorari to the Court of Appeals for the Fifth Circuit was denied by the U.S. Supreme Court.[110] Birmingham had exhausted its appeals, and statutory residential segregation had come to an end in Birmingham and the nation.

In the end, racial zoning died in part because it was unable to cope with the dynamics of city and neighborhood change. The black community had continued to grow in Birmingham between 1926 and 1950, but racial zoning did not facilitate growth in the housing stock available to blacks. Increased demand with next to no change in supply created increased pressure in the city for more black housing. Such pressure was likely to be greatest in white neighborhoods where a large black population was nearby and where a number of middle-class blacks could economically outbid whites for housing.

In Atlanta, public officials could cope with neighborhood change dynamics by brokering racial change. The political leadership in Birmingham was not willing to do this. Relative moderates such as Mayor

Jimmy Morgan were interested in the alternative approach to neighborhood change crafted by Atlanta mayor William Hartsfield, who successfully negotiated accommodations between blacks and whites that permitted the black community to grow while maintaining segregation. But in Birmingham politics, such moderation was no match for the rabid racism of Bull Connor, whose political base was built on the white, lower-middle-class neighborhoods of the city.[111] Nor could the city's law department, which had known for some time that racial zoning was indefensible in the courts, continue to succeed in discouraging or defusing legal challenges to racial zoning. The finest legal minds in Alabama, as Connor called them, were guided more by their racial ideology than their legal sense. They could not see, as did the law department, that going to war over racial zoning would be a losing battle.

In adopting a hard line on racial zoning, Birmingham wittingly or unwittingly supported a climate of violent reaction to neighborhood racial change. As in other cities in the postwar period, violence was used by whites to challenge black attempts to expand African American housing choices. By both toughening the racial zoning law in 1949 while failing to ever try or convict terrorists who bombed black homes, Birmingham sent a message that the use of violence was a legitimate means to reinforce racial boundaries. In fact, the city used the bombings as the basis for defending racial zoning in the courts, maintaining that racial zoning was necessary to the creation and preservation of racial peace. Moreover, bombs continued to be used against blacks moving into white neighborhoods even after the racial zoning law was declared unconstitutional. From 1956 through the middle of 1958, a series of bomb attacks occurred in the Fountain Heights neighborhood, lying just to the east of Enon Ridge. Each of these attacks involved the entry of blacks into predominantly white neighborhoods.[112]

In contrast, Atlanta sought to lessen the tension associated with racial change while still maintaining racial segregation. Mayor Hartsfield's approach of negotiated neighborhood change successfully defused the potential for violence.

In general, the struggle over racial zoning not only ended racial zoning in the United States but also established a pattern of racial politics that set the stage for Birmingham's civil rights struggles of the 1950s and 1960s. Bull Connor's radical racism won out over the more moderate approaches favored by other segregationists. By 1961, Birmingham's three city commissioners, including Connor, were unanimous in their determination to resist the civil rights movement and to do so with the tacit cooperation of the city's white terrorists.

Given this support from city government, the city continued to be rocked in the 1950s and 1960s by racially motivated bombings, giving the city its nickname of Bombingham. Beyond the bombings listed in table 3.2, forty-three race-related bombings or attempted bombings occurred in Birmingham between 1950 and 1965, with the best-known being the bombing of the Sixteenth Street Baptist Church on September 15, 1963.[113]

Although Birmingham's history of terroristic bombing began with the challenge to racial zoning, the black community's willingness to confront the risk of bombing also began at this time. Clearly, the people who followed in the footsteps of the Matthews family must have known of the real possibility that their homes would be bombed. Courage in the face of such risk became an important element of the civil rights movement in Birmingham. In 1956, after he survived being thrown in the air by a bomb planted at his home, Reverend Fred Shuttlesworth, founder of the Alabama Christian Movement for Human Rights, was seen by Birmingham blacks as divinely sent to lead them in the civil rights movement.[114] Thanks to the black experience with the racial zoning bombings of the late 1940s and early 1950s, standing up to a bomber became a badge of honor in Birmingham's black community.

In general, the struggle over racial zoning established the pattern for Birmingham's civil rights history of the 1950s and 1960s. The city's blacks would challenge various forms of racial discrimination, the city's public officials would resist change with all their might, and the city's terrorists would plant bombs designed to stifle black protest. This struggle over racial zoning helped shape Birmingham's reactionary response to threats to existing race relations, thereby making the city a target for the civil rights movement in 1963 and subsequently producing a national response that led to significant pressure for change in race relations and the 1964 Civil Rights Act.

4 "The Spirit of
Racial Zoning"

In the 1950s, in the period immediately after the demise of racial zoning, Birmingham's attention, as in other cities throughout the nation, turned to plans for urban redevelopment. Although a number of cities were interested in urban redevelopment prior to Congress's adoption of the urban renewal program in 1949, it was after passage of that act that Birmingham began to seriously think about urban redevelopment as a planning tool and more generally to look at comprehensive urban planning as a desirable activity of local government.[1]

Aside from adoption of the 1926 zoning ordinance and implementation of a public housing program in the 1930s, Birmingham had not embraced planning. Although the 1919 Manning plan had influenced the planning of the civic center area surrounding the city's downtown Woodrow Wilson Park, it had never been adopted by the city. The 1925 Olmsted Brothers report had not been implemented either (see chapter 2). In 1943, with an eye toward postwar planning, the Birmingham City Commission created the city's first permanent planning body, the Birmingham Planning Board, as an organization to advise the city commission on planning issues.[2] But by 1950, the city still lacked a comprehensive plan and had no planning staff, save a draftsman and the venerable J. D. Webb. In that year, Webb was completing forty-five years of employment with the city, including seventeen years as city engineer, a job whose duties included what passed for planning in Birmingham.[3] The city had no housing code, which meant that no regulations required dwelling units to possess a bathtub, shower, or water-heating facilities. Moreover, the city lacked the legal authority to regulate the subdividing of land, making it impossible, for example, to enforce uniform requirements for the width and siting of streets or the installation of sidewalks.[4] For a brief time, Alabama law prohibited

Birmingham and Jefferson County from receiving federal funds for public housing. Stirred by the city's real estate interests, Birmingham's legislative delegation had obtained passage of a 1945 state act prohibiting receipt of federal funds for public housing. After considerable clamor from returning veteran's groups, newly elected legislators pledged repeal, but before they could act the Alabama Supreme Court ruled in 1946 that the ban on federal funds for housing was unconstitutional.[5]

Passage of the 1949 Housing Act, however, began to change the prospects for planning in Birmingham. Birmingham could easily identify neighborhoods with blighted conditions that were likely to fit the federal criteria for urban renewal. Moreover, Birmingham's progrowth coalition, both in government and in business, could quickly identify potential redevelopment projects that would benefit from the slum clearance approach taken by the 1949 legislation for addressing the nation's urban problems.

Within months of Congress's adoption of the urban renewal program in 1949, Birmingham's attention was focused on three urban renewal projects: the medical center site, located on the city's south side; the Ensley community; and the Avondale community. The three sites had two characteristics in common. First, each of them was a slum area containing some of the city's worst housing and neighborhood conditions. Second, each of the neighborhoods was predominantly black. While the blighted conditions in each of these areas could justify their selection for urban renewal, their selection was also driven by the fact that the white community of Birmingham was directly affected by the location of these predominantly black, poor neighborhoods. The city therefore felt the need to modify existing land uses and conditions in order to serve the interests of its white residents. Consistent with the general themes of housing and community development practices in the United States, it was not the potential benefits to the poor that propelled urban renewal in Birmingham. Instead, it was the perceived "social cost" of the poor that caught the attention of public and private leaders in the white community.[6] Although the city no longer had racial zoning at its disposal, urban renewal gave Birmingham a capability that racial zoning could not offer: the ability to relocate blacks when they got in the way of the white community.

Southside Medical Center Urban Renewal

From urban renewal's inception in Birmingham, expansion of the University of Alabama Medical Center, located about six blocks south of the city's central business district, took center stage.[7] The medical center was established in 1944 when the state legislature created the Medical College of Alabama as a four-year school of the University of Alabama. It was located in Birmingham at the Jefferson-Hillman Hospital, occupying a single block as the city's oldest hospital. By 1952, the medical center had grown from one block to four and one-half blocks with the addition of a veteran's hospital, completed in 1952; the Jefferson County Public Health Building; and the Crippled Children's Hospital (see fig. 4.1).[8] Continued growth was expected as planning had already begun for a tuberculosis hospital and a hospital where black physicians could practice.[9] In addition, land was needed to provide park space and parking for the medical center.[10]

Standing in the way of the medical center's expansion was one of the poorest neighborhoods in Birmingham. The medical center was located in census tract 44, located between the railroad reservation that runs east-west through the center of the city and Ninth Avenue South and between Fifteenth and Twenty-Second Streets (see map 3.2). Tract 44 was part of the larger, Southside black community that also included tracts 42, 43, 45, and 46 and that in 1950 housed about 21,000 blacks, or about 16 percent of the city's 130,025 black residents.

The Southside black community had originally been a racially mixed area that in the late nineteenth century housed laborers who worked in the nearby mills located just east of downtown Birmingham. Between the 1880s and the early part of the twentieth century, however, white working-class households moved out to the residential suburban areas such as Woodlawn and East Lake on the city's east side, and West End on the city's west side. Consequently, as a core area of the city, the Southside evolved by the early 1900s into a poor, predominantly black neighborhood.[11]

In subsequent years, social surveys identified this area as a significant concentration of slum housing. In 1912, as noted in chapter 1, *The Survey*'s profile of Birmingham illustrated the city's housing problems with photographs of slum housing on the city's Southside.[12] Twenty-five years later, the 1937 Jefferson County Board of Health survey con-

Figure 4.1. Medical Center urban renewal site before redevelopment. This 1952 photo shows the existing medical school in the vicinity of Twentieth Street and Sixth Avenue and the urban renewal area running south to Tenth Avenue and west to Fifteenth Street. (*Annual Report of the Housing Authority of the Birmingham District*, June 30, 1952, Birmingham Public Library Department of Archives and Manuscripts)

cluded that of twenty-two blighted areas in Birmingham, Southside was the third-most blighted in the city.[13]

Conditions had not changed much by 1950, and in that year the Jefferson County Board of Health once again surveyed the city's blighted areas. Although the report noted that nearly every area in which blacks predominated was blighted, the board of health cited several areas that it deemed "particularly bad," including tracts 43 and 44 in the city's Southside community. In particular, the report recommended that a portion of tract 44 be cleared for expansion of the medical center.[14]

In 1950, the census tract 44 portion of Southside was 76 percent black, and it had a median household annual income of $1,241, the second-lowest of any tract in the city. Its residents were employed, but neighborhood residents were more likely to work in low-paying jobs as household workers, service workers, and laborers (see table 4.1).

Residents of tract 44 lived in some of the worst housing in the city. According to the 1950 census, 81 percent of the dwelling units in the neighborhood were dilapidated or lacked a private bath; nearly 62 percent were more than thirty years old; only about 5 percent had central

Table 4.1. Comparison of tract 44 and city-wide social statistics, 1950

Economic and employment status	Tract 44	City
Median Income	$1,241	$2,423
Labor force participation (%)	60.3	55.1
Unemployment Rate (%)	5.7	4.8
Occupational status: Percentage distribution	Tract 44 (%)	City (%)
Professional, technical, and kindred workers	15.0	8.7
Managers, officials, and proprietors	2.1	8.7
Clerical and kindred workers	3.8	13.9
Sales workers	2.5	8.3
Craftsmen, foremen, and kindred workers	7.2	14.5
Operatives and kindred workers	21.7	19.1
Private household workers	14.3	6.6
Service workers, except private household	18.0	9.4
Laborers, except miners	13.3	9.9
Occupation not reported	2.2	0.8
Total employed	100.0	100.0
Characteristics of dwelling units	Tract 44	City
Percentage owner-occupied	7.2	46.8
Percentage no private bath or dilapidated	81.4	38.5
Percentage built 1919 or earlier	61.7	39.2
Percentage with 1.01 or more persons/room	37.1	21.2
Percentage with no central heating	94.9	69.5
Median monthly rent	$15.09	$22.90
Median annual rent/median annual income	0.146	0.113

Source: U.S. Bureau of the Census. U.S. Census of Population, 1950, vol. 3, Census Tract Statistics, chap. 5. Washington, D.C.: U.S. Government Printing Office, 1952.

heat; and over one-third were crowded. Of fifty-eight census tracts in the city, only three had higher proportions of their dwellings that were dilapidated or lacked private baths.

The 1950 board of health report recommended that the "fringe area" of downtown Birmingham, including tract 44, as well as tracts 26, 28, 45, and 46, "be cleared of all slums and most standard dwellings to provide expansion for business and industry."[15] It reserved special attention for tract 44 and expansion of the medical center. The report recommended that the medical center be doubled in size through acquisition of the blocks immediately to the west and south of the existing medical center. The board of health also suggested that the city apply to the federal government for Title I urban renewal funds as a means to acquiring, clearing, and redeveloping the land so that it could be reused for medical purposes.

The federal urban renewal program gave cities significant assistance in transforming the land use of targeted neighborhoods. In particular, Title I was targeted at enabling cities to clear residential areas, such as the Southside, deemed to be slums.[16] It subsidized two-thirds of the difference between the cost of city acquisition, clearance, and improvement of urban renewal sites and the revenue earned from the sale of the land to private developers. In the case of the medical center, the initial plan projected a total cost of $4.98 million for acquisition, clearance, and improvement and a sales price of $3.34 million for the renewal area, thereby requiring a net outlay by the city of $1.64 million. Two-thirds of this amount would be funded by the federal government, leaving the city directly responsible for only $547,000 or about 10 percent of overall project costs.[17]

Responding to the opportunity presented by the urban renewal program, Birmingham leaders, public and private, began an initiative that focused primarily on redevelopment of the medical center area. In late 1949, within five months of the passage of federal urban renewal legislation, Colonel Harold Harper, executive secretary of the Housing Authority of the Birmingham District (HABD) began discussions with city and county officials about the advantages of urban renewal.[18] Prior to serving as a colonel in the U.S. Army in World War II, Harper was employed in real estate in Birmingham. After January 1, 1950, he would serve as the agency's executive director.[19] Harper reported that interest was being expressed about using the new program to enable slum clearance in three sites: the area adjacent to the Southside Medical Center, the Ensley community, and areas bordering Georgia Road on the city's east side.[20] At the same time, Birmingham city officials, such as mayor Cooper Green, wondered where the city would get the money to pay for its share of urban renewal costs.[21]

George Denison, director of the Jefferson County Board of Health, also assumed a leadership position. On April 19, 1950, one week after its publication, Denison presented his agency's survey of blighted areas to the Birmingham Planning Board. Since urban renewal funds were to be spent in clearing slum areas, the report was necessary to document the blighted conditions in these areas. Upon hearing the presentation, the planning board's members unanimously supported a resolution adopting the board of health's recommendations for seeking federal funds for urban renewal, including redevelopment of the medical center area.[22]

The following month, at the request of the Birmingham City Commission, the planning board voted to appoint a committee to make recommendations on urban renewal sites.[23] Three months later, in August 1950, the planning board's chairman, real estate businessman James Sulzby Jr., recommended three urban renewal sites to the board: the medical center site, the Ensley community, and the Avondale community. Members of the planning board unanimously approved these sites.[24]

Planning board chairman Sulzby was one of about two dozen individuals, representing four key interest groups in Birmingham, who assumed leadership in pushing the medical center expansion project forward. Dr. James J. Durrett, dean of the University of Alabama Medical College, along with health officer Dr. George Denison, represented the medical center and the broader medical community in Birmingham. The second key interest group was the housing authority, for which urban renewal and the Southside Medical Center expansion represented an opportunity to expand its mission beyond public housing development. Key housing authority officials assuming leadership positions included Harper and several other staff and board members of that agency. The third group consisted of the heads of the two planning agencies in the city—the president of the Birmingham Zoning Commission, George Byrum; and James Sulzby Jr., the chairman of the Birmingham Planning Board.

But the single largest source of leadership in planning the medical center expansion came from the city's real estate community. Eleven of twenty-three key leaders were real estate professionals, primarily realtors, and two others were lenders. At least eight of the twenty-three leaders, including planning board chairman Sulzby, had served as presidents of the primary real estate association in Birmingham, the Birmingham Real Estate Board.[25] Just as they had in the early 1920s, when Birmingham real estate interests had united to propose comprehensive and racial zoning, thirty years later the city's real estate interests led the push for urban renewal.

After recommending that Birmingham proceed with urban renewal of the medical center area, as well as the Avondale and Ensley sites, the planning board, along with the housing authority, began to formulate specific plans. In November 1951, the housing authority announced plans for expansion of the medical center area from four and one-half to nine and one-half blocks and construction of 750 units of public housing for blacks to be located just west of the medical center expansion area. The public housing would be used to replace dilapidated housing occupied by black residents of Birmingham.[26]

By February 1952, the housing authority, the planning board, and key real estate business leaders supported urban renewal, but the Birmingham City Commission was still skeptical about the city's financial participation in urban renewal. In 1952, among twenty-three cities with 1950 populations of between 250,000 and 500,000 inhabitants, Birmingham ranked last in per capita general expenditures, finishing behind such southern cities as San Antonio, Memphis, Louisville, and Atlanta.[27]

Nevertheless, private and institutional interests succeeded in persuading Birmingham's city commissioners that urban renewal was well worth the city's expenditure.[28] At a February 18, 1952, city hall meeting, members of the Birmingham Planning Board; Dr. George Denison of the board of health; Dean James J. Durrett of the medical school; Hill Ferguson, past president of the Birmingham Real Estate Board and influential member of the University of Alabama Board of Trustees, which oversaw the medical school; and Robert Jemison, dean of realtors and developers in Jefferson County, persuaded the three Birmingham city commissioners to view urban renewal and medical center expansion more positively. Dean Durrett contended that if the medical center was not able to expand, its facilities would be scattered and some of them might be located outside of the Birmingham area.[29] Soon thereafter, the Birmingham City Commission, led by mayor James Morgan, began to aggressively seek federal urban renewal assistance, not only for the medical center expansion but also for the Ensley and Avondale urban renewal projects. By summer of 1952, the U.S. Housing and Home Finance Agency (HHFA), which oversaw the urban renewal program, had advanced money to the city for planning the expansion of the Southside Medical Center.[30]

Under Title I, communities were required to develop a detailed redevelopment plan for a specific urban renewal site that was consistent with a general plan for the entire city.[31] The city lacked a general plan, however, as the 1919 Manning plan was never adopted and was clearly out of date. The planning board had been slowly developing a general plan, but lack of appropriations from the city commission forced the board to rely primarily on the voluntary services of its members, with assistance from the city engineer and a full-time draftsman.[32]

On February 8, 1952, ten days before the Birmingham City Commission was persuaded to pursue urban renewal, the Birmingham Planning Board published its attempt at a general plan. Aptly titled *Preliminary Report*, it outlined general improvements for the city's traffic circulation system and public facilities.[33] Consistent with its announced urban renewal policy, the *Preliminary Report* identified the Southside Medical Center, Ensley, and Avondale as target areas for the city's urban renewal program.

The *Report* conveniently provided a map that showed the location of the three sites on a general land use map of Birmingham. Strikingly, one of the map's land use classifications is Negro Residential, which along with Single-Family and Multiple-Family constituted the map's residential designations. Nearly one year after the U.S. Supreme Court had overruled the city's racial zoning law, and thirty-five years after the Supreme Court had declared racial zoning unconstitutional, Birmingham was still employing race in its land use map.

The map does, however, serve the purpose of displaying the proximity of the three urban renewal areas to Birmingham's black neighborhoods and therefore highlights the potential impact these three projects would have on those neighborhoods. As noted, the Southside Medical Center lay near a black neighborhood. Site B, in the Ensley community, was located among a large concentration of black households, while Site C, in the Avondale neighborhood, was also located within a predominantly black neighborhood. Like the Southside Medical Center area, the 1950 board of health study had identified the black neighborhoods in Ensley and Avondale as blighted.[34]

On January 13, 1953, nearly one year after issuance of the *Preliminary Report,* the housing authority's proposed urban renewal plan for the medical center expansion was presented to the Birmingham City Commission. The housing authority had contracted with the Harland Bartholomew planning firm, and Bartholomew told the city commissioners that planning for an expanded medical center would mean more to the city than a "great industry" because "as more and more of our people get into hospital insurance plans they will call on more and more hospital service." Moreover, the benefits from growth in the city's health sector would have a significant multiplier effect: "Patients coming to the hospital are visitors. And visitors spend money."[35]

While the January 1953 plan called primarily for expansion of medical facilities, including several hospitals, clinics, and medically related commercial facilities, no mention was made of the public housing that the housing authority had described eighteen months earlier as part of the Southside plan. In June 1952, however, the city commission elected not to proceed with plans for 1,050 units contained in three additional public housing projects, one of which the housing authority had planned to build in an area adjacent to the Southside Medical Center expansion area.[36] With the medical center projected to displace 529 black and 150 white families, the increased availability of public housing would have been of direct service to those families.[37]

Previously, the federal government had allocated 3,000 units of postwar public housing to Birmingham, of which 1,950 units had either been built or approved. Charles Marks Village, designated for whites, and Joseph Loveman Village, designated for blacks, each contained 500 units and each was completed in 1952. The remaining 950 units, for black occupants, were to come from the planned Tuxedo Court public housing project, to be located in the Ensley community. Mayor Cooper Green claimed that newspaper ads showed plenty of housing was available and said he wanted to see what happened to the housing market after the two new 500-unit public housing projects were opened.[38] The executive committee of the city's mortgage bankers association responded by adopting a resolution approving the city's position on further public housing. The bankers noted that such action was consistent with their belief that "there is no need for additional public housing for the City of Birmingham."[39]

The mortgage bankers' approval of the city's stance was joined by the *Birmingham News,* which noted that the two current black public housing developments (Smithfield Court with 512 units and Southtown with 480 units) had no vacancies and that rental housing available for blacks was in limited supply. Nevertheless, the *News* maintained that without a crisis in unemployment the public construction of such units could be postponed.[40] Consequently, despite available information that black rental housing remained in short supply and the fact that the city commission and planning board had already expressed support for three urban renewal projects, each of which targeted slum clearance in predominantly black neighborhoods, the city commission decided to close off additional opportunities for constructing badly needed housing.

Despite the city commission's sanguine approach to the issue of housing for blacks, the issue of relocation and rehousing of over 500 black households in the Southside neighborhood quickly became critical in the city's debate over the expansion of the Southside Medical Center. The Housing Act of 1949 required that jurisdictions employing federal urban renewal funds develop plans for the relocation of households displaced by urban renewal projects. Such households should be afforded the opportunity to live in "decent, safe, and sanitary housing . . . at rents or prices within their financial means." Recognizing that low-income families would have the greatest difficulty moving into decent, affordable housing in the private sector, the Housing Act granted highest priority to such families for occupancy in federally subsidized public housing. Local communities were therefore urged to "examine their local public housing program and plan in relation to the requirement for permanent rehousing of the low-income families to be displaced by the Title I projects. *Such examination of rehousing needs is particularly important with respect to the needs of minority group families which may be living in project areas*" (emphasis added).[41]

Given this proviso, the housing authority's 1952 survey of residents living in the Southside Medical Center expansion area should have alerted city officials to the critical role to be played by the relocation is-

sue in public discussion of this project. The survey found that the majority black population in the neighborhood not only lived in substandard dwelling units but also lacked the income to afford replacement
housing in the private market. In its preliminary report, the housing
authority found that of 756 households in the project area, 533 of whom
were black, only 87 owned their homes. Of the white residents, the
housing authority estimated that three-fourths could afford to buy or
rent a home in the private market, compared to only one-fourth of
black households living in the neighborhood. In addition, only nine
of 160 white households paid less than twenty-five dollars per month
for rent, compared to 330 of 596 black households.[42]

Clearly, Southside black residents exhibited a substantial need for
inexpensive rental housing and the housing authority soon realized
that low-income public housing would likely be a necessary source of
replacement housing.[43] But demand for the three existing public housing developments available to blacks was already very high. In the first
ten months of 1952, the housing authority processed 2,186 applications for residency in Birmingham's three black public housing developments, including the 500-unit Joseph Loveman Village that opened
for occupancy that year. Although Loveman was able to accommodate
473 of these applicants, Smithfield Court and Southtown combined to
house only an additional 151 families. Consequently, only 624 of 2,186
applicants, or 28 percent of the black demand for public housing in
Birmingham, could be accommodated by the three existing projects.[44]

With such a high level of existing, unmet demand, Birmingham's
public housing was hard-pressed to meet the rehousing needs of the
Southside's black residents *and* meet the continuing high need for
housing the city's other black households. According to the housing
authority's statistics, in fiscal year 1951–52, even though 75 percent
more whites lived in public housing than blacks, whites were 261 percent more likely than blacks to move out of public housing. Whereas
only twenty-three black households moved out of public housing because of excess income or because they were buying a home, 101 white
households moved out for these reasons. While the post–World War II
housing boom was opening up new opportunities for Birmingham
whites, similar opportunities were not available to blacks, forcing
them to stay in public housing.[45]

The Birmingham branch of the NAACP called attention to the

unmet demand for black public housing in Birmingham: "there are waiting lists of great length for each of the three existing public housing projects for Negroes."[46] Moreover, HHFA staff speculated whether the 500 units reserved for blacks at Joseph Loveman Village would be occupied too soon to benefit black residents relocated from the medical center site.[47] After all, George Denison had written the city commission in 1949 that it was important to build Birmingham's next public housing project in a location that did not require clearance of black housing units: "Because of demolition of Negro housing units already referred to, we feel that construction of a single housing project of 1,000 units without immediate compensatory condemnation of more Negro dwelling units is justified. *Furthermore, there is a great need for more Negro zoned residential areas* [emphasis added], and it is felt that the area described could be developed with a minimum expense to the City and the Housing Authority."[48] Denison thus believed that racial zoning had greatly limited the opportunity for blacks to find desirable housing.

Although Birmingham's white leaders, including the housing authority's staff, were aware of the difficulty in rehousing the Southside's black population, there was little they were willing to do about it. As noted, Birmingham city commissioners, in the summer of 1952, elected not to pursue more public housing beyond the planned 950-unit Tuxedo Court development. In a March 16, 1953, meeting at the medical center office of Dean James J. Durrett, key leaders of the medical center expansion project planned for a March 30 public hearing, which was required under the federal urban renewal legislation.[49] The participants devoted a lengthy part of the meeting to discussing the relocation of black households, particularly homeowners. They lamented the difficulty previous efforts had encountered in attempting to identify areas of the city that could be developed for black homeowners. But as the meeting's minutes note, although the idea of encouraging realtors and homebuilders to help with the relocation problem was discussed, "no definite action was taken." Instead, the housing authority's assistant director for redevelopment wrote that the chief backers of the medical center expansion were not well organized on the point of a "wholesome method of working with the Negro families."

Roberta Morgan, who attended the meeting and served as execu-

tive director of the Jefferson County Coordinating Council of Social
Forces, volunteered to confer with the Interracial Division about the relocation issue.[50] Morgan oversaw the staff of the Interracial Division,
which had been established in 1951 by the white elite of Birmingham
to provide an interracial forum with twenty-five white and twenty-five
black members that was under the control of local white leadership. In
response to her request, the housing subcommittee of the Interracial
Division focused its efforts on identifying sites in Birmingham that
could be developed as a "high class Negro subdivision," with an emphasis on home ownership.[51]

The housing authority's staff had learned, however, that most of the
blacks living in the Southside Medical Center area could not afford to
purchase a home and the most likely form of housing they could afford
was public housing. Of the 679 families that the housing authority's
1953 relocation plan envisioned moving from the neighborhood, 529
were black, and 482, or 91 percent, were poor enough to be eligible for
public housing.[52]

The housing authority expected that all of these families could move
into the three public housing developments designated for blacks. The
authority projected that 278 vacancies would occur annually in the
1,492 public housing units designated for black occupancy, for a
turnover rate of about 18 percent.[53] The housing authority also projected that relocation would take place over a five-year period, so that
on average 106 (529/5) black families per year would be moved from
the Southside Medical Center area to the black public housing developments. Hence, 38 percent (106/278) of Birmingham's already inadequate annual supply of vacated black public housing would be absorbed by the release of 106 new black rental families each year.
Although the housing authority could claim that room would be available in the public housing market for the displaced Southside households, it was also clear that relocation would come at the expense of the
many black households already applying for public housing. Moreover,
it did not take into account the fact that the city was planning two other
urban renewal projects in black neighborhoods, each of which required significant relocation of black households.

By encouraging black residents from the medical center area to
move to the three existing public housing projects for blacks, the
housing authority was effectively holding the line on segregation by

relocating residents to predominantly black neighborhoods. The three black public housing projects were located in neighborhoods that were predominantly black.[54] Relocation was not expected to lead to blacks moving into white neighborhoods.

It was at the March 30, 1953, public hearing that black leaders and Southside black residents had a rare opportunity to express themselves about being forced to relocate outside of their neighborhood. Only one black leader, attorney Arthur D. Shores, vice chairman of the Interracial Division of the Jefferson County Coordinating Council of Social Forces, was identified by the housing authority as participating in planning for the medical center project.[55] Opening remarks were made by Birmingham mayor Cooper Green; Fairfield and Mountain Brook developer Robert Jemison Jr.; John Gallalee, president of the University of Alabama; housing authority executive director Harold Harper; Birmingham Planning Board chairman James Sulzby Jr.; Frank Spain, president of the Birmingham Chamber of Commerce; and planning consultant Harland Bartholomew. Harper addressed the issue of relocation, stating that "those who reside in the area and who are entitled to low income housing will be taken care of and housed in the existing low income housing projects, both white and colored, and those whose income is too high, will be housed and cared for by private enterprise, either as home owners or as tenants."[56]

After the opening remarks, Reverend John W. Goodgame Jr., pastor of the black Sixth Avenue Baptist Church, spoke to the audience of several hundred that had gathered at the city auditorium. Sixth Avenue Baptist Church on the city's Southside, with 4,200 members, was one of the largest churches in the city. Goodgame, who had pastored Sixth Avenue since 1937, had succeeded his father, Reverend John W. Goodgame Sr., who had served as the church's minister for twenty-nine years beginning in 1908.[57] Reverend Goodgame supported the redevelopment project but asked how the neighborhood's black residents would be provided for: "Where can they go, where have you provided for them to go? Just turn them loose and say go where you will? We find ourselves hemmed in in Birmingham. We cannot move right or left because of certain regulations and laws that prohibit us from enjoying the fruits of our labor in the City of Birmingham, but if you say go, we must go."[58]

Black attorney Oscar W. Adams Jr., son of the *Birmingham Reporter* editor who opposed racial zoning in the 1920s, and a 1947 graduate of Howard University Law School, represented a group of twenty-four black citizens affected by the Southside urban renewal project. He echoed Goodgame's questions about where blacks relocated outside of the neighborhood would go: "I want us to consider today the fact that it is most difficult for a Negro to find suitable residential property in the City of Birmingham. He has been forced to confine himself into particular areas because of legal restrictions in some cases, and because of physical violence in the form of bombings in other cases."[59] Reverend J. B. Carter, a black resident of the medical center expansion area and a presiding elder of the African Methodist Episcopal Church, also expressed similar sentiments when he told the public hearing audience: "We don't see just now any opening where my group could go. . . . We want no social equality. I will tell you what that black man is looking for. He is trying to get next to a paved street; he is trying to get next to an electric light; he is trying to get next to adequate police protection."[60]

These statements reflected the historical concern of Birmingham blacks, going back to the early debates over racial zoning. Blacks in Birmingham were restricted as to where they could live, and the choices they faced were ones typically lacking in public services, such as streets, lights, and police protection, all three of which were highlighted in Oscar Adams's Senior's 1923 testimony against racial zoning (chapter 2). Racial zoning had ended, but its effects on limiting black choice were still in place, as was the fear that violence would greet black attempts to move outside of areas designated for them. When these conditions were combined with the substandard services faced by blacks in their neighborhoods, they were understandably distressed at the idea of so many blacks being removed from their homes.

The Birmingham News urged the black residents who felt threatened by the project to take comfort in the "health and happiness" that the medical center expansion would mean for thousands of people. The News further stated that the housing authority had said there will be sufficient vacancies in the city's public housing for eligible families.[61]

In contrast, Emory Jackson of the Birmingham World was quick to note the connection between the racial relocation aspects of the Southside Medical Center project and racial zoning. On May 29, 1953, Jackson editorialized that the Medical Center project, which he titled

"Birmingham's Racial Relocation Plan," "appears to be a clever re-working of the spirit of the invalidated racial zoning laws."[62] And in an editorial titled "Spirit of Racial Zoning," Jackson wrote: "Negro fami-lies would be removed from this area but under the proposal would not be permitted to return as home owners. White families who were removed or other white ones could get back into the proposed multi-housing units."[63] Specifically, Jackson was reacting to the housing au-thority's plan to construct private multifamily housing for white occu-pancy and to the city commission's deletion of language prohibiting racial discrimination in the disposition or use of urban renewal land.[64] Although racial zoning was legally dead, Birmingham was attempting to achieve racial zoning's purpose by using the city's general planning powers, aided by the federal urban renewal subsidy, to create white-only housing in a neighborhood that was predominantly black.

With no influence or representation on the city commission, the housing authority, or the Southside Medical Center Citizens Advisory Committee, Birmingham's blacks took their case to the courts and to the federal government. Thirty-eight black Southside property owners, three black churches, and a white property owner filed suit. They al-leged that use of the city's eminent domain powers was illegal because portions of the urban renewal project were planned for private devel-opment and therefore the project did not meet a public purpose.[65] The suit, which was not directed at racial discrimination but at the protec-tion of private property rights, did not succeed in arresting Birming-ham's urban renewal efforts. Even if it had succeeded, it would not have benefited the 90 percent of black families slated for relocation who were renters.[66]

The bulk of the black protest against the medical center urban re-newal project focused on a NAACP-led effort to influence the Eisen-hower administration and the federal Home and Housing Finance Agency to deny Birmingham's application for federal urban renewal funds. On May 28, 1953, at the same time that Birmingham was com-pleting its medical center urban renewal application, the Birmingham branch of the NAACP, through Clarence Mitchell, director of the NAACP Washington bureau, wrote Albert M. Cole, HHFA adminis-trator, urging no federal assistance unless Birmingham committed to seeing that any housing built on the urban renewal site was available to all qualified persons, regardless of race. Accompanying the letter

were petitions signed by 749 residents in the Southside neighborhood, twenty-four businesses, and two churches.[67] The Birmingham
NAACP also contended that while Birmingham paid lip service to relocation of Southside's residents into decent, safe, and sanitary housing, the HABD had not developed specific plans for carrying out this
objective. The Birmingham NAACP objected to the discrimination
faced by black physicians who would not be allowed to practice medicine in the main hospital at the medical center but would have their
practice confined to a planned black hospital.[68] Finally, the Birmingham NAACP objected to the absence of any blacks on the HABD board
and the city's planning and zoning board.[69]

The Birmingham branch of the NAACP responded to the city's urban renewal proposal by organizing a five-person committee, chaired
by attorney Oscar W. Adams Jr. On July 23, 1953, at the request of the
HHFA, housing authority officials met with that committee at the
Masonic Temple building, which housed the NAACP's southeast regional office, on Fourth Avenue and Seventeenth Street in Birmingham's black business district.[70]

The meeting followed growing HHFA concern about the Southside
project and the NAACP reaction to it. In late May 1953, George Nesbitt,
special assistant for racial relations to Nathaniel Keith, HHFA's director of the Division of Slum Clearance and Urban Redevelopment
(DSCUR), wrote Keith that it was "difficult to view this project other
than as [a] 'Negro clearance' proposal. . . . Nothing appears in the record reflecting that consideration was given to DSCUR's recommendation that housing open to Negro families be provided nor is there
any reflection of consultation with Negro groups."[71] Consequently,
Nesbitt recommended against approving the Southside redevelopment plan. When HHFA staff had earlier asked Birmingham officials
about including black housing on the medical center site, housing authority urban renewal director Samuel Gibbons replied that the area
"could not be expanded for that purpose."[72]

HHFA concern was further expressed when on June 18, 1953, Frank
S. Horne, assistant to the HHFA administrator, wrote Albert Cole that
"we should strongly recommend rejection of this proposal and recon-
sideration if and when basic revisions are made."[73] On the next day,
Cole wrote Clarence Mitchell "that there are a number of questions to
be resolved before this redevelopment proposal is acceptable to this

Agency for a loan and grant contract."[74] In a June 29, 1953, phone call, HHFA officials told Samuel Gibbons that the federal government was "very concerned" over the plans to place white-only housing in the medical center project and that the HHFA office in Washington, D.C., was being "bombarded with objections to the Medical Center development in the form of letters and telegrams." The HHFA officials told Gibbons that the housing authority should determine what could be done to "eliminate the objections or to get Negro leadership to express themselves as being favorable to the program."[75] In a separate communication, HHFA area supervisor E. Bruce Wedge wrote Harold Harper that numerous protest letters from black residents and the NAACP opposition to the medical center project "seriously jeopardize compliance of the subject project with the 'racial equity procedure' of the urban renewal program's rules."[76]

With Wedge's letter, the housing authority finally felt compelled to meet with Adams and other local NAACP representatives. But despite the pressure from Washington, HHFA officials also gave Birmingham redevelopment officials a way out of their problem. In a June 30, 1953, phone call, HHFA officials stated "that they had confidence in our ability to work out all matters satisfactorily," and "if worst came to worst, we could drop the two blocks between 9th and 10th Avenues, eliminating all housing."[77] And, indeed, at the July 23 meeting, housing authority director Harold Harper told Oscar W. Adams Jr., Emory Jackson, NAACP Birmingham branch president W. C. Patton, attorney Orzell Billingsley Jr., and NAACP regional coordinator Ruby Hurley that the housing authority was dropping the multifamily housing project and was reducing the size of the expansion from 12½ to 11½ blocks.[78]

Harper also told the NAACP representatives that the Jefferson County Coordinating Council of Social Forces was working on purchasing land from Republic Steel Corporation for a "high-class exclusive Negro residential area."[79] After expressing initial resistance, Republic Steel's land manager, W. S. Sanford, agreed to sell fifty acres for a black subdivision. W. I. Pittman, president of the Coordinating Council of Social Forces, persuaded Sanford to sell the land when Pittman explained the significant local and regional benefits that would derive from expansion of the medical center.[80] The value of making this arrangement had been enhanced by Robert C. Robinson, assistant to HHFA area superyisor E. Bruce Wedge, who had previously told the housing authority on July 3, 1953, that if the land for a black subdivision could be arranged, "he felt sure . . . [that the racial relocation issue] . . . would be settled."[81]

HHFA appeared willing to accept development of a higher-income black subdivision as a "solution" to the racial relocation problem, even though most of the black residents of the Southside Medical Center neighborhood were very poor. Thadford Forrest, a black realtor assisting with the acquisition of the Republic Steel property, expected to sell thirty homes in the new subdivision to blacks for $10,000 to $15,000, with several going for as high as $20,000 to $25,000.[82] Considering that in 1950, a home valued at $10,000 was at the 85th percentile of all owner-occupied dwellings in Birmingham, the description of this subdivision as "high class" was apt. At the same time, the fact that 90 percent of the black residents of the Southside Medical Center project area were eligible for low-income public housing meant that the availability of housing for blacks at the Republic property was of little comfort.

The "Negro subdivision" solution, an approach that was employed in other southern cities as well, was attractive to the white ruling class as a "dual solution" because it maintained racial segregation while addressing the shortage of housing for black middle-class families.[83] The Dallas Interracial Committee, for example, actively pursued the development of a black subdivision in suburban Dallas and in the early 1950s, a successor organization, the Dallas Citizens Interracial Association Incorporated, developed and constructed the 730-home Hamilton Park subdivision for middle-class blacks.[84]

In Birmingham, that city's Interracial Division also staked much hope on the black subdivision proposal. The committee had previously discussed development of a black subdivision as a means for addressing the Smithfield racial zoning controversy, and it once again trotted out this solution to handle the criticism of the housing authority's relocation plan for the Southside Medical Center project.[85] By buying into Birmingham's dependence upon the black subdivision as a solution to the black housing problem, the HHFA was permitting the city to refashion an old solution to fit a new issue.

Other than the proposal to take housing out of the medical center project and reintroduce plans for a black subdivision, no other concessions were made. Harper simply reported at the meeting what federal law required—that urban renewal displacees have top priority for entry into public housing and that individuals will receive the appraised value of any real property they own in the urban renewal area. Harper claimed that the housing authority had no direct influence over segregated medical facilities as this would be under the control of the University of Alabama Medical Center and the city's segregation ordinances. He also contended that he had no control over the absence of blacks on the housing authority board or the planning board as the members of these boards were appointed by city government.[86]

In response, W. C. Patton wrote HHFA officials, "we do contend that the Birmingham plan has every appearance of being a plan to clear the members of a minority group from a section of the city which now has high real estate value."[87] Patton also contended that turnover in the three public housing projects available to blacks was insufficient to provide relocation opportunities in the broader context of a shortage of decent housing for blacks in Birmingham. Moreover, the problem of relocating black households had been made harder because the planned construction of 950 units of black public housing at Tuxedo Junction in Ensley had recently been prevented by congressional cuts in federal public housing expenditures.[88]

The NAACP followed up on its accusations by holding two early August public meetings in the Southside neighborhood. Speakers included W. C. Patton; Oscar W. Adams Jr.; Emory Jackson; Reverend Hiram W. Scruggs, president of the Southside Protective Home Owners League; and Ruby Hurley.[89] Two weeks later, Adams, Hurley, Scruggs, Reverend John W. Goodgame, Orzell Billingsley Jr., and Reverend J. L. Ware, president of the Birmingham Baptist Ministers Conference, traveled to Washington, D.C., to join NAACP Washington bureau director Clarence Mitchell for a meeting with Albert Cole, the Eisenhower-appointed administrator of HHFA.[90] The Birmingham group told Cole that the city's decision to delete housing from the urban renewal plan did not address the issue of segregated hospital and park facilities. The delegates told Cole that one of the existing hospitals in the medical center required black patients to use the freight entrance and that while badly needed housing was deleted from the plan, proposed park facilities would likely be segregated: "It is ironic that space which could be used for badly needed housing will be converted into badminton courts—for whites only."[91] Finally, the NAACP-led group told Cole, as they had told others, that the city's relocation plan failed to address the housing needs of the families who would be displaced.

In early October, Cole traveled to Birmingham to hold a public hearing, at which three speakers, Ruby Hurley, Reverend J. L. Ware, and Reverend W. P. Vaughn spoke against the Southside Medical Center expansion project. Vaughn, who pastored Tabernacle Baptist Church, had resigned from the Interracial Division to protest the committee's attitude toward the urban renewal project.[92] Emory Jackson, in the *Birmingham World,* had challenged the twenty-four black members of the Interracial Division to state whether they had participated in an alleged statement supporting the Southside Medical Center expansion project.[93] Jackson learned from HHFA slum clearance director James W. Follin that HHFA had no record of a statement from the Interracial Division, but instead mayor James Morgan had reported to HHFA that some of the committee members favored the project. Jackson then criticized the Interracial Division for its weakness in the face of the relocation issue and the Southside Medical Center expansion project.[94]

Instead, the Interracial Division continued to address black housing issues, including relocation of blacks from the Southside Medical Center neighborhood, by attempting to launch a middle-class black subdivision.[95] Such effort, including the attempt to develop a subdivision on the Republic Steel property, never succeeded, however, as the Interracial Division and its housing subcommittee never obtained financing for the project. In southern cities such as Houston, San Antonio, Miami, and Atlanta, white investors were critical to the success of new housing for blacks, but in Birmingham the lack of financing doomed that city's effort at developing a black subdivision.[96] A. Key Foster, who chaired the housing subcommittee, was quoted at a 1955 meeting of the subcommittee, at which a subdivision for black homeowners was discussed, as saying: "Well, once again, we're just talking. We need some money in this."[97] Ironically, Foster was a vice president at Birmingham's First National Bank.[98] But while Foster thought the Republic Steel location "could be made into a beautiful residential section for Negroes, including a golf course," he also distrusted the group of blacks who wanted to develop the property: "I am afraid that their plan is not well conceived and I feel that somebody should guide them in their thinking."[99] In the end, the Interracial Division contributed nothing to the racial relocation issue created by the medical center expansion. Under pressure from segregationists, the division was dissolved in 1956.[100]

At the October public hearing, HHFA Director Cole heard speakers Vaughn, Ware, and Hurley criticize the Southside Medical Center urban renewal project, while none of the eight white speakers expressed opposition.[101] Ruby Hurley criticized the housing authority's relocation plan for its dependence upon the three existing public housing projects available to blacks. After citing the high level of need for public housing among Birmingham's black residents, she stated that, "the three existing housing projects which have lengthy waiting lists cannot possibly meet the need, therefore we endorse the continuation and extension of the public housing program."[102] Hurley criticized the Southside Medical Center urban renewal proposal for not having a plan that provided assurance that the 529 black families would be able to move into decent and affordable housing. Moreover, she reminded her listeners that when relocated black households are able "to move into new areas of housing," they should be granted equal protection under the law. Birmingham needs this reminder, she said, because, "we remember the bombing of a Negro home [the Monk home] here just twenty-four hours after a federal court had ruled that a racial zoning ordinance was unconstitutional, the subsequent burning of homes which had been previously bombed and the disability of the local police to find the perpetrators of these crimes."[103] The NAACP was reminding the city of the link between racial zoning and the city's new "Racial Relocation Plan." If the city wanted to use urban renewal to clear blacks out of certain neighborhoods, then it would have to provide them with an opportunity to live in decent, affordable homes somewhere else.

The city, for its part, was attempting to identify blacks who would support the Southside Medical Center urban renewal project. In June, HHFA officials Maslem and Robinson had told the housing authority that HHFA had not received any communications from black leaders that supported the Southside Medical Center project. The housing authority staff said they "would explore the matter very carefully and decide what should be done locally to eliminate the objections or to get Negro leadership to express themselves as being favorable to the program."[104] By the fall of 1953, several cracks, perceived or actual, appeared in the black opposition to the urban renewal project and the city attempted to make the most of them. After meeting with NAACP representatives on November 13, 1953, Mayor James Morgan sought to imply that the NAACP supported the Southside Medical Center project: "the group here this morning seemed pleased. They seemed to understand the problems."[105]

Within the same week, Mayor James Morgan also identified Oscar W. Adams Jr. as supporting the Southside Medical Center urban renewal project.[106] Earlier, Adams had been listed as one of the planned speakers at the October public hearing presided over by Cole, but he ended up not speaking at that event.[107] Adams, who also represented black homeowners affected by the Southside urban renewal project, later said that his clients were eager to sell and did not want to see the project halted.[108] Emory Jackson hinted at Adams's ambivalence on the relocation issue when his paper's "Around the Town" column featured the following cryptic statement: "Attorney Oscar W. Adams, Jr., is scheduled to deliver the 'Men's Day' Message at Hunter A.M.E. Zion Church, Tuscaloosa, Sunday October 25th. Some leaders have seen information which will embarrass some leaders who have talked on both sides of the housing fight."[109]

As already discussed, Jackson was less subtle in criticizing the black members of the Interracial Division for remaining silent on the Southside Medical Center's relocation plan. His paper's "Around the Town" column also criticized the Metropolitan Council of Negro Women, the City Federation of Women's Clubs, and the Alabama State Federation of Civic Leagues for their silence on the removal of blacks from the Southside.[110]

The Birmingham branch of the NAACP responded to Mayor Morgan's claim that the group supported the urban renewal project by issuing a statement denying that the organization had withdrawn its objection to the Southside Medical Center project and its relocation plan.[111] Nevertheless, on November 25, 1953, James W. Follin announced that HHFA had approved Birmingham's Southside Medical Center urban renewal application.[112] Follin did attach one condition to this approval, however. In a letter to housing authority director Harold Harper, Follin noted that the housing authority had deleted its original plan to build whites-only housing on the urban renewal site. He then warned Birmingham that he would disapprove any plan amendment that permitted housing in the redevelopment area, unless "appropriate provision were made for equitable and fair provision for the housing needs of Negro families."[113] At the same time, however, Follin noted that the Hill-Burton Act, which provided federal assistance for hospital construction, permitted segregated hospital facilities as long as the facilities and services for whites and blacks were of "like quality."[114]

The Eisenhower administration, therefore, encouraged Birmingham to avoid using the medical center site for housing that would exclude blacks but dismissed issues concerning the availability of adequate relocation housing for black residents and the racial discrimination faced by black medical personnel and patients. In a September 1953 memo to Cole, Follin had written that turnover in Birmingham's public housing stock was insufficient to accommodate blacks moving out of the Southside area and that in debating urban renewal legislation in 1949, the Senate had rejected an antisegregation amendment. Therefore, HHFA was not in a position to question segregation of the planned medical facilities.[115]

In response to the HHFA decision, Ruby Hurley wrote Mayor Morgan reminding him of the November 13, 1953, meeting that Morgan had interpreted as indicating NAACP support for the medical center project. Hurley's interpretation of that meeting was that regarding relocation and police protection for displaced blacks moving into "fringe or new areas," Morgan had pledged that the city would "do the right thing." Writing in mid-December, she noted, however, that the local Democratic Party had just run racially inflammatory advertising in connection with a poll tax amendment. This caused her to conclude that the Democratic-dominated city was not likely to interpret its implementation of the urban renewal act in any way that benefited blacks.[116]

Regarding the relocation of blacks from the Southside Medical Center neighborhood, the city's own documents demonstrate that the relocation plan was inadequate. Fourteen months after HHFA had approved the housing authority's Southside Medical Center urban renewal application, Mayor Morgan wrote A. R. Hanson requesting funds for 750 additional units of public housing. The attached data, Morgan wrote, "indicate a substantial deficit of units, particularly for Negro families." He elaborated on the deficit of housing for blacks by stating:

Our City is sponsoring a substantial Title I program of Slum Clearance and Urban Renewal, one project [Southside] being well under way and another [Avondale] expected to enter the Loan and Grant stage in about 90 days. Both of these project areas are occupied primarily by non-white families, most of them in the lower income bracket. Most of these families will not be able to afford standard dwelling units unless they can obtain low-rent public housing. *It is recognized that a limited number of displacements can be housed each month in the units that become available through turnover in existing low-income housing, but if the Title I program is to move with dispatch, additional low-rent units are necessary for non-white families.* (emphasis added)[117]

A December 1957 HHFA report described what happened to the first 527 families that were relocated from the medical center site. Of the 527 families, 484 were black. Of these, 403 were eligible for public housing, but only 76 had moved into public housing. Of the remainder who had not left town or been evicted, 100 moved into standard rental housing, 69 purchased standard homes, and 112 moved into substandard housing. Of the 43 white families relocated, none moved into substandard housing. Of the 146 urban renewal projects in the nation at that time, only five had more households relocated into substandard housing than did the Southside Medical Center project.[118]

The NAACP did follow up with a June 1954 suit in Federal District Court, filed by local black attorney Peter A. Hall and NAACP attorney Thurgood Marshall. The suit charged that blacks were not being treated equally by the city's relocation plans because they had access only to public housing developments designated for blacks.[119] The suit was summarily dismissed by the U.S. District Court on January 28, 1955, as having no legal merit.[120]

In May of 1955, the NAACP Birmingham branch dropped any plans to appeal this decision as over thirty of the thirty-six property-owning plaintiffs had dropped out of the suit in order to be able to obtain the money they had been paid for their properties. One of the homeowners, Reverend J. B. Carter, who had spoken against the Southside Medical Center relocation plan at the March 30, 1953, public hearing, pleaded for the release of the funds from the sale of his house and was quoted as "tearfully pleading 'I am in dire need of the money. I am not young anymore. I must have my money in the morning. I am facing an embarrassing situation.'"[121] By a vote of 17 to 4, the branch concluded that continuation of the court fight was too costly. Branch president Reverend R. W. Hayden recommended that the court suit be dropped "since the branch has no money and it would require thousands of dollars to continue this fight to the Alabama State Supreme Court and the United States Supreme Court."[122] By that time, relocation of residents was proceeding and the project would be completely closed out, with ten and one-half of the acres sold to the University of Alabama, by 1959.[123]

Despite long odds, Birmingham's black community had challenged the city's attempt to give racial zoning new meaning within the context of the federal urban renewal program. The Birmingham branch NAACP had joined with the city's black newspaper to oppose the city's efforts to remove blacks from the Southside neighborhood and had shown solid political acumen by enlisting the aid of NAACP's Washington, D.C., office and attempting to influence the Eisenhower administration to apply pressure on Birmingham's city government. Aside from preventing the construction of whites-only housing on the Southside Medical Center renewal site, the black community's effort failed. Its power was simply too limited to influence the city, either directly or indirectly through its allies in Washington. Even though staff members of the HHFA's Racial Relations Branch urged otherwise, HHFA and the Eisenhower administration were not willing to block local government, whether it be Birmingham or Chicago, from using "slum sites in areas of Negro occupancy in order to reinforce Negro containment."[124] Not until the 1960s and 1970s would the Birmingham black community's external allies in Washington, D.C., have the power and the will to influence Birmingham's city government. In the meantime, Birmingham would continue to be able to use not only the public housing and urban renewal programs but also the interstate highway programs to sustain racial segregation in Birmingham.

5 Urban Renewal
and Highways

The Southside Medical Center expansion project represented the successful use of the urban renewal program to expel the black population from a neighborhood coveted by the city's white establishment. The Avondale and Ensley urban renewal projects, as well as the city's federal highway projects of the 1950s and 1960s, also demonstrate how the white community could use the federal government's urban planning programs of that era to preserve racial segregation and to enhance the interests of the white establishment and white neighborhoods. As such, both the Avondale and Ensley urban renewal projects represent the use of "the blight that's right" to select urban renewal sites. This principle, employed in other cities' urban renewal programs as well, identified projects not only by the needs demonstrated in the neighborhood but also by the utility of that neighborhood for meeting the white establishment's economic and social interests.[1] In Avondale, the city selected a black neighborhood for redevelopment in great part because that neighborhood represented a blighting influence on a major thoroughfare connecting Birmingham's airport with its downtown. In Ensley, the city demonstrated how it could use the urban renewal program, in conjunction with the interstate highway program, to strengthen the boundary between a white and a black neighborhood. This case was not unique, as evidence exists to show that Birmingham used other segments of the interstate highway system to separate black from white neighborhoods. Moreover, it also is clear that the city adopted a policy of deliberately routing interstate highways through black neighborhoods in order to avoid routing them through white neighborhoods. The impact of the city's use of the federal urban renewal and highway programs was twofold. First, these programs had a profound impact on the city's black neighborhoods, causing them to lose significant portions of their population in the

1960s. The second impact was ironic because it was opposite to what the city's white leaders and neighbors wanted. With the significant dislocation of the city's black population by urban renewal and highway construction, significant neighborhood racial change began to take place in Birmingham in the 1960s. The city's march to becoming a majority black city, something its white leaders dreaded, began with the forced movement of its black residents into previously white neighborhoods in the 1960s.

The Blight That's Right:
The Avondale Urban Renewal Project

On November 28, 1953, three days after the U.S. Housing and Home Finance Agency (HHFA) gave final approval to the Southside Medical Center expansion project, the same agency allocated funds to the housing authority to complete the last phase of planning for Birmingham's second urban renewal project, located in the Avondale neighborhood on the city's east side (see map 5.1).[2] Census tract 24 (see map 3.2) of the Avondale neighborhood, like Southside, was a low-income, predominantly black neighborhood. At $1,822, the neighborhood's 1950 median household income was about 50 percent higher than the Southside neighborhood's median income, but overall, the neighborhood ranked fourteenth from the bottom among Birmingham's fifty-eight census tracts. Nearly three-quarters of all dwelling units lacked a private bath or were dilapidated.[3] In 1950, the census tract was 70 percent black, with the Avondale urban renewal project area zoned for black occupancy since adoption of the 1926 zoning map.[4] A housing authority study found that of 2,600 people living in the project area 2,392, or 92 percent, were black.[5]

Like other black Birmingham neighborhoods, the Avondale urban renewal area was isolated from white neighborhoods by nonresidential land uses. The 1926 zoning map, along with the zoning map contained in the Birmingham Planning Board's 1952 *Preliminary Report,* showed the triangle-shaped urban renewal area as wedged between the Central of Georgia Railroad on the north, major east-west arterial First Avenue North on the south, and industrially zoned land to the west. Of the 740 dwelling units in the neighborhood, 75 percent were dilapidated or lacked a private bath. Many houses were served by yard privies, and an open sewer ran down Forty-fourth Street, a dirt road through the neighborhood.[6]

What distinguished Avondale from other black, blighted neighborhoods was its visibility to Birmingham's white elite. Running through the neighborhood was Georgia Road, the main artery leading from the city's airport, located in East Birmingham, to the city's central business district. It was along Georgia Road that business and other travelers drove to downtown. They saw a two-lane street lined with wooden slum dwellings built nearly to the curb, with only a sidewalk separating them and their occupants from the street. According to a *Birmingham News* editorial, which included photographs of the neighborhood's substandard housing and dirt streets, "This is the entrance to the city for air travelers."[7] The community newspaper, *East End News,* editorialized that whatever one thinks about urban renewal, cleanup of the neighborhood "is going to make a big difference in the appearance of this part of the city." "Any way you look at it, the area between First Ave. and the Central of Georgia Railroad and in the 39th, 40th, and 41st St. blocks, is a scar on the face of Birmingham. It is hard to get to Birmingham from the Airport or from the entire Eastern section without passing near or through this blighted area."[8] In addition to improving the view associated with travel to Birmingham's downtown, the Avondale urban renewal project would also widen Georgia Road to four lanes, thereby improving its capacity to handle traffic.[9]

Birmingham's white elite also saw the Avondale urban renewal neighborhood as strategically important to the development of the city's black schools. In 1952, the Birmingham Planning Board declared in its *Preliminary Report* that no black high schools served the black residential areas located east of downtown between the Woodlawn neighborhood and the central business district. Black students in these neighborhoods were attending an overcrowded Parker High School in Smithfield, just west of downtown; and a new high school at the Avondale urban renewal site would relieve Parker's overcrowding while "eliminating the long ride and downtown transfer now necessary for Negro children living east of 26th St."[10]

The Birmingham Board of Education also saw the Avondale urban renewal site as a good location for a new black elementary school. The existing one, the Thomas School, was located near Sloss Furnaces and served the black children living in Sloss Quarters; it was less than a

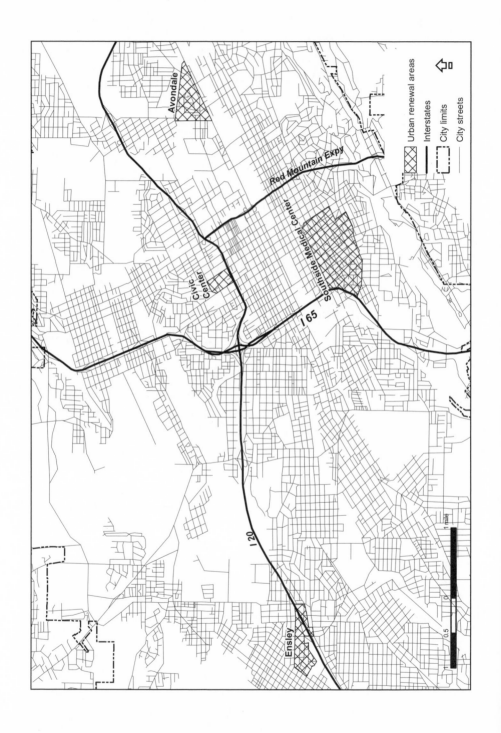

Avondale

Red Mountain Expy

Civic
Center

Southside Medical Center

I 65

I 20

Ensley

Urban renewal areas
Interstates
City limits
City streets

0.5   0   1 mile

mile east of downtown Birmingham.[11] The Birmingham Planning Board reported that the families of children attending the Thomas School were leaving the neighborhood.[12] This outmigration was occurring at the time that the Sloss-Sheffield Company, operator of Sloss Furnaces, was phasing out its company housing.[13]

In general, the city's urban renewal plan for Avondale revolved around the city's need to improve the appearance of this highly visible neighborhood, to widen the city's main thoroughfare linking the airport and downtown Birmingham, and to use the urban renewal program to subsidize the construction of two badly needed schools for black children. Finally, urban renewal permitted the city to do what it could no longer do with its illegal racial zoning law: designate the area for black occupancy. Throughout the project's planning, the city intended for this area to be occupied by blacks, and the federal urban renewal program facilitated this by subsidizing two-thirds of the project's costs.[14]

The city also continued its racial zoning tradition of concentrating black residents in industrial areas. Lying just south of the Central of Georgia rail line, the Avondale project was located just east of a large area of heavy industry, including Virginia Bridge and Iron, American Casting, and Birmingham-Goslin Manufacturing.[15] Because of the Avondale project's proximity to these industrial uses, HHFA staff questioned whether the area's reuse as residential was appropriate. Carl Feiss, of HHFA's Division of Slum Clearance and Urban Redevelopment (DSCUR), believed Avondale was unsuitable for residential development and that the division should disapprove Birmingham's urban renewal plans for the area. George Nesbitt, special assistant for racial relations to DSCUR's director Nathanial Keith, agreed that the Avondale neighborhood had physical problems. He attributed this to Birmingham's efforts to locate blacks in the city's industrial areas: "The city thought of its 'land leavings' when it considered land for housing open to Negroes." Nesbitt further argued that Birmingham was using urban renewal in Avondale to solidify black occupancy in the area so as to "check and offset Negro expansion in better areas."[16] Nesbitt also questioned the adequacy of relocation plans, especially for households not eligible for public housing. He requested a more detailed analysis

Map 5.1 (*opposite*). Birmingham urban renewal areas

of where displaced blacks would go in the private market, stating that "these details are most necessary in connection with Birmingham, a city in which racial restrictions in existing housing are still sanctioned by local public officials and in which violence in connection with Negro expansion is frequent."[17]

Despite such concern, on March 28, 1956, HHFA approved the Avondale project for $3.64 million in urban renewal funds. The project, which affected 675 families in 740 dwelling units, would provide new housing for 390 new households, all of them black; two new schools, both for blacks; a neighborhood park; a widened Georgia Road; and land for commercial and industrial development. Over two-thirds of the families in the neighborhood were eligible for public housing.[18] In this case, in contrast to the Southside Medical Center, additional units of public housing were being built to meet the relocation needs of the neighborhood's residents. The Kingston public housing project, later named Morton Simpson Village, was located in the Kingston neighborhood two blocks north of the Avondale urban renewal site. It would house five hundred households.[19]

The Avondale urban renewal project was not without controversy and delay, but unlike the Southside Medical Center case, Birmingham's black community did not mount any significant opposition to this development. The housing authority had appointed a Negro Citizens Advisory Committee, whose members contacted residents and property owners to head off opposition to the project. The committee's chairman, John L. Streeter, pronounced HHFA's approval of the project "wonderful for the city and the people."[20]

This is not to say, however, that Birmingham blacks did not question the Avondale project. In her October 1953 speech denouncing the Southside Medical Center urban renewal project, NAACP regional secretary Ruby Hurley also criticized the Avondale project: "We look with disfavor on the present plan to redevelop the Avondale area which is a section bound on two sides by industry and one side by a railroad, hardly suitable for a school, a park, and a housing project. We ask, why does the City continue to attempt the use of zoning techniques to relegate Negroes to the least desirable sections of the town?"[21] As in the case of the Southside Medical Center, Birmingham blacks saw the Avondale project as another extension of racial zoning. Like the 1926 zoning ordinance, the Avondale urban renewal project would target black housing for a predominantly industrial area that the Birmingham city government felt was unsuitable for white occupancy. In the words of Arnold Hirsch, Birmingham was using urban renewal and public housing to create a "second ghetto," which reinforced the first ghetto that was codified by Birmingham's racial zoning ordinance.[22]

Additional reaction came from the black residents of the Kingston neighborhood, just north of Avondale, who protested the loss of their homes so that a five-hundred-unit public housing development could be built to rehouse those displaced by the Avondale project. One hundred nineteen residents of predominantly black Kingston signed a petition protesting the declaration of their neighborhood as a slum, stating that, "Most of us have devoted years of effort and have spent our hard-earned money in acquiring a piece of land which we may call our own and on which we can live decently as law-abiding citizens of our great city."[23] Even though the city had at least planned to meet Avondale's relocation needs by building more public housing, that housing came at the expense of an existing black neighborhood in Birmingham. The city had compounded the displacement associated with urban renewal by locating replacement housing in an existing black neighborhood. This approach, of course, begged the question of where the Kingston neighborhood displacees were to go while the public housing created for the Avondale displacees was being constructed.[24]

Nevertheless, despite these protests, the broader black community did not challenge the Avondale project in the same way it had confronted the Southside Medical Center project. Although the Avondale project was designed to enhance racial segregation, the fact that it did not feature the displacement of blacks by whites or by segregated facilities, such as at the Medical Center, meant that opposition to Avondale in the black community was less abundant than in the Southside urban renewal project.

In contrast to the Southside Medical Center project, the Avondale urban renewal project faced delay and controversy that was primarily attributable to Birmingham's limited public revenues. In July 1955, Birmingham mayor James Morgan announced that the city lacked $850,000 for its share of the project, as well as for other planning requirements that were related to Birmingham's continued eligibility for federal urban renewal and public housing funds. Morgan's position was supported by fellow commissioner Wade Bradley, thereby representing a majority opinion on Birmingham's three-member city commission.[25] The housing authority, along with several unnamed "influential citizens," responded by urging the city commission to reconsider its decision to drop the Avondale project.[26] Among the influential citizens lobbying the city commission was chamber of commerce president James A. Head, who ran an office supply business in downtown Birmingham. The *Birmingham News* paraphrased Head as saying, "Industrial and business executives who come to Birmingham to study possible sites for their operations have been 'disappointed' as they drive through run-down neighborhoods lying between Municipal Airport and downtown hotels."[27]

By the end of July 1955, HHFA responded to Birmingham's reluctance to pursue the Avondale project by delaying plans for development of the five-hundred-unit public housing project in the Kingston neighborhood.[28] In response to these pressures, by August 1, 1955, the Birmingham City Commission voted to raise money for the city's portion of the Avondale urban renewal costs by asking voters to approve a $1.275 million bond issue in September 1955. The bond issue would be used to support public investment in both the Avondale and Southside urban renewal projects.[29] Both the Birmingham Chamber of Commerce and the *Birmingham News* announced their support for the bond issue.[30]

The Birmingham Real Estate Board, which supported the Southside Medical Center urban renewal project, opposed the Avondale urban renewal project. On August 2, 1955, Real Estate Board president Joe Meade, along with a delegation of board members, told the city commission of their opposition to the Avondale project, as well as to other projects that entailed public housing. The board claimed that private enterprise in combination with a city-adopted housing code could be counted on to clean up the city's slums. Meade also asked the city commission to separate the Avondale-Southside bond issue into two issues, so that citizens could vote on them separately.[31] The Real Estate Board supported urban renewal, but like realtors in other cities at that time, vigorously opposed government ownership of rental housing.[32]

Despite realtor opposition, on September 13, 1955, Birmingham voters approved the Avondale-Southside bond issue by a margin of 5,952 votes to 5,365.[33] Two days later, HHFA permitted Birmingham to resume planning for the Kingston public housing project.[34] Finally, in

March 1956, in response to Birmingham's financial support for the project, HHFA gave final approval to the Avondale urban renewal project.[35]

Birmingham's lack of planning capacity, attributable to its limited public expenditures, also delayed progress on the Avondale project. By the time serious planning for Avondale began in late 1953, Congress had adopted the Housing Act of 1954 and that act's Workable Program provision. Signed by President Eisenhower on August 2, 1954, the Workable Program amendment required communities planning to use urban renewal, public housing, or HHFA's Section 220/221 mortgage insurance funds to refrain from engaging in ad hoc slum clearance. Instead, communities were to develop a comprehensive approach to the entire city that would aim as much at slum prevention and rehabilitation as at slum clearance.[36] The Southside Medical Center project was exempted because federal approval had been obtained before August 2, 1954, but subsequent urban renewal projects, including Avondale, were bound by this provision. Birmingham spent little on planning and therefore was not in a good position to quickly enact many of the planning requirements imposed by the Workable Program legislation.

The Workable Program amendment required cities using federal urban aid funds to achieve seven objectives: "1) Adequate Codes and Ordinances, 2) [a] Comprehensive Community Plan, 3) Detailed Neighborhood Analyses, 4) Adequate Administrative Organization, 5) Financing Ability, 6) Housing for Displaced Families, 7) Full-Fledged Citizen Participation."[37] Birmingham had made only limited progress in meeting these seven objectives, and HHFA was specifically concerned about Birmingham's lack of progress in developing a comprehensive plan. In early 1955, as the city was preparing its first Workable Program application, HHFA's Bruce Wedge wrote Hugh Denman of Birmingham's Housing Authority:

that there be satisfactory evidence as to the existence of an adequate continuing local planning program and the elements of a General Plan for the locality as a whole must be found to adequately meet the Agency requirements before a Loan and Grant Contract can be executed. The progress made to date in Birmingham on the General Plan would appear to preclude the meeting of these requirements

in the near future. . . . In order that progress on the Avondale, Site
C Project will not be delayed by failure of the City to meet the General Plan minimum requirements, it is urged that your authority
make every effort to improve the current situation.[38]

So that it could proceed with the Avondale urban renewal project, the
city began work on a comprehensive land use plan. In so doing, the city
continued to plan for neighborhoods on the basis of race.[39]

In April 1955, the city responded to the new Workable Program requirements by hiring its first full-time city planner, George Foss.[40] By
fall of 1955, Foss had prepared a future land use map and a "narrative
description of [a] proposed future land use map" for the twenty-square-
mile area surrounding the Avondale urban renewal area.

The land use plan, which was adopted by the Birmingham Planning
Commission on November 16, 1955, recommended that the neighborhood be considered the minimum planning unit, "the extent of which
is primarily the service area of an elementary school." The 1955 land
use plan used the neighborhood unit concept and that concept's employment of the local elementary school as a means to assure the racial
character of a neighborhood. Under the neighborhood unit concept,
the elementary school serves as the center for a neighborhood, and the
school's enrollment requirements are used to determine the population size of the neighborhood.[41] Each neighborhood was classified by
the elementary school that served it and whether the school was for
whites or for blacks.

Taking the neighborhood unit concept a step further, however, the
planning commission's land use plan stated, "Inasmuch as the elementary school is the nucleus of the neighborhood, this entire analysis is based on the assumption that segregation in the schools of Birmingham will be maintained regardless of court decrees or the activity
of pressure groups."[42] Given the 1954 U.S. Supreme Court ruling
against segregated public schools, the Birmingham Planning Commission was using neighborhood planning as a mechanism by which
it could maintain segregated public schools. The plan divided the fourteen neighborhoods of the northeastern Birmingham area into eight
black and six white neighborhoods.[43] The land use plan used the racial
designations of the 1926 racial zoning law. It refrained from defining,
for example, what an A-2 district was, leaving it to the reader to know

that A-2 was the classification indicating a single-family neighborhood for black occupancy.

For the predominantly black Avondale urban renewal neighborhood, the planning commission recommended the area be designated for continued black occupancy. This was consistent with the planning board's 1952 recommendation to place a black elementary and high school on the site. The future land use narrative noted, however, that a small white population lived in the neighborhood along Fifth Court, just west of Fortieth Street. Such an enclave, the commission noted, was too small to be a separate neighborhood, and since the black elementary school required a minimum population to justify its construction, the plan implied that the white families should be replaced by black families.[44] When a consultant to the Birmingham Planning Commission completed a 1957 future land use plan for the entire city, he was less circumspect about recommending that the small white population in the Avondale area be replaced: "The area west of 40th Street is now occupied by white families and is too small to form a separate white neighborhood. This area should convert to use by colored families in order to establish a large enough neighborhood population to justify the construction of a minimum size elementary school."[45]

In designating white and black neighborhoods, the 1955 land use plan was careful to distinguish a "master plan" from zoning. The U.S. Supreme Court had declared racial zoning unconstitutional, but the Birmingham Planning Commission acted as if it thought that the master plan could still be employed to separate the races. The 1955 land use plan proceeds to say that the city commission should not adopt the plan, but that instead the master plan should be used as "a guide which suggests how the various existing and proposed physical features, such as highways, parks, public improvements, institutions, dwellings, commerce and industry should be related to each other."[46] It was through these devices that the planning commission proposed to maintain racial segregation in Birmingham.

The Avondale case demonstrates how the planning commission, in cooperation with the housing authority and the school board, could use public improvements (for example, new schools) to fix the racial characteristics of the neighborhood, even in a situation where a handful of whites occupied the neighborhood. In other neighborhoods, the planning commission planned to employ other comprehensive planning tools, including public schools, to enforce racial segregation. In the Inglenook neighborhood, the planning commission recommended the conversion of a four-block area into a park, so that it could "act as a buffer strip between colored and white properties."[47]

In the Kingston neighborhood, lying just north of Avondale, the planning commission noted the presence of whites as well as blacks, but "due to its proximity to industrial areas none of this neighborhood area is suitable for zoning as Residential A-1," the designation for a single-family white neighborhood.[48] Consistent with the 1926 racial zoning map's juxtaposition of black neighborhoods with industrial uses, the 1955 land use plan continued to see industrial use as appropriate to black, but not to white, neighborhoods.

In the Gibson School neighborhood just east of Kingston and northeast of the Avondale urban renewal area, the planning commission confronted a zone of transition between these black neighborhoods and the predominantly white Woodlawn neighborhood lying just to the east of the Gibson School. The Gibson School was a white school, but according to the land use plan, the neighborhood was zoned for black multifamily housing. The land use plan states, however, that with the recent development of single-family homes, the neighborhood should be designated for *white* single-family dwellings, as well as white multifamily dwellings. With this recommendation, the planning commission was seeking to use the land use plan to convert a neighborhood from racially mixed to white so that the local white school could draw on a catchment area that was entirely white.[49]

In another mixed neighborhood, at the northern edge of Woodlawn, lying due east of the Avondale urban renewal area, the planning commission proposed the use of urban renewal funds to take out an area occupied by blacks so that the entire neighborhood would become white.[50] The area had been undergoing racial transition, and one year after the planning commission report was issued, on December 31, 1956, the home of Otis and Catherine Flowers was bombed. The home had previously been occupied by a white family.[51] This was one of three bombings that took place in 1956, the first year since 1951 in which racial bombings occurred.[52]

HHFA's report on the progress of Birmingham's 1955 Workable Program offered both praise and criticism of Birmingham's planning effort, but while acknowledging the city's completion of the 1955 plan, it made no judgment on the city's plans to use land use planning to maintain racial segregation.[53]

Despite HHFA's approval of Birmingham's first Workable Program, two of the three Birmingham city commissioners decided that the program's requirements were too costly. The expected bill for meeting the Workable Program's planning requirements was rising, the city's adoption of a housing code requiring property owners to furnish bathtubs and hot water was met with opposition, and the expected cost of the city's participation in the Avondale urban renewal project was high. This prompted Mayor James Morgan and Commissioner Wade Bradley to conclude in July 1955 that it was time not only to discontinue the Avondale project but also to entirely drop out of the Workable Program, thereby making the city ineligible for further urban renewal and public housing funds.[54] Reacting to increased HHFA scrutiny of local planning, Bradley said, "It is just another step in local government becoming subservient to the federal government." Mayor Morgan responded: "This time they've gone too far. They've been very good to us in the public housing line. But there are too many regulations." These regulations cost too much money because they require the city to employ a "high-priced planning organization." Moreover, the newspaper quoted the mayor as saying that the scarcity of "genuine planners" makes them "cost more than they're worth."[55] With the chamber of commerce fearing the loss of the urban renewal program in Avondale, however, the city commissioners were persuaded to continue to participate in HHFA's Workable Program, thereby permitting continued participation in the urban renewal program.

Despite the city's decision to meet HHFA's terms for remaining eligible for federal urban renewal and public housing funds, the city continued to make plans under the Workable Program for the strengthening of racial segregation in the city's neighborhoods. Soon after the planning commission adopted the land use plan for Northeast Birmingham, the Birmingham City Commission appropriated funds to hire a consultant, Don Oesterling, an employee of the housing authority, to prepare a future land use plan for the entire city.[56] The 1957 plan, which built on the foundation laid by the 1955 Northeast Birmingham land use plan, consisted primarily of one- to two-paragraph descriptions and prescriptions for each of the city's eighty-one neighborhoods, fifty of which the plan identified as black and thirty-one as white. Although it refrained from using the racial land use codes left over from the 1926 racial zoning law, the 1957 plan, in an approach similar to the one taken in the 1955 Northeast Birmingham land use plan, emphasized the maintenance of racial segregation in the city's neighborhoods.[57]

For example, in its discussion of the white Graymont neighborhood, the 1957 land use plan emphasized the value of Elyton Village, a whites-only public housing project located just west of black Smithfield, "as a buffer to encroachment from adjoining Negro neighborhoods."[58] This development, completed in 1940 as Birmingham's first public project for white occupancy, thereby joined nearby McLendon Park, acquired by the city in 1923, as another racial buffer between white Graymont and black Smithfield (see chapter 3).

In the eyes of the federal government, however, Birmingham's 1957 future land use plan was inadequate. HHFA had given the housing authority authorization to proceed with the Avondale urban renewal project after the city had produced the 1955 Northeast Birmingham land use plan.[59] HHFA was no longer satisfied with a plan that did not include a professional analysis of population and employment trends or "other current land use planning practices." HHFA had no reaction, however, to the 1957 plan's focus on maintaining racial segregation.[60]

In order to get planning funds for Birmingham's third urban renewal project, in the Ensley–Pratt City community, HHFA told the city there must be a comprehensive plan. After some effort was made to find the nearly $250,000 required for such a study, in March 1958 the city commission agreed to contract with Harland Bartholomew and Associates for a comprehensive plan. Commissioners J. T. Waggoner and James Morgan voted for the plan, while Commissioner Bull Connor dissented.[61]

At the same time, the city's downtown business leaders also embraced comprehensive planning. In April 1957, downtown merchants and property owners, concerned with downtown's declining fortunes, also pressured the city commission to adopt a comprehensive plan by forming the Birmingham Downtown Improvement Association.[62] The BDIA's first action in 1957 was to call for a master plan, and later that year BDIA contributed thirty thousand dollars to the completion of the study.[63] With this act, Birmingham's downtown business inter-

ests began to increase the attention they paid to planning and its utility in furthering their interests.

At about the same time, in February 1958, with Birmingham promising to contract for a comprehensive plan, HHFA released funds for
the Ensley–Pratt City feasibility study. It was that study that enabled
Birmingham to apply another tool to the maintenance of racial segregation: the interstate highway system.[64]

Ensley Urban Renewal Project and Birmingham's Interstate Highway Program

Like Avondale, the Ensley community, located in west Birmingham
(see map 5.1), was infiltrated by industry. Ensley was founded by Enoch
Ensley, who established a land company in 1886 to develop the area
into a major manufacturing center. By 1900, the town of Ensley had
been incorporated and had become the center of Tennessee Coal and
Iron's (TCI) operations in the Birmingham District.[65] By 1910, the town
had merged with the City of Birmingham along with a number of
other suburbs, including Avondale, in the Greater Birmingham annexation of that year.[66]

As in other industrial areas of Birmingham, heavy concentrations of
blacks lived in Ensley, with the 1926 zoning map showing many black
households living in an area approximated by census tract 32 (see map
3.2).[67] Of 7,925 persons living in that tract in 1950, 6,478, or 82 percent,
were listed by the U.S. Census as African American. Many of these
black residents lived in the Tuxedo neighborhood located near the
junction of two streetcar lines, at the intersection of Twentieth Street
Ensley and Ensley Avenue.[68] Between the World Wars, blacks gathered
on Saturday nights at a second-floor music hall located in a building at
the intersection of these two streets, and the name of this area—
Tuxedo Junction—was memorialized in the 1939 Glenn Miller hit
written by Birmingham-born Erskine Hawkins.[69]

The majority of the residents in Tuxedo and the surrounding area
were poor. With a median annual income of $1,951 in 1950, tract 32 had
the seventeenth-lowest income of Birmingham's fifty-eight census
tracts. The majority of dwelling units were over thirty years old in 1930,
and 72 percent lacked a private bath or were dilapidated.[70] In its 1952
plan, the Birmingham Planning Board reported that nearly all of the

975 dwellings in Tuxedo were substandard, representing the largest concentration of inadequate housing in the city.[71]

Lying just to the south of the Tuxedo neighborhood and the rest of black Ensley was the hilltop neighborhood of Ensley Highlands. Enoch Ensley had foreseen the development of the Opossum Valley floor with industry and Flint Ridge with residences: "I intend to fill this valley, from the foot of the chert ridge [Flint Ridge] yonder to the Pratt Railroad with manufacturing plants. I'm going to build four blast furnaces and a steel plant. The whole of this chert ridge I'll use for residences."[72] While the dwellings of the black poor were concentrated in close proximity to Ensley's heavy industry, middle-class whites occupied the Ensley Highlands neighborhood, whose homes were developed for the foremen and superintendents working in the Ensley industrial plants.[73] In 1950, Ensley Highland's (tract 31) median income was $3,674, the seventh-highest in the city. Racially, Ensley Highlands was nearly all white, while tract 32 in Tuxedo was over 80 percent black. Occupationally, while 55 percent of Ensley Highlands' male workers in 1950 worked in professional, technical, managerial, or craftsmen occupations, only 21 percent of Tuxedo's males worked in these categories. Instead, 65 percent of Tuxedo's workers were either laborers or operatives. Among women workers, nearly half in Ensley Highlands worked in clerical positions, while two-thirds of the women workers in tract 32 were service workers, two-thirds of whom worked as private household workers. Sixty-four percent of Ensley Highland's residences were owner-occupied, compared to 27 percent of Ensley's dwellings.[74] Ensley Highlands was the home of a professional and managerial class that literally oversaw the black working classes who lived and labored below in the Tuxedo neighborhood. If Tuxedo's workers climbed the hill to work in Ensley Highlands, it was to clean the homes and care for the children of Ensley Highlands' residents.

The effective boundary between the Tuxedo neighborhood in Ensley and Ensley Highlands had been codified in the city's 1926 zoning code as Pike Road, which runs east to west between the two neighborhoods.[75] This same thoroughfare was then employed by the census bureau as the dividing line between tracts 31 and 32 (see map 3.2). Finally, the City of Birmingham attempted to employ the Ensley urban renewal project, along with the federal interstate highway program, to create a more formidable barrier between the black Tuxedo and white Ensley Highlands neighborhoods.

Preliminary planning for the Ensley urban renewal project had begun soon after passage of the 1949 Housing Act creating the urban renewal program. It was not until early 1958, however, that HHFA approved funding of a feasibility study for a 2,300-acre area that included the Tuxedo neighborhood and vicinity, and that extended from the Ensley community in the south to the Pratt City community in the north, taking in portions of census tracts 32, 33, 12, and 11 (see map 3.2).[76] The feasibility study, prepared by planning consultant De Leuw, Cather and Co. of Chicago, studied seven different areas within the Ensley–Pratt City community, including Tuxedo. The consultant found that of these communities, Tuxedo had the highest concentration of substandard housing—603 of 920 residential structures were substandard.[77] Tuxedo also had the highest concentration of "overly crowded blocks."[78] Moreover, it was subject to significant stormwater backups with nearly every rainfall. The area was serviced by a system of open ditches, and in some instances ditches running under houses appeared to be carrying sanitary sewage as well as stormwater.[79] Finally, many of the streets in Tuxedo were unpaved.[80] In other words, Tuxedo, with its blighted physical conditions associated with poor housing, coincided with an area in which the city had elected to provide inadequate public services.

But in addition to blight—De Leuw, Cather pointed out three other "seriously deteriorated" areas in Ensley–Pratt City—the consultant also noted that of these four neighborhoods, Tuxedo was "the southernmost of four seriously deteriorated areas, and was chosen as the initial project in order to prevent the spread of blight southward into presently sound neighborhoods."[81]

It was not only the serious blight that propelled Tuxedo's selection as the first urban renewal project in the Ensley–Pratt City communities. Its location adjacent to the white Ensley Highlands neighborhood also prompted the recommendation that this be the neighborhood of primary urban renewal attention. As in both the Southside and Avondale projects, it was not merely the incidence of slum conditions in black neighborhoods that directed the city's attention but also the impact that those neighborhoods' blight was perceived to have on surrounding areas controlled by white residents and institutions.

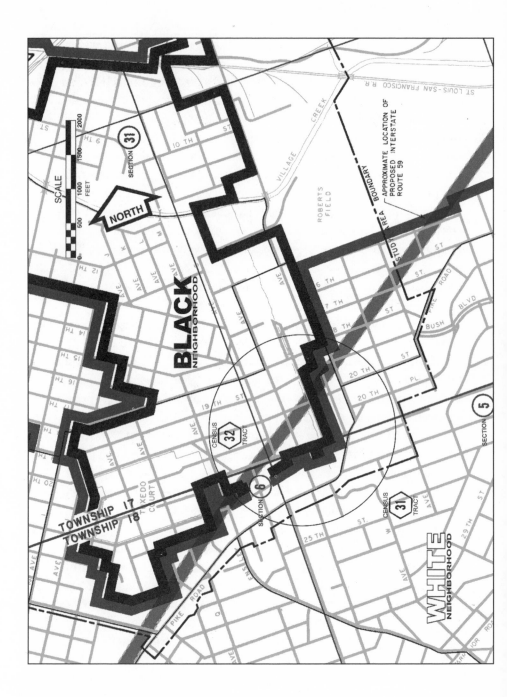

Planning for urban renewal in the Tuxedo neighborhood was complicated by the implementation of the federal interstate highway system, adopted by Congress in the Highway Act of 1956. Despite the fact that both programs would absorb significant quantities of urban real estate in the 1950s and 1960s, the Highway Act made no provision for coordination with the urban renewal program.[82] The city had not envisioned that a federal highway would be placed through the Ensley urban renewal project.[83] By 1958, the Alabama Highway Department had adopted preliminary routes for the two interstate highways that pass through Birmingham. One of them, Interstate 59, including an interchange, was planned to run through the Tuxedo neighborhood urban renewal site.[84] Given the amount of urban renewal land (roughly 40 percent) that would be dedicated for use by the new highway, HHFA questioned whether the new interstate and interchange were compatible with the urban renewal project.[85]

The De Leuw, Cather report responded to HHFA's concern by showing how the interstate, in conjunction with the urban renewal project, not only eliminated slums and blight but also enabled conservation of Ensley Highlands. This would be accomplished through clearance of the remnant of the black neighborhood that remained south of the new interstate. The De Leuw, Cather planners had mapped the black and white neighborhoods in the Ensley community and had displayed in their report the fragment of the black Tuxedo neighborhood that lay between Avenue S and Avenue V between Twenty-first Street to the south and Interstate 59 to the north (see map 5.2).[86] The southern and eastern boundaries of this black neighborhood correspond exactly to the outlines of the area delineated for black occupancy in the 1926 zoning map.[87] This can be seen most strikingly in map 2.1, which overlays the 1926 racial zones with the completed interstate highway system. This map shows the small southeastern portion of the black neighborhood in Ensley, in the western part of Birmingham, lying just to the south of Interstate 59. With elimination of this neighborhood for black occupancy, I-59 became a racial boundary fully separating the Tuxedo neighborhood to the north from Ensley Highlands to the south.

Map 5.2 (*opposite*). Map showing proposed Interstate 59 as racial boundary between the black Ensley neighborhood and the white Ensley Highlands neighborhood. (Source: De Leuw, Cather and Company, *Ensley–Pratt City Urban Renewal Study*, August 1958, Chicago, exhibit 2)

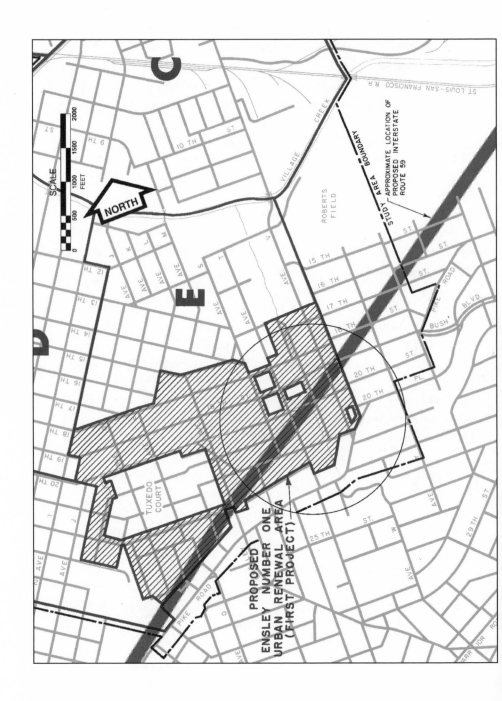

SCALE

NORTH

FEET

0 500 1000 1500 2000

ST LOUIS-SAN FRANCISCO R R

APPROXIMATE LOCATION OF
PROPOSED INTERSTATE
ROUTE 59

STUDY AREA BOUNDARY

ROBERTS FIELD

VILLAGE CREEK

ENSLEY
PROPOSED NUMBER ONE
URBAN RENEWAL AREA
(FIRST PROJECT)

TUXEDO COURT

PIKE ROAD

PIKE ROAD

BLVD.

BUSH

WARRIOR RO

The De Leuw, Cather report was explicit about using the urban renewal and interstate highway projects to create a boundary between the Tuxedo neighborhood and Ensley Highlands. The projects "will also remove the deteriorated areas which would otherwise remain between the expressway and the sound neighborhoods to the south. This represents an example of the value of close coordination between urban renewal and urban highway projects."[88] The report's emphasis on the protection of "sound neighborhoods" was consistent with the emphasis placed by the Housing Act of 1954 and the Workable Program on the *prevention* of slum and blight and not merely the clearance of slums.[89] It was also consistent with HHFA's interpretation of the 1954 Housing Act's objectives. In October 1959, Bruce Wedge wrote Mayor Jimmy Morgan on the importance of land use planning as a tool to enable neighborhood conservation: "To meet sound planning principles, these [land] uses should encourage the development of sound residential neighborhoods within the community."[90]

With the 1954 Housing Act's legitimation of neighborhood conservation, Birmingham deflected any criticism of spending urban renewal funds to clear a future interstate highway site by emphasizing that the two programs were used jointly to protect a neighborhood from nearby slum and blighted conditions. As in the 1920s, Birmingham could once again employ a "sound planning principle" to maintain racial segregation. With the 1926 racial zoning plan, the concept that zoning protected property values enabled Birmingham to justify its use as a device for segregating the races. By the 1950s, the conservation of "sound neighborhoods" had become another sound planning principle, and once again Birmingham was able to employ it in the pursuit of maintaining racial segregation.

Although modifications were made in the Tuxedo urban renewal project between the De Leuw, Cather report in 1958 and HHFA's January 1961 approval of the project, its role in creating a solid buffer between the Tuxedo and Ensley Highlands neighborhoods was fully realized. The urban renewal area shown in map 5.3 was made significantly smaller (85 acres) than the one recommended by De Leuw,

Map 5.3 (*opposite*). Map showing Ensley number one urban renewal area.
(Source: De Leuw, Cather and Company, *Ensley–Pratt City Urban Renewal Study*, August 1958, Chicago, exhibit 15)

Cather (176 acres), but the triangular-shaped black neighborhood south of the interstate remained in the urban renewal area.[91] Moreover, Interstate 59, as indicated in map 2.1, was routed along the same alignment as the De Leuw, Cather report had expected in 1958.

Interstate 59's effectiveness as a racial barrier is reflected in a 1978 neighborhood analysis prepared by the Birmingham Planning Commission. By that time, Interstate 59 is shown as the boundary between the Tuxedo neighborhood lying to the north and Ensley Highlands lying to the south. Moreover, the 1970 U.S. Census block data collected by the planning commission show the sharp contrast between the two neighborhoods. Of 5,446 residents living in Ensley Highlands in 1970, only nine persons were black. In contrast, of the 3,974 persons living in Tuxedo, 96 percent were African American.[92]

Despite the fact that the Ensley urban renewal project was used to maintain racial segregation between the Tuxedo and Ensley Highlands neighborhoods, no significant protest emanated from the black community. In contrast to the Southside Medical Center's public hearing, the Ensley project's public hearing on February 22, 1961, was uneventful, with no one speaking in opposition to the project, even though eight hundred dwelling units would be cleared.[93] The urban renewal plan called primarily for the development of new housing. Multifamily residential dwellings were located north of the interstate, and two-family residential dwellings were located south of the interstate in Ensley Highlands. A new elementary school, Tuxedo School, was built on a site adjacent to the Tuxedo Court public housing development, whose construction had begun in the spring of 1959. Nearly 40 percent of the urban renewal project's land area, or thirty-four acres, was used for right-of-way for the new interstate. Federal and city funds were used to address the area's flooding problems, to install a completely new utility system, to develop a new street system, and to pave previously unpaved streets.[94]

As in Avondale, concern in the black community was probably eased by the fact that the Ensley urban renewal project was built in tandem with a public housing project. In this case, Tuxedo Court, originally slated to consist of 950 households, was completed in 1960 with only 488 dwelling units. According to the relocation report prepared for the Ensley urban renewal project, there would be "a more than adequate supply of low rent public housing units" for families displaced by the urban renewal project, with many of them moving into Tuxedo Court.[95] What the report failed to mention, however, was that the start of construction at Tuxedo Court in 1959 required demolition of 521 dwelling units at a time when no new public housing had been completed in Birmingham since 1952. Since 1952, clearance had begun in both the Southside and Avondale urban renewal projects, creating further demand for new public housing. Although construction of Tuxedo Court helped assuage the relocation needs created by the Ensley urban renewal project, that construction also displaced over 500 predominantly black households.

The Ensley urban renewal project was not unique. An examination of map 2.1 shows at least one major instance in which interstate highway alignments created racial boundaries that corresponded to racial zoning lines drawn on the 1926 zoning map to separate white and black neighborhoods. Interstate 65 is located just east of a large area zoned for blacks that ran from Enon Ridge in the north, to Smithfield, and past the Elyton neighborhoods in the south.

For the segment of I-65 that runs just south of its intersection with I-59, I-65 marks the western boundary of the Birmingham central business district. In fact, this corridor running between Tenth and Eleventh Streets was deliberately selected to serve as a western boundary for downtown Birmingham. A January 1961 consultant's report, prepared by Leslie Williams of Philadelphia, recommended this alignment because, "Routing the Interstate between 10th and 11th Streets forms a suitable central district western boundary without cramping or limiting room for expansion and developments within the central area of Birmingham."[96] If the highway were located east of the Twelfth Street railroad tracks, the report contended, "this would involve the demolition of valuable properties between 12th and 13th Streets. It would unduly limit future expansion of the Central Business District."[97]

Moreover, the report noted, by locating the interstate between Tenth and Eleventh Streets, "substantial clearance of slum housing could be accomplished along the right-of-way of the freeway."[98] What the report does not mention is that this slum housing was primarily occupied by black households. By 1960, census tract 28, which I-65 bisected, was 98 percent black (see table 5.1). Any housing removed from this corridor was occupied by blacks, and any housing remaining west of I-65

Table 5.1. Black population by census tract, 1940–1970

Tract	1940 % Black	1950 % Black	1960 % Black	1970 % Black	Neighborhood
1	0.3	1.6	0.0	0.3	
2	1.6	0.0	0.0	0.7	
3	4.0	3.1	3.9	4.2	
4	15.1	15.8	16.8	16.5	
5	27.4	27.6	25.2	57.7	East Birmingham
6	81.2	87.5	92.5	97.9	
7	98.1	98.8	99.3	99.7	
8	17.4	32.8	40.6	56.8	
9	86.0	87.4	91.6	98.9	
10	51.9	73.9	81.2	75.4	
11	54.0	53.8	57.2	61.2	
12	47.0	45.0	53.9	67.7	
13	82.6	84.9	88.5	99.5	
14	96.7	98.0	99.9	99.9	
15	16.8	17.0	30.1	93.7	Fountain Heights
16	7.8	9.3	9.1	21.9	
17	32.8	39.9	38.2	42.7	
18	44.0	49.9	55.1	51.2	
19	20.0	30.5	40.5	36.1	
20	7.5	3.8	4.8	2.8	
21	1.2	0.1	0.0	0.0	
22	15.5	16.3	18.9	19.8	
23	16.7	18.2	16.2	22.0	
24	68.7	70.8	60.7	85.2	Avondale
25	47.0	50.3	51.9	51.3	
26	84.4	71.6	77.6	72.0	
27	17.3	11.1	12.2	20.8	
28	88.7	91.6	98.4	98.7	
29	97.5	97.4	99.1	99.7	
30	2.6	1.8	2.4	34.3	Graymont–College Hills
31	0.6	0.4	0.0	0.0	
32	80.1	81.7	79.9	89.0	

Table 5.1 *continued*

Tract	1940 % Black	1950 %Black	1960 % Black	1970 % Black	Neighborhood
33	60.9	69.8	83.2	96.2	
34	7.9	10.0	11.7	11.4	
35	8.1	13.2	25.3	28.3	
36	14.8	10.9	7.8	8.4	
37	0.2	0.3	0.1	0.1	
38	16.9	8.9	6.5	5.7	
39	65.2	49.3	42.0	44.6	
40	2.7	2.0	1.7	3.1	
41	62.2	61.9	69.8	73.0	
42	95.2	91.4	79.4	82.7	
43	88.8	89.8	99.7	98.6	
44	75.7	76.4	48.5	28.1	
45	92.8	94.3	96.4	96.8	
46	94.2	96.0	98.5	99.3	
47	9.6	7.8	2.5	1.7	
48	7.6	7.0	3.9	2.2	
49	7.0	7.0	9.8	7.7	
50	4.8	2.8	2.1	17.1	
51	86.2	88.6	98.5	99.5	
52	15.7	25.8	16.2	33.1	
53	—	20.9	12.8	12.3	
54	—	0.3	0.0	8.3	
55	—	56.2	58.3	64.7	
56	—	10.6	0.0	0.1	
57	—	42.8	44.7	59.1	
58	—	4.7	5.9	0.0	
59	—	—	0.7	0.2	

Sources: U.S. Bureau of the Census, *Population and Housing, Statistics for Census, Tracts, Birmingham, Alabama.* Washington, D.C.: U.S. Government Printing Office, 1942; U.S. Bureau of the Census, *U.S. Census of Population: 1950* vol. 3, *Census Tract Statistics,* chap. 5. Washington, D.C.: U.S. Government Printing Office, 1952; U.S. Bureau of the Census, *U.S. Censuses of Population and Housing: 1960, Census Tracts,* Final Report PHC(1)-17. Washington, D.C.: U.S. Government Printing Office, 1961; U.S. Bureau of the Census, *Census of Population and Housing: 1970, Census Tracts,* 970, Final Report PHC(1)-26, Birmingham, Ala., SMSA. Washington, D.C.: U.S. Government Printing Office, 1972.

was occupied almost exclusively by blacks. By eliminating the black neighborhood that most closely bordered the west side of the central business, I-65 became a buffer between Birmingham's west side black neighborhoods and the city's central business district.[99]

The consultant's advice was followed, and I-65 was constructed just west of downtown Birmingham along the corridor running between Tenth and Eleventh Streets. That alignment also had an impact on the racial boundary between the Southside Medical Center and the black neighborhood lying to the west. When the second phase of the Southside Medical Center's expansion was undertaken in the 1960s (see chapter 6), the University of Alabama at Birmingham expanded west to Interstate 65. With I-65 becoming the boundary between UAB and the black Tittusville neighborhood, the highway served as a significant buffer between the neighborhood and the university.

There appear to be at least two other instances in which interstate highways were aligned with existing racial boundaries. In the area north of I-65's intersection with I-59, I-65 closely aligns with the 1926 zoning map racial boundary that separated the black Enon Ridge neighborhood west of I-65 from the white Fountain Heights neighborhood just east of the interstate. In the 1950s, as the interstate highway system was being planned, the Fountain Heights area was undergoing racial change, and the white reaction was sometimes violent. From 1950 to 1960, the black population of this neighborhood, as represented by census tract 15 (see map 5.4), increased by nearly two-thirds, from 1,374 to 2,219 (see table 3.1). Beginning in April 1956 and lasting through July 1958, seven black-occupied homes were bombed and one burned in Fountain Heights, and a eighth bombing was attempted.[100]

Birmingham city commissioner Bull Connor blamed the bombings on "the firms and salesmen who sell homes to Negroes in white sections."[101] Blacks took exception to the view that Fountain Heights was to be an all-white domain. The *Birmingham World* editorialized: "A third unoccupied home in the community of Fountain Heights has been bombed. This community has not been totally all-white in nearly a half-century. It is becoming less so in recent years. That is what the bombing is all about. . . . one has the right in this country, in this city, even in Fountain Heights, however risky it may be, to live where he can buy, build, own or rent."[102]

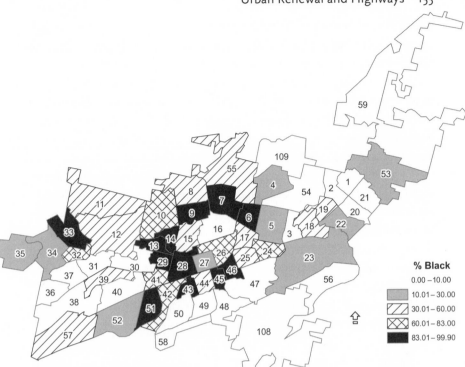

Map 5.4. Birmingham, Alabama, 1960 census tract map. (Source: 1960 U.S. Census)

Although no evidence has been uncovered that shows that Birmingham's city commissioners, including Connor, deliberately located Interstate 65 to serve as a buffer between Fountain Heights and the black neighborhoods lying to the west, the interstate was located on the precise boundary employed thirty years earlier when the 1926 racial zoning map was drawn. In this part of the city, I-65 was built along Sixth Street, which on the 1926 zoning map, running north from Eleventh Avenue North to Village Creek, a distance of about one mile, was the boundary line between black Enon Ridge to the west and Fountain Heights to the east.[103] The Sixth Street routing for I-65 was announced in May 1958, during the two-year period that the Fountain Heights bombings were taking place.[104] Location of the interstate on this historic racial boundary, along with the fact that it was being planned at the time of the Fountain Heights bombings, certainly creates suspicions that the interstate was purposefully located to help keep blacks out of Fountain Heights. Regardless of whether or not the decision was racially motivated, I-65's location on the historic boundary between black Enon Ridge and white Fountain Heights had the effect of serving as a racial buffer.

Like Fountain Heights, College Hills was a predominantly white neighborhood that feared racial change at a time in the late 1950s when Birmingham's interstates were being planned. Occupying the northern part of census tract 30 (see map 5.4), College Hills lies just southwest of the North Smithfield neighborhood that had been the site of the bombings of the late 1940s and early 1950s (see chapter 3). With the demise of racial zoning, the potential for black occupancy in College Hills only increased, and by 1957 white residents of College Hills were petitioning Birmingham's city commissioners to create a new racial dividing line. Mayor Morgan and city commissioners Robert Lindberg and James Waggoner responded that the U.S. Supreme Court's decision on racial zoning prevented them from establishing such a line, but Morgan and his fellow commissioners pledged in February 1957 that they would "'explore all possible routes' to aid white property owners in the preservation of the character of their neighborhood."[105]

At the time, Birmingham and the State of Alabama were considering two fairly distinct alignments for Interstate 59 west of downtown Birmingham. One of these would have exited downtown Birmingham at Eleventh Avenue North and then proceeded at a sharp southwest angle toward the industrial suburb of Bessemer. This is the alignment shown in the Bureau of Public Roads's *Yellow Book* maps published in 1955 (see map 5.5). In 1955, the U.S. Bureau of Public Roads published the *General Location of National System of Interstate Highways*, generally known as the *Yellow Book*.[106] That volume showed the national interstate highway map as well as maps of one hundred urban areas that had been submitted by state highway departments and approved by the U.S. commissioner of public roads. The second alignment would continue west along the Eleventh Avenue North corridor before it shifted to the southwest towards Ensley.[107] By March 1958, the latter alignment was selected.[108]

The significance of the Eleventh Avenue alignment lies in the fact that it coincides exactly with the racial zoning boundary that had been drawn prior to the demise of racial zoning (see map 3.1). By running the interstate between the North Smithfield and East Thomas (just west of North Smithfield) neighborhoods to the north and College

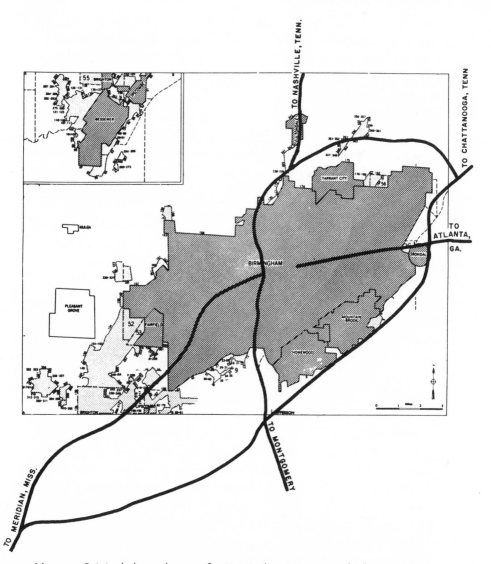

Map 5.5. Original planned routes for Birmingham's interstate highways. (U.S. Department of Commerce, Bureau of Public Roads, *General Location of National System of Interstate Highways,* 1955)

Hills to the south, I-59 became a racial buffer between these neighborhoods. Although no evidence has been uncovered to indicate that the interstate was purposely used to create a racial buffer along Eleventh Avenue, both the location of the route and the timing of the decision suggest that racial motives were at hand.

Regardless of intent, the location of the interstate highways had a lasting impact on the map of Birmingham's neighborhoods. In the 1961 Birmingham comprehensive plan, prepared by Harland Bartholomew and Associates, the lines separating white Ensley Highlands from black Tuxedo, white Fountain Heights from black Enon Ridge (referred to as Melville Court in the Bartholomew plan), downtown Birmingham from black neighborhoods to the west, and white College Hills from black North Smithfield all coincided with the routing of Birmingham's interstates 59 and 65.[109] And when Birmingham's neighborhood map was redrawn in the 1970s, with the adoption of the city's citizen participation program, these neighborhoods and the interstate highway boundaries between them were recognized again (see chapter 7). Consequently, today's map of Birmingham's neighborhoods largely reflects the neighborhood boundaries established by the location of the interstate highways in the city.

In most instances, neighborhood racial change has negated the racial segregation role played by these boundaries. One key exception is Interstate 65, which separates the University of Alabama at Birmingham campus from the Tittusville neighborhood lying just to the west. The interstate serves as a significant psychological, if not physical, barrier between the city's largest employer and the poor black neighborhood to its west. In recent years, UAB has reached out to the Tittusville neighborhood, an effort that is made more difficult by the highway that runs between the two.[110]

Routing of Interstate Highways through Birmingham's Black Neighborhoods

Map 2.1 also shows several instances in which the city's interstate highways bisected historically black neighborhoods, often so they could bypass white neighborhoods. On Birmingham's east side, Interstate 59 departs from its generally northeast to southwest trajectory to loop north and bisect the predominantly black portion of East Birmingham shown in map 2.1. While the East Birmingham neighborhood through which the interstate was routed was predominantly black, the neighborhoods lying to the south were predominantly white.[111] This routing of the interstate permitted the predominantly white Woodlawn neighborhood to be largely bypassed by the interstate, while retaining connections to the interstate at its eastern and northern edges. Not surprisingly, the Woodlawn Chamber of Commerce, which represented the many businesses in that neighborhood, favored this route.[112] From a traffic engineering viewpoint, bypassing the Woodlawn neighborhood was not an easy achievement as it required a sharp turn in the highway, thereby reducing the interstate's speed limit and increasing the danger of an accident as automobiles and large commercial trucks, accustomed to traveling sixty or more miles per hour, must slow significantly to negotiate the bend in the road. Although large warning signs greet drivers on this stretch, located just south of the Birmingham Airport, the danger is apparent.

Further east from East Birmingham lies another black neighborhood through which Interstate 59 ran. This neighborhood, located in the western part of the East Lake community of Birmingham, is shown on the city's 1926 zoning map as lying just south and east of the Forest Hill Cemetery, which today lies just south of the Birmingham Airport. Once again, the interstate takes an upward bend as it traverses this black neighborhood, thereby avoiding a more southerly route which would have taken it through Wahouma Park, a city park that separated this black neighborhood from the white neighborhoods to the south.

In 1960, Mrs. Lala Palmer, a resident of eastern Birmingham and spokesperson for a community organization there, publicly decried the "many curves and twists" of the proposed interstate that resulted in the bisection of the East Birmingham and East Lake black neighborhoods. Her preferred alternative, she noted, "is practically straight, yet both routes begin at essentially the same point and end at the same point." According to a telegram Mrs. Palmer sent to the Alabama Highway Department, the impact of the "curves and twists" was that the interstate "would almost completely wipe out two old Negro communities [in] eastern Birmingham with their 13 churches and three schools."[113]

Although Mrs. Palmer was not an engineer, her preferred routing for the interstate approximated the route originally recommended by the Alabama Highway Department and the U.S. Bureau of Public Roads. As can be seen in the *Yellow Book*'s Birmingham map (see map 5.5), the original plans for Interstates 59 and 20 (which join together in the eastern part of Birmingham) showed that they would move from east to west in a straight line, not in the curvilinear route that was eventually selected.

The original route avoided three problems associated with the selected route: 1) it lacked the sharp turn in Interstate 59/20 that was created as the interstate passes the Birmingham Airport; 2) the straight line route was approximately 1.25 miles shorter and more direct than the route that was finally selected; and 3) the original route avoided running through the heart of the black neighborhoods in East Birmingham and western East Lake.[114] Apparently because the initial proposed route went right through the middle of predominantly white Woodlawn, however, running through that neighborhood's residential and commercial districts, the Alabama Highway Department selected a less direct and probably more expensive route that required lower speeds. It should not surprise, therefore, that Woodlawn business interests were pleased with the changes made in the routing of the interstate, changes that were made at the expense of the two black neighborhoods through which the interstate would be routed.

The location of the city's interstates through black neighborhoods was not limited to the city's east side. As noted in chapter 3, Smithfield, which lies just to the west of downtown Birmingham, was one of the more affluent black neighborhoods in Birmingham in 1960. Since the latter part of the nineteenth century, Smithfield had been the home of many of Birmingham's black professionals. This remained so into the late 1950s as members of Birmingham's black elite began building new ranch-style homes along the 1000 and 1100 block of North Center Street on top of a hill with a good view of the city (see map 3.1). The 1100 block of Center Street is the same block where two black-occupied homes were bombed on August 13, 1949. The new residents in this area included civil rights attorney Arthur Shores, former Birmingham Black Barons shortstop Art Wilson, funeral home operator Earnest Poole, and insurance executive John Drew.[115] It was through this newly developing suburban-style area that Interstate 59 was routed.

One of those who would be displaced was insurance executive John

Drew, who lived at 1108 North Center Street. He wrote his congressman in 1963 to complain of the difficulty he was having in finding a
new house, given "that we are 'land-tight' and have not found suitable
replacement areas for our homes. My problem, together with many
other Negro homeowners, is not prevention of this worthwhile highway, but to ask consideration for more time in which to find other locations."[116] Because few areas in the city had been zoned for blacks, particularly in areas that were not located near industry and that were
zoned for single-family dwellings, middle-class blacks in Birmingham
traditionally had difficulty locating suitable neighborhoods.

In contrast to Drew, James Hutchinson opposed the new highway's
location. Hutchinson, who lived on Eleventh Avenue, the route that
would be taken by the interstate, wrote a series of letters in late 1963
complaining that "from Center Street the route curves making [an] almost U shape with [a] large interchange on Six[th] Street area. All of
this bisect[s] an exclusive residential area." At the same time, "The
other route is near straight, disturb[s] less home[s]. . . . Most folks
think this route [the selected one] was politically inspired."[117]

That Mr. Hutchinson and his neighbors thought the choice of the
route through their neighborhood was politically inspired is not surprising. John Drew and his wife, Deenie, were both members of Birmingham's black elite, while at the same time playing a significant
role in the city's civil rights movement in the 1950s and 1960s. Martin
Luther King Jr., in his trips to Birmingham, often stayed with the
Drews. Moreover, by the 1950s Drew's neighborhood on Center Street
was known as Dynamite Hill, a reference to the racial zoning–related
bombings of the late 1940s and early 1950s, as well as the August and
September 1963 civil rights–related bombings of civil rights attorney
Arthur Shores's house.[118] It's not surprising that anyone in the neighborhood thought that the interstate was being routed through Dynamite Hill for political purposes. Dynamite Hill residents would probably have been further convinced that politics played a role in the
interstate's location had they read the response of Rex Whitton, federal
highway administrator, to Senator John Sparkman's inquiry regarding
the Hutchinson correspondence. Whitton wrote Sparkman that "the
present location was proposed by the State and approved by the Bureau
of Public Roads based on a thorough evaluation of all engineering, economic and *sociological* factors involved" (emphasis added).[119]

Impact of the Interstate Highway System
on Birmingham's Black Neighborhoods

The construction of Birmingham's interstate highways during the 1960s had a significant impact on the city's population loss during that decade. Nearly all of the city's interstates had been completed or were under construction by 1971, and between 1960 and 1970 Birmingham's population declined for the first time in the city's history, from 340,887 to 300,910, a decrease of nearly 40,000 inhabitants.[120] Although over 75 percent of this decrease is accounted for by the loss of whites, the city's black population also declined by 8,725. The impact of the city's population loss was widespread. Between 1960 and 1970, forty-eight of the city's sixty-one census tract neighborhoods lost population. Of these forty-eight, the top ten losers are shown in table 5.2 in rank order of population loss. Overall, these neighborhoods lost 24,337 inhabitants, or 61 percent of the city's net loss of 39,977.

Of the ten neighborhoods shown in table 5.2, eight were predominantly black neighborhoods in 1960, and only one had a population less than 40 percent black in 1960. Of the nine neighborhoods with a significant black population, eight had key interstate or other federal highways (the Red Mountain Expressway) built through them in the 1960s. Moreover, one of these black neighborhoods, located in census tract 43, experienced significant population loss in the wake of the federally funded urban renewal expansion of the Southside Medical Center as the University of Alabama at Birmingham (see chapter 6). In addition, the predominantly white neighborhood located in census tract 49, just south of tract 43, also lost substantial population to the expansion of UAB.

The city's largest population loser was tract 28.2, a black neighborhood located just west and north of downtown Birmingham in what is today the southern part of the Fountain Heights neighborhood. With the construction of I-65, I-59, and the interchange of these two highways, this neighborhood lost 4,587 inhabitants, nearly all of whom were black. Overall, the neighborhood lost two-thirds of its population between 1960 and 1970, reflecting a population loss nearly twice as great as the next-highest population loser.

In general, therefore, the interstate highways built or started in Birmingham in the 1960s are associated with significant population

Table 5.2. Change in Birmingham census tract population, 1960–1970, top ten losers (includes 1960 census tracts only)

Rank	Tract #	1960 % Black	1960 Population	1970 Population	1960–70 Difference	Key highway or redevelopment projects
1	28.2	98.40	7,045	2,458	−4,587	I-65 and I-65/I-59 Interchange
2	9	91.60	8,338	5,655	−2,683	I-65/ North Birmingham
3	43	99.70	3,614	950	−2,664	I-65/UAB Urban Renewal
4	26	77.60	4,773	2,143	−2,630	I-59/Central Birmingham
5	45	96.40	4,759	2,175	−2,584	Red Mountain Expressway/ Southside
6	18	55.10	6,179	4,042	−2,137	I-59/Woodlawn
7	49	9.80	6,930	5,075	−1,855	UAB Urban Renewal
8	8	40.60	8,098	6,288	−1,810	I-65/ North Birmingham
9	29	99.10	7,999	6,228	−1,771	
10	6	92.50	4,889	3,273	−1,616	I-59/East Birmingham

Sources: U.S. Bureau of the Census, U.S. Censuses of Population and Housing: 1960, Census Tracts, Final Report PHC(1)-17. Washington, D.C.: U.S. Government Printing Office, 1961; U.S. Bureau of the Census, Census of Population and Housing: 1970, Census Tracts, Final Report PHC(1)-26, Birmingham, Ala., SMSA. Washington, D.C.: U.S. Government Printing Office, 1972.

losses in eight of the city's predominantly black neighborhoods. Although the interstates also ran through the city's white neighborhoods, they did not absorb the population loss experienced by the city's black neighborhoods. The population loss, in turn, undoubtedly had an impact on the overall decline of the city's black population between 1960 and 1970.

Black households displaced by the interstates had to move somewhere, and while some may have left the city, many others moved to neighborhoods within Birmingham. With this migration came a significant change in Birmingham. Whereas the city's racial zoning law and racial bombings had dampened neighborhood racial change in the 1940s and 1950s, by the 1960s several Birmingham white neighborhoods underwent significant racial change.

As table 5.1 shows, in neither the 1940s nor the 1950s did any neighborhood have a 25 percentage point or greater increase in black population. Between 1960 and 1970, however, census tracts in three neighborhoods (East Birmingham, Fountain Heights, and Graymont–College Hills) had their black populations increase by this much, and tract 24 in Avondale, located on the city's east side, had an increase in black population of nearly 25 percentage points. In Fountain Heights (tract 15), where bombings had been employed to keep blacks out in the 1950s, the black population had increased by only 13 percentage points in that decade, but between 1960 and 1970 the neighborhood went from one-third black to nearly 100 percent black as whites left that neighborhood in droves. Most certainly the large number of blacks displaced from tract 28.2, lying just to the south of tract 15, had a significant impact on the demand by blacks for housing in Fountain Heights and therefore on the flight of whites out of that neighborhood. Map 5.6 shows the 1970 distribution by race in Birmingham.

The Birmingham case demonstrates the importance of the interstates and more generally of the federal government in shaping the racial patterns of the post post–World War II city. As shown in table 5.2 and in the historical narrative, Birmingham's interstate highways had a deleterious impact on the city's black neighborhoods, causing a disproportionate number of them to lose one-third to two-thirds of their 1960 population. Apart from the cost and inconvenience of forced relocation, such population loss had an undoubtedly negative impact on these neighborhoods, threatening the viability of any neighborhood businesses and commercial areas that served them. When the impacts of the city's interstate highway programs are combined with the impacts of the city's urban renewal programs, particularly its efforts to replace the city's large Southside black neighborhood with the Southside Medical Center and the University of Alabama at Birmingham, it is apparent that the federal government had a profound impact on black neighborhoods.

Second, the Birmingham case illustrates how local and state government manipulated the interstate highway program into separating white and black neighborhoods. Although the interstate highway program had no explicit racial agenda, its implementation at the local and state level along with the complicity of the federal government permitted Birmingham and Alabama officials to use it to separate the races in the same way that the city had used racial zoning for twenty-five years to maintain racial segregation. What is especially startling about the Birmingham case is how the interstate highway program was employed to replicate the same racial boundaries that had been put into place by the city's 1926 racial zoning law.

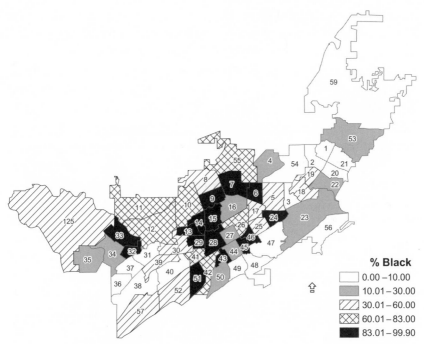

Map 5.6. Birmingham, Alabama, 1970 census tract map. (Source: 1970 U.S. Census)

In this respect, the Birmingham case also illustrates the moral ambiguity of planning and the ways in which planning permits legally and morally legitimate concepts to be transformed into coded concepts and terms that are used to discriminate against the disadvantaged. In the case of Birmingham's interstate highway program, planners used "slum prevention," which had been legitimated in the 1954 Housing Act, as a defense for using Interstate 59 and the Urban Renewal program to separate the largely black Tuxedo neighborhood from the all-white Ensley Highlands neighborhood. Slum prevention enabled a northern planning firm to justify the employment of federal interstate highway and urban renewal monies to erect what was in effect a large wall to separate a middle-income white neighborhood from a lower-income black neighborhood. The idea that planners could employ slum prevention to defend the maintenance of racial segregation in a city whose residents had already employed bombing to "prevent" neighborhood racial change reflects badly on the profession of planning and its claim to moral legitimacy. Instead of being a sharply delineated moral instrument, slum prevention became a broad tent underneath which both planning and Bull Connor could hide.

Third, and very ironically, the city's interstate highway program helped propel the very neighborhood racial change that Birmingham, as well as other cities, had sought to prevent. Because the interstate highways disproportionately affected black neighborhoods, a large number of the city's blacks were forced to relocate to other neighborhoods. While the city had been able to use racial zoning and bombing to hold the line on racial change in the 1940s and 1950s, the interstate highways, along with urban renewal, unleashed a demand for black housing that could not be met exclusively by existing black neighborhoods, and consequently in the 1960s significant neighborhood racial change began in Birmingham, a process that would continue in the 1970s such that by 1980 Birmingham became a majority black city. Birmingham therefore demonstrates how the employment of urban renewal and the interstate highway program in our nation's cities unleashed forces that led to rapid neighborhood succession and racial change.[121]

6 Civil Rights and
  City Planning

Despite its embrace of federal subsidies for urban renewal, public housing, and interstate highways, by the late 1950s Birmingham had been able to adapt these programs to its long-run objective of maintaining the racial status quo. As with zoning in the 1920s, Birmingham could adopt seemingly progressive planning reforms while using these reforms to maintain a system of racial segregation and inequality. With local public officials determined to maintain racial segregation in all ways of life and local vigilantes prepared to use violence to thwart black progress, Birmingham in 1960 appeared prepared to carry on as it always had.

In a great sense, Birmingham was attempting to remain locked in the 1920s. Howard Bowles, president of the Southern Institute of Management, told members of the Birmingham Sales Executive Club in May 1959 that Birmingham was still selling an image of the 1920s, an image of "steel, heavy industry, smoke and soot" and that businessmen throughout the nation did not like that image.[1] Despite the city's efforts to hang onto the past, however, its economic, social, and political systems were in the midst of significant change. In 1963, these forces came together and began the process of change that would affect profoundly the way the city was operated and the way the city used planning as a constructive or destructive force in the city's black neighborhoods.

By the 1950s, Birmingham's economy, which had been firmly grounded in mining and processing iron and coal, was declining. Mining diminished most rapidly, with the number of residents employed in coal or iron mining declining from 16,126 in 1950 to 5,812 in 1960. The decline in mining employment was part of a 30 percent national decline in mining jobs between 1950 and 1960 that was caused by mechanization and the importation of foreign coal.[2] But mining in the

Birmingham area also declined as local manufacturers began to sub-stitute imported iron ore for the Red Mountain hematite. In the early 1950s, U.S. Steel began to import Venezuelan iron ore, and soon after other iron ore mining operations ceased; by 1971, Birmingham's iron mines had ceased operation.[3]

Although employment in iron and steel fell less precipitously than employment in mining, the 1950s marked the beginning of a decline in primary metals employment, which eventually caused the diminu-tion of Birmingham's role as a major manufacturing center. Employ-ment in primary metals (chiefly iron and steel), which peaked in 1950 at 28,704 residents working in that industry, declined to 27,135 in 1960. Thereafter, employment declined precipitously so that by 1980, slightly fewer than 19,000 area residents worked in iron- and steel-related firms, down one-third from the 1950 high. Although employ-ment in overall manufacturing continued to grow after 1950, it too leveled off by 1980 and declined by 12 percent in the 1980s. By 1990, manufacturing accounted for only 14 percent of total employment in the area, down from 26 percent in 1950. By 1999, only about 11 per-cent of Birmingham's metropolitan area employment was in manu-facturing.[4]

A national trend away from steel employment in the older steel manufacturing centers (Pennsylvania, Ohio, New York, California, and Alabama) toward new centers in Indiana, Michigan, and Texas contributed to Birmingham's decline as a iron and steel center after 1950. Growth in Texas steel manufacturing employment was espe-cially significant. Between 1958 and 1977, while steel manufacturing employment in Alabama (most of which was in the Birmingham met-ropolitan area) declined by 5,200 jobs, employment in Texas steel mills increased by 4,500 jobs.[5] The rise of the Texas mills hurt Bir-mingham's ability to supply the rapidly growing southwest portion of the southern steel market. Also beginning in the 1950s, foreign steel, first from Western Europe and then from Japan, began to make major inroads in the southern steel market, significantly ahead of its pene-tration of the overall U.S. market.[6]

In 1958, as the city began to undertake the comprehensive planning process required by the Housing and Home Finance Agency's (HHFA) Workable Program, it reflected on its faltering economy. In a Septem-ber 1958 feature on a report prepared by Harland Bartholomew and

Associates, the *Birmingham News* asked the question: "What has sty-mied the district's growth, kept it from forging ahead in recent years as rapidly as other cities over the Southeast?"[7] The Bartholomew report found that Birmingham's recent growth in manufacturing employ-ment placed it last among five major cities that also included New Or-leans, Memphis, Louisville, and Atlanta. In the interest of improving the city's pace of growth, the report urged the city to diversify its econ-omy, claiming that Birmingham's reliance on its iron and steel base limited its growth and stability. The report estimated that 75 percent of Birmingham's jobs were in iron and steel and related activities. The re-port contended that Birmingham's future growth depended upon its ability to attract new industries and residents and therefore upon the quality of community facilities, including schools, parks, adequate streets, and convenient parking.

Taking aim at Birmingham's historic low taxes, the Bartholomew report concluded that the creation of quality community facilities re-quired a change in the city's attitude toward taxes and public expendi-tures: "Low taxes and low bonded debt are desirable, but not at the price of inadequate provision of needed public improvements."[8] The Bartholomew report found that Birmingham had the lowest assessed property valuation per capita and the lowest property tax rate of the five cities. The report also added that public improvements, such as off-street parking, could help build the volume of retail trade in Birming-ham. Although Birmingham's per capita income was comparable to per capita income in the other four cities, its volume of retail sales placed it last.[9] Moreover, Birmingham's downtown was no longer com-peting as well for retail trade. In 1948, downtown Birmingham cap-tured 36.5 percent of metropolitan retail trade; by 1958, this percentage had fallen to 26.8.[10]

Birmingham also lagged behind the other four southern cities in wholesale trade, with only slightly more than half as many employees per capita in wholesale trade as Atlanta to the east.[11] Located 150 miles apart, Atlanta and Birmingham had been rivals since Birmingham's rapid growth at the beginning of the twentieth century. As late as 1950, the two cities had nearly the same population (326,037 in Birmingham and 331,314 in Atlanta). But in the 1950s, Atlanta's economy took off, while Birmingham's slowed. Birmingham's population grew to only 340,887 in 1960, while Atlanta's grew to 487,455, a nearly 50 percent increase in population.[12] Only about 16,000 additional Birmingham metropolitan area residents were employed in 1960 than in 1950, while the number in Atlanta increased by nearly 123,000 in the same decade.[13] By 1971, former Atlanta mayor Ivan Allen Jr. could write fairly that Birmingham was Atlanta's "former rival."[14]

Overall, Birmingham was losing out to its southern rivals because its growth in manufacturing was slowing and it was not developing as an important trade center. As early as 1950, William P. Engel, who would soon be elected president of Birmingham's Chamber of Commerce, reported to the Kiwanis Club of Birmingham that the city could no longer assume it had no southern rivalries in manufacturing, with both Memphis and Atlanta rapidly adding new industrial employment.[15] Sheldon Schaffer, head of Birmingham's Southern Research Institute's Industrial Economics Section, made the same point twelve years later in an address to the Rotary Club, noting that a U.S. Department of Commerce survey of manufacturing growth rates showed that Birmingham placed forty-sixth on a list of fifty-three southern metropolitan areas. In addition, Schaffer told his audience, Birmingham was "failing to advance with any noteworthy speed as a regional trade and economic center." Handicapping Birmingham was the fact that its economic trade area consisted of "slowly growing or . . . declining rural and industrial counties" while Atlanta served as a trade center for about eighteen growing metropolitan areas in the South.[16] The growth that was occurring in the South at that time was not uniform. Instead, much of the economic growth was focused either in the South Atlantic states of Virginia, the Carolinas, Georgia, and Florida or in the West South Central states of Louisiana, Texas, and Oklahoma. In contrast, cities in the South Central states of Alabama, Mississippi, Arkansas, and Tennessee were experiencing slow growth.[17] Birmingham's economy was slowing because its trade service area was also growing slowly.

Birmingham's economic slowdown, combined with its low property tax rate, also spelled trouble for municipal finance. In 1957, the city began to run budget deficits, using surpluses from previous years to cover the gap between revenues and expenditures.[18] In 1961, the city finished the fiscal year $800,000 in the red. In 1962, closure of the city's parks to avoid compliance with a October 1961 court order mandating racial integration was insufficient to eliminate another significant budget deficit.[19] The rapid growth that had spawned the city's nick-name, the Magic City, had stopped.

Although Birmingham's economic woes were explained in part by increasing competition from other southern steel centers, the contin-ued concentration in iron and steel reflected a longtime disinterest among the city's economic elite in diversifying the local economy. Through at least the 1960s, the Tennessee Coal and Iron (TCI) sub-sidiary of U.S. Steel was the most important political and economic force in Birmingham.[20] Along with other Big Mules—the city's lead-ing banks, attorneys, insurance companies, and utilities—TCI–U.S. Steel discouraged new industrial operations from coming to Birming-ham. In 1947, an article in the *Saturday Evening Post* quoted an anony-mous spokesman for TCI–U.S. Steel as saying: "We are here to make steel. . . . We are not here to build a city. We sell our products through-out the South. If a plant that uses steel wants to set up in Chattanooga or Atlanta or Jackson, Mississippi, that's their business, not ours. If Birmingham wants them, it's Birmingham's business to go out and get them."[21]

Rumors of TCI–U.S. Steel's influence in controlling Birmingham's growth abounded. In a 1945 letter to Birmingham mayor Cooper Green, George W. Blanks, an examiner in the Birmingham office of the Reconstruction Finance Corporation, reported being told by General Motors officials that their corporation was planning to locate a plant southwest of Birmingham in nearby Bessemer, but the firm's plans were thwarted by TCI–U.S. Steel. Blanks also heard that Ford Motor Company had planned to locate in the Birmingham area, but TCI–U.S. Steel again interfered.[22] Four years later, Mayor Green wrote Henry Ford II, president of Ford Motor Company, that he had heard Ford Mo-tor had decided to build an assembly plant in Atlanta rather than Bir-mingham because TCI–U.S. Steel had refused to sell steel to Ford. Green reported that Rheem Manufacturing Company had recently shut down its Birmingham operations because of TCI–U.S. Steel's fail-ure to meet its steel needs.[23] In response to Green's letter, a Ford Motor Company representative stated that the decision to locate the Ford plant in Atlanta was not affected by TCI–U.S. Steel.[24]

Regardless of whether the General Motors or Ford Motor Company stories are true or not, TCI–U.S. Steel's reputation for limiting indus-trial growth had an impact on Birmingham. The post–World War II creation of the Young Men's Business Club (YMBC) was a response to TCI–U.S. Steel's dominance in Birmingham, and in the early 1960s YMBC members provided the leadership for reforming the city's politics.[25] According to an early member, YMBC was organized mainly in response to a belief that the Birmingham Junior Chamber of Commerce

> was probably too much under the control and domineered by the senior Chamber of Commerce. . . . The senior Chamber of Commerce at that time was, I consider, conservative and interested in maintaining the goodwill of the major industries in town that were in control at that time and they were not too aggressive in any new ideas and new projects. They didn't want anybody to rock the boat. They didn't want any new industry to come in. . . . The Tennessee Coal and Iron Company of the U.S. Steel operation did not want a union in Birmingham and they did not want surplus labor so that they would have to compete with other industries in their wage scales. They preferred to keep things as they were. One illustration of this was the fact that sometimes in the 40's the Ford plant considered placing their plant in Birmingham and they were notified so I was told that they would not be supplied steel from TCI if their plant was based in Birmingham. That's the plant that has been for some time in Atlanta.[26]

TCI–U.S. Steel and the other Big Mules used their influence to prevent Birmingham from actively working to attract new industries. As James Cobb describes in his book *The Selling of the South,* in the period after the end of World War II, cities and states throughout the South used special tax incentives to attract industry.[27] But TCI–U.S. Steel and the other Big Mules discouraged Birmingham from using such enticements. Louis Pizitz, a leading downtown merchant, wrote Mayor Cooper Green in 1945:

> I was on the Board of the Birmingham District Development Corporation and attended a meeting where the President of the Steel corporation and some men from other big corporations were present and when I brought up the question that we have got to give

them [small industries] something to bring them here, and these men all said not to give them anything.[28]

Although the Birmingham Chamber of Commerce formed the Committee of 100 in 1950 to attract new industry to Birmingham, the city failed to avail itself of special industrial recruitment legislation that Alabama adopted at that time.[29] In 1949 and 1951, Alabama adopted legislation that permitted local governments to issue tax-exempt bonds to finance the construction or expansion of industrial plants and exempt these plants from ad valorem property taxes. The Cater Act of 1949 and the Wallace Act of 1951, sponsored by state representative George Wallace, served to stimulate cities throughout Alabama to use their bonding and taxing authority to attract industry.[30] By 1963, at least fifty-nine cities in Alabama had made use of the Wallace-Cater acts to attract new industry.[31] Birmingham was not among them.

Birmingham's failure to pursue economic opportunities was reported by the Southern Institute of Management in its 1960 "Birmingham Metropolitan Audit." Commissioned in 1959 by business leaders who wanted to convey to the nation a more positive image of Birmingham than the press portrayed, the audit was based on a series of interviews with local leaders.[32] Report number two of that study, titled "The Personality of Birmingham," noted that "there exists a hesitation to do things," and that "hesitation to make decisions, to get a job done, to take the offensive, shows up as a major weakness in most of Birmingham's civic, social and intellectual structure." Among the most serious forms of inaction was a "reluctance to compete for employees," which, according to the study, had, "in the public mind . . . caused the blackest mark to be etched against certain industrial companies. There is a wide feeling that these companies have resisted location of new industries and expansion of existing ones."[33] In this apparent reference to TCI–U.S. Steel and other Big Mule firms, local leaders revealed their perception that the Birmingham's iron and steel companies were hurting the local economy.

TCI–U.S. Steel and the other Big Mules continued to resist employment of the Wallace-Cater Act incentives through 1964. That year, under a new mayor, Albert Boutwell, Birmingham business leaders, including Elton B. Stephens, president of a large magazine subscription company, led an effort to adopt the Wallace-Cater incentives. Frustrated by the resistance of the city's traditional industrial interests, Stephens wrote Boutwell in 1963, encouraging him to support the use of the Wallace-Cater incentives: "Somebody has got to act and do something or the City is going backwards—as it has been doing for a long period of time. You know, and I know, that the industrial might is going to put undue pressure on you to not do this. Are you going to let the industrial might continue to run the city, or are we going to do what is best for all of the people?"[34]

The Committee of 100, whose leadership was dominated by Big Mule iron and steel, banking, and utility executives, opposed adoption of the Wallace and Cater Acts.[35] In 1963, the Committee of 100's chairman, Caldwell Marks, testified against adoption of the acts, stating that "I think we would be giving an unfair advantage to new plants against those that are already here and paying taxes."[36] Like the Committee of 100, Mayor Boutwell opposed adoption of the Wallace and Cater Acts. Nevertheless, in 1964 the Birmingham City Council finally authorized and appointed a seven-member Industrial Development Board that would review industry applications for assistance under the Wallace and Cater Acts.[37]

Despite adoption of the Wallace-Cater incentives, true diversification of Birmingham's economic base began primarily because of the growth of the Southside Medical Center, which was enabled by the urban renewal program of the 1950s that permitted expansion of the center and the University of Alabama Medical School (see chapter 4). As early as 1963, the medical center had become the city's second-largest employer, lagging only behind TCI–U.S. Steel, and by 1966 the center would become the University of Alabama at Birmingham.[38] But in the early 1960s, the medical center's impact on the local economy was only beginning to be realized. Local businessmen—particularly those such as Stephens who did not have direct ties to iron and steel but who were invested in Birmingham's service economy—were worried about the city's economic future. To them, failure to expand and diversify Birmingham's economy was a critical issue because their investment dollars, unlike TCI–U.S. Steel's, were tied to the economic health of the community.[39]

As Birmingham entered the 1960s, it also faced the prospect of serious social change in the form of that city's emerging militant civil rights movement, led by Reverend Fred Shuttlesworth and the Alabama Christian Movement for Human Rights (ACMHR), which Shuttlesworth had helped organize. Beginning in 1956, when the State of Alabama obtained an injunction against the NAACP, the ACMHR provided new leadership to the civil rights movement in Birmingham. In that year, Alabama Attorney General John Patterson had sued the NAACP for failing to register as a "foreign corporation," and rather than divulge membership lists, the NAACP elected to cease operations in the state.[40] In contrast to the NAACP, which preferred legal challenges to segregation, Shuttlesworth, who had been membership chairman of the NAACP, and the ACMHR employed both the law and direct action in which Shuttlesworth and his followers attempted to use physical nonviolence to resist segregation.

The ACMHR contrasted with the local NAACP in several other respects as well. First, many of the traditional leaders in the black community, including W. C. Patton, who had led the protest against the expansion of the medical center (see chapter 4); attorney Arthur Shores; and Reverend J. L. Ware, head of the Birmingham Baptist Ministers' Conference in Birmingham, who along with Shores had led the fight against racial zoning (see chapter 3), opposed the ACMHR, believing it too militant.[41] Second, the ACMHR membership tended to reflect a more lower-middle-class makeup than the NAACP's middle-class and professional constituency. Shuttlesworth's church, Bethel Baptist, was located in the Collegeville neighborhood of North Birmingham, where many residents worked in nearby pipe mills and iron furnaces.[42] Shuttlesworth said of ACMHR: "Many of the upper class persons who worked in the NAACP are professional people who seem to feel that it is almost taboo to align actively with us. Our professional people need to understand that the gap between the class[es] and the masses must be closed. The classes evolved up from the masses and where would you go and what would you do without the masses?"[43] With ACMHR, Shuttlesworth was able to significantly broaden the base of core activists in the black civil rights movement in Birmingham.

Launched at a June 5, 1956, meeting attended by more than one thousand people, ACMHR built upon the Montgomery, Alabama, and Tallahassee, Florida, boycotts against segregated seating on city buses by showing that direct-action techniques could be used to confront other forms of racial segregation. With these techniques, Shuttlesworth and the ACMHR showed that black communities could develop a people's movement to undertake social change. Moreover, they demonstrated that it was possible for blacks in a community such as Birmingham to generate their own resources for challenging segregation.[44] Using both their own money and their own bodies, Shuttlesworth and ACMHR showed the power of a people's movement in taking on one of the most racist political regimes in America.

In December 1956, Shuttlesworth and the ACMHR requested that the Birmingham City Commission comply with the U.S. Supreme Court's affirmation of a lower court ruling that ended segregated bus seating in Montgomery, Alabama. Shuttlesworth warned that if the city did not discontinue segregated seating on city buses, the ACMHR would ride the buses without regard for the city's segregation ordinance. In response, on Christmas night, 1956, while Shuttlesworth was lying in bed, his house was bombed. Although the blast caused severe damage, Shuttlesworth emerged from the rubble unhurt. He was convinced, as were his parishioners and supporters, that God had spared him so that he could lead the movement against racial segregation in Birmingham.[45] In September 1957, Shuttlesworth and his family attempted to integrate whites-only Phillips High School. There he was beaten by a mob of white men, but once again he survived.[46] In these and other confrontations over integration of public facilities and public schools, Shuttlesworth and the ACMHR demonstrated a fearlessness and willingness to take on the forces of segregation, even when it meant endangering their lives. Just as blacks had risked their lives to obtain better housing in the late 1940s and 1950s, the born-again civil rights movement in Birmingham was risking attacks by the Ku Klux Klan to put an end to racial segregation.

In the years between 1956 and 1963, Shuttlesworth and ACMHR employed legal and direct-action strategies to challenge Birmingham on issues of hiring black police officers, integrating the city's beaux arts–style Terminal Station, integrating Birmingham's downtown retail stores, and integrating the city's schools, parks, swimming pools, and playgrounds. It was ACMHR's attempt to integrate the city's parks, along with the Freedom Rides of 1961, that finally captured the attention of the city's white business establishment and encouraged them to begin to think about ways of changing the city's government and ending legal racial segregation.

On Mother's Day, May 14, 1961, unrestrained by the Birmingham police, a mob of white vigilantes attacked civil rights Freedom Riders as they got off a bus at the Birmingham Trailways bus station. Under a prearranged plan with the Birmingham police and the city's public safety commissioner, Bull Connor, terrorists from the Ku Klux Klan and the American States' Rights Party were given fifteen minutes to violently club and kick white and black Freedom Riders. The Congress of Racial Equality (CORE) had organized the Freedom Rides to test the degree to which southern communities were in compliance with U.S. Supreme Court and Interstate Commerce Commission orders to desegregate buses, terminals, and restaurants serving interstate passengers.[47] The next day, in contrast to the bombings of black homes in which the perpetrators remained anonymous, a picture of white vigilantes beating a Freedom Rider was printed in the *Birmingham Post-Herald* and newspapers throughout the world. The *Birmingham News*, which had supported Bull Connor in his most recent reelection campaign, asked on its front page, "Where Were the Police?"[48] In Japan at a convention of the International Rotary Club, incoming Chamber of Commerce president Sydney Smyer read the news of the Mother's Day beatings and quickly learned the impact they would have on the city's reputation as a place to do business. Smyer noted that among the conventioneers, "When you said you was from Birmingham, boy, they didn't have anything to do with you."[49] Recognizing what the city's racial politics meant for its business climate, Smyer and other Birmingham businessmen began to move away from their support for Connor and racial segregation.

Smyer was president of the Birmingham Realty Company, the successor to the Elyton Land Company, which had founded Birmingham in 1871.[50] He was also a segregationist who had helped organize the Dixiecrat revolt in 1948 when delegations from Alabama and other southern states walked out of the Democratic convention to protest the adoption of a civil rights plank in the party's platform and to hold their own convention in Birmingham later that summer.[51] In 1954, he was elected president of a Methodist layman's association organized to prevent racial integration of the Methodist Church, but he had left this group by 1956.[52] But in 1961, when he returned to Birmingham after the Mother's Day beatings, Smyer used his power as Chamber of Commerce president to establish a study committee to investigate the problems of race in Birmingham. Joining him were other business leaders from the Chamber of Commerce, the Committee of 100, the Birmingham Downtown Improvement Association, and the city's black community.[53]

The study committee was significant in several key ways. First, the committee was biracial. In the past, blacks were not invited to participate with whites in civic affairs. Only the Interracial Division of the Jefferson County Coordinating Council of Social Forces had invited blacks to participate, but in 1956 white segregationists successfully pressured the Community Chest to cease funding the division.[54] Smyer's committee therefore represented a significant change in the white establishment's approach to racial issues. Second, the committee's existence furnished evidence that at least some businessmen in Birmingham saw that the city's policies of racial segregation and brutality hurt the local economy. Reportedly, the Mother's Day beatings had cost the city a $40 million manufacturing plant. Smyer, along with William Engel, one of the city's leading realtors, and office supply store owner James Head, who chaired the Chamber's Committee of 100, agreed that Birmingham's already shaky economy could be hurt even more by the negative publicity associated with violent resistance to racial integration.[55] Birmingham's declining economic fortunes helped set the stage for its business leaders to reconsider whether racial segregation was in the city's economic interests.

Economic and social change also persuaded Smyer and others to look toward political change as a means by which they could redirect the local economy and local racial policies. Specifically, Smyer and a group of young, progressive attorneys, many of them members of the Young Men's Business Club, saw that it was time to remove Bull Connor from public office by eliminating the commission form of government, thereby preventing Connor from being reelected commissioner of public safety. Also, by eliminating the commissioner of public safety position, Connor could be kicked out of office immediately; otherwise his term of office did not end until 1965. Connor was clearly Birmingham's most powerful public official, and in his position as public safety commissioner he was able to use the police and the local courts as tools for maintaining racial segregation. David Vann, one of the young, progressive attorneys who helped oust Connor, wrote of him:

> The distinctive differences between Birmingham and other cities probably boiled down to one man, Eugene "Bull" Connor. There were undoubtedly more erudite leaders in racial demagoguery. The Bilbos, the Talmadges, the Strom Thurmonds, and the Faubuses were all better educated and more sophisticated. Lester Maddox in Atlanta was perhaps even more colorful. But none brought in one man the folksy, almost grandfatherly touch, the available expert legal and professional advice, and the command of one of the best trained municipal police departments in America. Without police enforcement, not only by arrests, but also by an instilled fear of physical abuse by the police, racial segregation could not be sustained. In Birmingham the police were under the command of an elected public safety commissioner, who considered that he had a mandate to use that Birmingham Police Department as a primary instrument for maintaining racial segregation in the city.[56]

Nearly three months before the 1961 Freedom Rider beatings, Smyer asked the Birmingham Bar Association to prepare a report on Birmingham's government and to recommend whether the city should discard the commission form of government it had operated under since 1910.[57] One year later, the Birmingham Bar Association recommended replacing the commission form of government with a mayor-council form of government in which a mayor with veto power was elected along with a nine-member city council, all of whom would be elected at large. The bar association justified these recommendations as necessary to encouraging the city's suburbs, chiefly Mountain Brook and Homewood, to merge with the city.[58]

At the same time that the bar association was studying alternative forms of government, a key issue emerged that further convinced Birmingham's business community that Connor must go. In 1958, Shuttlesworth and the ACMHR had filed suit to desegregate the city's nearly 1,300 acres of parks, golf courses, community centers, and swimming pools. On October 24, 1961, U.S. District Court judge H. H. Grooms ruled that segregation of parks was unconstitutional and that the city's parks should be desegregated by January 15, 1962. In response, the Birmingham City Commission cut the parks budget by 80 percent, thereby forcing the city's Park and Recreation Board to close the parks. All parks were closed, and 125 park employees were laid off effective January 1, 1962.[59] The city's business leaders responded by pleading with the city commission to keep the parks open.

In a great sense, the parks closure issue brought Birmingham face to face with the ambiguities of the American planning tradition. In Birmingham, as in other cities, parks were an important symbol of the city's ability to plan for itself in a way that made the city a better place to do business. The development of urban parks lay at the roots of city planning in nineteenth-century America and remained so into the twentieth century, as exemplified by the schools and parks element of Birmingham's 1961 Comprehensive Plan. Since the nineteenth century, American business leaders were among the chief advocates of using parks to relieve congestion and enable a city's residents to enjoy the ennobling effects of nature, while adding to the value of the city's real estate investments.[60]

At the same time, the segregation of parks represented the last bastion of racial zoning. As a land use, parks were still segregated even though the U.S. Supreme Court had struck down the racial zoning of privately owned land in Birmingham in 1951. Consequently, the segregation of parks represented the other side of American planning tradition—a tradition begun in the 1920s when Birmingham and other cities had adopted racial zoning as part of their comprehensive zoning ordinances. Parks had also been used by the city, as McLendon Park was used in the 1920s, as a means to discourage black movement into white neighborhoods. The Birmingham City Commission feared that by ceding the ability to control who entered the city's parks, their efforts to maintain racial segregation and a white-dominated city would fail. Mayor Art Hanes, who was the city's nominal leader but was controlled by Bull Connor, told his constituents: "I don't think any of you want a nigger mayor or a nigger police chief. But I tell you, that's what'll happen if we play dead on this park integration."[61]

In asking the city commission to keep the parks open and therefore to permit their integration, Birmingham's business leaders chose to follow a more progressive planning position than the one exemplified by racial zoning. Whereas at one time, Birmingham's business leaders

had seen racial segregation as protective of property values, the closing of the city's parks cast new light on segregation. The traditional
business support for parks was now in conflict with racial segregation.
To support the city's parks, therefore, the city's business leaders were
forced by the city commission to support racial integration.

More generally, the parks closing controversy once again reveals the
internal contradictions in city planning. City planning is about building beautiful cities and parks that meet the needs of residents to be
close to nature while making the city attractive to doing business. At
the same time, city planning is about protecting property values, including the property values of whites who believed that the presence
of blacks could devalue their neighborhoods. Consequently, city planning could be used to justify and perpetuate racial segregation. But in
the case of the parks closing, these two planning traditions came into
direct conflict with each other, forcing the city's business leaders, who
were sympathetic to both perspectives, to make a decision as to which
element of the planning tradition they supported. The tension between these viewpoints and the need for the business leaders to present to the world a city that was a good place to do business led them
to advocate a position few of them would have previously favored: integration of the city's parks.

Nobody personified the internal tension of planning more than Sidney Smyer. In addition to being a leading businessman and a segregationist, he had a passion for the importance of planning. His firm, the
Birmingham Realty Company, owned considerable land in Jefferson
County as well as in Birmingham, and he sought to protect those holdings by serving as a charter member of the Jefferson County Planning
Commission in 1947.[62] In 1956 and 1957, he attempted to get the Jefferson County legislative delegation to sponsor a bill creating a metropolitan planning commission that would address planning problems
throughout the metropolitan area.[63] He bemoaned the lack of progress
in establishing a comprehensive plan in Birmingham and wrote in
1955 that, "After looking over the long range plan of Atlanta, I am more
convinced that we in Birmingham and Jefferson County are far behind
in our overall planning."[64] Two years later he was among the charter
members of the Birmingham Downtown Improvement Association,
an organization that was instrumental in enabling Birmingham to
contract for its first comprehensive plan.[65] As a businessman, Smyer

knew the value of planning as a protector of property values, a primary source of wealth to his firm. Just as it was in the 1920s when racial zoning was introduced, a belief in racial segregation was consistent in Smyer's mind with a belief in using planning and zoning to preserve property values. But by the 1960s he realized that the maintenance of racial segregation had significant economic costs for his firm and his city. Consequently, he adopted a more progressive view toward integrating the city's parks in order to maintain the city's image as a good place to do business.

The ACMHR's suit to integrate the parks, along with the city commission's response, created a wedge that separated the city's business leaders like Smyer from Bull Connor and the Birmingham City Commission. In response to the city's plan to close the parks, leading business groups, as well as other community organizations, petitioned the city commission to reconsider its decision. The Birmingham Downtown Improvement Association, the Committee of 100, the Chamber of Commerce, the Junior Chamber of Commerce, and the Young Men's Business Club, as well as both daily newspapers, the Birmingham Ministerial Association, and the Jefferson County Board of Mental Health, all opposed closing the parks.[66] James Head, chair of the Committee of 100, coauthored a "Plea for Courage and Common Sense" that was signed by 1,260 petitioners, including business leaders such as Sydney Smyer, and that called for the city commissioners to live up to their campaign promises to expand the city's parks and playgrounds.[67] Ironically, at the instant that the city was planning to close the parks, the December 1961 Comprehensive Plan, prepared by Harland Bartholomew and Associates, was recommending that the parks be increased by 1,700 acres.[68] That recommendation followed Harland Bartholomew's conclusion in September 1958 that enhancement of the parks was vital to expansion and diversification of the city's economic base. In order to preserve racial segregation, the city commission was ignoring the comprehensive plan's park expansion objectives.

Consistent with Harland Bartholomew's recommendation, the city's business leaders also feared that closing the parks would hurt the city's slowing economy.[69] According to a statement made by the Committee of 100: "This is the type of action which will reduce the jobs available in metropolitan Birmingham. It also will cripple our efforts to create new job opportunities for which we must compete with other Southern cities. The situation which confronts us is that serious."[70]

Their pleas fell on deaf ears, however. On January 9, 1962, James Head was joined by four other leading citizens—Bernard Monaghan, chief executive of Vulcan Materials; Henry King Stanford, president of Birmingham-Southern College; David Wright, minister of the prestigious St. Mary on the Highlands Episcopal Church; and Mayer Newfield, attorney—as they asked the city commission to reconsider. Connor, and the other commissioners, rejected the five and the petition they carried, saying, "I bet half the people on this list don't even live in Birmingham." Connor treated the visitors to a one-hour lecture on desegregation. Most significantly, the visitors, along with other members of Birmingham's business and community elite, came away from the city commission meeting humiliated by Connor. They recognized that Connor and his fellow commissioners were out of control. Stanford stated, "I never had such an experience in my life." Whereas Birmingham's business leaders had formerly acquiesced to Connor's leadership—or in the case of U.S. Steel, actively encouraged it—the controversy over closing the parks and the humiliation they suffered made it much easier for them to support a change in government and the ouster of Bull Connor.[71]

After a sixty-day stay was granted by Judge Grooms, the parks were finally closed in March 1962, one month after the bar association made its recommendation for a mayor-council form of government.[72] But recommending a change in government and achieving it were two different things. In the 1950s, the Alabama state legislature adopted the Mayor-Council Act, which gave the city's residents the power to change its type of government in a referendum. In 1953, Birmingham's state senator Hugh Kaul had sponsored legislation that would enable changing Birmingham's form of government from the city commission to the council-manager form. Birmingham's mayor Jimmy Morgan responded by persuading the legislature to require a third alternative, a mayor-council form of government, to be included in any referendum on a change in the city's government. In this way, the Birmingham City Commission hoped to split the vote against the city commission form of government, thus enabling it to stay in place.[73] Ironically, the availability of the mayor-council alternative propelled the change of government in 1963.

In August 1962, attorney David Vann recognized the opportunity provided by the state enabling law to change Birmingham's form of government. As he drove to work on August 14, he heard local radio announcer Dave Campbell argue that Birmingham residents should either petition for a new form of government or accept the one they had. Challenged by what he heard, Vann examined his law books and found that the Mayor-Council Act required only 10 percent of Birmingham voters to sign a petition to trigger a referendum. Vann served as head of the Jefferson County Democratic Campaign Committee, a group that was organized in 1960 to support John Kennedy for president and had remained together as an alternative to the conservative-dominated regular local Democratic Party. Vann and the committee were already preparing for an August 28 special election for new Jefferson County representatives to the state legislature. Members of the Young Men's Business Club had filed suit in 1961 to reapportion the state legislature so that cities such as Birmingham would have fair representation in what had been a rural-dominated legislature. The U.S. District Court in Alabama responded in 1962 by ordering the legislature to reapportion itself, and soon thereafter the August 28 election was called to elect ten new Jefferson County legislators.[74]

Vann also knew that if he succeeded in getting a referendum on the form of government, the switch to a mayor-council form of government had a chance of succeeding. In June 1962, George Wallace had won the Democratic primary for governor but had lost in Birmingham. Vann noticed that a new voting pattern had emerged in Birmingham with black and middle-class white districts voting together, while Wallace carried working-class white districts. In Vann's words, the 1962 gubernatorial race "had produced an unconscious coalition of voters of middle class, upper class, and blacks voting for the same candidates."[75] Between 1956 and 1962, four thousand new black voters had been added to Jefferson County's rolls, resulting in a nearly 50 percent increase in the number of black voters.[76]

But in order to succeed, the white members of Vann's emerging coalition had to remain "unconscious" of their growing alliance with black voters. In 1961, moderate white Tom King ran for mayor against Bull Connor's hand-picked candidate, Art Hanes.[77] King attempted to court progressive business support by criticizing the city and the Chamber of Commerce for failing to compete with Atlanta for air service. King was disturbed by Birmingham's slowing economy and wanted to focus the city's energies on attracting new industry. But Hanes turned King's criticism of the airport into a racial context. He claimed King was trying "to make Birmingham into another Atlanta," which, according to King's friend and supporter Charles Morgan Jr., could be translated to mean, "Atlanta's progress came at too high a cost: integration."[78]

By playing the race card, Hanes, with Connor's support, was able to shift the white vote against King. With the support of the growing black vote, King had led the field in the primary. But Connor and his colleagues were quick to exploit the fact that King had won the black vote and used that fact against him in the campaign.[79] Moreover, King had been tricked into being photographed shaking the hand of a black man hired to set him up. The resulting photograph, taken in front of Birmingham's city hall, was used to campaign against King in the city's white working-class districts.[80] Finally, the Freedom Ride into Birmingham took place several weeks before the June 1961 mayoralty runoff, further inflaming racial attitudes and ultimately costing King the mayor's seat.[81]

Vann and his colleagues recognized that in order to succeed, they had to prevent Connor from using the perceived threat of the black vote to divide the white electorate, thereby defeating any proposal to change the city's form of government. In Vann's words, the unconscious coalition of blacks and whites that was forming in the city was such that you "couldn't get them all together in the same room."[82]

After reviewing the Mayor-Council Act, Vann called fellow attorney Abe Berkowitz, who had been a member of the Birmingham Bar Association's committee that recommended a change in government. Berkowitz and others had been making speeches to drum up support for switching to a mayor-council form of government and had worked with Vann and other young attorneys on the Tom King mayoral campaign.[83] Berkowitz agreed to help, and he organized a meeting later that day that included leaders from the Democratic Campaign Committee, the Birmingham Chamber of Commerce, the Birmingham Real Estate Board, the PTA Council, and the Birmingham Labor Council.[84] With encouragement from Don Stafford, president of the labor council, the group decided to proceed with a petition campaign that would take place two weeks later on August 28. Sidney Smyer proposed that the group identify twelve leading Birmingham citizens who would sponsor the petition. But of the twenty-five top leaders identified as potential sponsors, none wished to take a public stance favoring the petition. Smyer responded by saying, "If we can't get 25 silk-stocking people, let's get 500 anybodies." By Wednesday, August 22, the group organized more than five hundred individuals who supported the petition campaign. They reasoned that if they could get five hundred supporters in less than a week, they could get six thousand to seven thousand signatures at the polls on August 28.[85] Meanwhile, the city's elite leaders offered their financial support to what became known as Birmingham Citizens for Progress.[86]

On Tuesday, August 28, Birmingham Citizens for Progress volunteers set up petition booths at polling places across the city. By the end of election day, they had collected more than eleven thousand signatures, with only 7,500 signatures required to call an election. Bull Connor organized a petition signing at the Jefferson County Courthouse in which movie cameras shot pictures of twenty-five blacks signing the petition. Later, he and Commissioner J. T. Waggoner claimed that five thousand of the eleven thousand signatures belonged to black voters. Vann and fellow attorney Erskine Smith had prepared for this tactic by setting up petition booths only in predominantly white neighborhoods.[87]

The referendum campaign that followed was fought over the race issue. Connor and the other commissioners charged that the Birmingham Citizens for Progress was using the referendum to bring racial integration to Birmingham. David Vann had been Justice Hugo Black's law clerk in 1954 when the former Alabama senator had voted to end legalized segregation in *Brown v. Topeka Board of Education*. While initially arguing that the mayor-council referendum was about government efficiency and not about racial integration, the Citizens for Progress shifted its argument by contending that the Mayor-Council Act had been created by segregationists in the 1950s and that establishment of a progressive form of government would make merger with Birmingham more palatable to the city's suburbs. Merger with predominantly white suburbs such as Mountain Brook and Homewood, they pointed out, would help assure that whites would continue to dominate Birmingham politics.[88]

Despite their efforts to paint the November 6 election as a referendum on race, Connor and the other commissioners shot themselves in the foot by attempting to buy the votes of city employees. On October 17, the three Birmingham commissioners held a secret meeting in which the city's firefighters were promised an 8 to 10 percent pay raise if they supported and campaigned for the commission form of government. One of the firefighters asked if they would get the raise regardless of the outcome of the referendum. Mayor Hanes responded: "Absolutely not. You don't get your raises unless *we* are here to give it to you." Tom Lankford, photographer for the *Birmingham News*, whose editorial boss, Vincent Townsend, supported the mayor-council form of government, secretly taped the meeting, and the next day a transcript appeared in the *Birmingham News*. An unidentified messenger gave a copy of the tape to David Vann, who used it to run a number of radio ads. In the closing days of the campaign, Birmingham's citizens were treated to Citizens for Progress commercials that featured Bull Connor and his fellow commissioners attempting to bribe the firefighters.[89]

Despite the revelation of blatant corruption, the November 6 referendum gave the mayor-council form of government a plurality of only 729 votes out of 37,176 cast. The commission form scored well in the same working-class white neighborhoods where Connor had garnered the bulk of his votes in the past, while the mayor-council form did well in the city's affluent and middle-class white neighborhoods and in the city's black neighborhoods, where it was favored by an overwhelming majority. Birmingham had rejected Connor and the other city commissioners, and for the first time the city's black voters had a hand in shaping the outcome of a city election.[90] After the polls had closed, David Vann read a statement: "We have seen one of the most dramatic demonstrations of democracy that any of us will ever witness."[91] But the commissioners lost by only a small margin. Politically, Connor and his supporters were not dead yet.

Not surprisingly, therefore, Connor, along with fellow commissioner J. T. Waggoner, entered the race for mayor in the March 5, 1963, election. Joining them in the race for mayor were 1961 mayoral candidate Tom King and Albert Boutwell. Boutwell had replaced Connor's mentor, Big Mule attorney James Simpson, as Jefferson County's state senator in 1946 and served in that post until 1958, when he became lieutenant governor. He was unsuccessful in his bid for the governorship in 1962 and returned to private life in Birmingham.[92] As a state senator, he led the legislature's response to the Supreme Court's 1954 *Brown v. Topeka Board of Education* decision by coauthoring a freedom of choice law that permitted students to enroll in segregated schools.[93] Boutwell was a segregationist, but unlike Connor, he campaigned in favor of maintaining law and order as well as segregation: "I am determined that we are going to defend, I hope maintain, segregation, but we are not going to be a city of unrestrained and unhampered mockery of the law."[94] To a longtime segregationist like Sydney Smyer, who led the effort to encourage Boutwell to run, Boutwell was the best candidate to offset Connor.[95] With impeccable segregationist credentials, it was harder to tag Boutwell as favoring integration, although Connor attempted to do so.[96] At the same time, he could be relied upon to maintain order and to not permit a repeat of the Mother's Day attack on the Freedom Riders.

On March 5, 1963, Boutwell and Connor led the race for mayor with Birmingham voters awarding Boutwell 39 percent of the vote and Connor earning 31 percent.[97] Because no candidate received a majority, a runoff between the top two vote getters, Boutwell and Connor, was required. On April 2, Boutwell beat Connor by nearly 8,000 votes, earning 29,630 to Connor's 21,648.[98] Once again, the unconscious coalition of affluent and middle-class whites and recently enfranchised blacks mustered enough votes to carry the day, and the approximately 10,000 black votes, nearly all of which went for Boutwell, supplied the margin of victory.[99] On April 3, Vincent Townsend's *Birmingham News,* which along with the *Birmingham Post-Herald* had supported Boutwell, marked the Boutwell victory with the headline: "New Day Dawns for Birmingham."[100]

A new day was dawning in Birmingham, but it was not the day that Townsend and his newspaper imagined. First, Connor and the other commissioners challenged the legality of the election, arguing that they were elected to four-year terms in 1961 and that their terms should therefore not end in 1963. Two separate state laws governing changes in municipal government were in conflict on this issue, and consequently Alabama's courts had to resolve the contradiction.[101] With the law unclear, Birmingham's commissioners, including Connor, remained in office, while the newly elected mayor and city council also asserted their right to govern. Birmingham's progressive business leaders, who had hoped to move the city forward with a new form of government, were now confronted with having two governments in apparent power. The situation would not be resolved until the Alabama Supreme Court could reach a decision on the commissioners' challenge to the immediate expiration of their terms.

Second, a series of civil rights demonstrations began on April 3 that catapulted Birmingham into the front pages of the nation's newspapers. Building on demonstrations and a downtown "selective buying campaign" led by black Miles College students in 1962, the original intent of the spring 1963 demonstrations was to once again disrupt the Easter shopping season in downtown Birmingham through lunch counter demonstrations and a boycott of downtown merchants. In both 1962 and 1963, attention was focused on protesting downtown merchants who refused to serve blacks at their lunch counters and refused to employ them. After the temporarily successful 1962 spring boycott dissolved, Reverend Fred Shuttlesworth asked Martin Luther King Jr. and the Southern Christian Leadership Conference (SCLC) to help ACMHR lead a campaign for equal access and employment opportunity in Birmingham's downtown stores.[102] After being asked several times, King agreed to come to Birmingham, and the ACMHR-SCLC campaign began on April 3.

In targeting downtown merchants, ACMHR-SCLC was attempting to use the black community's purchasing power to make a dent in the city's economy. At the same time, wittingly or not, the ACMHR-SCLC was also taking aim at the segment of Birmingham's business community that was vulnerable to a boycott as well as willing to make plans to improve downtown's and the city's ability to grow and prosper. Since at least 1957, when downtown merchants helped form the Birmingham Downtown Improvement Association, merchants had worried about their economic prospects. Later that year they put up the money to help pay for a master plan that would lead the city and its downtown into the future.[103] At a time when the city's political leaders were attempting to preserve the past, the city's downtown merchants and investors were looking to the future, making them more willing, if ever so slightly, to accept change in order to meet their economic goals. And in accepting change, unlike the city's political leaders, they were also willing to do something that whites had never done in Birmingham: negotiate with blacks.

But moving the business community to negotiation did not come easy. ACMHR-SCLC's campaign continued through April but with diminishing success. The boycott failed to seriously deter black shoppers, and the demonstrations failed to rally blacks to protest discrimination by downtown merchants. By the end of April there were few protestors left willing to be arrested.[104] Finally, on May 2 the campaign took a new turn when ACMHR and SCLC leaders enlisted schoolchildren to march in the streets of Birmingham and fill the city's jails.[105]

The impact was electric. At noon on May 2, black children from area schools poured out of downtown black churches and onto the streets. For almost four hours, groups of ten to fifty children, singing civil rights songs and expecting to be arrested, marched over various routes. Bull Connor, who remained as public safety commissioner until the Alabama courts resolved how long his term would last, had been told that the month-long protest movement had run out of people willing to be arrested. Suddenly he was confronted with hundreds of schoolchildren marching in downtown Birmingham, all willing to be arrested. Connor, who had tried not to react with violence, ordered his fire department to occupy intersections to contain the marchers with fire hoses ready to spray the demonstrators. By the end of the day, police vans and school buses had been used to arrest hundreds of demonstrators. On Thursday evening of May 2, two thousand people filled Sixth Avenue Baptist Church to celebrate, nearly one week after a movement rally had been attended by a significantly smaller crowd. Martin Luther King Jr., who had not been able to decide whether the children's marches should proceed, announced to the crowd: "I have been inspired and moved today. I have never seen anything like it."[106]

On Friday, May 3, the children continued to march, but Bull Connor could no longer stand and watch. The arrests on May 2 had nearly filled the city's jail. The firemen once again took their positions between the demonstrators and downtown. But on May 3, they were ordered to use their fire hoses to spray the demonstrators. Film and photographs of Birmingham fire fighters spraying helpless demonstrators were shown around the world, as were photographs of the police department's canine corps German shepherds lunging at onlookers caught in the melee. The city's reaction to the demonstrators also provoked the crowds of black bystanders, who responded by throwing bottles and bricks at police and firemen. Seeing that events could get out of control, civil rights leaders ended the demonstration. Within forty-eight hours, two new elements had been added to the civil rights struggle in both Birmingham and the nation: 1) the employment of masses of schoolchildren, an act that provoked the city to respond with fire hoses and police dogs; and 2) the beginnings of mob violence as black onlookers reacted to Bull Connor's efforts to stop the children from marching.[107]

Concerned with the negative international publicity created by the city's efforts to punish children, the Kennedy administration sent Assistant Attorney General Burke Marshall to Birmingham. On Friday night, May 3, Sidney Smyer once again gathered a biracial group of businessmen who had previously met in April, to no avail. The group, which would meet over the next few days, included white downtown merchants, led by Roper Dial of Sears, Roebuck, who had served as president of the Birmingham Downtown Improvement Association; attorneys David Vann and Abe Berkowitz; Sidney Smyer; the *Birmingham News*'s Vincent Townsend; and black leaders including millionaire businessman A. G. Gaston, insurance executive John Drew, attorney Arthur Shores, Miles College president Lucius Pitts, SCLC's Andrew Young, and Fred Shuttlesworth, who attended the first meeting. Mayor Albert Boutwell sent his aide, Billy Hamilton, to give unofficial representation to the new government. With the turn of events and the increasing negative publicity for Birmingham, both Smyer and the Kennedy administration felt compelled to reach a settlement that would end the demonstrations and restore order. In addition, the city's downtown merchants were feeling the pinch of the black boycott of their stores along with white fears of shopping downtown in the midst of demonstrations.[108]

Over the next few days the demonstrations and talks continued. The white business leaders were uncertain as to whether Connor would remain in office—after all, his fate and that of the other commissioners was in the hands of an Alabama Supreme Court whose members had been elected statewide as candidates committed to segregation. Consequently, the white business leaders concluded that they could not negotiate on behalf of the city government, and the black leaders concurred. Negotiations focused instead on issues that Birmingham's business leaders could control, such as desegregation of downtown stores and black employment opportunities in those stores, not on desegregation of parks and schools or the hiring of black police officers.[109]

Despite their willingness to negotiate desegregation of their stores and the promotion of a few of their black employees to clerk positions, the city's downtown merchants still felt they needed the endorsement of the Big Mules. According to David Vann, the merchants recognized their vulnerability if responsibility was assigned to them for any settlement with King and Shuttlesworth. Their stores and merchandise were vulnerable to white backlash, and so the city's bankers and realtors would be asked to endorse a settlement.[110] Consequently, Roper Dial urged Sidney Smyer to call a meeting of the Senior Citizens Committee, a group that Smyer had formed the previous fall when the SCLC held its annual convention in Birmingham and Shuttlesworth had spread the rumor that Martin Luther King Jr. was coming to Birmingham to lead demonstrations. The committee consisted of seventy-seven of the city's leading white business leaders along with twelve black leaders, but Smyer invited only the white members to meet on Tuesday, May 7.[111] Kennedy cabinet members had called their business colleagues on the committee, giving them the courage to stand in favor of negotiations with SCLC even though Birmingham's leading economic power, Arthur Wiebel of TCI–U.S. Steel, objected to settling.

Their courage was strengthened by fears of further disturbances and shame for their city. Jefferson County sheriff Mel Bailey said that the jails were full and that further arrests would require confining people behind barbed-wire fences at the city's football stadium, Legion Field. With local law enforcement being tested by the demonstrators, Governor George Wallace had sent 375 state troopers to Birmingham, and business leaders feared what the governor and his troopers might do. Sidney Smyer told the Senior Citizens Committee that he would assume full responsibility for a negotiated settlement and that their names would not be published for a week. In return, he asked that they authorize a subcommittee to implement the remaining negotiations. With at most three dissents, the senior citizens gave Smyer authority to proceed with negotiations that would desegregate stores and increase employment opportunities for blacks, as well as set up a biracial committee that would attempt to resolve other civil rights issues.[112] For the first time, the city's leading business interests supported negotiating with spokespersons for black residents. In their eyes, such an outcome was not welcome but was made necessary by the events that had overtaken the city and the corner into which Connor, King, and Shuttlesworth and their followers had boxed them. Smyer made this clear when he proclaimed, "I'm a segregationist, but I'm not a damn fool."[113] Despite being cornered, however, Birmingham's white business leaders would still dictate the terms of the immediate agreement as well as its implementation in the years to come.

On Tuesday night, May 7, Sidney Smyer led a delegation that included David Vann, Roper Dial, and Edward Norton of Royal Crown Cola in a meeting with black leaders Arthur Shores, Lucius Pitts, John Drew, and Andrew Young. Billy Hamilton represented Mayor Boutwell, and Burke Marshall represented the Kennedy administration. Smyer's delegation agreed to Young's proposal for "immediate 'token' employment of Negroes," establishing a timetable for desegregation of public accommodations, and proposed that other issues be considered by a biracial committee. Still up in the air was how to deal with the charges filed against the demonstrators. Young wanted them dropped, but the white leaders were opposed. The two groups compromised by agreeing that white leaders would not stand in the way of black leaders raising money to pay for bail. How the black leaders would raise the money had yet to be worked out, however. Nevertheless, Lucius Pitts recommended that the promises be accepted and that if the demonstrations were halted the black community would be "in a good position to effect continual change in the community."[114]

By Wednesday morning, May 8, Martin Luther King Jr. had agreed to the deal and to halting the demonstrations so that a final deal could be worked out that included the bail money. His SCLC associate Ralph Abernathy believed that the national press would interpret a moratorium on the demonstrations as an act of good faith and advised King to end them. In addition, SCLC feared the presence of Governor Wallace's state troopers and the possibility of casualties, for which Wallace had promised to hold the black leaders accountable. The likelihood of deadly violence occurring was compounded by reliance on children and the increasingly violent response of black bystanders to the City of

Birmingham's use of force. On Tuesday, May 7, police, firemen, and black onlookers fought battles with fire hose spray and rocks being exchanged and police chasing people and beating them with billy clubs.

Fred Shuttlesworth, who had been hospitalized soon after the melee when firemen had slammed him into a brick wall with the force of their hose, confronted King on Wednesday for making a unilateral decision to end the ACMHR-SCLC demonstrations without a publicly announced agreement. Shuttlesworth met King at John Drew's house, located on Center Street in North Smithfield, high on Dynamite Hill overlooking downtown Birmingham. The meeting between whites and black leaders the night before had concluded at Drew's house. Shuttlesworth told King, "You and I promised that we would not stop demonstrating until we had the victory." Shuttlesworth, who had been organizing the black community and risking his life for civil rights since 1956 and who had to invite King three times to come to Birmingham, now felt betrayed by what he perceived as King's usurpation of power and authority. Moreover, in fall 1962, Birmingham's downtown merchants had agreed to desegregate their stores, only to renege on their promise after the SCLC and the threat of Martin Luther King Jr. led demonstrations had gone away. Threatening to call his own demonstrations, Shuttlesworth left Drew's house in anger. After Attorney General Robert Kennedy spoke with Shuttlesworth, however, Shuttlesworth ended his call for demonstrations. Instead, he was willing on Friday, May 10, to sit with King and Abernathy at a press conference to read the terms that had been hammered out by Smyer and the black leaders and agreed to by King. In the meantime, a deal had been struck whereby the United Auto Workers and other unions would post the bond money needed to release the more than one thousand children who were still in jail.[115]

The settlement accomplished much, both for the nation and for Birmingham, but it also had its costs. The struggle to achieve civil rights in one of the nation's most racist and segregated cities had created massive national and international publicity that defamed segregation and roused a nation to support passage of national civil rights laws, including the Civil Rights Act of 1964. The achievement of a settlement helped to propel the civil rights movement and solidify Martin Luther King Jr.'s reputation as a national leader.[116] Locally, the movement to change the city's government resulted in the ouster of Bull Connor from office. The campaign to unseat him finally succeeded on May 23, 1963, when the Alabama Supreme Court ruled that Birmingham's adoption of a new form of government had ended Connor's and the other commissioners' terms of office.[117] Moreover, the settlement between whites and blacks that ended the spring 1963 demonstrations represented the first occasion that the city's black residents and the city's white leaders had been able to ever sit down and negotiate.

But the settlement also represented a clear compromise that Shuttlesworth had hoped to prevent. In his press conference on Thursday, May 9, from which Shuttlesworth was noticeably absent, Martin Luther King Jr. was content to say that lunch counters and other public facilities would be desegregated at a certain but unnamed date. Employment of blacks in downtown stores would be gradually upgraded. Concerns regarding desegregation and opening of the parks, hiring of black police officers, and other issues would be dealt with by the biracial commission that would be appointed. The *New York Times* commented that black demands for action in Birmingham had been replaced by a willingness to accept promises from the white community.[118]

With the departure of Connor and the end to the demonstrations, Birmingham's white business leaders had once again captured the momentum they had lost the day after the April 2 election when Connor refused to step down and the demonstrations began. With little in the way of firm commitments, the white business leaders, most of whom were supporters of segregation, could proceed to negotiate freely to set the terms and priorities they deemed most critical. Moreover, with the complicity of Martin Luther King Jr. and SCLC, Birmingham's black middle class, which preferred negotiations to demonstrations, had displaced Shuttlesworth and ACMHR as spokespersons for the black community.

The black leaders who had negotiated with Sidney Smyer—John Drew, Lucius Pitts, A. G. Gaston, and Arthur Shores—represented Birmingham's traditional black middle-class leadership that had frequently been at odds with Shuttlesworth's direct-action approach to social change. Gaston and Pitts had opposed the spring 1963 demonstrations, and in fall 1963, Gaston, along with Shores, criticized Martin Luther King Jr. for "outside interference" in negotiations with local white leaders over such issues as the hiring of black police officers.[119]

Pitts had previously argued against the employment of direct-action techniques, short-circuiting an early 1962 Miles College student-led boycott of downtown merchants by informing the merchants of the students' plans and arranging a biracial meeting.[120] Shores had received Shuttlesworth's public censure as a "Calhoun" for asking fees five times the amount proposed by ACMHR for representing Shuttlesworth's suits to desegregate the city's parks.[121] Drew, as well as Shores, had refused to support ACMHR when it was created in 1956.[122] Drew and his activist wife, Deenie, had played a more neutral role regarding Shuttlesworth and the spring 1963 demonstrations, but they were solid members of the city's black middle class.[123] Andrew Young, who had helped negotiate the settlement to the spring 1963 demonstrations later wrote, "By and large, the leadership fell right back into the hands of the middle class, and had they not been involved at all through the process, they wouldn't have been prepared to bring leadership in the period of reconciliation that followed."[124]

After May 1963, Shuttlesworth lost the important role he had played in building a people's movement in Birmingham, and without his leadership that movement's emphasis on direct action by the black lower middle class was supplanted by the negotiation approach favored by the black middle class. In part, this was Shuttlesworth's doing as he took a new pastorate in 1961 in Cincinnati, even though he committed to remain head of ACMHR and continue to lead civil rights efforts in Birmingham.[125] In part, as well, his confrontation with Martin Luther King Jr. over ending the demonstrations led to a waning of his stature in the SCLC at the same time that King's attention was drawn to the national civil rights movement. In 1963 and 1964, Shuttlesworth asked King to return to Birmingham to lead more demonstrations, but his pleas went unheeded. In October 1963, King and Shuttlesworth addressed a mass meeting with King talking about another boycott, but there was no follow-up. By spring 1964, King's attention was on a civil rights campaign in St. Augustine, Florida.[126] In Birmingham, the black middle class, which had always been discomforted by Shuttlesworth's tactics, used his residency in Cincinnati as an opportunity to label him as an outsider.[127] Meanwhile, Shuttlesworth complained that Gaston, Drew, and Shores were delaying progress by negotiating in private with Mayor Albert Boutwell.[128] Boutwell, however, would not meet with Shuttlesworth, repeatedly ignoring the latter's call for a meeting.[129] In response, Shuttlesworth threatened further demonstrations, but without King's support these threats were in vain. For seven years Shuttlesworth had labored in the vineyard of protest and direct action, but with King's ascension to national leadership, Shuttlesworth was unable to rally the ACMHR troops he had worked so hard to organize.

This meant that the militant, direct-action tactics of Shuttlesworth that had aroused the black community's grassroots and demonstrated its ability to set the terms of debate were supplanted by a methodical approach in which a few middle-class blacks slowly negotiated civil rights. Shuttlesworth's ability to organize larger groups of lower-middle-class blacks into participating in these direct-action campaigns would be lost. Prior to the introduction of children in the spring 1963 demonstrations, 339 adult protestors had been arrested in April 1963.[130] While many of these ladies and gentlemen undoubtedly remained active in the civil rights movement, the loss of Shuttlesworth's leadership made it less likely that they would participate in direct-action campaigns of this scale again. Instead, leadership had been restored to the same black middle-class leaders who had opposed ACMHR as too militant.

From the perspective of planning and community development, as well as social change in general, this meant that a grassroots-based movement that called for serious change had been defused by businessmen's reform and the complicity of the black middle class, both in Birmingham and in the national civil rights movement. Businessmen-led reform and the civil rights movement had successfully ridded the city government of Bull Connor, but the same forces also led to the demise of Fred Shuttlesworth as a key leader in the city. Although it is difficult to speculate on what Shuttlesworth would have done if he had stayed in Birmingham, clearly the local people's movement he had built rapidly diminished in influence after 1963, thereby creating a vacuum in the black community that the traditional black middle-class leadership was eager to fill. With the loss of Shuttlesworth and his ability to employ direct-action tactics to rally the black folk against the forces of political and economic oppression, Birmingham's black community sacrificed the only source of power they had ever been able to effectively employ. At the same time, white business leaders—who still were segregationists, even if they weren't fools, as Sidney Smyer expressed it—used the change in government and the spring 1963 negotiations to reassert their power over the city's affairs. They used this opportunity to get the city's economy moving again; they were much less interested in pushing for increased equality for the city's black residents.

At the same time, the city's white vigilante element once again asserted its ability to employ terrorism to threaten the black community. In prophetic response, however, the city's black community engaged in the first of many urban riots of the 1960s that reflected growing national African American discontent with the status quo. On Saturday, May 11, one day after King and Shuttlesworth announced the settlement with the white business leaders, the Ku Klux Klan organized a large rally in a field thirteen miles south of Birmingham. Later that night, a bomb exploded at the home of Reverend A. D. King, brother of Martin, in Ensley. Soon after, another bomb exploded at the A. G. Gaston Motel, near downtown, where the SCLC and ACMHR leadership had directed the Birmingham demonstrations. Both bombs were targeted for Martin Luther King Jr., who had left earlier that day for Atlanta. When police arrived at the Gaston Motel, enraged black residents hurled bricks and bottles at the officers. Black rioters then proceeded to burn down and ransack a twenty-eight-block area, while city police, state highway patrolmen, and Dallas County, Alabama, sheriff Jim Clark's vigilantes tracked them down and beat them. Several Italian-owned groceries that served the black neighborhood were burned, but the out-of-control fires enveloped black homes as well. No one was killed, but at least fifty people were injured.[131]

Although it was not apparent at the time, the Birmingham riot of May 12 and 13 followed a pattern that would be matched in other cities in the 1960s and later, as black residents of inner-city ghettos responded to a provocation by ransacking their neighborhood. An era of "commodity riots" had begun. While such riots occurred most famously in the 1960s in such places as Watts, Detroit, and Chicago, latter-day versions continue to take place nearly forty years later. Birmingham was not unique—the black rage that brewed there was to be found in cities across the nation and throughout the remainder of the twentieth century. While Birmingham represented a major victory in the national civil rights movement, the May 12–13 riot also made Birmingham a harbinger of urban strife to come.

The bombing and violence would not end in May, however, but for the first time in the city's history of bombings going back to the 1940s there would be casualties. On Sunday, September 15, 1963, soon after court-ordered school integration had begun in Birmingham, a bomb exploded at the Sixteenth Street Baptist Church, killing four black girls—Cynthia Wesley, Carole Robertson, Denise McNair, and Addie Mae Collins. Once again rioting broke out as angry blacks threw objects at the police. A police officer shot one black youth with his shotgun while two white teenagers shot a black teenager in the head and killed him.[132] As in past bombings, no arrests were made, and it appeared that once again Birmingham's bombers would go free. In the 1970s, however, Alabama attorney general William J. Baxley reopened the case, which led, in 1977, to the murder conviction of Ku Klux Klan member Robert Chambliss. Other Klan members were suspected of participating in the bombing, but they were not brought to trial at that time.

With Chambliss's conviction, the thread that had run through Birmingham's history of bombings became clearer. Although never convicted of the racial zoning bombings of the late 1940s and early 1950s, Chambliss had been questioned about his role in those bombings and had actually told black homeowner Willie German that he was a member of the Klan and that German's house would be bombed if he did not move (see chapter 3). What had begun as a series of bombings designed to preserve the city's racial zoning law had now been transformed into one of the most significant events in the nation's civil rights history. City planning had established the foundation for the city's racial zoning law, which Bull Connor and the city's vigilante bombers had sought to preserve in the North Smithfield neighborhood. The racial bombings that began in North Smithfield in 1947, and that numbered over forty by the end of 1963, had culminated in the Sixteenth Street Baptist Church bombing. That incident demonstrated to the American public the immorality of racism and segregation. The bombings would continue to serve as powerful landmarks of the nation's civil rights struggles even in the twenty-first century as two others, Thomas Blanton Jr. and Bobby Frank Cherry, were convicted in 2001 and 2002 of assisting Chambliss in the Sixteenth Street bombing.[133]

Meanwhile, after the Alabama Supreme Court's May 23, 1963, decision, the Boutwell administration and the new nine-member city commission assumed full authority for the city's governance. On July 23, the city commission unanimously repealed all the city's segregation ordinances, including the one requiring segregation in parks and recreational facilities.[134] Ten days earlier, Mayor Boutwell announced that he had appointed 212 members to the city's Community Affairs Committee (CAC), the biracial committee called for in the settlement to the spring 1963 demonstrations.[135] Despite much fanfare, the CAC had little lasting impact, and by its first anniversary was fading in importance. As of July 1964, the CAC had been without a chairman for two months, and only the Municipal Expansion and Group Relations Committees of the CAC's original ten committees remained active.[136] In October 1963, the Group Relations Committee recommended that Mayor Boutwell "issue a public statement immediately that the city will employ Negro police when they have qualified under Civil Service regulations and are certified."[137] Boutwell responded that when a black applicant qualifies he will be hired, but the first black officer was not appointed until March 1966, nearly two and one-half years after the Group Relations Committee made its recommendation and nearly twenty years after Atlanta had hired its first black police officer.[138] More generally, Boutwell contended that the city had a very limited role in promoting equal opportunities for its black residents.[139] While the most egregious examples of segregation and racism had been eliminated, by fall of 1963 it was clear that despite the spring demonstrations and the business-approved reforms that followed, attitudes toward race had still not moderated significantly.

The lack of progress in race relations would have two major impacts on the city and city planning. First, city building and planning efforts would continue to concentrate on issues of greatest importance to the business leaders who shaped the city's agenda. These were primarily issues of municipal expansion and downtown development. Increasing economic opportunities for black residents assumed little importance for the city's business elite. Second, meaningful African American participation in the city's planning process would be greatly limited. As the city moved to adopt the Great Society's reforms, it would begin to move toward including blacks in the development of policies and plans, but only in a very limited way. By 1970, blacks would begin to have a voice in city planning, but only a very small voice, especially when compared to the role that business leaders saw for themselves in shaping the city's urban agenda.

The CAC's municipal expansion committee focused its efforts on expanding the city's boundaries through merger with the suburbs, particularly the affluent Homewood and Mountain Brook suburbs that lay in Over the Mountain to the southeast of Birmingham. In July 1964, the CAC's Municipal Expansion and Development Committee recommended that the city pursue consolidation with the surrounding suburbs.[140] Leadership on the thirty-two-member municipal expansion committee consisted primarily of business executives and attorneys, including seven presidents or former presidents of leading Birmingham companies.[141] Reflecting the importance of the suburbs, two-thirds of the committee's members lived in Birmingham's suburbs, with fifteen residing in Mountain Brook, the richest of the suburbs.[142]

The 1964 merger campaign was similar to one fought in 1959. In both cases, the city's primary aim was to merge with the elite suburbs of Homewood and Mountain Brook, and in each instance leading citizens of these two suburbs helped lead the merger movement. In 1964, as in 1959, a significant number of Mountain Brook's elite continued to see their destinies tied with Birmingham's and consequently pushed for consolidation.[143] Even the *Shades Valley Sun,* a suburban newspaper serving Mountain Brook and Homewood, urged voters in those two cities to vote for consolidation with Birmingham, as did the Shades Valley Junior Chamber of Commerce.[144]

As in 1959, the strong support of many Mountain Brook business leaders for consolidation failed to resolve the issue of school integration. In 1959, the prospect of school integration in Birmingham in the wake of the U.S. Supreme Court's 1954 *Brown v. Topeka Board of Education* decision split the residents of Homewood and Mountain Brook, becoming the most important issue affecting the consolidation debate that year.[145] Residents of both suburbs raised the school integration issue. W. D. Powell, a Homewood city councilman, maintained: "If we stay out, we won't have integration. We're further away from integration if we stay out."[146] With no blacks residing within its boundaries, Mountain Brook recognized that it had the opportunity, if it stayed outside of Birmingham, to not only postpone but also to successfully resist school integration.[147]

In response, Birmingham expansionists argued that Homewood and Mountain Brook could maintain school segregation even if the two suburbs were consolidated with Birmingham. Jefferson County state senator Larry Dumas proposed legislation permitting schools to secede from their existing school districts when the districts were forced to integrate.[148] But Mountain Brook residents, whose children were attending Jefferson County schools at that time, felt safer developing their own school system. A member of the Mountain Brook school committee noted that, "there is no legislation that can insure us this protection [from integration] and we should not surrender it."[149] Recognizing the importance of the school issue, on the eve of the May 12, 1959, consolidation referendum, the Mountain Brook City Council voted to move forward with development of an independent school system.[150]

Consolidation advocates also maintained that there was a larger racial issue that suburban residents should consider, especially those who had businesses interests in Birmingham. According to consolidation leader George Peach Taylor: "Even more important [than schools] is the total fight at the ballot box. If you overlook that battle—you're overlooking the main issue."[151] Elsewhere Taylor said that suburbanization "would allow block voting minorities to take over the government of Birmingham. . . . We must unite at the ballot box through merger if we are to protect our present standards of living and Southern customs."[152]

By 1963 school integration had come to Birmingham, and Mountain Brook's fear of desegregation had not subsided.[153] Recognizing this, in 1964 the Birmingham City Council adopted a Contract in Trust, which made a series of service commitments to the five suburbs (Homewood, Mountain Brook, Fairfield, Irondale, and Midfield) toward which merger campaigns were aimed. In Mountain Brook's case, special language was added to help that suburb retain its segregated schools. Invoking Alabama's Independent School District Act of 1959 (the Dumas Bill of the 1959 merger campaign), Birmingham's contract called for a vote on the establishment of an independent school district in the event that Mountain Brook residents agreed to merge with Birmingham.[154]

Despite the Alabama attorney general's opinion that the Independent School District Act could withstand legal scrutiny, Mountain Brook school board members and other local leaders, including successful 1964 mayoral candidate William Given Jr., remained skeptical of the legislation's ability to protect them from school desegregation.[155] In the closing days of the merger campaign, school desegregation once again became the most important issue in the minds of Mountain Brook voters. On August 25, 1964, the residents of Mountain Brook voted, by a margin of 3,177 to 2,923, not to consolidate with Birmingham.[156] Anticonsolidation forces, led by mayors and city councils, were also able to defeat the merger proposals in the other suburbs.[157]

The merger attempts of the late 1950s and mid-1960s made it clear that Birmingham was unlikely to annex its affluent, predominantly white suburban neighbors. Unlike other Sunbelt cities, such as Jacksonville, Florida, or Houston, Texas, Birmingham was unable to significantly expand its boundaries and increase its population in the first twenty-five years after World War II. In general, Sunbelt cities have distinguished themselves from cities in the Northeast and Midwest by being able to expand their boundaries, thereby continuing to capture a significant share of the metropolitan area's population. But between 1950 and 1970, Birmingham was performing increasingly like a northern city. Birmingham ranked forty-second out of sixty-four cities in percentage increase in land area, two places ahead of Chicago. Birmingham's 8 percent reduction in population made it and Louisville the only two Sunbelt cities to experience population loss during this period.[158]

Birmingham's inability to annex was created by two interrelated factors, both linked to race. First, the city had a large black population— for nearly the entire twentieth century, the city's population had been about 40 percent black. Other Sunbelt cities that were able to significantly expand their boundaries and populations had much smaller black populations.[159] Second, Birmingham's school district coincided with the city's boundaries. Therefore, the student population was at least 40 percent black, making it more likely that white children would have to go to school with sizeable numbers of black children. Other Sunbelt cities avoided this situation by either having countywide school districts (such as all cities in Florida, as well as Charlotte, North Carolina) or having independent school districts that enabled newly annexed areas to remain in suburban school districts (Dallas, Houston, and San Antonio).[160] School integration was the key issue that stopped the city's merger initiatives in 1959 and the 1960s. In one last-ditch effort in the 1970s—the One Great City proposal—fear of school integration once again was the major impediment to the city's merger with its suburban areas. Only in the 1970s and 1980s, when the city began to focus its attention on annexing black suburban areas, as well as unpopulated areas, was it able to expand its boundaries, but such annexations obviously bypassed white, middle-class neighborhoods.[161]

Birmingham's failure to annex its suburbs also meant that its politics would be dramatically altered. Although the influence of black votes in the 1962 change in government referendum and 1963 elections was clear, the number of black voters in the city had historically been very low. In 1960, Jefferson County's nearly twelve thousand registered black voters constituted only 10 percent of the county's adult black population.[162] But by constituting 40 percent of the city's total population, the city's black population had a high potential for influencing local politics. At the same time that the city was realizing its inability to merge with its predominantly white suburbs, the 1965 Voting Rights Act made it possible for many more blacks to register to vote. In 1964, the number of black voters in Jefferson County had doubled to 24,000; in 1966, 50,000 additional black voters were added to the rolls. Consequently, the mid-1960s marked the beginning of a major change in Birmingham's electoral politics—a change that would have important impacts on the way in which planning affected the black community in that city.[163] Much of this change, however, would not be realized until the 1970s.

In the late 1960s, as Birmingham's *suburban strategy*—which was based on merger—unraveled, business leaders maintained their attention on a *downtown strategy* that focused on revitalization of the central business district. Downtown revitalization held out the possibility of enhancing the city's prosperity by focusing on its centralized assets that business leaders hoped could compete with the decentralized suburbs that surrounded the city. In late 1961, the Harland Bartholomew firm completed the comprehensive plan that it had begun in 1958 (see chapter 5). The plan proclaimed the downtown area to be the "most important piece of real estate in Birmingham" and proposed strategies for preserving downtown's role in serving the retail and commercial needs of the city. To make better use of the existing buildings in downtown, as well as to keep development within a concentrated area, the

Bartholomew report recommended "the construction of an upper (second story level) promenade which will unite the major foci of pedestrians within the core-department stores and important retail shops, offices, banks and major parking terminals."[164] The *Birmingham News* feature on the Bartholomew plan headlined the second-story promenade as "Sky City—Birmingham's Jet Age Heart-To-Be."[165] Despite Mayor Art Hanes's appointment in early 1962 of a committee to implement the Bartholomew plan, the Sky City concept for downtown never caught on.[166] Consequently, after the city's business leaders reasserted control over the government in 1963, a new effort began to develop a set of strategies for downtown revitalization.

These efforts built on what the Birmingham Downtown Improvement Association (BDIA) had started in 1957, when it had encouraged the city to undertake a comprehensive plan (see chapter 5). In 1963, the BDIA launched a major downtown planning effort entitled "Operation New Birmingham."[167] Among BDIA's leaders in 1963 were several downtown merchants who had participated directly or indirectly in the black-white negotiations triggered by the spring 1963 demonstrations: Roper Dial of Sears, Roebuck; Emil Hess, owner of Parisian's department store; and Isadore Pizitz, owner of Pizitz department store.[168] Also serving on BDIA's board was Vincent Townsend, regarded as Birmingham's most powerful political actor, who used his influence and his newspaper, the *Birmingham News,* to direct the city's attention to downtown revitalization.[169] In a December 1963 *News* political cartoon, the city's symbol, Vulcan, whose statute sits atop Red Mountain overlooking the city, says of downtown's failure to revitalize—"That's Our Number 1 Problem!"[170] Coming just six months after the spring 1963 demonstrations, the riot that followed, and three months after the bombing of the Sixteenth Street Baptist Church, businessmen saw the city's problems as primarily economic, reflecting not the overall welfare of the city's mixed population but rather the welfare of its downtown commercial core.

With the city's chief problem so defined, business leaders looked to city planning to provide the city and its downtown with a new, upward direction. Instead of turning to the city's planning department, however, in early 1963 the BDIA convinced members of the local American Institute of Architects chapter to donate six thousand hours to develop a plan for revitalizing downtown.[171] The project, titled Operation New

Birmingham, was initially unveiled at the March 1964 annual meeting of the BDIA, where John Evins, BDIA president, linked downtown revitalization to the city's merger campaign: "I would like to recommend that the municipalities immediately join in face to face communication with each other and with the legislative delegation, and then cooperate to coordinate or merge."[172] In early 1965, BDIA presented the architects' master plan, the Design for Progress, which called for the creation of what would become the Birmingham–Jefferson County Civic Center. BDIA also recommended that additional funds be spent on beautification of Twentieth Street, downtown Birmingham's main thoroughfare, and construction of a new public library, downtown parking garages, a trade mart, and two downtown residential developments, Park East and Park West.[173]

By mid-1965, Operation New Birmingham (ONB) was formalized as an implementing body for the Design for Progress plan, and Vincent Townsend was named chairman. ONB boasted an enlarged membership, consisting primarily of businessmen, serving on twelve committees, all chaired by whites. Only a handful of blacks, all members of Birmingham's black elite, including A. G. Gaston, Mrs. A. G. Gaston, John Drew, L. S. Gaillard, W. L. Williams, and Arthur Shores, served on ONB's committees. Shores, Gaillard, and Williams all served on the Downtown Housing Development Committee, whose charge included planning for the Park West development, a multifamily housing project intended to serve middle-class blacks wishing to live near the black commercial area just west of downtown Birmingham.[174]

By fall of 1965, Townsend had begun to marshal the resources he would use to revitalize the city's downtown. Two hundred local businesses, the city, and the county had pledged $160,000 to ONB for an "action fund."[175] By 1966, ONB merged with its parent organization, the Birmingham Downtown Improvement Association, while retaining the ONB name and widening its charge to include Jefferson County infrastructure issues.[176] Under the U.S. Department of Housing and Urban Development's (HUD) Workable Program requirement for receiving public housing and urban renewal funds, ONB was named in 1966 as the city's official citizen participation arm for city planning, replacing the moribund Community Affairs Committee.[177] Increasingly, ONB became not just a downtown business organization but a business-led arm of government. ONB hired two full-time staff members to serve as liaisons between Birmingham, the state, and the federal government for the purpose of obtaining grants for ONB projects.[178] It employed a public relations firm to launch a national Operation Sell Birmingham campaign, hired a Washington, D.C., consultant to lobby on behalf of the city and county, and was provided with an office in city hall.[179]

At the same time, ONB actively implemented the Design for Progress agenda, making it very clear that business leaders were fixed upon a clear path to improving the city's business fortunes, primarily through major publicly supported construction projects. In September 1965, Vincent Townsend announced that the first steps had been taken to create the Birmingham–Jefferson County Civic Center, which would be a "center of beauty, culture, and commerce—second to none in the country."[180] In the same speech, Townsend made clear how the business agenda had triumphed over the anti–civil rights agenda expressed just two years earlier: "We are embarked on a journey into the future. We will fly the banners of private enterprise. We will marshal all the dollars that are available. . . . We must have an economy that produces thousands of new jobs . . . jobs based on sound economic policies. We have been frustrated long enough. We have been bemused too long by those who have sought to divide and control us. We must continue to cast them aside, whether they be at home or abroad."[181] By March 1966, the Birmingham–Jefferson County Civic Center Authority had been created, and by July 1969, ground had been broken on the civic center (see map 5.1). The facility would include a sports arena, an exhibition hall, a concert hall, and a theater, all of which were completed by 1977.[182] In the early 1970s, the city created the Birmingham Green, a beautification project for Twentieth Street, by burying telephone lines, planting trees, and widening pedestrian areas.[183] Funds for both projects, as well as for other Design for Progress projects, were included in a $50 million bond issue approved by voters on June 4, 1968, with greatest support coming in the city's black neighborhoods.[184] In addition, the U.S. Department of Housing and Urban Development committed urban renewal funds for the civic center project.[185]

At the same time that Birmingham's business leaders were focusing their attention on downtown redevelopment, the federal government was enabling the Southside University of Alabama Medical Center to expand into the University of Alabama at Birmingham. In the spring 1963 mayoral election, candidate Albert Boutwell spoke in favor of the medical center's $30 million expansion program and supported expansion of the center's educational program to create a four-year undergraduate college. He viewed the center as vital to increasing employment and economic expansion in Birmingham.[186] Soon after Boutwell took office as mayor, Joseph F. Volker, the center's vice president for health affairs, wrote Boutwell asking to discuss the possibility of the center acquiring additional adjacent land through the federal urban renewal program.[187] Volker, who came to the medical center in 1948 as dean of the dental school, saw it as the basis for creating an urban university. In his international research and consulting, he had noted the urban origins of European universities, and he also believed that medical centers were more successful when located in universities.[188] Given this vision, the existing fifteen-block campus was too small, particularly since the medical center's projections showed that the fifteen blocks would be completely utilized by 1974.[189] In response to the expansion plans, Boutwell in December 1964 announced the creation of the Mayor's Committee for the Medical Center.[190]

In contrast to a decade earlier when the first medical center expansion took place, blacks were able to participate in the decisions regarding the second expansion. Once again, members of Birmingham's black elite, including L. S. Gaillard Jr., A. G. Gaston, and Arthur Shores, were named to serve on the committee, as well as a realtor, a physician, an insurance agent, dentist John Nixon, and attorney Orzell Billingsley Jr.[191] The vast majority of the 140 citizens, however, were white. Nevertheless, at the committee's February 23, 1965, meeting, the black realtor on the committee, Wilbur Hollins, seconded a motion requesting the city, the housing authority, and the federal government to employ the urban renewal program to expand the medical center from fifteen to sixty city blocks.[192] In December 1964, the city council had voted 5 to 4 to name Hollins to the planning commission. He was the first black to serve on a major city board or authority. In his favor, council members Alan Drennen and George Seibels stated that Hollins's appointment was important because of proposed urban renewal projects involving black residents.[193] By seconding the motion, Hollins was saying that Birmingham's black leaders supported expansion of the medical center.

By spring 1965, the city council had approved the medical center urban renewal application, and on November 10, 1965, HHFA urban renewal administrator William Slayton had approved over $6.1 million in federal funds for the expansion.[194] With the expansion, the medical center would occupy much of the city's Southside neighborhood (see map 6.1), stretching from Twentieth Street West to Interstate 65 and from the Fifth Avenue South to Twelfth Avenue South. As with the first medical center expansion of the 1950s, most of the households living in the existing neighborhood were black. Of 996 families, 815 were black. Of 719 single persons, 417 were black.[195] Of 1,027 buildings in the proposed expansion area, 873 had deficiencies, including 528 that were deemed structurally unsound.[196] By 1966, the medical center would be renamed the University of Alabama at Birmingham, and the College of General Studies would be established to award four-year bachelor's degrees.[197] Birmingham had its first public university.

Despite the impact that urban renewal would have on what remained of the predominantly black Southside neighborhood, no significant protest against the proposal took place. This probably reflected the fact, at least in part, that by spring 1965, hospitals and clinics at the medical center had been desegregated. On behalf of ACMHR, Oscar Adams Jr. in May 1964 informed Volker that he might file a suit to desegregate the medical center. In response to the possible suit, as well as federal public health service threats to withhold federal funds for new medical facilities, the center's hospitals and clinics were desegregated in April 1965, soon after the housing authority had applied for federal urban renewal funds for the center's expansion. Black insurance executive John Drew praised "the sincere efforts on the part of the hospital staff to provide equal facilities and service to all our people."[198] Adams, whose father had fought racial zoning in 1923 and who himself had opposed the first medical center merger in 1953, could at least know that although many black Southside residents would have to relocate, the medical center's hospitals and clinics were no longer segregated.

Although black participation in the second Southside Medical Center expansion had been limited to a few members of Birmingham's black elite, another federally assisted city project encouraged more significant citizen participation. At the same time that he was appointing the Mayor's Committee for the Medical Center, Boutwell was applying

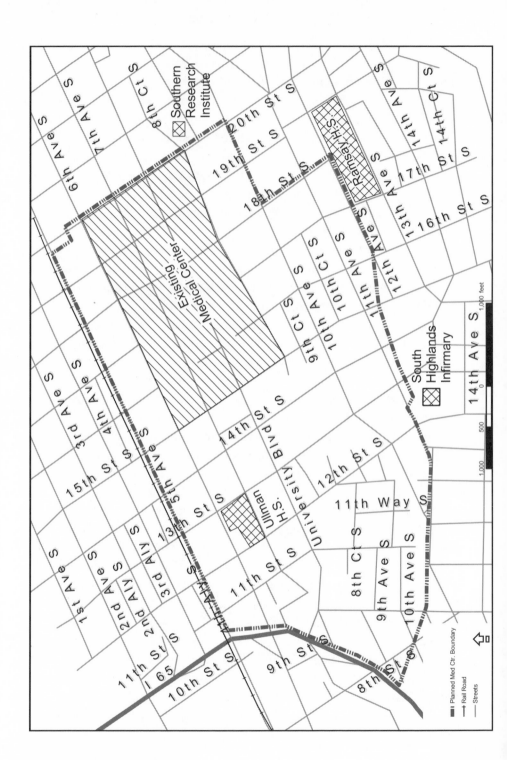

for a project development grant under the federal Economic Opportunity Act of 1964, President Lyndon Johnson's War on Poverty.[199] By June 1965, the city, in cooperation with Jefferson County, created a nonprofit community action agency, the Jefferson County Committee for Economic Opportunity (JCCEO), to implement programs under the Economic Opportunity Act.[200] The federal Office of Economic Opportunity (OEO) wanted to prevent control of JCCEO by Alabama governor George Wallace and delayed approval of funding for JCCEO until Birmingham and Jefferson County agreed to appoint at least six people living in low-income areas to the forty-one-member JCCEO board of directors. Candidates for these positions were to be democratically nominated by neighborhood advisory councils and appointed by the Birmingham and Jefferson County governments.[201]

In 1966, Congress amended the Economic Opportunity Act to require that at least one-third of community action agency board members be directly elected by residents of the poor neighborhoods served by the agency. The new law required that sixteen of forty-eight JCCEO board members be elected directly by the public, with the remaining thirty-two members coming equally from public agencies and community groups. Previously, Birmingham and Jefferson County leaders had been able to name all of the JCCEO board members. But as a result of OEO's interpretation of the new law, Birmingham and Jefferson County were required to accept both democratic election of poor persons to the JCCEO board and the selection of public and community agency representatives to the JCCEO board.[202]

Several striking outcomes must be noted. First, OEO's citizen participation demands met no resistance from the Birmingham city government. Second, the push for increased participation by the poor in JCCEO did not come from Birmingham's poor and their representatives but rather from the federal government.[203] Third, JCCEO's black constituency confined its political activism to specific problems with the community action agency's job training program. In the 1960s and early 1970s, Birmingham blacks did not use the JCCEO forum as an opportunity to challenge the authority of Birmingham's white political establishment.[204]

Map 6.1 (*opposite*). Southside Medical Center urban renewal area, 1965, showing planned medical center boundary. (Source: *Birmingham Post-Herald*, February 24, 1965)

In turn, Birmingham's political leaders essentially left JCCEO alone. Even when the 1967 Green Amendment presented cities with an opportunity to assume greater fiscal control over community action agencies, Birmingham elected not to do so; taking instead a position of "just keep us informed and pull no surprises."[205]

The quiet acceptance of grassroots citizen participation in the War on Poverty program would not be repeated, however, with Birmingham's Model Cities funding application. By the time the city submitted a Model Cities application in 1968, the black community demanded direct control over the planning of its neighborhoods. The purpose of the Model Cities program was to enable cities to concentrate various federal resources in the most depressed urban neighborhoods. Despite the program's similarity to the OEO's antipoverty program, the Boutwell administration elected not to apply for the program's first round of funding in 1967. In early 1968, however, newly elected mayor George Seibels decided to compete for the second round of Model Cities funds.

City councilman Seibels had been elected mayor in November 1967. Despite his willingness to challenge Bull Connor in 1963, Boutwell had been criticized for lacking leadership. Certainly, the community advisory committee that he nominated with great fanfare in 1963 had fizzled. In addition, as a segregationist who had defeated Connor, both the city's white working-class and black communities viewed him with distrust.[206] In the fall 1967 primary, Boutwell finished third to Seibels and attorney George Young, with Seibels defeating Young in the November 1967 runoff. Unlike Boutwell, Seibels was no segregationist. His personal style made him a good spokesperson for the city at a time when the business community, including ONB, was very concerned with the city's public image. As a Republican, Seibels was also very comfortable with the city's business leaders, as they were with him. At the same time, Seibels courted the black vote and was the city's first mayor to attend black social affairs.[207]

The city's Model Cities application targeted the Ensley community and its ten neighborhoods (see map 6.2), including the predominantly black Tuxedo neighborhood, south of which Interstate 59 had been constructed as a racial barrier (see chapter 5), as well as predominantly white Wylam, the city's westernmost neighborhood.[208] The Ensley community was undergoing racial change. According to a report prepared

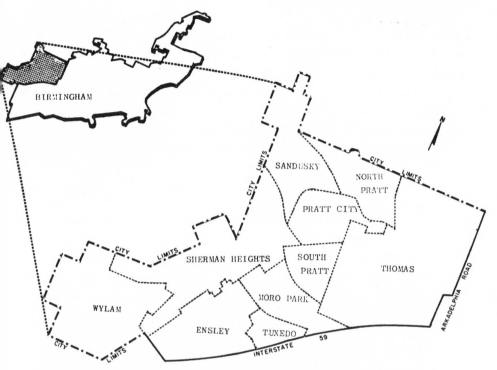

Map 6.2. The Ensley community proposed Model Cities neighborhoods. This map, prepared by the City of Birmingham for its Model Cities application, shows the location of the Ensley community and its neighborhoods. (Birmingham Public Library Department of Archives and Manuscripts)

by Yale Rabin, a planning consultant brought in by neighborhood residents, the Ensley population was over two-thirds black, up from the 1960 U.S. census estimate of 54 percent black reported in the city's Model Cities application.[209]

Perhaps because of its mixed race composition, the city government took greater interest in retaining control of the Model Cities application than it had shown with its laissez-faire approach to JCCEO. Greater city government authority was possible since the Model Cities program, in contrast to the Community Action Program, placed local authority for decision making in city government rather than CAP-like community action agencies.[210] Birmingham did not anticipate significant citizen participation, and when pressure for such participation came from Ensley's black residents, the city resisted a shift of power from city hall to the neighborhood. Instead, it relied on a thirty-two-member mayor's task force that originally consisted of six community agency heads, including JCCEO's black executive director and a representative of the Birmingham chapter of the NAACP, two black newspaper editors, and more than twenty local government officials. The city then undertook three meetings with citizen groups. At the last of these meetings, held on March 21, 1968, residents elected thirty persons to also serve on the mayor's task force.[211]

Despite these efforts, the city's citizen participation procedure received sharp criticism. Marie Jemison wrote Mayor George Seibels urging him to make the neighborhood representatives elected at the March 21 neighborhood meeting the representatives for the Model Cities area. She regarded the city's chief planner, James Wright, as unsympathetic to the needs of Ensley's residents.[212] On April 5, 1968, the mayor's task force met for the last time to approve the "planning approach" for the Model Cities application. Although task force members adopted the general approach favored by the city, they appeared "uncertain" and expressed concern that the city's planner had spent insufficient time in the neighborhood. As one black member of the task force observed: "Negroes are tired of coming to City Hall and okaying what you've already done. Some of the people from the neighborhood should have been included in the groundwork. If we're going to be a part of this task force, we want to be part of it all the way."[213]

Several weeks after the city's submission of its Model Cities application to HUD, disgruntled black members of the mayor's task force, represented by attorney Harvey M. Burg, obtained a copy of the application from the city. This was the first opportunity the citizens of the task force had to review the application. The NAACP Legal Defense Fund, at Burg's request, provided the black citizens with the services of planning consultant Rabin, who noted a number of flaws in the application, including allegedly underestimating the black population of the Ensley proposed Model Cities area.[214]

Rabin and the black task force members complained that the application made no commitments concerning the responsibilities, resources, and powers of the proposed Model Cities Neighborhood Board, and failed to provide for selection of a majority of the board members by the residents of the Model Cities neighborhood. As an alternative, Rabin and the black residents proposed that a citizens board be set up. Three individuals would be elected from each of the ten neighborhoods in Ensley to serve on the board, and they would receive technical assistance from a full-time planner hired by the board. The citizens from the board, along with the citizens board planner, would have the right to sit on the City Development Agency (the designated decision-making body under Model Cities) and to make policy recommendations.[215]

After several rounds of proposals and counterproposals, the city refused to concede responsibility to the neighborhood residents for electing their own representatives to the neighborhood board, preferring to keep this power in the hands of the mayor.[216] Consequently, as promised, the black task force neighborhood representatives took their case to HUD secretary Robert Weaver.[217]

Finally, in November 1968, HUD informed Mayor Seibels that Birmingham had not been approved for the Model Cities planning grant.[218] Although no reasons were given, it is clear that the application represented an important transition point in the development of citizen participation in Birmingham. In contrast to the JCCEO experience in 1965 and 1966, by 1968 Birmingham blacks pushed hard for self-determination in citizen participation and planning. They were not content with whites appointing black representatives.

At the same time, the Model Cities case indicates that the white political community in Birmingham had not moved as far on citizen participation as the rise of black citizen participation in JCCEO might indicate. By permitting "too much" black self-determination, Birmingham city government appeared to fear that it would alienate white residents and business leaders in the proposed Model Cities neighborhood. Evidence shows that the city was in danger of losing white support for the Model Cities application if the program appeared "too black." Residents of the primarily white Wylam neighborhood asked to be taken out of the Model Cities application, and Mayor Seibels and the city council agreed to do so if the planning grant application was funded.[219] According to the citizen complaint filed with HUD, the city canceled a planned May 23, 1968, meeting with attorney Harvey Burg, representing the black task force neighborhood representatives, because of a petition reportedly signed by white Wylam residents opposing the Model Cities program.[220] The Ensley Chamber of Commerce, which had no black members, voted to oppose the Model Cities application.[221]

Consequently, by the late 1960s, while the black community moved toward self-determination in citizen participation, the white power structure still feared that such participation, especially in programs involving whites as well as blacks, would alienate the white community. Moreover, the business community, led by Operation New Birmingham, was firmly in control of the city's planning agenda, which it focused on suburban annexation and downtown revitalization. The downtown merchants and property investors had launched the Birmingham Downtown Improvement Association in 1957 to address downtown's declining economy and to push the city to develop a master plan. Many of these same leaders, especially Smyer, were moved by the city's response to the Freedom Riders and closing of the parks to push for a change in government that led to Connor's departure from local politics. In 1963, the downtown leaders had negotiated an end to the ACMHR-SCLC demonstrations while launching a major planning initiative for revitalizing downtown.

The 1960s were a period of great change in Birmingham, but despite the ouster of Bull Connor and the rising influence of blacks in electoral politics, business leaders retained control of the planning agenda. The city's black neighborhoods remained outside the business community's primary agenda of expanding the local economy and revitalizing downtown. In the 1970s, however, indigenous organizations in the city's black neighborhoods, aided by advocate planners and the federal government, began to assert their right to shape the planning of their neighborhoods.

7 The African American Planning Tradition in Birmingham

Although the 1970s mark the period in which Birmingham's black neighborhoods asserted their power to help guide the fate of their neighborhoods, the seeds for this change were planted decades earlier with the establishment of indigenous black neighborhood organizations that attempted to provide the public services that were denied by the white-controlled city government. These organizations are part of an African American planning tradition that enabled Birmingham's black neighborhoods to respond creatively and positively to their exclusion from the planning process.

The African American planning tradition in Birmingham, as well as other cities, stands in contrast to the much better publicized view of city planning as a government activity. When planning is seen as a government activity, as opposed to a broader-based community activity, the histories of planning primarily recount the histories of government actions in planning. Viewed as a government activity, the history of city planning in Birmingham was one of the key events recounted in earlier chapters: Warren Manning's *The City Plan of Birmingham*, published in 1919; the adoption of the city's first zoning ordinance in 1926; the 1925 Olmsted Brothers plan for the city's parks; the first forays into direct public investment in housing in the 1930s; the urban renewal projects of the 1950s and 1960s; and the city's first comprehensive plan of 1961. These are the kinds of typical guideposts that mark most histories of planning in U.S. cities.

Viewed from the perspective of the African American community in Birmingham, however, there is quite a different and less well known planning tradition. This tradition includes the black community's opposition to racial zoning in the 1920s; its determination to see that Smithfield Court was a development built to high standards; its courageous efforts to challenge racial zoning and move into neighborhoods where blacks were welcomed only by dynamite; its efforts to challenge the racial resegregation imposed by the Southside Medical Center urban renewal project of the 1950s; and its efforts to end segregation in the city's parks as well as other public facilities. In a sense, therefore, the African American planning tradition in Birmingham is an anti-planning tradition, one in which the black community found itself in opposition to plans made by the dominant white community that affected the black community.

In searching for an African American planning tradition in Birmingham, one must also look to the neighborhoods where blacks lived. For Birmingham blacks, necessity required them to develop their own institutions for the planning and implementation of public improvements in their neighborhoods. Operating either apart from or at odds with each other, Birmingham's white and black planning traditions maintained separate existences until they became intertwined in 1974 with the adoption of a Citizen Participation Plan. This plan has since become nationally recognized for the degree of citizen involvement in its planning and community development process.[1] The adopted Citizen Participation Plan represented a triumph of African American neighborhood-based planning over the top-down approach favored by the white planning regime because it placed significant responsibility for community development planning within the hands of Birmingham's neighborhoods, both black and white.

Historical Roots of African American Planning in Birmingham

Since at least the 1920s, black neighborhood-based organizations have existed in Birmingham. These neighborhood organizations are known in Birmingham as civic leagues. They were (and to a limited extent, continue to be) organizations established in black neighborhoods with the primary objective of improving the quality of life in the neighborhood, particularly with respect to basic public services, such as streets, public safety, parks, recreation, water and sewers, and community centers.[2] Civic leagues existed in black neighborhoods throughout Birmingham and Jefferson County. At least fifty-four Birmingham civic leagues are recorded as being active between 1945 and 1975, and an additional thirteen were located in Jefferson County black neighborhoods outside of Birmingham (see tables 7.1 and 7.2). In addition, in 1933, eleven civic leagues, all in the Birmingham area, founded the Alabama State Federation of Civic Leagues, an umbrella organizations for civic leagues.[3]

Civic leagues were the primary organizations in the black Birmingham community that defined membership on the basis of location. Unlike other organizations, they took in anyone who lived within a neighborhood.[4] Consequently, civic leagues operated within a set of specific neighborhood boundaries.[5] In the Woodland Park Civic League, which remains active, membership is defined as "all adult residents within the area bounded by Fourteenth Avenue on the north, the L and N Railroad tracks on the southeast, and a line extending adjacent to the south property line of the Elmwood Cemetery, Center Street on the east, and Montevallo Road on the west and surrounding areas."[6] To obtain funds, dues were charged to neighborhood residents, and block or street captains were assigned the task of collecting the money. The amount of dues varied but was typically between twenty-five cents and one dollar per month for each member. Individuals behind in their dues sacrificed their voting privileges.[7]

Given the importance of religion in the black community, it is not surprising that civic league meetings were typically conducted in neighborhood churches. Some leagues, such as the South Woodlawn Civic League, rotated their meetings in a variety of neighborhood churches, with an eye, evidently, toward avoiding identification with any single church.[8] Others, however, met at the same church. In the early 1950s, for example, the Grasselli Heights Civic League always met at the Bryant Chapel AME Church.[9] Finally, a minority of civic leagues had access to nonsectarian facilities. The Enon Ridge Civic League, for example, would meet at the Beulah Moore (later the Enon Ridge Civic Day) Nursery in the neighborhood.[10]

Activities of the civic leagues primarily focused on neighborhood improvement and relied chiefly on two key approaches: petitioning local government for improved services and self-help. Until the late 1960s, the former approach required the black civic leagues to approach the all-white Birmingham city government to request services for their neighborhood. This was by no means an easy experience. The Harriman Park Civic League waited four months to get an appointment with Birmingham Public Safety Commissioner Bull Connor.

Table 7.1. Birmingham civic leagues (date of founding in parentheses, where known)

Avondale Community Civic League	North Westside Civic League (1957)
Brownsville Civic League*	Norwood Civic League (merged with Druid Hills Civic League in 1970)*
Collegeville Civic League*	
Community Civic and Commercial League (1956)	Oak Ridge Civic League*
	Oxmoor Civic League
Druid Hills Civic League* (1968) (merged with Norwood Civic League in 1970)	Powderly Civic League* (1944)
	Powderly Hills Civic League (1955)
East Birmingham Civic League*	Pratt City Civic League (1925)
East Thomas Civic League*	Riley Station Civic League* (aka Riley and Travellick Civic League)
Enon Ridge Civic League*	
Ensley Civic League* (1932)	Roosevelt Civic League*
Evergreen Community Civic League*	Roseland Heights Civic League
Fountain Heights Civic League*	St. Marks, Rosewood North and West Civic League (1952) (aka Rosewood, St. Marks, and East Thomas Civic League)
Gate City Civic League*	
Grasselli Heights Civic League*	
Harriman Park Civic League* (1950)	Sand Ridge Civic League*
Hillman/Hillman Gardens Civic League*	Sherman Heights Civic League*
Honeysuckle Hills Civic League	Smithfield Civic League*
Hooper City Civic League*	South Elyton Civic League (1934)
Ishkooda Civic League (1969)	South Goldwire Civic League
Jones Valley Civic League*	South Woodlawn Civic League* (1966)
Kingston Civic League*	Tarpley City Civic League*
L and N City Civic League	Tittusville Civic League* (1966)
Martin Quarters Civic League	West Finley Avenue Civic League
Mason City Civic League*	West Goldwire Civic League*
Minnieville Civic League	West Oak Ridge Civic League*
North Birmingham Civic League*	Woodland Park Civic League* (1964)
North Ensley Civic League	Woodlawn Civic League*
North Pratt Civic League* (1954)	Wylam Heights Civic League*
Northside Civic League (1949)	Zion City Civic League* (1966)

Source: Birmingham World, 1945–75.

Note: List assumes 1999 boundaries of city. Hence, civic leagues such as Brownsville or Roosevelt that were formed prior to those neighborhoods being annexed to Birmingham are included in the list of Birmingham civic leagues.

* indicates existence of 1992 neighborhood association with same or similar name as reported in City of Birmingham, Citizen Participation Plan, April 21, 1992.

When the meeting finally took place, Connor kept his back turned to the petitioners until the league's president, Benjamin Greene, said that Connor could at least look at them. The league's representatives made their presentation but received no commitment from Connor.[11]

Even after Connor's departure in 1963 and the change in Birmingham's government (see chapter 6), civic league pleas could fall on deaf ears. As discussed in chapter 6, the business community directed the city's planning efforts, which focused on major bricks-and-mortar public improvement designed to revitalize the downtown and invigorate the local economy. In 1972, Preston Gadson, president of the Sherman Heights Civic League, located in the Ensley community, made several trips to city hall to petition for better municipal services, "but always without getting anything he asked for." Gadson had asked for equipment for a small park in the neighborhood but received only a small amount of what had been requested. Emory Jackson, the *Birmingham World*'s editor, wrote of this case, "The City of Birmingham can come up with proposals for the Civic Center, Birmingham Green, the Airport Expansion, equipment for the Police Department, and other projects, but the money runs out when it comes to the poor, Blacks and the unpowered."[12] Gadson's neighborhood, which could have been helped four years earlier by the failed Model Cities proposal, continued to suffer as Birmingham's priorities were shaped by the business-dominated agenda of Operation New Birmingham.

The other key civic league strategy was self-help. Faced with an unresponsive local government, civic leagues would provide their own public services or raise funds to pay for those services directly.

A number of civic leagues, for example, initiated neighborhood beautification campaigns. The Grasselli Heights Civic League worked to beautify the neighborhood by contacting owners who had not maintained vacant lots. In cases where lot owners did not cooperate, civic league members undertook the cleanup themselves, utilizing a heavy-duty lawnmower purchased with civic league funds.[13]

In other neighborhoods, civic leagues launched cleanup campaigns. In the spring of 1959, the Enon Ridge Civic League announced a cleanup campaign in March and Paint Up Month in June. Civic league president E. H. Fort announced that first, second, and third place prizes would be given for the best-kept yards. Fort also said that the civic league's community development committee reported that

Table 7.2. Birmingham civic leagues by year of founding

1920s (1 Civic league)

  Pratt City Civic League (1925)

1930s (2 Civic leagues)

  Ensley Civic League (1932)

  South Elyton Civic League (1934)

1940s (2 Civic leagues)

  Northside Civic League (1949)

  Powderly Civic League (1944)

1950s (5 Civic leagues)

  Community Civic and Commercial League (1956)

  Harriman Park Civic League (1950)

  North Pratt Civic League (1954)

  North Westside Civic League (1957)

  Powderly Hills Civic League (1955)

1960s (6 Civic leagues)

  Druid Hills Civic League (1968)

  Ishkooda Civic League (1969)

  South Woodlawn Civic League (1966)

  Tittusville Civic League (1966)

  Woodland Park Civic League (1964)

  Zion City Civic League (1966)

Note: In addition to the Pratt City and Ensley civic leagues, the following Birmingham civic leagues formed the Alabama State Federation of Colored Civic Leagues in 1933: Enon Ridge, Woodlawn, East Thomas, Avondale, Roosevelt, North Birmingham, and Smithfield.

Birmingham city government "promised favorable consideration" to the league's request for street and traffic lights.[14]

The Mason City Civic League announced a Cleaning Up, Paint Up campaign for June 1957. The household making "the most noticeable improvement" would receive an award at the end of the drive.[15] In late summer of 1967, the Tittusville Civic League sponsored a Clean Up Project, in which special attention was to be given to "dead end streets and alleys."[16]

The Harriman Park, Fountain Heights, and Roseland Heights Civic

Leagues each constructed community centers for their neighborhoods.[17] The Harriman Park Civic League raised $1,500 to purchase two lots in 1972 for the community center that was eventually built with Birmingham Community Development Block Grant funds.[18] The Fountain Heights Recreational Center, opened in 1975, was located in the Fountain Heights neighborhood, which twenty years earlier had begun to undergo racial change and by 1970 was nearly all black.[19] The Fountain Heights Center's purpose was to tie together four Northside neighborhoods—Fountain Heights, Enon Ridge, and two neighborhoods lying just to the east of Fountain Heights, Druid Hills and Norwood, both of which were undergoing racial change in the 1960s and 1970s.[20] Charlie Pierce, president of the Druid Hills–Norwood Civic League, placed an ad in the *Birmingham World* asking for support for the Fountain Heights recreation center, declaring that these Northside neighborhoods had decent park facilities, but none were usable in cold or rainy weather: "The youth of the Northside need indoor basketball facilities and indoor skating rinks. Where there is provision for recreational facilities, the city is making a solid attempt to provide an alternative to antisocial behavior on the part of youth. Where there is no such provision, the city is not making this solid attempt."[21]

Other civic leagues focused on improving the recreational opportunities in their neighborhood. In the early 1940s, the founder and head of the Alabama State Federation of Civic Leagues, W. L. McAlpine, was instrumental in persuading the City of Birmingham to create the first city-owned park for blacks, Memorial Park, dedicated on May 31, 1942.[22] In 1951, the South Elyton Civic League sponsored a fundraising campaign to light Memorial Park in hopes of fighting juvenile delinquency by offering recreation to youth both day and night. Other civic leagues also attempted to obtain recreational facilities and parks for their neighborhoods, including the Honeysuckle Hills, Enon Ridge, North Pratt (which opened a playground in 1956), Riley and Travellick, Mason City, and Powderly Hills Civic Leagues. The Powderly Hills Civic League held fundraisers to provide lights for the neighborhood baseball park.[23] In 1973, the Woodland Park Civic League negotiated with the Birmingham School Board to use the playground facilities at the neighborhood school. This required the civic league to take out an insurance policy.[24]

The Beulah Moore Day Nursery was an important community

facility in the Enon Ridge neighborhood. In 1952, the Birmingham Community Chest discontinued its support for the nursery. In response, "furious Enon Ridge residents" called a community mass meeting that was sponsored by the Enon Ridge Civic League. Joining with the Tuggle Hill Redemption Corporation and the Alabama State Colored Federation of Civic Leagues, the civic league explored ideas for keeping the nursery open.[25] Within the year, the Enon Ridge Civic League took over operating the nursery, and by spring of 1953, the Enon Ridge Civic Day Nursery had been licensed by the Alabama Department of Health. It was one of only two black nurseries licensed by the state and the only one in Jefferson County.[26]

Other civic leagues worked on public safety issues. Several civic leagues located in what is today Southwest Birmingham had faced, prior to their annexation into Birmingham, serious shortages of fire hydrants. In the 1950s, the Grasselli Heights neighborhood had no fire hydrants.[27] Consequently, the Grasselli Heights Civic League devoted attention to petitioning Jefferson County public officials for the installation of fire hydrants and to raising money to purchase them after a house had burned in that neighborhood.[28] The Hillman Civic League, located in a neighborhood near Grasselli Heights, also needed fire hydrants and in 1948 initiated a fundraising effort to purchase them, as well as streetlights.[29] In 1954, the nearby Mason City Civic League also began planning to obtain fire hydrants for the neighborhood.[30] As in Hillman, the Riley and Travellick Civic League needed streetlights, and in September 1955 it met with city officials to ask for streetlights for the neighborhood.[31]

Water and sewer issues were also addressed by civic leagues. In the Harriman Park neighborhood to which he moved in 1948, Benjamin Greene found unpaved streets, no sanitary sewers, and one water meter serving all the residents of his street.[32] After the neighborhood was annexed by the City of Birmingham in 1949, the Harriman Park Civic League successfully petitioned city government to obtain suitable water mains, sanitary sewers, and a gas line.

As discussed in chapter 1, storm drainage was also a problem in black neighborhoods, with open ditches creating flooding problems when heavy rains occurred. The Jones Valley Civic League petitioned city government to address the neighborhood's drainage problems but did not have much success until David Vann became mayor in 1975.[33]

Storm drainage was a key problem also targeted by the Harriman Park Civic League, but as in Jones Valley, it was not until the 1970s that the neighborhood was able to obtain adequate storm sewers.[34]

Several civic leagues sought basic improvements to streets and transit. In the late 1940s, the Riley and Travellick Civic League initiated a fundraising campaign for street and drainage improvements. Nearly $4,200 was raised through such means as direct solicitation of residents and a plate-dinner sale.[35] On February 1, 1949, the Riley and Travellick Civic League began a campaign to raise $5,000 for street improvements. Seventeen street solicitors, twelve of whom were women in the neighborhood, were assigned to solicit their neighbors on seven streets, with the goal of raising the $5,000 by March 15. At weekly meetings held at Noble Chapel C.M.E. Church, the street solicitors reported on their fundraising progress. By the May 3, 1949, meeting, the civic league had raised $4,188.83 for street improvements. The civic league also sponsored a plate dinner at which $79.50 was raised to purchase a pipe for a neighborhood street. The neighborhood, which at that time had not been annexed into Birmingham, was rewarded for its fundraising efforts by a visit from Jefferson County engineer E. H. Gilmore, who "commended the organization for their splendid work they are doing in soliciting money for street improvements."[36]

A nearby civic league, located in the Grasselli Heights neighborhood, also faced the problem of unpaved streets and in 1948 announced that it had raised $2,000 for its street improvement project.[37]

The Riley and Travellick Civic League again mounted a street improvement campaign in the late 1950s. The civic league encouraged homeowners to contribute to the street improvement fund and also reported that stop signs would be placed in the neighborhood. As money was solicited, the civic league's standing committee scheduled a meeting with Birmingham city officials to discuss lights, sewage, and bridges in the neighborhood.[38] At the same time, the civic league was pushing voter education and registration. On June 30, 1957, the civic league invited Reverend Fred L. Shuttlesworth to speak, thereby demonstrating its willingness to participate in more general civil rights activity. By the fall of 1957, when the street improvement campaign was ended, the civic league's president had announced that Thirty-seventh Street "had been worked" and that Myrtle Avenue and Fortieth Street in the neighborhood had been paved. Also, the civic league's efforts to solicit city assistance had paid off as stop signs and traffic lights had been installed in the neighborhood. The traffic lights were installed at six intersections. By December 1957, the civic league reported that $1,467.20 had been spent on street improvements and that a balance of $1,189.49 was still available.[39]

The Honeysuckle Hills Civic League, organized in a 180-family neighborhood located about three miles southwest of downtown Birmingham, petitioned city government and transit officials to obtain bus service for the neighborhood. Working with the Honeysuckle Hills Housewives League, the civic league reported that after many attempts, they had received "favorable answers" to their requests. The housewives league was also pushing to get adequate telephone service for their neighborhood, with only one family having phone service.[40]

Despite the fact that black neighborhoods were often located near areas zoned for industrial and commercial uses, zoning was not an issue that civic leagues emphasized. By the 1960s, however, as increasing numbers of blacks moved into formerly white neighborhoods, black residents learned that their new neighborhoods were sometimes zoned for multifamily dwellings. Although such zoning had been in place prior to racial transition, it did not become an issue until neighborhood racial change began and brought with it increased developer interest in capitalizing on the process by developing apartments in these neighborhoods.[41]

In 1972, the black residents of Druid Hills and Norwood, formerly white neighborhoods just north of downtown Birmingham, learned that these areas, especially Druid Hills, had been substantially zoned for multifamily housing since 1926. In response, the Druid Hills–Norwood Civic League organized a successful petition campaign to have the neighborhood downzoned from a multifamily to a single-family designation. Although the civic league was opposed by the Birmingham Real Estate Board, a majority of Birmingham City Council members supported the zoning change. Part of the civic league's success was attributable to the fact that the city council then included attorney Arthur Shores, Birmingham's first black city council member. According to Emory Jackson's account, Shores's "probing questions" of the proponents and opponents of the Druid Hills zoning change "clarified the real issue."[42]

The successful Druid Hills–Norwood Civic League petition was vindication for Emory Jackson's long-held belief that black electoral power was the key to influencing Birmingham city government and obtaining improvements for black neighborhoods. In a speech before the Alabama State Federation of Colored Civic Leagues in early 1945, Jackson was described as calling "attention to the need for increased voting as a means of improving community levels."[43] Twenty-seven years later, in remarking on the city council's positive response to the Druid Hills–Norwood Civic League's petitioners, Jackson wrote of the changes that were beginning to happen in Birmingham: "The new interest in improving neighborhoods through concern for families and homes ought to help Birmingham. . . . What is happening at the City Council meetings these days obviously have their [sic] beginnings at the ballot box. One of the largest concentration of voters is in the Norwood Druid area."[44] As discussed in chapter 6, however, black participation in twentieth-century elections in Birmingham was a long time coming. Since the 1930s, the black community had sought to increase black voter registration and participation and the civic leagues played a significant role in helping blacks to overcome the obstacles to registration and voting.[45]

In 1949, the North Birmingham Civic League sponsored a citizenship clinic and was pleased to report that seventy-six of eighty residents participating in the clinic had been able to register to vote.[46] In 1960, the Enon Ridge Civic League revitalized its voter registration campaign by organizing "traveling voter-registration clinics" to provide "house-to-house workshops" on the procedures for registering and voting.[47] The South Elyton Civic League, located in an established neighborhood about two miles southwest of downtown, had paved streets and sewers, as well as Memorial Park. Consequently, in the 1950s and early 1960s, it focused its attention on registering and preparing black voters. In the early 1960s, J. Mason Davis would speak at South Elyton Civic League events on political issues and, using a practice voting machine, instructed residents on the mechanics of voting.[48] At least twelve other civic leagues also devoted a portion of their efforts to encouraging voter registration and voting.[49]

In general, residents of Birmingham's black neighborhoods responded to the lack of public services by creating their own neighborhood-based organizations to address these deficiencies. The record of these organizations was mixed. They were up against a local government, particularly before the change in 1963, that was not elected by the black vote and was generally uninterested in spending public money in black neighborhoods. As discussed in chapter 1, the disparity between similarly situated black and white neighborhoods in the quality of local public services was substantial; therefore, a movement based on self-help and vote-less persuasion is likely to produce a mixed record of success.

Moreover, at least one key black opinion center in Birmingham, the *Birmingham World,* argued that the civic leagues were sometimes too accommodating to segregation as they focused their energies primarily on obtaining separate but equal, or at least comparable, public services. At a time when *Birmingham World* editor Emory Jackson was growing increasingly dissatisfied with local black leadership, particularly in the Birmingham branch of the NAACP, the *World's* "Around the Town" column commented on a 1951 South Elyton Civic League Mayor of Tittusville contest designed to raise funds for recreational equipment and improvements for Memorial Park. The description was followed by a note that said:

> While such money is being raised Negroes are wrongly denied the use of the four city-owned golf courses, admitted only by permits to Vulcan Park, denied an opportunity to use Kiddyland Park and provided only makeshift parks. Yet these civic leagues apparently continue to raise money to bolster these racial discriminations instead of using funds to open up new opportunities.[50]

Similarly, the column criticized the Enon Ridge Civic League in early 1952 for focusing its energies on saving the Beulah Moore Day Nursery and not looking at the larger picture:

> Despite efforts of the league to save the Beulah Moore Day Nursery, they are likely to go for naught. League members should ask some of those leaders in the save the nursery fight whether they are qualified voters. The league has an ambitious program for recreational facilities under private funds sponsorship. However these leaders are overlooking one of their best weapons—the proposed equal schools suit being worked up by the NAACP. Tuggle School [the public elementary school for black children in Enon Ridge] is over-

crowded with no gym, no playground, no lunch room and etc. A number of timid leaders are afraid of going to bat for their children where it will help most.[51]

The *Birmingham World* also criticized the Enon Ridge Civic League for paying too little attention to voter registration. Several months after criticizing the "timid leaders" of the Enon Ridge Civic League, the "Around the Town" column commented, "The Enon Ridge Civic League is having interesting weekly discussions but none of them reportedly promoting voter registration."[52]

The Enon Ridge Civic League's efforts to save the nursery reflected a tradition of self-help that was vitally important to the black community in Birmingham. Wrapped as it was in the self-help philosophy espoused by Booker T. Washington, that tradition encouraged the civic leagues to lose sight, just as Washington's vision lost sight, of the need to end the systemic discrimination that prevented blacks from moving to a position of equality with white Americans.[53]

The *Birmingham World*'s criticism of the civic leagues came at a time of organizational crisis in black Birmingham. The NAACP Birmingham branch, whose membership had grown dramatically throughout most of the 1940s as the branch's leadership spearheaded the attack on racial zoning, had experienced a sharp decline in membership in the late 1940s and early 1950s. One factor explaining that decline was the increasing violence visited on blacks by whites, particularly the racial bombings (see chapter 3) that sought to terrorize blacks attempting to move into white neighborhoods.[54]

Although the civic leagues may have lacked the militancy that Jackson felt they needed to combat racial discrimination, they were effective. They provided a positive response to the inadequate public services faced by Birmingham's black neighborhoods and to a political situation where blacks had no real power. Because of limitations placed on black voter registration, no immediate prospect of exercising any real or direct influence on local politicians existed other than through the civic leagues. By the early 1970s, when Birmingham's traditional white- and elite-dominated approach to planning came under question, civic leagues were prepared to put forth an alternative, neighborhood-based approach to planning and community development. This was an approach built upon decades of African American

experience at organizing black neighborhoods for community improvement.

The 1970s: The Role of the Black Community in
Shaping Birmingham's Citizen Participation Plan

The 1970s began with two nonblack organizations attempting to work
with the civic leagues to improve the quality of life in Birmingham's
black neighborhoods. These two organizations had contrasting agen-
das, and their interaction with black neighborhoods greatly influenced
the design of Birmingham's 1974 Citizen Participation Plan.

In the late 1960s and early 1970s, Operation New Birmingham
(ONB) continued to expand the role begun in 1963 (see chapter 6)
as the business community's primary organization for organizing
Birmingham's city planning and economic development, especially
downtown revitalization. ONB created the Community Affairs Committee (CAC) in response to growing black concern about police brutality and other racial inequities that persisted in Birmingham in the
late 1960s.[55] The CAC's creation was prompted by an April 1969 incident in Ensley in which two white Birmingham police officers arrested
a black man on a charge of disorderly conduct. Witnesses claimed that
the policemen beat the suspect as well as two black women who were
at the scene. The president of historically black Miles College, Dr. Lucius Pitts, who had participated in the negotiations to end the spring
1963 demonstrations, responded to the incident and student concerns
at his college by organizing an April 14 meeting of Birmingham's black
leadership to discuss police brutality. The group took action by sending a telegram to local police and elected officials demanding an end to
police brutality; greater citizen oversight of police activities; and the
appointment of blacks as judges, members of the city's personnel
board, and lawyers for the city's legal staff and the district attorney's
staff.[56]

The group also demanded an immediate meeting with city and
county officials, who responded by calling a meeting for April 16. After listening to an expanded list of fourteen demands, city and county
officials spoke defensively, claiming that incidents of police miscon-
duct were being handled appropriately. ONB's president, Albert Mills,
proposed that a committee be established that would bring whites and

blacks together to fashion solutions to the continuing racial problems in the city. On April 19, Mills announced the creation of the Community Affairs Committee that would consist of nine white leaders, nine black leaders, and nine local government officials. Its purpose, said Mills, would be "to involve the entire citizenship in a responsible redress of the frictions of today's complicated society."[57]

As a sign that relations between blacks and whites were shifting, black leaders were affronted by the appointment by whites of the nine black CAC members. Dr. James Montgomery and Calvin Woods were dispatched to tell white leaders, "we were going to appoint our own leaders." The incident, according to one historian, "graphically depicted the rise in a new kind of black leadership in Birmingham, not radical in the traditional sense of the word, but insistent that the black community determine its own direction."[58] The CAC's first meeting took place on May 2, 1969, and subsequently the committee met every Monday for breakfast.

Soon after its formation, the CAC began its work in Birmingham's black neighborhoods by responding to residents of Collegeville, a black neighborhood in North Birmingham, who had approached Birmingham's mayor and city council for help in addressing neighborhood crime. Working with Collegeville neighborhood leaders, CAC subcommittee members sought action from local government agencies to address a list of fourteen problems that had been identified by the neighborhood.[59] Building on this experience, ONB, through the Birmingham Regional Planning Commission, obtained in 1970 U.S. Department of Housing and Urban Development comprehensive planning assistance funds. Staff was hired, and the Collegeville program was expanded to a broader Neighborhood Planning Program that, by 1971, included sixteen other neighborhoods.[60] In each case, neighborhood representatives met with ONB staff members, prioritized problems, and, in conjunction with ONB staff members and CAC subcommittee members, met with public officials to request actions to address these problems.[61] In many instances of working with civic leagues, ONB's Neighborhood Planning Program essentially carried on the efforts of the civic leagues by focusing on obtaining improved public services through solicitation of appropriate government agencies.[62] The major difference was that civic leagues and other black neighborhood groups now had the clout of ONB and the CAC behind them. According to an unnamed ONB official, public agency heads "realize CAC has as strong a representation as any group as far as influence is concerned."[63] Through the Neighborhood Planning Program ONB had further expanded its business-led role in public affairs by assuming responsibility for helping neighborhoods get better public services from city hall.

At about the same time that ONB was expanding its Neighborhood Planning Program, Greater Birmingham Ministries (GBM), a church-based, ecumenical organization, began efforts to achieve "systems change" in Birmingham's black neighborhoods. In the early 1970s, GBM established the Block Partnership Program, in which it matched largely white, suburban churches with primarily black neighborhoods in Birmingham. GBM often worked with neighborhood civic leagues, including groups in the same North Birmingham area where ONB had begun its Neighborhood Planning Program. In contrast to the downtown-oriented ONB, however, GBM's neighborhood initiatives were led at this time by a United Methodist Church minister, George Quiggle, whose approach to community organization was influenced by the writings of Saul Alinsky as well as his own theological beliefs. Under the Block Partnership Program, resources from both the suburban church and the black neighborhood were used to address needs identified by neighborhood residents.[64]

In the summer of 1973, HUD's Birmingham area director, Jon Will Pitts, wrote a memo to Birmingham mayor George Seibels that propelled the city, ONB, GBM, and the city's neighborhoods to redefine the role played by black, as well as white, neighborhoods in shaping the city's planning and community development agenda. At this time, prior to passage of the 1974 Housing and Community Development Act, HUD continued to certify the Workable Programs of cities seeking HUD assistance. Eight months earlier, in November 1972, responding to citizen protest over ONB's perceived role as an exclusive representative of community groups, Birmingham's city council tried to clarify its contract with ONB so that it did not appear that ONB stood between citizens and city government.[65] Unsatisfied with this change, however, Pitts wrote Seibels in July 1973 that the city needed to revise its community development process so that citizens will have direct access to the mayor's office; so they will be "integrally involved, on a con-

tinuous basis, in all phases of the community development process";
and so that citizen participation is "under direct City control."[66]

Since 1966, ONB's members, consisting of over two hundred leaders from the private and public sectors, had served as the city's Citizens' Advisory Committee in compliance with HUD's Workable Program requirements.[67] HUD's requirement that citizen participation be
under direct control of city government and that it provide citizens
direct access to city hall had the effect of placing ONB's role in citizen participation in doubt. HUD also made clear that ONB's Neighborhood Planning Program was not a sufficient substitute for direct
citizen involvement in community development. HUD area office director Pitts wrote the Birmingham Regional Planning Commission—
the agency through which ONB received HUD funds for the Neighborhood Planning Program—that the program was "more effective in
dealing with complaints than in involving citizens in the community
development process."[68]

Pitts's letter forced the City of Birmingham to revise its citizen participation program as well as to revise the role that ONB played in that
program.[69] In response to HUD, Birmingham's Community Development Department prepared a three-tier Citizen Participation Plan under which citizens in each of Birmingham's ninety-one neighborhoods
could participate in their area's Neighborhood Citizens Committee
and elect officers for their committee. These officers would also serve
as representatives to a Community Citizens Committee (the middle
tier), which represented each of the sixteen communities in Birmingham.[70] Each of the sixteen communities elected a chairman, who sat
on a twenty-five-member citywide Citizens Advisory Board (the top
tier). The remaining nine members were appointed by Birmingham's
mayor. Under the proposal, ONB had "primary field responsibility for
developing, organizing, and maintaining viable citizen participation
groups in the neighborhoods and communities throughout Birmingham."[71]

Birmingham mayor George Seibels publicly announced the Citizen Participation Plan in January 1974 and instructed the city's Community Development Department to put it into effect immediately.[72]
Although City Commissioner David Vann proposed an alternative citizen participation plan, his call for a public hearing on citizen partic-

ipation was rejected by a council majority in early February 1974.[73] Soon thereafter, three Community Development Department staff members, along with three ONB staff members, began the process of taking the new Citizen Participation Plan to the neighborhoods.

After ranking Birmingham communities by the order in which they should be contacted about the Citizen Participation Plan, ONB recommended that the process begin in the predominantly white Woodlawn community, located on the city's east side. The Community Development Department's staff, however, selected North Birmingham as the inaugural community for the program, even though ONB had slated that community as the fourth one to be visited.[74]

Chuck Lewis, a former Peace Corps volunteer who as a city planning graduate student at Virginia Polytechnic Institute had written a research paper on citizen participation, helped staff the Community Development Department's citizen participation effort. He was concerned that the Citizen Participation Plan was too dependent upon mayor-appointed nominees and that ONB participation made it more difficult to sell citizen participation in Birmingham's black neighborhoods.

Several of ONB's leaders, including its president and several vice presidents (one of whom was black millionaire A. G. Gaston), had formed the Birmingham Action Group (BAG) to promote the candidacy of two conservative white city council incumbents and black incumbent Arthur Shores. They were being challenged in the fall 1973 municipal elections by three black candidates. ONB rented tables and chairs for one of three telephone centers, each located in a white neighborhood. Through a telephone and media campaign, BAG sought to reelect the incumbents, who, according to a *Birmingham Post-Herald* editorial, "are notable for their cautious approach to social problems and for their willingness to go along with programs which often require heavy expenditures for projects which are largely civic cosmetics." ONB jumped into the election because it wanted to assure that the Birmingham City Council would continue to support the business-oriented capital expenditures for which it had begun advocating ten years earlier in the Design for Progress (see chapter 6). The effort succeeded as the increase in the white vote helped the white incumbents win reelection.[75]

Given this history, Lewis knew that ONB's involvement in citizen participation would be suspect in the black community.[76] Consequently, he went to Reverend George Quiggle, whom he had first known when Lewis worked as a community organizer several years earlier in a black public housing development. Lewis, knowing that Quiggle and GBM had many contacts in Birmingham's neighborhoods, told Quiggle of his concern about the mayor's Citizen Participation Plan and asked if there wasn't something that could be done.[77] According to Quiggle, "Chuck didn't have to say much; we knew what to do."[78]

On February 28, 1974, community development and ONB staff met in the black Collegeville neighborhood with twenty-one representatives of that neighborhood.[79] Among the neighborhood leaders attending the meeting were several individuals who had been local leaders in ONB's pilot Neighborhood Planning Program, including Benjamin Greene, president of the Harriman Park Civic League, and Lula Menefee, president of the Collegeville–Harriman Park Coordinating Council.[80] At the meeting, the neighborhood representatives asked questions about a number of issues: What would ONB's role be in the Citizen Participation Plan? Why did the mayor have the power to appoint one-third of the citywide Citizens Advisory Board? Why not use existing groups to represent the neighborhoods?[81]

Clearly, the neighborhood leaders at the Collegeville meeting were not happy with the strong role played by ONB and the mayor in the citizen participation program and the relatively weak role played by existing neighborhood groups. These concerns were further expressed at a general meeting held in Collegeville on March 7, 1974, attended by about 125 residents of that neighborhood.[82] A similar meeting took place that night in Fountain Heights in North Birmingham. According to the *Birmingham News,* speakers at both meetings stressed that the mayor's Citizen Participation Plan assumed that the black community was unorganized, thereby ignoring the community organizations already in place. According to this account, civic league presidents attended the meetings, one of them asking: "Why can't we use the organization we already have? Why do YOU have to organize us?" Harriman Park Civic League president Benjamin Greene said, "We don't want an extension of City Hall into our neighborhoods."[83] The board of directors of the Alabama State Federation of Civic Leagues opposed the mayor's Citizen Participation Plan "because no one has seen fit to include the grassroots leaders to the top level position of this program to help formulate the policy and goal. We also feel that it is useless to organize another civic organization in a community that is already organized with a civic league with qualified people who know their community needs and can get their own priority."[84]

The neighborhood residents at the March 7 meetings called for a public hearing on the mayor's Citizen Participation Plan.[85] Five days later, Birmingham's city council, at the urging of Mayor Seibels, called for a public hearing to be held on April 1, 1974.[86] Collegeville neighborhood leaders, including Benjamin Greene, Lula Menefee, and Rosa Kent, who held a number of neighborhood leadership positions, called on their neighbors to attend the April 1 public hearing.[87] Black neighborhood leaders prepared for the public hearing by meeting at Evergreen Baptist Church. Assisting in the organization of these meetings were Reverend George Quiggle and Greater Birmingham Ministries.[88] Through the presence of a spin-off organization, the Legal Evaluation and Action Project (LEAP), GBM's organizing assistance had also been evident at the March 7 Collegeville and Fountain Heights meetings.[89] At Evergreen Baptist Church, equipped with fifteen typewriters, black neighborhood leaders planned their presentations for the April 1 public hearing.[90]

Because of an expected large turnout, city officials moved the April 1 public hearing from city council chambers to Birmingham's Boutwell Auditorium. Over five hundred people attended the meeting, thirty of whom spoke. None of the thirty speakers favored the mayor's Citizen Participation Plan. Most of the speakers came from Birmingham's black neighborhoods, and at least eight of the thirty were associated with various civic leagues.[91]

Generally, the speakers reiterated what had been said publicly at the meetings in the Collegeville and Fountain Heights neighborhoods. According to a *Birmingham News* article, "the most frequent complaint was that a city-sponsored network would displace already established and trusted organizations and might produce groups less responsive to needs of citizens now represented by organizations of their own choosing."[92] Birmingham's Community Development Department staff found that after the perceived lack of citizen input, the second-most frequently cited concern was the impact that the mayor's Citizen Participation Plan would have on existing neighborhood organizations. Other frequently cited concerns focused on the role of ONB; the impact the three-level Citizen Participation Plan would have on direct access to city government; concern with the mayor's authority to appoint nine members to the Citizens Advisory Board; and concern that traditional neighborhoods were not identified in the plan and were grouped with other neighborhoods on maps prepared by Birmingham's planners.[93]

Given the strong sentiments expressed at the April 1 public hearing, Birmingham's Community Development Department staff began incorporating citizen concerns into a revised plan. Chuck Lewis and his staff organized a follow-up citizens meeting on April 25, 1974, to which the thirty speakers at the April 1 public hearing and others were invited. Based on comments made on April 1, the approximately eighty individuals attending this follow-up meeting were divided into five groups, each of which focused on one of the major issues identified at the public hearing. The Community Development Department staff then used the comments made at this meeting to revise the Citizen Participation Plan.[94]

By June 27, 1974, the Community Development Department had revised the Citizen Participation Plan, generally following the recommendations made by the participants in the April 1 and April 25 meetings. ONB's involvement with citizen participation had been jettisoned; instead, Community Development Department staff would work with neighborhood groups. The new plan also called for all citywide Citizens Advisory Board members to be elected by community representatives; the mayor would no longer have the power to appoint any members. Existing neighborhood organizations, such as the civic leagues, were directly encouraged to participate in the Citizen Participation Program. The new plan kept the three-tier concept but made it clear that going through channels was unnecessary if citizens or neighborhoods wanted to go straight to city hall. Finally, the Community Development Department staff pledged to work with local citizens to determine the names and boundaries of the city's neighborhoods, each of which, under the plan, would continue to have a Neighborhood Citizens Committee, with officers elected by neighborhood residents.[95]

With the Citizen Participation Plan rewritten, the Birmingham Community Development Department staff completed the job they had previously begun of soliciting citizen opinion on the names and boundaries of Birmingham's neighborhoods. City staff interviewed citizens and met with neighborhood organizations to obtain information on residents' perceptions of neighborhood and community names and boundaries.[96] As a result of this effort, city staff developed a list of eighty-six neighborhoods, thirty-two of which were not among the ninety neighborhoods presented by the city in its initial Citizen Participation Plan.[97]

The city staff's careful work in obtaining citizen input helped to obtain support for the revised Citizen Participation Plan. Tony Harrison, president of the Enon Ridge Civic League, said that the city had, for the first time, placed on a map the oldest and most prestigious black neighborhood in Birmingham—Enon Ridge.[98] Benjamin Greene, Harriman Park Civic League president, said that the revised Citizen Participation Plan gave a neighborhood two things: a voice in what would happen in the neighborhood and an ability to identify its own borders.[99]

As a result, black neighborhoods, as well as white neighborhoods, were to be recognized by the names and boundaries their residents ascribed to them. In addition to Enon Ridge, eleven other black neighborhoods with civic leagues that were not on the original Citizen Participation Plan neighborhood map appeared on the revised map.[100] Collegeville, which had appeared on the existing city map as two neighborhoods, Douglasville and Hudson Park, now appeared with the boundaries and name known by the residents of that neighborhood.[101] In at least several instances, the neighborhood boundaries delineated under the revised Citizen Participation Plan corresponded to the boundaries previously employed by the civic leagues in those neighborhoods.[102]

As a result of these changes, Birmingham's black neighborhoods reflected the historical identities that their residents, often through the civic leagues, had given to them. Of the fifty-four civic leagues that have existed in Birmingham, thirty-six have the same name or a very similar name as neighborhood associations that are identified in the 1992 Citizen Participation Plan list of Birmingham neighborhoods (see tables 7.1 and 7.2).[103]

With these changes, Birmingham's black community switched its position on the Citizen Participation Plan from opposition to support. Birmingham's city council, however, had put the revised Citizen Participation Plan on hold during the summer of 1974. Soon after the Housing Act of 1974 was signed into law in August 1974, three city council members attended a National League of Cities conference in Atlanta on the act and provisions of the new Community Development Block Grant (CDBG) program. Having been told that cities would need a citizen participation plan in order to participate in the CDBG program, the three council members recognized that the city had prepared a citizen participation plan that simply needed to be adopted.

Within a week of their return to Birmingham, David Vann, one of the city council members attending the Atlanta meeting, called for a public hearing to review the revised Citizen Participation Plan.[104] At this public hearing, held October 1, 1974, the new plan was well received by the public, and the city council ratified it one week later.[105] Several weeks later, the eighty-five neighborhoods delineated in the Citizen Participation Plan each held elections for neighborhood association officers. In at least sixteen of these neighborhoods, elected officers included individuals who also participated in the neighborhood's civic leagues.[106]

The African American planning tradition in Birmingham was shaped by the circumstances of discrimination experienced by residents within the city's black neighborhoods. The roots of this tradition go back at least to the 1920s and 1930s and consist of a rich network of neighborhood-based organizations that were formed to provide or petition for basic public services to the residents of their neighborhoods. By the 1970s, when the City of Birmingham was forced by HUD to reform its elite-dominated approach to planning, its attempts to retain a top-down participation process controlled by the business-led Operation New Birmingham were thwarted by a black community whose planning history was enriched by a tradition of neighborhood self-determination. The actions of Birmingham's black neighborhoods in shaping the 1974 Citizen Participation Plan were aided by HUD's intervention, the city's Community Development Department's advocacy planning, and the community organizing efforts of Greater Birmingham Ministries. Without the involvement of the black community, however, these outside forces could not, by themselves, have created the firestorm of reaction in the spring of 1974 that resulted in the revision of the mayor's original plan. Instead, this energy and passion came from a community with a rich tradition of community planning that finally had the opportunity to impose its vision of planning on the larger community.

8 The Evolution of Black Neighborhood Empowerment

With adoption of the Citizen Participation Plan in 1974, Birmingham had reversed the city's longtime tradition of denying its black citizens the opportunity to participate in the planning process. But the question remained as to whether the representation that the city's residents, white and black, had obtained through the Citizen Participation Program would result in the city's neighborhoods obtaining significant influence in the planning process. In the 1970s, Birmingham's black residents were able to achieve a degree of influence they had not had before. By 1979, when the city elected its first black mayor, Richard Arrington, the black community had established itself as a voice in determining the degree to which city resources would be used to benefit the city's neighborhoods.

The Black Community and the Red Mountain Expressway

As discussed in chapter 5, the interstate highway system in Birmingham had significant impacts on the city's black neighborhoods. Despite expressed concerns about how the interstates were affecting black neighborhoods, the black community generally had no influence in the 1950s and 1960s on the location of the interstates. In the 1970s, this would change as the residents of Central City public housing project succeeded in redirecting a federal highway that would have taken their homes.

Plans for building the Red Mountain Expressway had begun in the 1950s. The Red Mountain Expressway was designed to enable traffic from the affluent Over the Mountain suburbs of Mountain Brook and Homewood, lying south and southeast of downtown, to more easily traverse Red Mountain (see map 1.1). Red Mountain had been a challenge to commuting since those suburbs were developed in the 1920s, but especially after World War II when the population of these two Shades Valley communities grew apace.[1] The city's 1952 *Preliminary Report* commended a 1945 Red Mountain Tunnel report and urged that engineering studies for a tunnel be prepared. In 1955, the state legislature created the Red Mountain Tunnel Authority.[2]

While the authority looked to the development of a toll-financed tunnel, passage of the Interstate Highway Act in 1956 encouraged local and state officials to look at federal funding of a Red Mountain highway.[3] Moreover, the Alabama Highway Department announced its support for a cut through Red Mountain rather than a tunnel.[4] In the spring of 1958, tentative plans for Interstate 65, Birmingham's north-south interstate, featured a route, running along Twenty-sixth Street, that directly connected Mountain Brook and Homewood with downtown Birmingham via the Red Mountain cut.[5] Although this route served the commuting interests of these neighborhoods, it also entailed the clearing of significant areas of downtown Birmingham, thereby engendering opposition from an ad hoc committee of downtown professional and business leaders and property owners. E. T. Brown Jr., an attorney and head of the temporary committee, contended that "The 26th-st route would destroy hospitals, parks, schools, and low-rent public housing."[6] The public housing to which Brown was referring was the Central City public housing development, built in 1941 for white families. The 910-unit housing project was located three blocks east of Birmingham's city hall.

Brown's committee looked to an alternative route that ran along Green Springs Highway and took Interstate 65 along the western, rather than the eastern, edge of downtown.[7] After considering both corridors, the State Highway Department announced in May 1958 that Interstate 65 would run west of downtown along Green Springs Highway, citing $43,800,000 in lower costs along with the concern that the Twenty-sixth Street routing generated more traffic than downtown Birmingham could handle. As noted in chapter 5, the routing of Interstate 65 along the western edge of Birmingham's downtown also took it through a predominantly black neighborhood. Consequently, protest from Birmingham downtown business interests resulted in the relocation of the city's north-south interstate to a primarily black neighborhood.

To meet the needs of the Over the Mountain commuters, the highway department also proposed building an expressway directly connecting Mountain Brook and Homewood with downtown Birmingham.[8] Although adjustments were made to avoid running the Over the Mountain connector through the public and private properties identified by the Brown committee, the highway department's new proposal—by 1961 dubbed the Red Mountain Freeway and soon thereafter the Red Mountain Expressway—remained on a Twenty-sixth Street alignment that took it through the eastern portion of the Central City public housing development.[9] Construction of the Red Mountain Expressway began in February 1963.[10] The first major phase of construction focused on completing the expressway between its beginning in Homewood at the intersection of Federal Highways 31 and 280 and its northern terminus at Third Avenue North on the southeastern edge of downtown Birmingham. But as early as April 1962, state highway planners anticipated a second major segment with the extension of the expressway from Third Avenue North, along the Twenty-sixth Street corridor, north to an intersection with Interstate 59 at about Twelfth Avenue North (later Tenth Avenue North).[11]

Actual completion of Red Mountain Expressway's first segment was delayed by disputes between Birmingham, Homewood, Mountain Brook, Vestavia Hills, and Jefferson County regarding each jurisdiction's share of the cost of building the expressway. Nevertheless, expressway advocates, led by businessman Elton B. Stephens, who chaired the Red Mountain Expressway Committee of the Birmingham Downtown Improvement Association, successfully lobbied Governor George Wallace in early 1964 for additional state assistance to relieve local governments of a portion of the cost of the new expressway.[12]

Despite the construction delay, the second phase of the Red Mountain Expressway was planned to cut through a portion of the Central City housing project, just has had been foreseen in 1958. The state's 1963 plan, prepared by consultants Harland Bartholomew and Harry Hendon Associates, took the expressway through the eastern portion of the Central City housing project, removing an estimated two hundred to four hundred dwelling units.[13] The highway followed Twenty-sixth Street North, which formed the eastern border of the Central City housing development. The highway department selected this alignment, rather than a more eastern route, to avoid the Birmingham Terminal Station, the city's main railroad station, located just east of Twenty-sixth Street North, between Fourth Avenue North and Seventh Avenue North.

Ironically, the terminal station was demolished in 1969, but by then the highway department had already planned the Red Mountain Expressway route. The highway department's 1963 report did not explore the possibility that the terminal station might be razed, even though in May 1962 Birmingham city commissioners raised this as a possibility in attempting to find a site for a new federal postal facility.[14] Nor did the 1963 report firmly establish that extension of the Red Mountain Expressway was even necessary to meet the objectives of enabling suburban commuters to drive to downtown Birmingham. In 1969, city engineer Alton McWhorter wrote to the Alabama Highway Department:

> The Red Mountain Expressway was conceived solely for the purpose of bringing into the central City of Birmingham people from over the mountain as an inducement for trade in the downtown Birmingham area, and it is my opinion that any overhead structure which is designed along this route will not serve such a purpose. It has been, and still will be, my recommendation that the Red Mountain Expressway be brought to grade at 4th Avenue, North, in accordance with the original intention and that the area between 4th Avenue, North, and 12th Avenue North, be widened for traffic at ground level to fulfill the purpose for which it was originally intended.[15]

In 1974, John Bryan also argued that the termination of the Red Mountain Expressway at Third Avenue North met the objectives of getting Over the Mountain suburban commuters into downtown and that therefore an extension to Interstate 59 was unnecessary.[16] As a city council member in the 1960s, Bryan had become very familiar with the early planning of the expressway.

Nevertheless, by early summer of 1974, the Alabama Highway Department was ready to construct the final phase of the Red Mountain Expressway. The highway department had acquired all of the property between Third Avenue North and Fifth Avenue North and 80 percent of the property between Seventh Avenue and I-59/20. The missing link was the Central City segment between Fifth and Seventh Avenues North.[17] Despite the immediate plans to acquire this segment, the highway department had made no plans for the relocation of the four hundred Central City households being displaced by the expressway. Responding to early criticism from the Birmingham Housing Authority and the city council, the highway department redesigned a ramp, thereby reducing the number of displaced households from 400 to 233 (later reduced to 218).[18]

As the news broke in summer 1974 that the highway department planned to demolish a portion of Central City, its residents began to protest the loss of their homes. They claimed they had never been notified of the upcoming demolition. The highway department replied that notices were mailed to "all concerned agencies, but the latest meeting was canceled due to lack of interest."[19] Residents claimed they never heard anything from the agencies. The public hearing, scheduled for June 3, 1970, was never held. No notice was sent to the Central City tenants association, and the legal notice contained no map showing the expressway's route.[20]

Protesting Central City residents dreaded having to move from their homes. Oliver Williams, an older resident, talked about the impact a move would have on him and his ailing wife, especially since Central City was accessible to a variety of services: "She's under a doctor's care for her nerves and doesn't want to move. It's handy for getting a bus to the doctor, for getting her medicine and going to the store. Besides we've got friends here. It's our home."[21] Malinda Cobb, another Central City resident, expressed the anguish of someone who had been moved by both highway construction and urban renewal. "If I'm moved this time it will make three times and I'm tired of it," she said, recalling her homes in East Lake and Avondale. "We had to just take what they gave us and that wasn't much."[22] With such concerns, Central City tenants attended a July 9, 1974, city council meeting to protest the expressway plans and to request a public hearing on the issue. The council scheduled a public hearing for July 22, 1974.[23]

At the July 22 hearing, several hundred Central City residents and supporters appeared to argue against demolition and relocation and to testify to their neighborhood's accessibility to medical services and to local schools. Said one man in a wheelchair: "We need Central City. We need every unit, every apartment. We need the clinic, the schools, the stores."[24] With the highway department willing to entertain replacement housing, the city council prepared to approve the Red Mountain Expressway extension if the displaced tenants could be moved to replacement housing.[25] Several days after the public hearing, Birmingham City Council Public Improvements chair Dr. E. C. Overton stated that the council will "probably favor" the Red Mountain Expressway if comparable housing in the same area is provided.[26]

Nevertheless, Central City residents planned to protest the emerging relocation plans. More than seventy persons in Central City met to discuss protesting the Red Mountain Expressway. Mrs. Vendetta Dowdell, an organizer of the meeting and soon to be elected president of the Central City Neighborhood Association in the first Citizen Participation Program elections, said of the housing authority and the highway department: "Do not believe they are not going to relocate us. They knew 10 years ago that we would have to move; why didn't they plan for relocation then?"[27] Instead of moving, the residents wanted the expressway moved one block east so that no buildings at Central City would be demolished.

About twenty Central City residents, including both blacks and whites, followed up their rhetoric with a protest march to the Birmingham City Council meeting on October 1, 1974. City council members were not pleased by the protest, challenging one of the protestors as to whether she actually had written her statement. Council member Nina Miglionico engaged in a shouting match with Central City resident Vendetta Dowdell after Ms. Dowdell asked for the city's position on the expressway route.[28] Council member Russell Yarborough declared that the tenant protest was "in poor taste." Reacting to the tenants' protest, the city council refused to guarantee that the residents would not have to move.[29]

At this time, the highway department had not presented the city with a relocation plan, but the city was already sending signals that it was likely to approve such a plan. To do otherwise would require the highway department to plan a new route. According to council member Overton: "it would take them six or seven years to draw up new plans for a new route, have them approved by the Federal Highway Administration and get the project ready for construction. The council is convinced that long a delay is not in the best interest of the city."[30]

Toward the end of 1974, the highway department's relocation plan began to take shape. Initially, in May 1974 and as late as August 1974, the housing authority had opposed the expressway extension, preferring that an alternate route be selected.[31] By December 1974, however, the housing authority had reversed course and supported the expressway. In cooperation with the highway department, the housing authority planned to move elderly tenants in Central City to replacement housing in the city's Southside neighborhood. The housing authority had acquired the site for the second phase of the medical center expansion. The elderly tenants would be placed in a high-rise development designed for elderly occupancy. Families displaced by the Red Mountain Expressway would be moved into the Central City units vacated by their elderly tenants.[32]

Such a plan had a clear racial subtext. The housing authority had built Central City in 1941 for whites, but the population had begun to change in the 1960s after President John Kennedy's 1962 executive order outlawing racial discrimination in federally assisted housing. By 1974, Central City had a substantial black population, mostly consisting of families, but also retained a significant white population, most of which was elderly.[33] By relocating Central City's elderly to an alternative site, the housing authority, in cooperation with the highway department, was resegregating Central City from white to black. Moreover, the relocation plan enabled Central City's white elderly to live in a high-rise building for the elderly. Although the housing authority could not enforce racial segregation in such a project, the fact that the replacement facility was unavailable to families reduced the prospect of the racial turnover that had occurred at Central City.

The relocation plan's ulterior motives exposed a key feasibility issue, however. Because the plan called for the relocation of Central City's elderly to the Southside high-rise, regardless of whether a household had lost a dwelling to the Red Mountain Expressway, the highway department's relocation funds would be used to relocate residents who had not lost their homes. Housing authority staff were uncertain whether the highway department would use relocation funds to pay for replacement housing for elderly households who had not been displaced by the expressway.[34]

With the city council appearing unsympathetic to resident protest and the housing authority creating a racial relocation plan, Central City residents began investigating a legal challenge to the Red Mountain Expressway plans. The Alabama State Tenants Organization (ASTO) organized tenants into a lawsuit and on December 19, 1974, filed suit in federal court against the Alabama Highway Department, the Birmingham Housing Authority, the U.S. Department of Housing and Urban Development, and the Federal Highway Administration. The plaintiffs alleged that the highway department had planned the Red Mountain Expressway and had begun right-of-way acquisition without proper attention to the requirements of the federal Uniform Relocation Act, the environmental impact statement requirements of the National Environmental Policy Act, the hearing and urban transportation requirements of the Federal Aid Highway Act, the antidiscrimination provisions of the Civil Rights Act of 1964, and the public housing provisions of the Housing Act of 1937.[35]

On June 19, 1975, federal district judge James Hancock ruled the suit was premature because the Red Mountain Expressway project "was completely dormant, if not dead."[36] The federal and state defendants argued that they were not yet required to meet their obligations under federal law because the City of Birmingham had not yet approved the project and had not displayed "sufficient local interest" to necessitate preparation, for example, of an environmental impact statement. Given that the highway department had already completed substantial acquisition of land for the expressway, this contention was dubious. While the federal court accepted the defendants' argument, it also told the defendants that federal law required that a environmental impact study would have to be completed.[37] Not surprisingly, the Central City tenants' attorney Robert Wiggins promised the Birmingham City Council that the tenants would appeal Judge Hancock's decision.[38] Wiggins proposed terms for an out-of-court settlement. Faced with further delays in the expressway's construction, Birmingham public officials and civic leaders throughout the late summer and early fall of 1975 attempted to reach an agreement with the Central City tenants.[39] When negotiations stalled, however, expressway proponents in November 1975 let the tenants' appeal of Judge Hancock's decision proceed.[40] Sixteen months later, in March 1977, the federal Fifth Circuit Court of Appeals vacated the federal district court's decision on three of the nine counts filed by the Central City residents. The court ordered that plaintiffs be able to refile these counts if the defendants failed to comply with state and federal laws pertaining to the extension of the Red Mountain Expressway.[41]

With this decision, the Alabama Highway Department realized that it must comply with federal requirements for consideration of alternatives to the proposed alignment and therefore it had to perform an environmental impact study. Although planning for the expressway had begun before enactment of the 1969 Environmental Protection Act, in the context of the tenants' suit, federal highway officials informed the Alabama Highway Department that a complete environmental impact study was now necessary.[42] By June 1977, therefore, the highway department had begun examining four alternative alignments and was preparing an environmental impact study that would include air and noise pollution studies as well as interviews with tenants. At the same time, Operation New Birmingham, the city's leading nonprofit, business-oriented advocate for downtown revitalization, announced that it would begin a campaign to finish the Red Mountain Expressway.[43] In response, hundreds of letters were sent to ONB asking that the expressway be completed. Many of these letters criticized what their writers perceived as an unfair situation in which taxpaying commuters were unable to use an expressway whose completion was blocked by individuals dependent upon federal housing subsidies.[44]

Throughout the summer of 1977 the Alabama State Tenants Organization and its attorney Robert Wiggins negotiated with the highway department on behalf of the Central City residents.[45] The tenants were armed with the ability to prolong the time needed to prepare an environmental impact study. Highway department attorney Donald Sweeney reported that if the negotiations failed and the tenants pursued litigation, the environmental impact study would have to meet stringent court-directed tests. Under these circumstances, the Federal Highway Administration would require a major study of five or six years' duration. If a settlement with the tenants could be reached, a shorter study would be more likely.[46]

At issue was the degree of authority tenants would have in the replacement housing. Tenants argued for a review committee consisting of tenants and highway department officials that would have decision-making authority over the location and design of the replacement housing.[47] Finally, in November 1977, Alabama governor George Wallace signed an agreement that had been worked out in September between the highway department, the tenants, the housing authority, and the city council. This agreement provided one-for-one replacement housing for the displaced tenants and provided tenants the right to influence decisions on the location and design of the replacement units. Specifically, a six-person committee would determine the location of the replacement housing and would advise architects on the design. The Alabama State Tenants Organization would appoint three of the six persons, two of whom would be residents of Central City, while the city council, the housing authority, and the State of Alabama would appoint one member each. In exchange for the replacement housing and influence over its site and design, the tenants agreed to forego any further litigation.[48]

Despite the agreement for replacement housing, difficulties in completing the environmental impact study delayed construction of the Red Mountain Expressway extension.[49] By the latter half of 1979, the highway department's second consultant was examining several alignment alternatives, including one through Central City.[50] But after studying the alternatives, the highway department in winter 1980 announced that it favored a route that would go east of Twenty-sixth Street North, bypassing Central City entirely. By taking a route over the former terminal station property, the expressway avoided Central City, thereby saving $16 million, much of which would have been spent on replacement housing.[51] Through the efforts of the Central City tenants and the Alabama State Tenants Organization, the Central City development had been preserved.

Moreover, under Albert Rohling, the successor of housing authority director Hugh Denman, the housing authority announced plans to renovate Central City. HUD awarded the housing authority nearly $19 million to modernize the development by improving unit exteriors, installing modern equipment in the apartments, and increasing the living space in each unit by an additional fifty square feet. Mayor Richard Arrington explained how a revitalized Central City would enhance downtown Birmingham: "We decided if we could improve Central

City, and by doing so, improve the quality of living, and making it aesthetically more acceptable, we would be accomplishing part of our plan to get more people into the downtown area."[52] By the mid-1980s, all 910 units of Central City (now known as Metropolitan Gardens) were renovated. The residents' highway revolt had generated a completely refurbished public housing project.

Denman's departure and Central City's renovation came in response to increasing criticism of the housing authority. In 1979, at age eighty-one, Denman retired. In the late 1970s, he and the housing authority had been the targets of community efforts to change the way in which public housing in Birmingham was operated.[53] George Quiggle, of Greater Birmingham Ministries, who had helped organize the black community for a more participatory Citizen Participation Plan, worked with other community activists to replace Denman and housing authority board members who supported Denman.[54] In 1974, the housing authority had no black board members; by 1978, however, four of the authority's five members were African American.[55] Among the board members that Quiggle and his colleagues persuaded the city council to appoint was Benjamin Greene, president of the Harriman Park Civic League and an activist who was instrumental in organizing the black community to support the city's Citizen Participation Plan (see chapter 7). Greene, who joined the housing authority in 1978, and Quiggle were key participants in the effort to force Denman's departure.[56]

Denman's departure was historically significant. Joining the housing authority's staff in 1953 as urban renewal director, he became authority director in 1960. He had presided over both phases of the medical center urban renewal project as well as the Avondale, Ensley, and Civic Center urban renewal projects. All of these projects had entailed the relocation of black households for the benefit of the white community. The partial demolition of Central City, with its attendant relocation scheme of moving white elderly residents to a Southside high-rise, represented his last effort to use planning to manipulate the city's racial characteristics. With his retirement and the transformation of the housing authority's board, the likelihood that the housing authority's programs would be used for the purposes of arranging Birmingham's racial geography had seemingly decreased.

Birmingham's Citizen Participation Program

With city commission approval of the Citizen Participation Program in October 1974, elections were held the next month for the presidents, vice presidents, and secretaries for each of eighty-six neighborhood associations. Overall, 647 persons ran for office, with at least two presidential candidates in each neighborhood and only a handful of neighborhoods in which only one candidate was running for vice president or secretary. With each neighborhood averaging about 3,400 residents and persons sixteen years of age or older eligible to participate in the neighborhood association elections, nearly 8,500 persons voted, for an average of nearly 100 voters in each neighborhood.[57] Although not a large turnout by election standards—25,000 had voted in a city council election two weeks earlier—it was a large number by citizen participation standards where a well-attended public hearing on a citywide issue might attract 500 persons.

Under the Citizen Participation Plan, the Citizens Advisory Board (CAB)—the top tier in the three-tiered program—directly advised the mayor and city council on Community Development Block Grant (CDBG) expenditures. Early on, the CAB and the city disagreed on how to allocate CDBG funds, with the city favoring targeting of funds to several neighborhoods and the CAB opposing targeting. In 1975, the city council responded by targeting $3 million to three neighborhoods but also allocating $2.05 million in CDBG funds to be distributed among the remaining eighty-three neighborhoods. This pattern was repeated in subsequent years, with funds distributed on a population- and need-based formula. The city also began funding the neighborhood allocation with the city's General Revenue Sharing allocation, a Nixon administration New Federalism program that was discontinued early in the Reagan administration. Funds could be spent on council-approved projects in each neighborhood's area. In addition, neighborhoods could request allotments of CDBG funds as well as an allocation from the city's capital improvements fund.[58] Minimal annual allocation to each neighborhood has been as high as $10,000 but was reduced in the late 1980s to $3,000. With the demise of General Revenue Sharing, the City of Birmingham used its own funds for the annual allocation.[59]

The Citizens Advisory Board also advised the mayor and city council on the allocation of capital improvement funds. Given the historic denial of public services to black neighborhoods in Birmingham, the CAB saw the city's capital improvement budget as an important means for meeting the infrastructure needs of all the city's neighborhoods. In spring of 1977, the city prepared a $62 million bond issue, its first bond issue since 1968.[60] Prior to the city council's meeting with the CAB to discuss the bond issue, Birmingham's citizen participation planner, Chuck Lewis, made available a comparison of the CAB's and the city's bond issue recommendations.[61] The CAB made clear its objections to the city's bond issue proposal. The next day the city council revised its original budget to spend more funds on sanitary and storm sewers and less on such "frills" as a $3 million Olympic swim center, refurbishment of the city's Sloss Furnaces, street lighting, a neighborhood business development, and city libraries.[62] The city council increased the bond issue for drainage from $1.6 to $5.6 million. Half of the sixteen neighborhoods receiving drainage improvements through the bond issue were predominantly black.[63]

The city also increased its allocation for sanitary sewers from $2.3 to $5.1 million with the bulk of the funds going to the predominantly black neighborhoods of Central Pratt, Smithfield Estates, South Pratt, North Pratt, Mason City, and Grasselli.[64] In Grasselli, which the city had annexed in 1976, 5,000 residents lived in 1,700 houses lacking sewers.[65] In the past, the Grasselli Civic League had to directly petition local officials for basic services, often to no avail.[66] But with the advent of Birmingham's Citizen Participation Program, Grasselli now had the support and the influence that a united consortium of neighborhoods like the CAB could provide.

On May 10, 1977, Birmingham voters approved all thirteen items in the city's $62 million bond issue. Voters were most supportive of the sanitary sewer and drainage issues, with 80 percent voting for the sanitary sewer bond issue and 85 percent casting votes for storm sewers.[67] Mayor David Vann attributed the victory to the city's "sinking fund" program that targets one-fourth of property taxes for bond use even before the bonds are approved and to the city's Citizen Participation Program. Bragging to envious mayors at a meeting of the U.S. Conference of Mayors, Vann said, "Somebody asked me how much I figured our

Citizens Participation program is worth and I told him 'About $62 million dollars.'"[68] Generally, areas with strong neighborhood associations were more likely to support the bond issue, especially those items that directly benefited neighborhoods. In particular, three areas with strong neighborhood associations—Grasselli, North Birmingham, and Collegeville—gave overwhelming support to the bond issue, with 95 percent of Grasselli voters supporting the various items.[69] All three were black neighborhoods, and more generally—although black and white neighborhoods supported the various bond issue items—support for all items ran higher in black neighborhoods than in white neighborhoods.[70]

Despite the influence exercised by the city's neighborhoods in the 1977 bond issue, fundamental disagreements between many of the neighborhoods, particularly the black ones, and the city emerged in conjunction with the Community Development Block Grant program. At a November 14, 1978, meeting, the Birmingham City Council agreed to target four and possibly five neighborhoods for concentrated assistance under HUD's Neighborhood Strategy Areas (NSA) initiative. Approximately $10 million of a $32 million CDBG allocation would be spent on the neighborhoods over a three-year period, 1979 through 1982.[71]

Under President Jimmy Carter, HUD was attempting to counter what was perceived as the geographic spreading of benefits under the Community Development Block Grant program. After two years of CDBG program experience under the Ford administration, a congressional staff report had noted that the practice of spreading benefits across a variety of eligible neighborhoods raises the issue of "whether or not areas targeted for treatment in order to renew, rehabilitate or conserve them are being programmed with a variety of activities at a sufficient level to reasonably insure that the proposed treatment will be successful."[72] A classic dilemma in community development was thereby posed. Is neighborhood revitalization best served by concentrating resources in small areas or spreading them out over a variety of jurisdictions? The concentration strategy seems more likely to stimulate visible revitalization, while the benefit-spreading strategy appeared more politically viable. To concentrate resources into a few neighborhoods meant making tough choices, with a number of neighborhoods left out entirely.

Responding to the congressional concerns, the Carter administration proposed new rules in October 1977 that established geographic targeting as an important objective in the allocation of CDBG funds within cities. By concentrating resources within limited areas, HUD believed that it would be easier to demonstrate success in stabilizing and revitalizing deteriorated neighborhoods. HUD adopted final regulations for the Neighborhood Strategy Areas program in March 1978 that called for the concentration of physical development activities within NSA neighborhoods.[73]

In selecting neighborhoods for the NSA program, HUD advised cities to target neighborhoods that were "not too big, not too bad, and not too many."[74] As political scientist Donald Rosenthal has written, such guidance implied that cities adopt a triage approach to selecting neighborhoods for NSA designation. Triage, a much-discussed urban strategy in the 1970s, assumed that with limited resources it was not economically efficient to invest in needy neighborhoods unless they also had a realistic opportunity for revitalization.[75] Although billed as a new idea, it really was a continuation of "the blight that's right" concept that had driven the selection of urban renewal areas throughout the nation and in Birmingham (see chapter 5). Under either name, scarce community development resources would be targeted to neighborhoods that displayed not only need but also potential for revitalization.

To select the NSA neighborhoods, Birmingham's planners employed a "rational, objective and well-organized" methodology that essentially implemented the triage concept.[76] With $10 million available over three years, Birmingham Community Development Department planners expected that the selection of four or five neighborhoods would achieve the appropriate concentration of resources. To identify neighborhoods that were in need and "not too bad," the city's Community Development Department categorized Birmingham neighborhoods by measures of economic need, physical blight, and potential for revitalization or coordination with major planning objectives.[77] Neighborhoods were then divided into four categories:

A. Neighborhoods with *greater* degree of low/moderate income households and blight, and with *greater* degree of residential revitalization potential.

B. Neighborhoods with *lesser* degree of low/moderate income households and blight, and with *greater* degree of residential revitalization potential.

C. Neighborhoods with *greater* degree of low/moderate income households and blight, and with *lesser* residential revitalization potential.

D. Neighborhoods with less than minimal degree of low/moderate income and/or blight.[78]

The Community Development Department concluded that neighborhoods in group D were not eligible for the NSA program and that during the 1979 to 1982 period, no neighborhoods in group C should be targeted for NSA funding. "While these neighborhoods have severe problems," concluded the city's analysis, "revitalization of these areas will be more difficult and will require additional information before undertaking concentrated projects." The Community Development Department planners then recommended that five neighborhoods be funded through the NSA program: Woodlawn, North Birmingham, Five Points South, Bush Hills, and Jones Valley.[79]

Although the Community Development Department analysis did not review the racial characteristics of Birmingham's neighborhoods, the racial implications of the planners' recommendations are made clear in table 8.1. The group A neighborhoods, with higher levels of economic need and revitalization potential, were a mix of both predominantly black and racially mixed neighborhoods, along with one predominantly white neighborhood, North East Lake.

Overall, however, the group B neighborhoods, which had lower levels of economic need but higher levels of revitalization potential, were 60 percent white, while the group C neighborhoods were only 7 percent white. Consequently, the city's community development planners recommended adoption of a Neighborhood Strategy Area program that placed many of the predominantly black neighborhoods in group C, which would not be targeted for NSA funding. Although the city's recommended list of NSA neighborhoods showed a balance of both black and white neighborhoods, the fact that predominantly black neighborhoods were more likely to be placed in group C meant that their chances of benefiting from the city's neighborhood revitalization

Table 8.1. Racial characteristics of Birmingham neighborhoods, 1980

| | Number | | Percentage | |
A Neighborhoods	White	Black	White	Black
Druid Hills	340	3,231	9.5	90.5
Enon Ridge	1	1,525	0.1	99.9
Grasselli Community	NA	NA		
Hooper City	29	1,644	1.7	98.3
North Birmingham	249	3,641	6.4	93.6
North East Lake	4,855	357	93.2	6.8
North Pratt	1,013	2,595	28.1	71.9
Sandusky				
Woodlawn	2,940	1,976	59.8	40.2
Wylam	2,302	1,804	56.1	43.9
Zion City	348	1,543	18.4	81.6
Total	5,590	5,323	51.2	48.8

| | Number | | Percentage | |
B Neighborhoods	White	Black	White	Black
Belview Heights	4,467	1,220	78.5	21.5
Bush Hills	2,120	3,185	40.0	60.0
Central Park	3,759	579	86.7	13.3
College Hills	18	2,123	0.8	99.2
East Lake	2,567	931	73.4	26.6
East Thomas	7	2,159	0.3	99.7
Ensley Highlands	4,348	997	81.3	18.7
Fairview	1,763	1,315	57.3	42.7
Five Points South	5,967	1,250	82.7	17.3
Germania Park	1,015	2,147	32.1	67.9
Green Acres	2,426	173	93.3	6.7
Inglenook	3,468	1,333	72.2	27.8
Jones Valley	410	2,505	14.1	85.9
Powderly	82	3,441	2.3	97.7
South East Lake	7,645	150	98.1	1.9
South Tittusville	84	3,691	2.2	97.8
Wahouma	1,483	413	78.2	21.8
Total	41,629	27,612	60.1	39.9

(continued)

Table 8.1 *continued*

C Neighborhoods	Number		Percentage	
	White	Black	White	Black
Acipco-Finley	99	3,897	2.5	97.5
Arlington-West End	3,380	4,788	41.4	58.6
Brown Springs	NA	NA	NA	NA
Central City	1,038	2,223	31.8	68.2
Central Pratt	90	3,232	2.7	97.3
Collegeville	18	6,306	0.3	99.7
East Avondale	316	824	27.7	72.3
East Birmingham	107	2,626	3.9	96.1
Ensley	2,359	5,483	30.1	69.9
Evergreen	40	2,945	1.3	98.7
Fairmont	616	2,616	19.1	80.9
Fountain Heights	63	5,039	1.2	98.8
Gate City	492	2,841	14.8	85.2
Graymont	633	4,005	13.6	86.4
Harriman Park	1	827	0.1	99.9
Kingston	156	5,221	2.9	97.1
Mason City	7	2,637	0.3	99.7
North Avondale	192	1,861	9.4	90.6
North Tittusville	15	6,205	0.2	99.8
Norwood	748	5,358	12.3	87.7
Oak Ridge Park	103	1,642	5.9	94.1
Oakwood Place	1,516	3,449	30.5	69.5
Riley	67	2,200	3.0	97.0
Rising Station	338	1,530	18.1	81.9
Sherman Heights	NA	NA	NA	NA
Smithfield	41	5,217	0.8	99.2
South Pratt	4	1,503	0.3	99.7
South Woodlawn	269	1,503	15.2	84.8
Southside	72	2,038	3.4	96.6
Thomas	824	1,319	38.5	61.5
Tuxedo	10	3,495	0.3	99.7
Woodland Park	2	1,248	0.2	99.8
Total	1,222	16,323	7.0	93.0

Source: 1980 Census Neighborhood Statistics Program, Neighborhood Strategy Areas, n.d., City Council Papers, box 28, file 4, Birmingham Public Library Department of Archives and Manuscripts.

Note: Neighborhood strategy areas in bold

programs were greatly reduced, even though they had greater economic need than the group B neighborhoods.[80]

At a November 20, 1978, public hearing on the city's Community Development Block Grant program, Reverend George Quiggle and Reverend William Hamilton, president of the Ensley Neighborhood Association, criticized the city's NSA plans. They argued that the plans had not been presented to the Citizens Advisory Board and that the NSA plan ignored the city's poor renters.[81] In identifying neighborhoods with revitalization potential, the city's planners had focused on neighborhoods with higher rates of home ownership, but Quiggle and Hamilton argued that this policy neglected neighborhoods with a higher percentage of poor renters.[82] Greater Birmingham Ministries (GBM) had been monitoring the city's CDBG spending since 1974 and had complained that too much money was being spent on infrastructure and not enough to provide decent housing.[83] Quiggle and Hamilton told the city council,

First, we are concerned that neighborhoods with a higher percentage of renting families, coupled with a higher percentage of substandard homes, have been omitted from the "rational, objective and well-organized" Neighborhood Strategy Area selection process.

. . . Most importantly and most clearly, the City (Community Development Department, Mayor and Council) has *already* rendered this meeting meaningless. You have already spent several months developing plans for 1979 programs, this evidenced by the statement concerning the selection of NSAs. The Mayor has had the Community Development Department's recommendations on his desk for several weeks, and just last week the Council voted approval that certain neighborhoods be designated as CDBG target areas for 1979. All of this *before* the first citizen hearing on how the moneys should be spent.

. . . we are *concerned* that the future is foreclosed on developing a meaningful policy and program for the poorest families who rent substandard housing.[84]

By the time the Citizens Advisory Board met on February 19, 1979, with the city council to review the CDBG proposal, two other neighborhoods, Mason City from group C and South Tittusville from group

B, had been added to the list of NSA target neighborhoods. This was done at the behest of the city council, which had been requested by the Citizens Advisory Board to include at least one group C neighborhood.[85] Mrs. Leola Terry of Mason City was pleased at her neighborhood's inclusion and defended the city's decision to fund her neighborhood: "Once you see Mason City, you see we need more money than that. Please don't throw us out because we feel we've been deserted for so long."[86]

Despite Mason City's selection, other neighborhood leaders were still frustrated by the selection process. Thomas Jenkins of the Thomas neighborhood expressed his concern at the CAB meeting when he said: "The Thomas community is disturbed that only one community was designated out of the C group area. We feel we have a lot of potential for revitalization. We want to know if the city is going to write off these areas that have more blight and less potential for revitalization—the group C communities?"[87]

At the February 19 CAB meeting, Greater Birmingham Ministries presented its recommendations on the CDBG program. GBM noted that the NSA selection process should make severity of need a key indicator; that group C neighborhoods that the city's Land Use Plan targeted for future residential development should be included as NSAs; and that the city should encourage the Bush Hills and Five Points South neighborhoods to avail themselves of HUD's Neighborhood Self-help Development program, for which they have demonstrated capacity, freeing up CDBG funds for neighborhoods with greater need. Despite the dissent over the NSA strategy expressed by GBM and neighborhood representatives, the CAB approved the city's proposed CDBG budget, provided that $400,000 be transferred from the NSA neighborhoods to housing programs for low-income households and for study, planning, and implementation of programs that would benefit group C neighborhoods.[88]

Taking further action on April 16, 1979, the CAB appointed the Ad Hoc Committee on Lower Income and Blighted Neighborhoods Planning to investigate how the city's CDBG program might better serve lower-income neighborhoods. Leading the new committee were William Sherman, president of the North Avondale Neighborhood Association; Paul Carruba, vice president of the Central City Neighborhood Association; and Benjamin Greene, president of the Harriman Park

Neighborhood Association and the Harriman Park Civic League. At a May 8 meeting organized by the three leaders, representatives from the thirty-two group C neighborhoods agreed to organize a Low-Income Planning Committee and to charge that committee with filing a complaint to HUD concerning Birmingham's allocation of CDBG funds. Sixty-seven of the seventy-five persons attending the meeting signed the complaint. Thirty-three of the sixty-seven signers were officers in their neighborhood associations.[89] Clearly the neighborhood leadership developed through the city's Citizen Participation Program was asserting itself.

The May 16, 1979, citizens complaint against the 1979–80 Birmingham CDBG budget was signed by citizens representing twenty-four of the thirty-two group C neighborhoods, as well as one group A and one group B neighborhood. Greater Birmingham Ministries provided technical assistance for the complaint. The complaint cited several key objections:

- By stressing home ownership, the city's CDBG program did not principally benefit low-income households who are more likely to be renters.
- Citizens were not provided sufficient opportunity to participate in the selection of and planning for the NSAs.
- Thirty predominantly black neighborhoods, including 14 of 17 neighborhoods in the city with over 45 percent substandard housing, were excluded from NSA designation because of their lack of revitalization potential.[90]

The complaint argued that the city's emphasis on home ownership was inappropriate because the 1979 Housing Assistance Plan reported that half of Birmingham's substandard housing was renter occupied. The complaint attributed the city's focus on home ownership to concern with the "outward movement of middle and upper-income home-owners."[91] By focusing on revitalization potential and home ownership, the complaint alleged that the city's NSA selection methodology placed too little weight on economic need: "Need was secondary and severity of need was not a factor in the selection process."[92] Specifically, the NSA selection process ignored the group C neighborhoods that "contain significant concentrations of deteriorated, dilapidated and unfit housing, the majority of residents are not home owners and they lack vacant dwellings or lots for development."[93] Because selection focused on home ownership and not on housing need, the complaint charged that the NSA process "affects blacks in particular," resulting in the large majority of group C neighborhoods being predominantly black.[94] The complaint concluded: "The relegation of 32 neighborhoods with 'greater' lower income households and blight to lowest priority for community development resources by virtue of their 'lesser' revitalization potential smacks of 'triage,' a policy of writing off the poorest neighborhoods as unsalvageable. There is here overwhelming evidence of needs which remain unaddressed by the City's chosen strategy."[95]

The complaint made several recommendations. The city should redirect its housing activities toward assisting poor renters and should drop the Five Points South and Bush Hills neighborhoods from the NSA program. As GBM had argued in February, the complaint maintained that these neighborhoods already had the capacity to obtain support from HUD's Neighborhood Self-Help Development program and did not require CDBG assistance. The complaint also urged HUD to require the city to replace Bush Hills and Five Points South with one or more group C neighborhoods that had a concentration of substandard housing. It further asked HUD to budget CDBG funds for the CAB's Ad Hoc Committee on Lower Income Neighborhood Planning to be spent on hiring a consultant to plan for and help build planning and development capacity in lower-income neighborhoods.[96]

The complaint's focus on the Bush Hills and Five Points South is indicative of the split between the group C neighborhoods and the city on CDBG priorities. Both Bush Hills and Five Points South were white middle- to upper-class neighborhoods that by the 1970s were undergoing significant change. Bush Hills, located just east of Ensley and west of College Hills, developed in the 1920s as higher-paid executives and blue-collar workers sought to escape the congestion and pollution of Ensley and its TCI–U.S. Steel mill. Young Dorothy Inman-Johnson's mother walked every day from her family's home in Ensley to the Bush Hills home where she worked as a maid.[97] By the 1970s, the neighborhood was undergoing racial change as Birmingham's black population moved west of Center Street into College Hills and then into Bush Hills. In 1980, the neighborhood's population was 60 percent black (see table 8.1). With one small exception, the neighborhood enjoyed a sound housing stock and in the 1970s continued to be attractive to middle- and upper-income households. Prior to the neighborhood's NSA designation in late 1978, the city had already funded public improvements there. In addition, the neighborhood had been targeted by the federally funded Neighborhood Housing Services program, a program that merged public and private investment to encourage homeowners to rehabilitate their dwellings.[98]

Five Points South had also been a middle- to upper-income neighborhood. The neighborhood is located on the city's south side and includes the University of Alabama at Birmingham campus, a commercial area along Twentieth Street South, and single-family homes between Thirteenth Avenue South and Red Mountain. The southern part of the neighborhood had been one of Birmingham's early streetcar suburbs, housing many of the city's elite in the late nineteenth and early twentieth centuries before they moved over the mountain to Mountain Brook and Homewood. The northern part of the neighborhood had been, prior to the development of the Southside Medical Center and UAB, a predominantly black neighborhood. With urban renewal, Five Points South was by 1980 over 80 percent white, and a good share of its land use was institutional. It was confronted with the challenge of retaining its single-family residential character in the face of pressure for apartments and expansion of institutional uses as well as the objective of retaining its commercial vitality. Although the neighborhood had once housed the city's elite, by the late 1970s an estimated 37 percent of the neighborhood's residential structures were considered substandard. A 1977 master plan detailed recommendations designed to address these problems.[99]

Although both these neighborhoods faced their share of urban challenges and both were undoubtedly critical to the vitality of Birmingham, their needs for basic infrastructure and decent housing paled in comparison to the predominantly black group C neighborhoods that had long been neglected by the city. From the perspective of the group C neighborhoods, no matter how critical Five Points South and Bush Hills were to revitalization, their needs failed to match the long-standing needs found in the predominantly black neighborhoods.

On May 14, 1979, two days prior to submission of the citizen complaint, HUD area manager John Wilson also expressed concern about how the city was planning to spend its CDBG dollars. Wilson's letter, which reflected a discussion between HUD and the city on April 30, 1979, summarized six issues presented at that meeting that pertained to the NSA selection process. Specifically, Wilson requested that the city provide "greater specificity of the NSA selection criteria, particularly as it applies to low and moderate income persons" (defined as individuals living in households earning 80 percent or less of metropolitan area median income) and that the city address the housing needs within the NSAs of homeowners who lack sufficient income to qualify for rehabilitation loans.[100] Although Wilson's letter questioned the city's NSA program, it did not forcefully question, as did the citizens complaint, the decision to target CDBG funds to neighborhoods with lesser need but greater revitalization potential. Nor did the letter suggest that the NSA selection criteria had a systematic bias against low-income black neighborhoods.

After receiving the citizen complaint, as well as the city's response to Wilson's May 14 letter, HUD responded by questioning several of the city's CDBG budget items. In the case of Five Points South, HUD persuaded the city to target money for housing development to low- and moderate-income households. In other cases, in both Five Points South and Bush Hills, the city converted CDBG funds from the low- and moderate-income category to the "prevention of slum and blight" category, which was permitted by federal CDBG legislation. Since the latter could be used in any neighborhood that had even the potential for slum or blight, it permitted more flexible spending of CDBG funds. Although HUD area office special assistant Sam Brannon agreed that it appeared that there were neighborhoods with greater needs than those selected, HUD would not require the reallocation of funds from group B to group C neighborhoods. Instead, HUD encouraged the city to put any funds that become available into neighborhoods that have greater need.[101]

Despite the changes, Greater Birmingham Ministries and the group C neighborhoods were not satisfied with HUD's actions. Indeed, the city's modifications were closer to the concerns laid out in Wilson's May 14 letter than they were to the citizens' May 16 complaint. Carolyn Crawford, who wrote the citizen's complaint and who chaired GBM's Housing Working Group and Systems Change Task Force, saw the city's response as a clarification rather than a change and criticized the city for not addressing the needs of poor renters.[102]

Despite HUD's 1979 acquiescence in the basic assumptions of Birmingham's NSA selection strategy, in June 1980 HUD seriously questioned the city's 1980–81 CDBG budget, which included the second year of spending for the seven NSA neighborhoods. During the period since HUD's June 1979 questioning of the city's CDBG priorities, the Low-Income Planning Committee, representing the group C neighborhoods, and GBM obtained technical assistance from the Center for Community Change in Washington, D.C., and prepared an administrative performance case study of Birmingham's CDBG program for the National Citizens Monitoring Project on Community Development Block Grants. The May 1980 case study was submitted as an amendment to the 1979 complaint. The case study reviewed the origins of the complaint as well as commented on what it perceived to be the inadequacy of a neighborhood analysis of the thirty-two group C neighborhoods prepared by Harland Bartholomew and Associates.[103] The city had responded to the NSA controversy by selecting Bartholomew to complete a $98,000 study of Birmingham's poorest neighborhoods. Although objecting to their lack of participation in the design of the study and selection of the contractor, group C neighborhood leaders, organized as the Citizens Planning Committee for Lower-Income Neighborhoods, worked with the city and Bartholomew in the spring and early summer of 1980 on the low-income neighborhood study.[104]

The following month, on June 27, 1980, John Wilson presented HUD's case to Birmingham, attaching two conditions to the city's 1980–81 CDBG budget. The first condition required the city to justify selection of the NSAs in terms of whether they met CDBG statutory guidelines for principally benefiting low- and moderate-income households. HUD believed that the NSAs consisted of areas that did not include low- and moderate-income households and ordered the city to justify their selection. If the city could not do so, then it would have to reprogram its CDBG funds to principally benefit these households.[105] The second condition required the city to provide a more extensive summary of its community development and housing needs, particularly with regard to low- and moderate-income households.

Both conditions were prompted by HUD's questioning of the "overall appropriateness of the program toward complying with the statutory purpose" of principally benefiting low- and moderate-income households.[106]

HUD rejected the city's August 19 response to these conditions. Instead, on September 11, 1980, Wilson wrote Mayor Richard Arrington that the city had excluded many areas in which 60 percent or more of residents had low or moderate incomes, while selecting NSAs that had only slightly more than 50 percent of households in this income range. HUD was not arguing that such neighborhoods as Five Points South and Bush Hills lacked economic need, but that the city had selected these neighborhoods while bypassing "large areas with severe needs."[107] Given the large degree of need that had accumulated in Birmingham's neighborhoods, most of which were black, HUD was telling the city that these neighborhoods could not be excluded from the CDBG program just because they lacked revitalization potential. HUD was effectively saying that the city would have to continue to pay for its years of accumulated neglect of its black neighborhoods.

HUD required the city drop Five Points South and Bush Hills from the NSA program and reprogram $1,375,000 targeted to these two neighborhoods to activities that would principally benefit low- and moderate-income persons. In addition, HUD required the city to reduce the size of the Woodlawn, Mason City, North Birmingham, and South Tittusville NSAs so that they included "only those areas with high concentrations of low and moderate income persons."[108] Overall, Wilson had taken a clear position that the NSA program's objectives were subservient to overriding legislative intent of the CDBG program to primarily assist poor households. Specifically, in his September 11 letter to Mayor Arrington, Wilson said, "While we encourage the use of NSA's, our mandate is to ensure that the overall CDBG program principally benefits low and moderate income persons."[109]

Quickly recognizing that the possibility of reprogrammed CDBG funds represented a significant opportunity to influence the city's CDBG program, on July 19, 1980, the Citizens Planning Committee for Lower-Income Neighborhoods met with Mayor Richard Arrington and his administrative assistant, Edward LaMonte. The committee recommended that resources be invested in increasing the capacity of neighborhoods to revitalize themselves. Based on their experience with the NSA selection process, the members recommended abolition of the Community Development Department. It should be replaced with an Office of Neighborhood Development that could provide planning and other technical assistance to group A, B, and C neighborhoods. Moreover, while the new office would assign neighborhood development specialists to group A and B neighborhoods, the city should subcontract with a nonprofit Citizen Planning Committee to assign neighborhood development specialists to work full-time with the group C neighborhoods.[110] This recommendation was clearly motivated by a desire to establish a technical assistance and planning organization that was independent of the city.

The city's Community Development Department responded with its own proposal, which instead of eliminating that department would reorganize and expand its staff. Although the Community Development Department believed that it could adequately serve the needs of the city's low-income neighborhoods, Mayor Arrington and the city council approved a reprogramming of CDBG funds. This enabled the expansion and reorganization of the Community Development Department while also providing $200,000 annually to Neighborhood Services, Inc. (NSI).[111]

NSI, which grew out of the Citizens Planning Committee for Lower-Income Neighborhoods that had served as the core group for the May 1979 citizens complaint, was incorporated in December 1980 and funded by the city's CDBG program in May 1981.[112] NSI was established to provide technical assistance to the city's poorest neighborhoods, most of which were on the group C list. According to the CDBG amendment, "The purpose of this assistance will be to help build the capacity of neighborhood groups to participate in the planning and implementation of Community Development activities within their neighborhoods."[113] NSI's initial board of directors was drawn from the presidents of Citizen Participation Program neighborhood associations in the forty-three group A and group C low-income neighborhoods identified in the NSA selection process.

NSI was intended to be a source of technical assistance that was controlled by the city's low-income and predominantly black neighborhoods. At the same time, the city responded to HUD's mandatory CDBG programming by expanding and reorganizing the Community Development Department so that it would be more responsive to the needs of low-income neighborhoods. The Community Development Department designated teams of one planner and two community resource officers to each of four areas of the city that included low-income neighborhoods. The teams were to provide expertise in meeting both the physical and human services needs of low-income neighborhoods.[114] Despite the shift in the Community Development Department's approach, NSI executive director Richard Berliner felt that NSI would serve a vital purpose: "Community Development has the same goals [as NSI]. But we respond to the presidents of the neighborhoods rather than the city and the mayor."[115]

Epilogue

With the rerouting of the Red Mountain Expressway, the recasting of priorities in the 1977 bond election, and the conditioning by HUD of the city's Community Development Block Grant budget, residents of Birmingham's black neighborhoods had established themselves as a source of influence in shaping the city's plans. In particular, the creation of the Citizen Participation Program in 1974 permitted black neighborhoods to organize themselves and to develop a cadre of leadership that could begin to influence the planning process in Birmingham. Significantly, the city's black neighborhoods had taken advantage of the changes wrought by the Citizen Participation Program to obtain not only veto power but actual influence to shape the city's policies. HUD's 1968 rejection of the Birmingham's Model Cities application was the first time black neighborhoods were able to stop the city from planning in a way that hurt their community or at least left black residents outside the decision-making process. But by the end of the 1970s black residents had not only been able to stop the city from doing what it wanted but also had developed the capacity and the strength to force implementation of alternative plans that better recognized the needs of black neighborhoods. These advantages were compounded by the election in October 1979 of Richard Arrington as Birmingham's first black mayor.

Richard Arrington was first elected to the Birmingham City Council in 1971. Raised in nearby Fairfield, Arrington had been forced to earn a master's and Ph.D. in zoology at universities outside of Alabama because there were no such opportunities for blacks in his home state. Returning to the Birmingham area in 1966, Arrington served as a faculty member and administrator at historically black Miles College in Fairfield, where he had taught from 1957 to 1963 prior to earning his Ph.D. In 1970, he left Miles to become executive director of the

Alabama Center for Higher Education, a consortium of eight predominantly black colleges in Alabama.[1]

During the summer of 1971, Arrington was approached by three young black men who asked him if he was interested in running for mayor of Birmingham. Arrington said no, but friends persuaded him to run for a seat on the city council. Running on a platform that included greater representation of blacks on city boards and paved streets and better services for black neighborhoods, in October 1971 Arrington became the second black elected to Birmingham's city council.[2] During his two terms on the city council, Arrington championed support for affirmative action and opposition to police brutality of black citizens.

Arrington's leadership on the police brutality issue propelled him into the 1979 mayoral race. Although Bull Connor had not overseen the city's police department since 1963, the transformation of that department to one that administered justice equally to blacks and whites did not come quickly. Connor's police chief, Jamie Moore, was protected by the Jefferson County Personnel Board, which oversaw the city's and the county's civil service system. Even though George Seibels was elected as mayor in 1967 promising to fire Moore, Moore did not leave office until 1972, when Operation New Birmingham leaders helped get him appointed as an assistant to Alabama's attorney general. At Moore's departure, Birmingham had only about ten black police officers.[3] Even after Moore's resignation, incidents of police brutality in which blacks were injured or killed by white Birmingham police continued throughout the 1970s. During this period, Arrington took strong and publicly visible stances against police brutality, including challenging mayor George Seibels to get better control of the city's police department.[4]

Although Arrington expected David Vann, who defeated Seibels to become mayor in 1975, to be more willing to crack down on police brutality, Vann disappointed the black community in a police brutality case that cost him the 1979 election. On a June night in 1979, Bonita Carter had inserted herself in a violent situation by attempting to move the car of Alger Pickett. Pickett had fired shots into a 7-Eleven store, wounding a clerk in the predominantly black Kingston neighborhood after being told that he would have to pay in advance to fill his car with gas. Pickett had taken refuge across Tenth Avenue and called out for someone to move his car from where he had left it in the 7-Eleven parking lot. The twenty-year-old Carter, who had just walked to the store with a friend, got in the car and drove it out onto Tenth Avenue. Two Birmingham police officers arrived at the scene just as Bonita Carter had responded to the store manager's shout to stop the car. Although bystanders warned police that the person in the car was not the shooter, without speaking to Carter, the police fired into the parked car and killed her.[5]

With an angry crowd gathering at the 7-Eleven following the shooting, Birmingham police chief Bill Myers asked Richard Arrington to accompany him to the scene. Arrington attempted to get the crowd to disperse, but to no avail. Afterward, blacks called for the dismissal of officer George Sands, who had fired the shots that killed Bonita Carter. Arrington was familiar with Sands, having previously filed police brutality charges against him, as had others, adding up to a dozen complaints in eight years on the police force. In only one instance did Sands get as much as a verbal reprimand. When Arrington made public the accusations against Sands, black support for Sands's firing strengthened.[6]

Mayor Vann responded by appointing a citizens committee to investigate the shooting. It represented the first time that civilians had been brought in to investigate accusations of police brutality. In the past the police department's Internal Affairs Division had done its own investigations without citizen participation or review. Four of the committee's members were white and four were black, including Emmett Lockett, who had been elected president of the Kingston Neighborhood Association the previous November. After holding hearings and listening to witnesses, the committee voted unanimously, with one abstention, that the shooting of Bonita Carter was not justified. Nevertheless, Vann refused to fire Sands. Instead, he contended that Sands had followed the police department's procedures, and that it was these procedures, not Sands, that were at fault. Vann, who had been elected mayor by obtaining substantial support in the city's black community, had now earned its enmity.[7]

Vann's decision not to fire Sands came just three months before the October 1979 mayoral election. Energized by an act of police brutality that suggested that Bull Connor's legacy of racism in the police department was not yet dead, blacks searched for a mayoral candidate to run against Vann. According to Arrington's campaign manager, the Bonita Carter affair generated a determination in the black community to see that there was change: "The import of that incident kept the black community so enraged that [blacks] said there . . . must be . . . political change."[8] In August 1979, when a group of black community leaders called a news conference to announce their effort to draft Arrington as a candidate for mayor, Arrington responded by announcing his candidacy for the position. With limited funds, Arrington's campaign made use of the Citizen Participation Program neighborhood associations to provide the leadership for his campaign. Although two blacks ran in the primary along with three whites, including Vann, Arrington earned a plurality of votes, and in the runoff on October 30, 1979, was elected mayor, eking out a slim margin of victory over white conservative Frank Parsons. Much of Arrington's support came from the city's black neighborhoods, with only 10 percent of white voters supporting him.[9]

Birmingham entered a new phase of its history when its citizens elected Richard Arrington as mayor, a phase that would last nearly twenty years as he was elected to five four-year terms, finally stepping down in July 1999. At the beginning of Arrington's tenure as mayor, the city's black neighborhoods, with their demonstrated ability to influence the planning process, seemed poised in 1980 to move forward. Nevertheless, the conditions in which the city found itself after 1979, especially in its black neighborhoods, represented significant challenges to the city's planning efforts. Specifically, three key challenges confronted Arrington and his governance of Birmingham: poverty, restructuring of Birmingham's economy, and suburbanization.

Poverty

Although the city's neighborhoods benefited from increased attention to basic housing and infrastructure needs in the Seibels, Vann, and Arrington administrations, poverty still pervaded the city, especially its black neighborhoods. By the 1990s, only 2.6 percent of Birmingham's black households lived in dwelling units with "severe physical problems," and another 14.6 percent lived with "moderate physical problems." Whereas in 1950, 85 percent of the city's black residents lived in substandard housing, by the 1990s a similar percentage lived in standard quality housing. Similarly, by the 1990s, less than 5 percent of the city's black residents cited poor city or county services or undesirable land uses in their neighborhood. Ten percent of the city's black residents said their neighborhood streets required major repairs, about the same percentage as for the entire city.[10]

At the same time, however, Birmingham was the tenth-poorest large city in the nation, with nearly 25 percent of its residents living below the poverty line.[11] Much of this poverty was concentrated. In 1990, 45,434 Birmingham residents lived in census tracts that had poverty rates of 40 percent or higher. Sociologist William Julius Wilson, in his book *When Work Disappears,* identifies such neighborhoods as "ghetto poverty tracts." In addition, another 103,866 Birmingham residents lived in neighborhoods in which between 20 and 39 percent of the population was below the poverty line. Wilson calls these "poverty tracts." Overall, 149,300 of Birmingham's 265,968 residents in 1990 lived in poverty or ghetto poverty tracts. Although 25 percent of the city's population was poor, 56 percent of the city's population in 1990 lived in neighborhoods with substantial poverty. Twenty years earlier, 39,241 residents lived in ghetto poverty tracts, and 122,060 lived in poverty tracts, totaling 54 percent of the population.[12] The percentage of the city's population living in poverty and ghetto poverty tracts remained stable during the 1970 to 1990 period, but the number living in ghetto poverty tracts increased by over 6,000 persons, or nearly 16 percent, between these two census years. Clearly, poverty and concentrated poverty were major challenges confronting the Arrington administration.

In 1990, Birmingham's ghetto poverty tracts were predominantly black, and many of them were identified by the city in 1978 as group C neighborhoods (see table 8.1). But the reallocation of Community Development Block Grant funds to meet the needs of these neighborhoods faced long odds. On the city's west side, black neighborhoods such as Smithfield, Ensley, Sherman Heights, Mason City, Graymont, Rising West Princeton (formerly Rising Station), and the western part of North Tittusville were ghetto poverty tracts, as were the black neighborhoods of Central City, Fountain Heights, and Southside, which lie close to downtown Birmingham. The Kingston neighborhood in East Birmingham, the Collegeville neighborhood in North Birmingham, and Gate City on the east side were also ghetto poverty tracts. Many of these neighborhoods featured public housing projects that have come to concentrate the very poor: Smithfield (Smithfield Court), Ensley (Tuxedo Court), Graymont (Elyton Village), Central City (Metropolitan Gardens), North Tittusville (Joseph Loveman Village), Southside (Southtown), Kingston (Morton Simpson Village), Mason City (Cooper Green Homes), Fountain Heights (Freedom Manor), and Gate City (Charles Marks Village). In fact, ten of the city's seventeen public housing projects were located in ghetto poverty tracts.[13]

Overall, 91.5 percent of the population in the city's thirteen ghetto poverty tracts was black. The poverty rates ranged between 40.1 percent in Mason City to 72.4 percent in Central City, where the Central City (later Metropolitan Gardens) public housing project was located at the eastern edge of downtown Birmingham. Six of the thirteen ghetto poverty tracts had poverty rates above 50 percent, including Central City, Collegeville, Graymont, Ensley, Rising West Princeton, and the western part of North Tittusville. According to the 1990 census, 21.3 percent of persons sixteen and older in the labor force of the thirteen ghetto poverty tracts were unemployed, compared to 9.3 percent in Birmingham and 6.1 percent in the metropolitan area. Fifty-nine percent of families in these thirteen ghetto poverty tracts were female-headed, compared to 34.2 percent in the city and 19 percent in the metropolitan area.[14]

For residents who lived in these neighborhoods, poverty in the 1990s was commonplace; unemployment was three times greater than the metropolitan area average; and the majority of families were headed by a single female. Birmingham was not unique in having such concentrated poverty; increasingly, many large cities are the sites of large concentrations of impoverished residents who are by and large removed from the mainstream economy.[15] Nevertheless, Birmingham stood out in 1990 among large cities as having one of the ten most impoverished populations in the nation. While the basic housing and infrastructure problems in the city's black neighborhoods had been largely addressed, poverty had increasingly become the most apparent problem in these areas.

Restructuring of the Birmingham Economy

Birmingham's economic organization, which contributed to poverty in the city, dictated the Arrington administration's second great challenge: the restructuring of the Birmingham economy. Overall, the city has successfully transformed itself from a manufacturing and mining center to a services center, but the impact of economic restructuring on employment opportunities has compounded the problems faced by the city's African American population. Birmingham was the leading industrial center of the New South, but by the 1950s, as discussed in chapter 6, its economic base of manufacturing, especially iron and steel, as well as mining, had begun to decline.

The impact of steel's decline in Birmingham was compounded by the racial caste system that kept black iron- and steelworkers out of the best jobs in the mills. By the time racial barriers to advancement were cleared away by the civil rights movement and changes in federal policies and laws, the decline in overall employment in the steel industry prevented Birmingham's blacks from making up for what they had lost through employment discrimination. Black employment in iron and steel plants had actually begun to decline after the organizing drives of the 1930s that unionized Birmingham's metal workers. As a price for obtaining the support of white workers, the Steel Worker Organizing Committee (SWOC, later the United Steelworkers of America) permitted the construction of separate lines of promotion for whites and blacks. With the Depression threatening their livelihoods, white steelworkers pushed for using the seniority system to protect their entry into semiskilled jobs formerly held by blacks but made available to whites after layoffs and call-backs had permitted white foremen to replace black workers with whites. Consequently, black employment in Birmingham's iron and steel plants was down by nearly 25 percent in 1940 compared to its 1930 level. White employment in these plants was the same in 1940 as in 1930. From 1950 to 1970, black employment in iron and steel fell by nearly 20 percent, while white employment was the same in 1970 as it was in 1950.

In effect, the employment declines in the local iron and steel industry that began in the 1950s had their primary impact on black employment opportunities. By the 1970s, when blacks had won significant employment discrimination cases and finally obtained the jobs to which their seniority entitled them, the era of massive plant shutdowns cost them their employment. Tennessee Coal and Iron, a subsidiary of U.S. Steel, had been the Birmingham district's largest employer. After reducing its workforce in the 1970s, it stopped operating in 1982, although one plant reopened two years later. Sloss Furnaces, which had been a visible hallmark of the city's iron industry, shut down in 1971 and by the early 1980s was a historical museum. Republic Steel also shut down in the 1970s, as did Pullman-Standard in the early 1980s.[16]

Fortunately for the city's economic base, the health industry has assumed an ever-increasing role in employing the region's workforce. If successful urban renewal is defined by the degree to which a particular project establishes a new economic base, then the Southside Medical Center expansion that became the University of Alabama at Birmingham may have been the most successful urban renewal project in the nation. By the 1980s, with the reductions in force at U.S. Steel and the growth of UAB, the university and its hospital had become the city's largest employer.[17] Without UAB, the decline in the steel industry would have been an economic disaster for Birmingham. With UAB, the city and region were able to shift to an economy that is a balance of manufacturing and services. In 1950, the health services industry in Birmingham employed 5,481 residents, or about 10 percent of the total number employed in manufacturing that year. By 1990, 42,691 residents were employed in health services, or about 72 percent of the number employed in manufacturing.[18]

The impact of the growing health industry on Birmingham can be seen by comparing metropolitan and national unemployment rates. In the national recession of the early 1980s, when Birmingham's iron and steel plants were closing down and laying off workers, local unemployment rates soared to 14 percent in 1982 and 13 percent in 1983. Nationally, the unemployment rate in these years was 9.7 percent and 9.6 percent. While the national economy was suffering through a period of deindustrialization, the process of plant closings was amplified in Birmingham.[19] During the 1990–91 recession, however, Birmingham's unemployment rate ran in the 5.0 to 5.3 percent range, while the national unemployment rate ran one to two percentage points higher.[20] By the 1990s, with plant closings behind it, Birmingham's increasingly service-based economy appeared better prepared to handle economic downturns. UAB had enabled the city to successfully shift away from a manufacturing-based economy to one with a more diversified and stable economic base.

Although the growth of UAB and the health industry in Birmingham enabled the metropolitan area to successfully restructure its economy, the impact on the city's black citizens, especially black men, was less apparent. In contrast to the iron and steel industry, which is male dominated, 85 percent of individuals employed nationally in the health occupations (excluding physicians and dentists) in 1998 were female. Overall, blacks are slightly underrepresented in these health occupations (8.9 percent versus 11.1 percent for all occupations).[21] The employment that Birmingham's black men lost in the iron and steel industry, therefore, has not been replaced by equivalent job opportunities in the health industry.

The contrast between Birmingham's booming health sector and the black neighborhoods left behind can be seen by comparing UAB with its neighbor to the west. Lying just west of UAB's western boundary, Interstate 65, North Tittusville is one of Birmingham's poorer neighborhoods. In 1978, the city included it with the thirty-two group C neighborhoods, even though North Tittusville is located adjacent to the city's largest growth engine, UAB. In 1980, 57 percent of the neighborhood's residents had incomes below the federal poverty line, and 99 percent of its population was black. Of the neighborhood's 1,640 families, nearly 60 percent were headed by a single-parent female. Despite the proximity to higher education, only 5 percent of the adult population had completed four or more years of college. Only about one-fourth of the neighborhood's residents owned their own homes.[22] By the 1990s, the North Tittusville neighborhood continued to be impoverished, although the percentage living below the poverty line had dropped to 36 percent. Of the approximately 3,500 dwelling units in the neighborhood, 500 were located in the Loveman Village public housing development. About 14 percent of all dwelling units were vacant.[23]

In 1990, North Tittusville neighborhood leaders, including the president of the North Tittusville Neighborhood Association, petitioned UAB officials for a partnership between the neighborhood and the university to address issues related to the neighborhood's impoverishment. The university responded with the commitment of faculty and students and the capitalization of the Tittusville 2000 Project with a $150,000 grant. In preparation for applying to HUD for federal funds, neighborhood leaders and residents identified a set of priorities for the neighborhood. Second on the list of twenty-two ranked priorities was a call for "more economic development."[24] The fact that a neighborhood located so close to the city's chief economic engine could identify economic development as being of high importance indicates the degree to which the economic benefits flowing from the urban renewal of the city's south side had failed to trickle down to the city's poor, black neighborhoods. If a neighborhood such as North Tittusville, for which geographic accessibility to employment is not an issue, could not enjoy the fruits of UAB's growth, then it is not surprising that the remainder of Birmingham's black neighborhoods were also not sharing in the benefits of the local economy's shift to health and education services.

Suburbanization

The Arrington administration's third key challenge was suburbanization. From the 1910 Greater Birmingham annexation—which added forty-eight square miles and 70,000 people—to 1950, Birmingham's share of Jefferson County's population remained nearly constant at around 58 percent. From 1950 on, suburban growth diminished Birmingham's share of the county's population so that by 1970 fewer than half of the county's residents lived in the city. By 1980, the percentage had dropped to 42 percent.[25] If Birmingham was to remain fiscally healthy, it needed to do a better job of capturing the region's population and economic growth. Although suburbanization did not directly affect the city's black community in the same way as poverty or economic restructuring, it did affect the ability of the city to retain its middle-class population and to retain tax revenue. With continued suburbanization, Birmingham would increasingly become a city of concentrated poverty with a tax base inadequate to meet the pressing needs of its black neighborhoods.

After the failure of the One Great City campaign in the early 1970s, however, it was clear that the specter of school integration would keep Birmingham's suburban neighbors from ever voting to join the city. As a consequence, mayors David Vann and Richard Arrington pursued an annexation strategy that focused less on adding population and more on adding land that had potential for future economic development. As a result, even though the city's population dropped from 300,910 in 1970 to 265,968 in 1990, the city's land area increased from 79.5 square miles to 148.5 square miles.[26] Focusing on peripheral areas that typically had small, black populations eager to live in Birmingham and to receive public services often denied them by Jefferson County, the city's objective was to annex areas of potential future suburban development that had not yet been incorporated.

Vann and Arrington accomplished this by employing a little-used 1907 state law. The law permitted cities to call annexation elections without petition from landowners or residents where the city promises to provide full public services, but where all private property and associated uses were exempt from property, occupational license, and business license taxes for a period of five to fifteen years, depending on use.[27] The obvious fiscal cost associated with tax-exempt annexation had kept Birmingham from considering this alternative. A city council staff member in 1970 had described tax-exempt annexation as "almost completely useless."[28] But in the eyes of David Vann, who in 1974 was a city council member chairing the council's annexation committee, tax-exempt annexation was "the only route for any major annexation efforts" and was especially useful for annexation of areas with potential for industrial and commercial development. A 1923 revision of the state annexation code had made it very difficult for Birmingham to annex industrial lands and industrial interests had successfully opposed revision of that law ever since.[29]

Vann was particularly interested in Pinson Valley, running northeast from Birmingham; Oxmoor Valley, running southwest from the city; and Cahaba Valley, running southeast of the city along the Jefferson County–Shelby County line. Birmingham's Metropolitan Development Board had identified the first two undeveloped valleys as prime areas for new industrial development, and the Birmingham Chamber of Commerce had identified development of Cahaba Valley as its number-one priority.[30] By annexing land in these areas, Birmingham could better afford to use the tax-exempt annexation method because unpopulated areas require fewer services. Moreover, argued Vann, the tax-exemption feature could be used as an incentive to get industries to locate in these newly annexed areas.[31]

In a six-month period, from November 1974 through April 1975, Birmingham engaged in four major tax-exempt annexation efforts. Two of these were in Pinson and Oxmoor Valleys. A third was in an area north of the city that included Smithfield Heights and Daniel Payne College. The fourth was in an area west of Birmingham that extended to Birmingport on the Warrior River, part of the yet-to-be-completed Tennessee–Tombigbee Waterway running from the Tennessee Valley to the Gulf Coast, near the line marking the northwestern boundary of Jefferson County.[32] Birmingham was successful in all but the Pinson Valley annexation. In that case, a popular vote for annexation was overturned by an Alabama Supreme Court decision that found that Birmingham had gerrymandered the annexation vote by selecting areas that surveys showed favored annexation.[33]

Vann and the city used the same strategy in each of these referenda. The city identified an area it wanted to annex and then identified the population enclaves most likely to vote for annexation. In most of these areas (Smithfield Heights–Daniel Payne, Oxmoor Valley, and Pinson Valley), the populations were primarily black, reversing the pre-1970 pattern of attempting to annex predominantly white suburban enclaves.[34]

Under Mayor Richard Arrington, Birmingham began anew its tax-exempt annexation efforts in 1985. Again, the city succeeded primarily when it annexed relatively unpopulated areas with small pockets of black residents.[35] The annexations of the 1980s continued the strategy of the 1970s. To reach Cahaba Valley, lying southeast of the city, Birmingham in 1985 first annexed land northeast of the city, using this annexation to obtain a site for the Birmingham Race Course, an effort to bring horse racing, pari-mutuel betting, and associated economic development to the Alabama-Georgia area. Soon after, Birmingham made several annexations that enabled its boundaries to move south between the suburbs of Irondale, Leeds, and Trussville and link up with Lake Purdy, owned by the Birmingham Water Works Board.[36] Finally, by connecting with property near Lake Purdy, annexation was then able to continue southwest to the intersection of Interstate 459 and Alabama 280. Birmingham was also able to achieve similar success in annexing land west of the city to Birmingport on the Warrior River and the Tennessee–Tombigbee Waterway and in extending city land further southwest into Oxmoor Valley.[37]

Although the annexations of the 1970s and 1980s nearly doubled the city's land area, the loss of population to the suburbs continued, and by 1990 only 40.8 percent of Jefferson County's population lived in the city.[38] The success or failure of Birmingham's annexation policy rests upon the degree of development these areas will capture after their annexation. Thus far, it appears that while the city has been successful in annexing areas that will enjoy significant commercial development, the city has been unable to annex land that is attractive for residential development.

In the case of commercial development, annexations have taken in portions of the rapidly developing Alabama 280 corridor, which runs southeast from the city on a line between Homewood and Mountain Brook. Annexation of this land gives Birmingham the opportunity to capture or retain commercial development that prefers to be in "edge city" type developments, such as that which lies at the intersection of Alabama 280 and Interstate 459. Developments in this area, which are now in Birmingham, include the South Central Bell–Alabama headquarters (which had moved out of downtown Birmingham), a Sheraton Hotel, the Colonnade, and the Summit shopping center, which produced $5 million in local tax revenue in its first eighteen months of operation.[39] In 1995, the city was able to entice HealthSouth Corporation, the nation's largest provider of rehabilitation services, to build a $38 million headquarters facility in this area.[40]

But the biggest test of Birmingham's annexation policy lay in Oxmoor Valley, which is located to the southwest of Birmingham. Portions of Oxmoor Valley were annexed in both the 1970s and 1980s. It was here, in a 7,800-acre mixed-use Oxmoor Valley development, that the city had hoped not only to stimulate commercial development but also to launch suburban residential development inside the city's expanded boundaries. The *Birmingham News* articulated Birmingham's suburban dream for Oxmoor when it wrote: "Imagine a new suburb—

inside the Birmingham city limits—the size and population of Homewood, complete with a city center that includes a police station, fire station, a school and lots of homes. It also would have high-tech industry,
research institutes and warehouses."[41]

Mayor Richard Arrington was very excited about Oxmoor's potential, claiming that "Oxmoor is the most important development Birmingham has."[42] Although Oxmoor has been successful in attracting
commercial development, its success in stimulating residential development is in doubt, especially with respect to the impact of Birmingham's public school system on housing demand in Oxmoor. The Oxmoor master plan identifies education as one of the major issues of
concern in planning the new community. An important planning objective was identified as the need to "consider the perceived 'negative'
aspect of the public school system as an opportunity to address and
solve an important social issue, while at the same time providing the
catalyst needed to market residential uses within Oxmoor."[43] If Oxmoor is to be comparable to Reston or Columbia, as called for in its
1990 plan, it must still address this basic issue.[44]

Unfortunately, in the 1990s the quality of the Birmingham school
system came under question, with 80 percent of the schools in the system on academic alert for low test scores and the state's superintendent of education considering takeover of the school system.[45] To make
the prospect of public schooling more appealing to prospective residents of Oxmoor, plans called for construction of a magnet school
affiliated with UAB, but delays in its construction postponed residential development.[46] Instead, $8 million of a 1993 bond issue set aside
for the Oxmoor school were reallocated in 1997 to meet existing school
needs. This came in response to criticism that the Oxmoor school would
serve affluent families, while ignoring the needs of existing schools
serving poor families. The city's decision also reflected the fact that
USX, the successor to U.S. Steel and the major landowner in Oxmoor,
had postponed plans to begin residential development in the area.[47]

Birmingham's suburban strategy, under both mayors Vann and Arrington, has been a mixed success. It has enabled the city to capture
some lucrative commercial development but failed as a tool for re-
capturing suburban growth. In the end, the city's more recent annexation efforts have failed to capture significant population gains for the
same reason the earlier annexation campaigns of the 1950s, 1960s,

and early 1970s had failed: people who have a choice do not want their children attending schools in Birmingham's predominantly black school system.

City Planning in Birmingham: Change and Continuity

After 1979, planning in Birmingham had entered a new era. The era in which planning had been used to segregate blacks into inferior neighborhoods had ended. The black community, through its indigenous civic leagues, had influenced the development of a citizen participation program in which residents could better influence the planning process, and through the community-organizing efforts of the 1970s, it had demonstrated its ability to influence city plans. In a sense, the election of Richard Arrington marked the passing of Birmingham's civil rights era. But new challenges now confronted Arrington and the black community. These challenges—poverty, economic restructuring, and suburbanization—had powerful implications for the city's black community. They would not be easily solved.

Birmingham's black community and its neighborhood-based planning tradition were also challenged by the Arrington administration and the ascendance of the black elite, as represented by Arrington, to political power. With Arrington as mayor, the politics of planning and race were no longer the same as prior to 1980. Instead, blacks and black neighborhoods faced the prospect that class differences in the black community would become more apparent and would dilute efforts to resolve problems, such as poverty, that confronted the entire black community. The same class differences that Glenn Eskew found had divided the black community in Birmingham's civil rights era became more visible after 1980, when blacks of all classes were no longer discriminated against by city government. When Bull Connor treated all blacks with contempt, it was easier for blacks from different backgrounds to come together. But a black mayor and, after 1985, a majority black city council meant that city government's actions that hurt black neighborhoods could no longer be construed as racist and therefore were more difficult for a broad group of black citizens to unite against.[48]

The demolition of Metropolitan Gardens (formerly Central City public housing) presents a prime example of this change in Birmingham's politics. In January 2000, Birmingham received a $35 million HOPE VI grant from HUD. Before resigning as mayor in July 1999, Richard Arrington pledged $22 million in funds that would directly or indirectly assist the HOPE VI project.[49] The plan called for demolition of the 910 public housing units at Metropolitan Gardens and their replacement by two mixed-income neighborhoods, one located on the Metropolitan Gardens site and the other located in the city's civil rights district, just to the northwest of downtown. The nonprofit Birmingham Urban Revitalization Partnership—headed by Arrington, Alabama Power chief executive Elmer Harris, and Reverend John T. Porter, for thirty-eight years the pastor of the city's largest black church— would develop the latter project.[50] Only 340 units of public housing were to be built on the two sites, resulting in a net loss of 570 public housing units. In addition, 489 market-rate units were to be constructed at both sites. Also supporting the project was Operation New Birmingham, which saw the new housing as consistent with its goal of adding 1,000 units of housing to downtown Birmingham.[51] Displaced families who did not move into the newly constructed public housing units were to either move into existing public housing in the city or receive federally funded Section 8 housing vouchers to move into private rental housing.[52]

Twenty-five years after black residents of this public housing project successfully resisted white-dominated city government attempts to plow the Red Mountain Expressway through it, the black-led Birmingham city government, in cooperation with black and white business and civic leaders, was planning to demolish the project. Once again, Operation New Birmingham was backing efforts to demolish the city's predominantly black downtown public housing project in order to advance its business-oriented downtown revitalization agenda. And just as in 1974, the residents of Metropolitan Gardens dreaded the thought of leaving their neighborhood and its convenience to downtown Birmingham.[53] But it is that convenience that has attracted city officials and business leaders to claiming this valuable real estate for uses that they believe will do more to enhance the business climate of downtown Birmingham. According to the housing authority's 1999 HOPE VI application:

The recognition of Downtown Birmingham as one of America's most livable cities has been stymied for years by the concentration of distressed public housing at its core. Parking garages have been built up around the units like a blockade, shielding Downtown from this site. And a general reluctance by developers, institutions, and corporate users to get too close to the perceived dangers of this site have resulted in disinvestment and distress in the intervening blocks.[54]

As in the 1950s, 1960s, and 1970s, when the city's urban renewal and highway construction programs created relocation problems for black residents, the demolition of Metropolitan Gardens promised to do the same. Lisa Isay, head of the Metropolitan Birmingham Services for the Homeless, expressed concern that the demolition of public housing "further hurts our chances of moving people from homelessness to public housing."[55]

Unlike the earlier decades, however, when Birmingham blacks could rally against the racism practiced by a white-controlled city government, they now faced a black-dominated city government that was cooperating with a coalition of both white and black economic and civic leaders who gave priority to downtown as a place to do business. Operation New Birmingham, created in the midst of the city's civil rights struggles to direct attention toward downtown revitalization, was rejected by the city's black community in 1974 as administrator of the city's Citizen Participation Program. In 1999, it was cooperating with the city's black-led government to support the demolition of Metropolitan Gardens. The challenge to the black community after 1980 was that while racism no longer shaped the relationship between the city's government and its black neighborhoods, differences in economic interest were likely to continue to affect the welfare of Birmingham's black neighborhoods. The business interests that have been reflected in the Operation New Birmingham agenda since its creation were now broad enough to include both black and white business leaders, but the interests of the city's black neighborhoods still appeared to come second.

As such, the political distribution of power in Birmingham resembles that found in other majority black cities such as Atlanta and

Detroit. Black politicians and business leaders in both cities have formed alliances with white politicians and business leaders to make certain that the interests of business are met first. Often this occurs at the expense of addressing problems that befall poor, predominantly African American neighborhoods in those cities.[56]

This challenge also reflected the continuing moral ambiguity of planning. The advocacy planning of the 1970s, which led local planners and other activists to defend the rights of blacks and the poor against threats posed by Operation New Birmingham and the Red Mountain Expressway, had not succeeded in establishing and sustaining a clear moral vision that would guide planning decisions.[57] Consequently, the question of whether the land served its residents or its investors continued to be unresolved, enabling planning to once again be used to assist in dislocating poor people who also happened to be black. Although many may argue that public housing for poor people is an inappropriate use for land located so central to the city's downtown core, it is also difficult to ignore planning's long history in Birmingham, and in other cities, as a tool for relocating marginalized populations, often African American, when they get in the way of the development plans of cities, institutions, and private businesses. The Metropolitan Gardens case is but one more example of how planning was used in the twentieth century to manipulate the residency of black households so that the needs of other groups can be met first. Whether the planning tool is zoning, urban renewal, or highway construction, the pattern has been the same. Furthermore, the pattern persists as exclusionary zoning has succeeded racial zoning and HOPE VI has succeeded urban renewal.[58]

Even though the 1980s and 1990s marked the ascendance of black political power in Birmingham, the Metropolitan Gardens case demonstrates that black, lower-income populations remain subservient to the overall economic needs of the business community. In the words of *Birmingham World* editor Emory Jackson, writing in reaction to the planned expansion of the Southside Medical Center in 1953, "Progress which pushes one group down because of race is the wrong type of progress."[59]

At minimum, one would hope that in the case of Metropolitan Gardens, as well as in other public housing projects and impoverished neighborhoods threatened by displacement, a relocation plan similar to the one worked out between the Central City residents and the State of Alabama in 1977 can be agreed upon. In that case, Governor George Wallace approved an agreement where public housing residents displaced by the Red Mountain Expressway would receive replacement public housing. The location and design of the housing would be approved by a committee whose membership included Central City residents (see chapter 8). Providing secure tenure in decent housing with tenants involved in the choice of design and location seems to be a minimally humane foundation upon which future urban revitalization can be grounded. Ironically, it is an agreement signed by the one-time segregationist governor of Alabama that provides city planning with a much-needed framework for assuring the civil rights of residents confronted by urban renewal.

Notes

Introduction

1. In the case of Birmingham, see Glenn T. Eskew, *But for Birmingham: The Local and National Movements in the Civil Rights Struggle* (Chapel Hill: University of North Carolina Press, 1997); Diane McWhorter, *Carry Me Home, Birmingham, Alabama: The Climactic Battle of the Civil Rights Revolution* (New York: Simon and Schuster, 2001).

2. See, for example, John F. Bauman, *Public Housing, Race, and Renewal: Urban Planning in Philadelphia, 1920–1974* (Philadelphia: Temple University Press, 1987); June Manning Thomas, *Redevelopment and Race: Planning a Finer City in Postwar Detroit* (Baltimore: Johns Hopkins University Press, 1997); Arnold Hirsch, *Making of the Second Ghetto*, 2d ed. (Chicago: University of Chicago Press, 1998); Thomas Sugrue, *The Origins of the Urban Crisis: Race and Inequality in Postwar Detroit* (Princeton: Princeton University Press, 1998).

3. See, for example, Yale Rabin, "Expulsive Zoning: The Inequitable Legacy of *Euclid*," in *Zoning and the American Dream: Promises Still to Keep*, ed. Charles M. Haar and Jerold S. Kayden, 101–21 (Chicago: Planners Press, 1989); Charles Haar, *Suburbs under Siege: Race, Space, and Audacious Judges* (Princeton: Princeton University Press, 1996).

4. Martin Luther King Jr., *Why We Can't Wait* (New York: Harper and Row, 1964), 43.

5. Eskew, *But for Birmingham*, 312.

6. See Bobby Wilson, *America's Johannesburg* (Lanham, Md.: Rowman and Littlefield, 2000); Eskew, "Bombingham," in *But for Birmingham;* "Fear and Hatred Grip Birmingham," *New York Times*, April 12, 1960; "Birmingham: Integration's Hottest Crucible," *Time*, December 15, 1958.

7. Henry M. McKiven Jr., *Iron and Steel: Class, Race, and Community in Birmingham, Alabama, 1875–1920* (Chapel Hill: University of North Carolina Press, 1995), 171.

8. Christopher Silver, "The Racial Origins of Zoning: Southern Cities from 1910–1940," *Planning Perspectives* 6 (1991): 189–205.

9. Raymond A. Mohl, "The Second Ghetto and the 'Infiltration Theory' in Urban Real Estate, 1940–1960," in *Urban Planning and the African American Commu-*

nity: In the Shadows, ed. June Manning Thomas and Marsha Ritzdorf (Thousand Oaks, Calif.: Sage Publications, 1997), 63.

10. George B. Nesbitt to J. W. Follin, urban renewal commissioner, July 25, 1956, U.S. Home and Housing Finance Agency (HHFA) Files, record group 207, box 749, National Archives II; "Negro clearance" reference is used to describe Birmingham's Southside Medical Center urban renewal project in George B. Nesbitt to N. S. Keith, director, Division of Slum Clearance and Urban Redevelopment, May 21, 1953, HHFA Files, record group 207, box 750, National Archives II.

11. A. L. Thompson, racial relations advisor, Housing and Home Finance Agency, to Carlos W. Starr, June 3, 1952, HHFA Files, record group 207, box 750, National Archives II.

12. Ebenezer Howard, *Garden Cities of Tomorrow* (Cambridge: MIT Press, 1965). Howard's book was originally published in 1898 as *Tomorrow: A Peaceful Path to Real Reform*.

13. Joe Feagin, "Arenas of Conflict: Zoning and Land Use Reform in Critical Political-Economic Perspective," in *Zoning and the American Dream*, ed. Haar and Kayden, 84–89; Haar, *Suburbs under Siege*, 8–9, 15–16.

14. H. M. Caldwell, *History of the Elyton Land Company and Birmingham, Alabama* (Birmingham: self-published, 1892), 3–4; Marjorie Longenecker White, *The Birmingham District: An Industrial History and Guide* (Birmingham: Birmingham Historical Society, 1981), 36–37; Martha Carolyn Mitchell, "Birmingham: Biography of a City of the New South" (PhD diss., University of Chicago, 1946), 18.

15. Warren H. Manning, *City Plan of Birmingham* (Birmingham, 1919).

16. *The Survey*, January 6, 1912, 1449–556.

17. Philip A. Morris and Marjorie Longenecker White, eds., *Designs on Birmingham: A Landscape History of a Southern City and Its Suburbs* (Birmingham: Birmingham Historical Society, 1989), 51; Edward LaMonte, *Politics and Welfare in Birmingham: 1900–1975* (Tuscaloosa: University of Alabama Press, 1995), 12.

18. *Birmingham Post*, July 13, 1926.

19. Federal Emergency Administration of Public Works, Housing Division, Statistical Section, "Status of PWA Housing Division Projects: December 15, 1936."

20. Charles E. Connerly, "Federal Urban Policy and the Birth of Democratic Planning in Birmingham, Alabama: 1949–1974," in *Planning the Twentieth-Century American City*, ed. Mary Corbin Sies and Christopher Silver (Baltimore: Johns Hopkins University Press, 1996).

21. William Julius Wilson, *The Truly Disadvantaged* (Chicago: University of Chicago Press, 1987).

1. Big Mules and Bottom Rails in the Magic City

1. W. David Lewis, *Sloss Furnaces and the Rise of the Birmingham District* (Tuscaloosa: University of Alabama Press, 1994), 24; Marjorie Longenecker White, *The Birmingham District: An Industrial History and Guide* (Birmingham: Birmingham Historical Society, 1981), 36–37.

2. Marvin Whiting, "James R. Powell and 'This Magic Little City of Ours': A Perspective on Local History," *Journal of the Birmingham Historical Society* 8 (1983): 39.

3. Lewis, *Sloss Furnaces*, 21–22, 32–33, 47–48, 50–57; Ethel Armes, *The Story of Coal and Iron in Alabama* (Birmingham: Chamber of Commerce, 1910), 111–20.

4. John T. Milner, *Report of the Chief Engineer to the President and Board of Directors of the South and North Alabama Railroad Co., on the 26th of November 1859* (Montgomery: Advertiser Steam Printing House, 1859), 13.

5. Armes, *Story of Coal*, 77–78; Lewis, *Sloss Furnaces*, 20.

6. Lewis, *Sloss Furnaces*, 83; John Hope Franklin, *From Slavery to Freedom* (New York: Alfred A. Knopf, 1967), 197.

7. John W. DuBose, ed. *The Mineral Wealth of Alabama and Birmingham Illustrated* (Birmingham: N. T. Green and Co., 1886), 109.

8. Lewis, *Sloss Furnaces*, 85; Jonathan M. Wiener, *Social Origins of the New South* (Baton Rouge: Louisiana State University Press, 1978), 159–60; Carl V. Harris, *Political Power in Birmingham, 1871–1921* (Knoxville: University of Tennessee Press, 1977), 187.

9. Lewis, *Sloss Furnaces*, 71; U.S. Senate, *Report of the Committee of the Senate upon the Relations between Labor and Capital*, vol. 4 (Washington, D.C.: Government Printing Office, 1885), 288. Elsewhere in his testimony Sloss complains about the high rate of turnover among his employees (286–87).

10. Lewis, *Sloss Furnaces*, 91.

11. DuBose, *Mineral Wealth*, 109.

12. Robert J. Norrell and Otis Dismuke, *The Other Side: The Story of Birmingham's Black Community* (Birmingham: Birmingfind, n.d.), 1–2.

13. Harris, *Political Power*, 34.

14. U.S. Department of Commerce, *Statistical Abstract of the United States, 1925* (Washington, D.C.: Government Printing Office, 1926), 42–45. The other cities were Baltimore, Chicago, New York, Philadelphia, St. Louis, and Washington, D.C.

15. "Big Mules" was a term coined by populist and Ku Klux Klan member Bibb Graves, who was twice elected governor (in 1926 and 1934). Graves said that Big Mule industrialists brought to mind a wagon heavily loaded with corn pulled by a small mule. As the small mule strained to pull the load, a big mule hitched behind the wagon ate the corn. William Warren Rogers, Robert David Ward, Leah Rawls Atkins, and Wayne Flynt, *Alabama: The History of a Deep South State* (Tuscaloosa: University of Alabama Press, 1994), 413; Diane McWhorter, *Carry Me Home, Birmingham, Alabama: The Climactic Battle of the Civil Rights Revolution* (New York: Simon and Schuster, 2001), 36–37.

16. Armes, *Story of Coal*, 361–62; White, *Birmingham District*, 92; C. Vann Woodward, *Origins of the New South* (Baton Rouge: Louisiana State University Press, 1971), 299.

17. Armes, *Story of Coal*, 515; Lewis, *Sloss Furnaces*, 290; Woodward, *New South*, 300.

18. Armes, *Story of Coal*, 516–19; Lewis, *Sloss Furnaces*, 290–93; Woodward, *New South*, 300–301.

19. Harris, *Political Power*, 59–89. Harris found that between 1871 and 1953, the city's mayors and city council or city commission members came from "middle-ranking economic-interest groups," while no mayor and few city legislators were employees of Big Mule firms.

20. Irving Beiman, "Birmingham: Steel Giant with a Glass Jaw," in *Our Fair City*, ed. Robert S. Allen (New York: Vanguard Press, 1947), 118.

21. *Louisville Courier-Journal*, January 1, 1939. For a 1920 comparison with other cities, see Harris, *Political Power*, 145. For 1952, see U.S. Department of Commerce, *Compendium of City Government Finances in 1952* (Washington, D.C.: Government Printing Office, 1953).

22. Robert J. Norrell, "Caste in Steel: Jim Crow Careers in Birmingham, Alabama," *Journal of American History* 73 (1986): 669-94.

23. William A. Nunnelley, *Bull Connor* (Tuscaloosa: University of Alabama Press, 1991), 12–17; McWhorter, *Carry Me Home*, 37–39.

24. In 1953, after being convicted of having extramarital sex with his secretary, Connor did not run for reelection. He was elected to the city commission again in 1957 when the white, working-class voting districts of Birmingham provided him with his margin of victory. See Eskew, *But for Birmingham*, 118–19.

25. Beiman, "Birmingham," 117–18; Eskew, *But for Birmingham*, 90–91; Leah Rawls Atkins, "Senator James A. Simpson and Birmingham Politics of the 1930s: His Fight against the Spoilsmen and the Pie-Men," *Alabama Review* 41 (1988): 3–29.

26. Nunnelley, *Bull Connor*, 29; McWhorter, *Carry Me Home*, 593 n. 39.

27. Eskew, *But for Birmingham*, 87–89, 119.

28. Paul B. Worthman, "Working-Class Mobility in Birmingham, Alabama, 1880–1914," in *Anonymous Americans*, ed. Tamara K. Hareven (Upper Saddle River, N.J.: Prentice-Hall, 1971), 203–7.

29. Martha Carolyn Mitchell, "Birmingham: Biography of a City" (PhD diss., University of Chicago, 1946), 67; Lewis, *Sloss Furnaces*, 307.

30. Blaine A. Brownell, "Birmingham, Alabama: New South City in the 1920s," *Journal of Southern History* 38 (1972): 28–29.

31. *Birmingham World*, August 12, 1949.

32. Armes, *Story of Coal*, 234.

33. Worthman, "Working-Class Mobility," 197–201; Mitchell, "Birmingham: Biography of a City," 67; Henry M. McKiven, *Iron and Steel* (Chapel Hill: University of North Carolina Press, 1995), 57–58.

34. Karl E. Taeuber and Alma F. Taeuber, *Negroes in Cities* (New York: Atheneum, 1972), 39–40, 190. An index of 0 indicates complete integration, and 100 means complete segregation. The Taubers' indices were calculated on blocks, thereby resulting in higher indices than if census tracts had been used.

35. Barbara Nunn, ed., *Like It Ain't Never Passed: Remembering Life in Sloss Quarters* (Birmingham: Sloss Furnaces National Historic Landmark, 1985).

36. Will Prather, interview in Nunn, *Like It Ain't Never Passed,* 3–4. Will Prather worked for Sloss for forty-two years, retiring in 1956.

37. Will Prather and Jeffrey Rush, interviews in Nunn, *Like It Ain't Never Passed,* 1–4.

38. Mrs. Fannie Brown, interview by New South Associates, June 29, 1989, Birmingham Public Library Department of Archives and Manuscripts (hereafter BPLDAM), transcribed by author.

39. *Birmingham News,* October 13, 1912.

40. John Fitch, "The Human Side of Large Outputs," *The Survey,* January 6, 1912, 1532.

41. Ibid.; Morris Knowles, "Water and Waste," *The Survey,* January 6, 1912, 1485–1500.

42. Quotation from county health officer as reported in Knowles, "Water and Waste," 1486.

43. United States Senate, Reports of the Immigration Commission, *Immigrants in Industries,* pt. 2, *Iron and Steel Manufacturing* (Washington, D.C.: Government Printing Office, 1911), 2:187.

44. Knowles, "Water and Waste," 1489.

45. United States Senate, Reports of the Immigration Commission, 188–89.

46. W. M. McGrath, "Conservation of Health," *The Survey,* January 6, 1912, 1510.

47. Harris, *Political Power,* 238–39.

48. *Birmingham Age-Herald,* July 21, 1916, July 25, 1916, July 28, 1916, March 13, 1918, June 7, 1918, June 3, 1918; *Birmingham News,* January 15, 1918.

49. *Birmingham Age-Herald,* January 7, 1920.

50. *Birmingham News,* January 11, 1920.

51. Ibid., March 2, 1920.

52. Harris, *Political Power,* 180.

53. Graham Romeyn Taylor, "Birmingham's Civic Front," *The Survey,* January 6, 1912, 1467; George H. Miller, "Fairfield, A Town with a Purpose," *The American City: A Monthly Review of Municipal Problems and Civic Betterment* (September 1913): 213–19.

54. White, *Birmingham District,* 122.

55. Marlene Hunt Rikard, "An Experiment in Welfare Capitalism: The Health Care Services of the Tennessee Coal, Iron, and Railroad Company" (PhD diss., University of Alabama, 1983), 75–122; White, *Birmingham District,* 256–60.

56. Knowles, "Water and Waste," 1489.

57. McKiven, *Iron and Steel,* 137.

58. Rikard, "An Experiment in Welfare," 323–27.

59. J. D. Dowling and F. A. Bean, *Final Statistical Report of Surveys of the Blighted Areas, Birmingham, Alabama, Showing Some Comparative Figures for the Years, 1933 and 1935,* Jefferson County, Alabama Board of Health, 1937, 5–6; U.S. Census, *Fifteenth Census of the United States: 1930* (Washington, D.C.: Government Printing Office, 1932).

60. Duncan Nolan, *Social and Economic Survey of the Birmingham District* (Housing Authority of the Birmingham District [HABD], 1943), 18.

61. Nolan, *Social and Economic Survey*, 20.

62. National Register of Historic Places Inventory—Nomination Form, Smithfield Historic District, Birmingham Historic Society Register Files, box 1, file 13, BPLDAM; Lynne Feldman, *A Sense of Place: Birmingham's Black Middle-Class Community, 1890–1930* (Tuscaloosa: University of Alabama Press, 1999).

63. Feldman, *A Sense of Place*, 174; Angela Davis, *Angela Davis: An Autobiography* (New York: International Publishers, 1974), 87–92; Norrell and Dismuke, *The Other Side: The Story of Birmingham's Black Community*.

64. New South Associates and John Milner Associates, *"More Than What We Had": An Architectural and Historical Documentation of the Village Creek Project Neighborhoods, Birmingham, Alabama* (U.S. Army Corps of Engineers Technical Report, November 27, 1989), 22–40; Marjorie L. White and Carter L. Hudgins, *Village Creek: An Architectural and Historical Resources Survey of Ensley, East Birmingham and East Lake, Three Village Creek Neighborhoods* (Birmingham Historical Society, 1985), 71–72.

65. Quoted in New South Associates and John Milner Associates, *"More Than What We Had,"* 89–90.

66. Ibid., 148.

67. Mrs. Anna McCray Penick, interview by New South Associates, June 29, 1989, BPLDAM, transcribed by author.

68. U.S. Department of Commerce, Bureau of the Census, *Statistical Abstract of the United States, 1953*, 74th ed. (Washington, D.C.: Government Printing Office, 1953), 771–73.

69. U.S. Department of Commerce, Bureau of the Census, *Census of Housing: 1950*, vol. 1, pt. 2 (Washington, D.C.: Government Printing Office, 1953), tables 17, 21a.

70. Ibid.

71. New South Associates and John Milner Associates, *"More Than What We Had,"* 49–52, 61.

72. Dorothy Inman-Johnson, interview by the author, May 31, 2000, Tallahassee, Fl., transcript available.

73. De Leuw, Cather and Company, *Ensley–Pratt City Urban Renewal Study*, prepared for the Housing Authority of the Birmingham District, August 1958.

74. Ibid., 16.

75. *Birmingham Post-Herald*, July 6, 1971.

76. De Leuw, Cather and Company, *Ensley–Pratt City*, 18, exhibit 14.

77. Dorothy Inman-Johnson, interview by the author, May 31, 2000, Tallahassee, Fl.

78. Ibid.

79. Ibid.

80. Mrs. Anna McCray Penick, interview by New South Associates, June 29, 1989, BPLDAM, transcribed by author.

81. Rosa M. Kent, interview by Birmingfind Project Interviews, March 16, 1981, Birmingham, file 809.2.4.2.5, BPLDAM.

82. Benjamin Greene, former president, Harriman Park Civic League, interview by the author, June 23, 1995, Birmingham.

83. John Culpepper, former president, Grasselli Heights Civic League, interview by the author, June 27, 1995, Birmingham.

84. Simmie Lavender, Jones Valley Civic League, interview by the author, May 4, 1995, Birmingham.

85. Mrs. Fannie Brown, interview by New South Associates, June 29, 1989, Birmingham, BPLDAM, transcribed by author.

2. Planning and Jim Crow

1. C. Vann Woodward, *The Strange Career of Jim Crow*, 3rd rev. ed. (New York: Oxford University Press, 1974), 97–102.

2. Edward LaMonte, *Politics and Welfare in Birmingham, 1900–1975* (Tuscaloosa: University of Alabama Press, 1995), 12.

3. Carl Harris, *Political Power in Birmingham, 1871–1921* (Knoxville: University of Tennessee Press, 1977), 167.

4. *Birmingham World,* May 29, 1942.

5. LaMonte, *Politics and Welfare,* 12.

6. Ibid., 13; Harris, *Political Power,* 167.

7. The General Code of the City of Birmingham, Alabama of 1930, 1930, §§ 5066, 5067, 5210, 5211, 5212, 5213, 5288, 5516, 5699, 6002. Quote from § 5516.

8. Woodward, *Strange Career of Jim Crow,* 100–101; Roger L. Rice, "Residential Segregation by Law, 1910–1917," *Journal of Southern History* 34 (1968): 181; Christopher Silver, "The Racial Origins of Zoning: Southern Cities from 1910–1940," *Planning Perspectives* 6 (1991): 192–95.

9. Rice, "Residential Segregation," 180–81; Silver, "The Racial Origins," 192–93; Woodward, *Strange Career of Jim Crow,* 100.

10. Silver, "The Racial Origins," 193; Christopher Silver, *Twentieth-Century Richmond* (Knoxville: University of Tennessee Press, 1984), 111.

11. Silver, "The Racial Origins," 194–95.

12. Rice, "Residential Segregation," 184.

13. Ibid., 182–86.

14. Quoted in *Buchanan v. Warley,* 245 U.S. 60, 69–70 (1917).

15. Rice, "Residential Segregation," 186.

16. Ibid., 187–88.

17. *Buchanan v. Warley,* 245 U.S. 60, 81 (1917).

18. *Buchanan v. Warley,* 245 U.S. 60, 82 (1917).

19. *Birmingham News,* January 5, 1911.

20. Ibid., August 17, 1913.

21. Ibid., August 24, 1913, August 31, 1913.

22. Ibid., July 13, 1914; Lynne Feldman, *A Sense of Place: Birmingham's Black*

Middle-Class Community, 1890–1930 (Tuscaloosa: University of Alabama Press, 1999), 48.

23. Silver, "The Racial Origins," 193; Rice, "Residential Segregation," 189.

24. *Birmingham Age-Herald,* March 18, 1916.

25. *Birmingham Ledger,* September 13, 1916; Carl V. Harris, "Reforms in Government Control of Negroes in Birmingham, Alabama, 1890–1920," *Journal of Southern History* 38 (1972): 571.

26. Silver, "The Racial Origins," 189–205.

27. Ibid., 196.

28. Yale Rabin, "Expulsive Zoning: The Inequitable Legacy of *Euclid,*" in *Zoning and the American Dream: Promises Still to Keep,* ed. Charles M. Haar and Jerold S. Kayden (Washington, D.C.: American Planning Association Press, 1989), 103–6; Roy Lubove, *The Progressives and the Slums* (Pittsburgh: University of Pittsburgh Press, 1962), 229–45.

29. Blaine A. Brownell, *The Urban Ethos in the South, 1920–1930* (Baton Rouge: Louisiana State University Press, 1975), 182.

30. Ibid., 183.

31. *Birmingham News,* February 10, 1914, February 11, 1914; *Birmingham Age-Herald,* February 11, 1914.

32. Warren H. Manning, *City Plan of Birmingham* (Birmingham, 1919).

33. Ibid., 2–4, 28 (facing).

34. Ibid., 41–44. In 1924, a municipal auditorium was constructed adjacent to Capitol Park, later renamed Woodrow Wilson Park, and currently named Charles Linn Park. In 1927, the city's library was built next to the park, followed by the completion in 1932 of the Jefferson County Courthouse. Later, city hall (1950) and an art museum (1959) were constructed adjacent to the park, thereby completing the concentration of civic buildings and park space that Manning had called for in his plan. See Marjorie Longenecker White, *Downtown Birmingham: Architectural and Historical Walking Tour Guide* (Birmingham: Birmingham Historical Society, 1980), 88–91.

35. Manning, *City Plan of Birmingham,* 30–32; Harris, *Political Power,* 166; Olmsted Brothers, *A System of Parks and Playgrounds for Birmingham* (Birmingham: Park and Recreation Board of Birmingham, 1925). The Manning Plan identified the lack of dedicated park land as a significant issue. Forty years later, the city's park land had doubled in area, from 640 to 1,283 acres, but the population had also nearly doubled, from 178,806 in 1920 to 340,887 in 1960, leaving the city with practically the same ratio of persons per acre of park land in 1960 as it had when Manning wrote his plan. See Harland Bartholomew and Associates, *The Comprehensive Plan: Birmingham, Alabama* (Birmingham, 1961), 119.

36. Warren H. Manning to Hill Ferguson, January 18, 1937, Hill Ferguson Papers, file 56.3, 10.40, BPLDAM.

37. *Birmingham News,* June 15, 1920.

38. Ibid., July 1, 1920.

39. Harris, *Political Power,* 42, 238–39.

40. *Birmingham Age-Herald*, November 3, 1920.

41. Ibid., April 8, 1921.

42. Ibid., April 10, 1921, April 15, 1921.

43. *Birmingham News*, November 9, 1920.

44. Ibid., January 21, 1923.

45. Ibid.

46. *Birmingham Age-Herald*, February 4, 1923.

47. *Birmingham News*, January 19, 1923.

48. *Birmingham Age-Herald*, June 16, 23, 1923.

49. *Birmingham Reporter*, January 20, 1923; Wilson Fallin Jr., "A Shelter in the Storm: The African American Church in Birmingham, Alabama, 1815–1963" (PhD diss., University of Alabama, 1995), 68, 70, 160; Robert J. Norrell and Otis Dismuke, *The Other Side: The Story of Birmingham's Black Community* (Birmingham: Birmingfind, n.d.).

50. *Birmingham Reporter*, January 13, 1923.

51. Ibid., January 20, 1923.

52. Ibid.

53. Ibid., January 13, 1923. For Wynn's statement, see *Birmingham Age-Herald*, January 8, 1923.

54. Kenneth T. Jackson, *The Ku Klux Klan in the City, 1915–1930* (New York: Oxford University Press, 1967; Chicago: Ivan R. Dee, 1992), 82, 239; Roger K. Newman, *Hugo Black: A Biography* (New York: Pantheon, 1994), 90–92; Blaine Brownell, "Birmingham: New South City," *Journal of Southern History* 38 (1972): 39–40.

55. Dorothy Autrey, "National Association for the Advancement of Colored People in Alabama, 1913–1952" (PhD diss., University of Notre Dame, 1985), 65.

56. Rice, "Residential Segregation," 182–88. William Warley was president of the Louisville branch of the NAACP.

57. Autrey, "The NAACP in Alabama," 64–69, 121–41; Robin D. G. Kelley, *Hammer and Hoe: Alabama Communists during the Great Depression* (Chapel Hill: University of North Carolina Press, 1990), 80.

58. Harris, *Political Power*, 58; Autrey, "The NAACP in Alabama," 138; Kelley, *Hammer and Hoe*, 182–84.

59. Act No. 435, *Acts of Alabama*, 1923.

60. *Birmingham Age-Herald*, December 28, 1923.

61. Ibid., April 25, 1924, July 11, 1924, September 28, 1924.

62. Ibid., October 12, 1924; February 18, 1925.

63. *Birmingham News*, March 12, 1925; *Birmingham Age-Herald*, March 13, 1925; *Birmingham News*, March 28, 1925.

64. William M. Randle, "Professors, Reformers, Bureaucrats, and Cronies: The Players in *Euclid v. Ambler*," in *Zoning and the American Dream*, ed. Charles M. Haar and Jerold S. Kayden (Chicago: Planners Press, 1989), 38–39, 42.

65. Mel Scott, *American City Planning since 1890* (Berkeley and Los Angeles: University of California Press, 1969), 194.

66. Silver, "The Racial Origins," 197–98.

67. It should be noted that in 1923, Whitten told the Birmingham city commissioners that Atlanta's racial zoning ordinance would probably not stand up in court. The record does not show whether Birmingham's choice of Knowles was influenced by Whitten's second thoughts about the Atlanta zoning ordinance. Knowles's actions, however, indicate that he was willing to accommodate racial zoning and would continue to do so in preparing the 1931 Charleston plan (*Birmingham Age-Herald*, February 4, 1923).

68. *Birmingham News*, March 29, 1925.

69. *Birmingham Post*, July 13, 1926.

70. City of Birmingham, *The General Code of City of Birmingham Alabama of 1930*, Ordinance 1101-C.

71. *Birmingham News*, December 2, 1926.

72. George D. Hott, "Constitutionality of Municipal Zoning and Segregation Ordinances," *West Virginia Law Quarterly* 33 (1927): 349.

73. Silver, "The Racial Origins," 196; Raymond A. Mohl, "The Second Ghetto and the 'Infiltration Theory' in Urban Real Estate, 1940–1960," in *Urban Planning and the African American Community*, ed. June Manning Thomas and Marsha Ritzdorf (Thousand Oaks, Calif.: Sage, 1997), 72 n. 5.

74. Silver, "The Racial Origins," 191.

75. Walter White, "The Supreme Court and the N.A.A.C.P.," *The Crisis*, May 1927, 83, 99–100.

76. Silver, "The Racial Origins," 197; Silver, *Twentieth-Century Richmond*, 112.

77. U.S. Department of the Interior, National Park Service, National Register of Historic Places, Inventory—Nomination Form. Smithfield Historic District, c. 1985; Feldman, *A Sense of Place*, 26.

78. White and Hudgins, *Village Creek: An Architectural and Historical Resources Survey of Ensley, East Birmingham and East Lake* (Birmingham Historical Society, 1985), 43.

79. The zoning map shows Tenth Avenue in East Birmingham as a commercial corridor with the black neighborhood beginning one block north at Eleventh Avenue (City of Birmingham, Alabama Zone Map, July 13, 1926, Birmingham Public Library).

80. John H. Adams to Honorable J. H. Jones Jr., president, Birmingham City Commission, November 25, 1935, James Marion Jones Papers, file 7.9, BPLDAM.

81. Leavy W. Oliver, "Zoning Ordinances in Relation to Segregated Negro Housing in Birmingham, Alabama" (master's thesis, Indiana University, 1951), 66.

82. Olmsted Brothers, *A System of Parks*, 18.

83. White and Hudgins, *Village Creek*, 45, 102.

84. Ibid., 11; Philip A. Morris and Marjorie L. White, *Designs on Birmingham: A Landscape History of a Southern City and Its Suburbs* (Birmingham: Birmingham Historical Society, 1989), 50–51.

85. City of Birmingham, Alabama Zone Map, July 13, 1926, Birmingham Public Library.

86. White and Hudgins, *Village Creek*, 12; *Birmingham Age-Herald*, September 26, 1926.

87. White and Hudgins, *Village Creek*, 13.

88. *Birmingham News*, March 13, 1997.

89. Census tracts were not used for Birmingham until the 1940 census.

90. Rabin, "Expulsive Zoning," 102.

91. *Birmingham World*, August 20, 1946.

92. City of Birmingham, Alabama Zone Map, July 13, 1926, Birmingham Public Library.

93. City of Birmingham, *The General Code of City of Birmingham Alabama of 1930*, Ordinance 1101-C, §§ 6, 7.

94. On at least two occasions, the city was challenged when it attempted to rezone commercial zones—which were open to both black and white occupancy—to white residential areas. In both instances, this occurred when blacks moved into an area previously occupied by whites, and neighborhood whites responded by petitioning the Birmingham City Commission to change the zoning from commercial to white residential. In June 1935, this occurred when a black resident moved into an apartment located in a commercial area just northwest of downtown Birmingham. See *Birmingham News*, June 15, 1935, June 16, 1935, June 17, 1935; *Birmingham Post*, June 15, 1935, June 17, 1935, June 19, 1935. In 1936, a property owner attempted to rent three duplexes and a single-family house in the Ensley portion of Birmingham to blacks. See First Federal Savings and Loan Association Zoning case, Law Department Papers, box 58, BPLDAM. The plaintiff's petition to the Birmingham City Commission noted that the city's proposal to rezone the property from commercial to white residential was "in the nature of a segregation ordinance which is forbidden by the Constitution of the U.S." In both cases, the city was persuaded by the plaintiff's challenge to the city's zoning ordinance to withdraw plans to rezone the properties to white residential.

95. Gail Radford, *Modern Housing for America: Policy Struggles in the New Deal Era* (Chicago: University of Chicago Press, 1996), 101.

96. W. J. Wynn, city attorney, to W. O. Downs, public safety commissioner, May 7, 1934, James Marion Jones Papers, box 5, file 6, BPLDAM.

97. Eugene H. Klaber, PWA, to W. J. Wynn, May 7, 1934, James Marion Jones Papers, box 5, file 6, BPLDAM.

98. *Birmingham Age-Herald*, June 2, 1934. "Members Biographical Data," record group 196, file 2900.703, box 214, National Archives II. Mrs. Beddow was married to Roderick Beddow, a prominent attorney who for a short period in 1931 was retained by the NAACP to defend the eight Scottsboro defendants convicted of raping two white women. See Dan T. Carter, *Scottsboro: A Tragedy of the American South* (Baton Rouge: Louisiana State University Press, 1979), 71.

99. Graham Lacy to E. K. Burlew, Office of Federal Emergency Administrator, February 5, 1935, record group 196, file HA2900.703, box 214, National Archives II; Bishop B. G. Shaw to Nathan Straus, March 10, 1938, record group 196, file H2902.7,

box 218, National Archives II; Norrell and Dismuke, *The Other Side: The Story of Birmingham's Black Community*; J. C. deHoll to A. R. Clas, director of housing, Federal Emergency Administration of Public Works (PWA), October 26, 1935, record group 196, file H2902.084, box 217, National Archives II.

100. Graham Lacy to A. R. Clas, director of housing, Federal Emergency Administration, September 13, 1935, record group 196, file 2902.8, box 219, National Archives II; Housing Authority of the Birmingham District incorporation document, August 28, 1935, record group 196, file 2902.303, box 219, National Archives II.

101. Recommendations and Resolution Adopted by the Inter-Denominational Ministers Alliance, January 1938, record group 196, file H2902.09, box 217, National Archives II.

102. Radford, *Modern Housing*, 100–105. These cities are Atlanta, Cleveland, Detroit, Louisville, Memphis, Montgomery, Alabama, Nashville, and New York City. Only in Chicago, where four PWA projects were constructed, were all projects built for whites.

103. *Birmingham Post*, October 17, 1934.

104. Montgomery Real Estate and Insurance Co., *Location for Slum Clearance Housing Project for White Occupancy, Birmingham, Alabama—Avondale*, September 9, 1935, record group 196, file H-2900, box 212, National Archives II.

105. J. D. Dowling, F. A. Bean, and John H. Adams, *Analysis of Family Study for Federal Low-Cost Housing Project for Negroes, Birmingham, Alabama*, November 28, 1934, record group 196, file H-2900, box 212, National Archives II.

106. Norrell and Dismuke, *The Other Side: The Story of Birmingham's Black Community*; Feldman, *A Sense of Place*, 34–35.

107. J. D. Dowling and F. A. Bean, *Final Statistical Report of Surveys of the Blighted Areas, Birmingham, Alabama*, Jefferson County Board of Health, 1937, 30–34. Variables employed in measuring blight were: population density; quality of physical features (incidence of substandard housing, community toilets, running water, bathing facilities, and lighting); crime (incidence of delinquency; number of police calls, petty crimes, major crimes); health (incidence of fire calls, illegitimate births, home/nursing visits, sanitation problems, clinic visits, public hospital cases; morbidity, infant mortality, general mortality, and maternal mortality); and relief (number of cases with Department of Public Welfare, T.B. Association, Children's Clinic, and other charitable agencies; number of pauper burials).

108. J. D. Dowling, *Analysis of Family Study for Federal Low-Cost Housing Project for Negroes, Birmingham, Alabama*, November 28, 1934, record group 196, file H-2900, box 212, National Archives II; *Birmingham Post*, October 24, 1934.

109. *Birmingham Post*, October 17, 1934; *Birmingham News*, October 18, 1934. The *Birmingham Reporter* ceased publication in 1934. Henry Lewis Suggs, *The Black Press in the South, 1865–1979* (Westport, Conn.: Greenwood Press, 1983), 42.

110. Horatio B. Hackett to Honorable Hugo L. Black, April 25, 1935, record group 196, file H-2900.09, box 214, National Archives II.

111. J.C. deHoll to E. W. Taggart, president, NAACP Birmingham branch, May 6, 1936, James Marion Jones Papers, box 5, file 2, BPLDAM.

112. *Birmingham Post,* October 20, 1937; Radford, *Modern Housing,* 189

113. Sallie Russell and others to Horatio Hackett, May 8, 1935; Sallie Russell and others to Harold Ickes, May 8, 1935, both in record group 196, file H-2900.09, box 214, National Archives II. In all, twenty-six homeowners signed the petition to Hackett and twenty-eight to Ickes.

114. The Housing Commission's survey found that of 524 households in the nine-block study site, only thirty-two of them owned their homes. J. D. Dowling, *Analysis of Family Study for Federal Low-Cost Housing Project for Negroes, Birmingham, Alabama,* November 28, 1934, record group 196, file H-2900, box 212, National Archives II.

115. Sallie B. Russell to J. C. deHoll, May 29, 1935, record group 196, file H-2900.09, box 214, National Archives II.

116. J. E. Bacon to A. R. Clas, director of housing, Federal Emergency Administration of Public Works, May 30, 1935, record group 196, file H-2902.09, box 217, National Archives II.

117. Recommendations and Resolutions Adopted by the Inter-Denominational Ministers Alliance, January 1938, record group 196, file H-2902.09, box 217, National Archives II.

118. Sallie B. Russell to Harold Ickes, June 27, 1935, record group 196, file H-2900.09, box 214, National Archives II.

119. J. C. deHoll, chairman, Housing Authority of the Birmingham District, to E. W. Taggart, president, NAACP Birmingham branch, May 6, 1936, James Marion Jones Papers, box 5, file 2, BPLDAM; *Birmingham Age-Herald,* November 13, 1935.

120. City of Birmingham Zoning Board of Adjustment, "True Copy of Resolution Passed by Zoning Board of Adjustment, June 28, 1935," James Marion Jones Papers, box 7, file 9, BPLDAM; W. J. Wynn, city attorney, to R. S. Marshall, superintendent, Park and Recreation Board, January 4, 1936, Law Department Papers, box 65, BPLDAM. The rezoning included the eastern portion of the first block (block 36) west of Center Street between Ninth Avenue and Ninth Court and the eastern portion of the northern half of the block (block 35) between Eighth Avenue and Ninth Avenue.

121. John H. Adams to Honorable J. M. Jones Jr., president, Birmingham City Commission, November 25, 1935, James Marion Jones Papers, box 7, file 9, BPLDAM.

122. *Birmingham News,* November 20, 1935; *Birmingham Post,* November 29, 1935.

123. *Birmingham News,* March 29, 1925.

124. *Birmingham Age-Herald,* November 30, 1935.

125. *Birmingham News,* November 30, 1935.

126. Ibid.

127. *Birmingham Age-Herald,* November 13, 1935.

128. Kelley, *Hammer and Hoe*, 124, 134. Among the issues with which the Birmingham branch became more active was the Scottsboro case, to which the branch had been too weak to respond in 1931 when the Scottsboro boys were arrested for allegedly raping two white women. By 1937, the branch's larger membership included black Communists who had belonged to the International Labor Defense (ILD) until that organization was dismantled during the period of the Popular Front.

129. In August 1935, the Housing Authority of the Birmingham District was incorporated as the public body that would oversee Birmingham's housing program. Creation of the Housing Authority had first required state enabling legislation to be adopted, which occurred in February 1935. The first chair of the Housing Authority was J. C. deHoll (*Birmingham News*, August 13, 1935); Housing Authority of Birmingham District incorporation document, August 28, 1935, record group 196, file H-2902.803, box 219, National Archives II.

130. Committee to Housing Authority of the Birmingham District, September 21, 1936; H. D. Coke, editor, *Birmingham World*, to Robert Weaver, Department of Interior, October 17, 1936; NAACP Birmingham branch, n.d., record group 196, file H-2902.09, box 217, National Archives II.

131. E. W. Taggart, and others, to President Franklin Roosevelt, October 12, 1936, record group 196, file H-2902.09, box 217, National Archives II.

132. H. A. Gray, PWA director of housing, to H. D. Coke, *Birmingham World*, October 20, 1936; H. A. Gray to Charles McPherson, secretary, NAACP Birmingham branch, October 31, 1936, record group 196, file H-2902.09, box 217, National Archives II; *Birmingham Post*, January 24, 1938.

133. H. D. Coke to Nathan Straus, January 11, 1938, record group 196, file H-2902.7, box 218, National Archives II. The *Birmingham World* began publication as a biweekly black newspaper in 1930. Birmingham Public Library, *Bibliography of Birmingham, Alabama, 1872–1972* (Birmingham: Oxmoor Press, 1973), 121.

134. Recommendations and Resolution Adopted by the Inter-Denominational Ministers Alliance, January 1938, record group 196, file H-2902.09, box 217, National Archives II.

135. *Birmingham World*, January 28, 1938.

136. Housing Authority of the Birmingham District Meeting Minutes, September 21, 1937, file H-2900.703, box 214, record group 196, National Archives II; James Marion Jones to Col. Horatio Hackett, assistant administrator, PWA, November 2, 1936, record group 196, file H-2900.703, box 214, National Archives II; James Marion Jones to Edgar Puryear, personnel director, Housing Division, PWA, August 11, 1937, James Marion Jones Papers, box 3, file 5, BPLDAM.

137. Memorandum to the Administrator from Donald Jones, United States Housing Authority, Department of the Interior, November 22, 1937, record group 196, file H-2902.8, box 219, National Archives II.

138. Nathan Straus to J. C. deHoll, February 11, 1938, record group 196, file H-2902.7, box 218, National Archives II.

139. Frank Spain, HABD chairman, to Birmingham City Commission, Feb-

ruary 15, 1939, James Marion Jones Papers, box 5, file 2, BPLDAM; J. C. deHoll to Nathan Straus, January 29, 1939, record group 196, file H-2902.7, box 218, National Archives II. White (aka M.D.L. White) and Henry Harris had split from the Alabama State Federation of Colored Civic Leagues in 1933 to form the Negro Democratic Council. Fearing that Communist Party voter registration efforts in the early 1930s would greatly increase the number of black voters, white politicians had urged creation of the council with the intent that it would control the black vote by selecting a limited number of blacks to vote. See Kelley, *Hammer and Hoe*, 183; Nell Irvin Painter, *The Narrative of Hosea Hudson* (New York: Norton, 1979), 263–65, 381.

140. Bishop B. G. Shaw to Nathan Straus, March 10, 1938, record group 196, file H-2902.7, box 218, National Archives II; Frank Spain, HABD chairman, to Birmingham City Commission, February 15, 1939, James Marion Jones Papers, box 5, file 2, BPLDAM.

141. Nathan Straus to Bishop Shaw, March 16, 1938, record group 196, file H-2902.7, box 217, National Archives II.

3. Planning, Neighborhood Change, and Civil Rights

1. *Birmingham News*, January 19, 1923.

2. For a good summary of the filtering and neighborhood change literature, see Anthony Downs, *Neighborhoods and Urban Development* (Washington, D.C.: Brookings Institution, 1981).

3. In the 1920s, neighborhood representatives referred to their neighborhood as Graymont and their organization as the Graymont Civic Association. See *Birmingham News*, March 29, 1925. By the late 1940s, the neighborhood and its association were known by the Graymont–College Hills name. See *Birmingham Age-Herald*, June 1, 1949; and J. R. Gardner, president, Graymont–College Hills Civic Association, to Cooper Green, November 2, 1949, Cooper Green Papers, file 9.20, BPLDAM. The College Hills area borders the campus of Birmingham-Southern College.

4. *Birmingham News*, March 29, 1925. In 1898, Smithfield, then a suburb of Birmingham, was about 45 percent white and 55 percent black. In 1908, two years before Smithfield was annexed by Birmingham, slightly over 80 percent of the neighborhood's residents were black, and by 1928 only three white households remained. See United States Department of Interior, National Park Service, National Register of Historic Places Inventory—Nomination Form, "Smithfield Historic District," c. 1985. Cooper Green, later mayor of Birmingham, recalled that the Graymont Civic Association met with a group of blacks and the city commission in 1923 to set the racial boundary between Graymont and Smithfield. Brief and Argument of Horace C. Wilkinson, in the United States Circuit Court of Appeals, Fifth Circuit, No. 13,158, *City of Birmingham, et al., vs. Mary Means Monk, et al.*, 1950.

5. Based on comparison between Graymont Civic Association boundaries described in *Birmingham News*, March 29, 1925, and the zoning commission's map published in the *Birmingham Post*, July 13, 1926.

6. *Birmingham Post*, July 13, 1926.

7. *Birmingham News,* May 19, 1923, May 20, 1923, May 30, 1923; *Birmingham Age-Herald,* January 30, 1924. Legion Field, where Bear Bryant's University of Alabama football team played many of its games, is located in McLendon Park.

8. Downs, *Neighborhoods and Urban Development,* 94.

9. United States Bureau of the Census, *United States Census of Population: Birmingham, Alabama, Census Tract Statistics* (Washington, D.C.: Government Printing Office, 1952). Tracts 13 and 14 had median annual incomes of $1,857 and $1,861, while tract 32, located in Ensley, had a median income of $1,951.

10. Robert J. Norrell and Otis Dismuke, *The Other Side: The Story of Birmingham's Black Community* (Birmingham: Birmingfind, n.d.).

11. For the same period, the white population had grown from 158,622 to 195,922, for a population increase of nearly 24 percent. See U.S. Bureau of the Census, *Sixteenth Census of the United States: 1940* and *Seventeenth Census of the United States: 1950.*

12. City of Birmingham, *The General Code of the City of Birmingham, Alabama* (Charlottesville, Va.: Michie Company, 1944), § 1591; *Birmingham Post,* July 13, 1926; *Birmingham News,* November 12, 1947.

13. George A. Denison, *Health as an Indication of Housing Needs in Birmingham, Alabama,* Jefferson County Board of Health, April 12, 1950, 8.

14. Field Report from Albert L. Thompson, racial relations adviser, Housing and Home Finance Agency, April 19, 1949, record group 207, box 750, National Archives II.

15. Dorothy Autrey, "National Association for the Advancement of Colored People in Alabama, 1913–1952" (PhD diss., University of Notre Dame, 1985), 121–41, 206–8.

16. Ibid., 202–18.

17. Ibid., 207.

18. *Birmingham World,* August 6, 1946.

19. Ibid., August 23, 1946.

20. Ibid., September 3, 1946. The Alabama State Federation of Civic Leagues was an umbrella organization for the neighborhood-based civic leagues that are profiled in chapter 7. Hosea Hudson's life as a Communist organizer in Birmingham is told in Nell Irvin Painter's *The Narrative of Hosea Hudson* (New York: Norton, 1994). Belzora Ward was identified by the Birmingham Police Department as a member of the Southern Conference for Human Welfare (SCHW) and a signer of a June 12, 1948, petition calling for an end to police brutality in Birmingham. See Report to Chief C. F. Eddins of the Investigation of the Bombings as of May 21, 1949, Police Surveillance Papers, Birmingham Police Department, file 6.4(b), BPLDAM. W. C. Patton would later serve as president of the Birmingham branch of the NAACP and played a significant role in protesting the "urban removal" of blacks from the city's south side in the 1950s (see chapter 4). Reverend J. L. Ware was an important spokesman for the black ministry in Birmingham and would later serve as president of the Birmingham Baptist Ministers' Conference. He was

also extensively involved in civil rights issues in the 1940s and 1950s, including the Southside urban renewal project. See Wilson Fallin Jr., "A Shelter in the Storm: The African American Church in Birmingham, Alabama, 1815–1963" (PhD diss., University of Alabama, 1995), 230–31, 246. The diversity of these supporters reflects the lingering effects of the World War II alliance of the Birmingham NAACP, CIO, and SCHW, which dissolved within two years as the NAACP distanced itself from individuals, such as Hudson, or groups, such as the SCHW, who had been accused of supporting communism. See Robin D. G. Kelley, *Hammer and Hoe: Alabama Communists during the Great Depression* (Chapel Hill: University of North Carolina Press, 1990), 222, 226.

21. *Birmingham World*, July 29, 1947; Glenn Eskew, "But for Birmingham: The Local and National Movements in the Civil Rights Struggle" (PhD diss., University of Georgia, 1993), 132; Lynda Dempsey Cochran, "Arthur Davis Shores: Advocate for Freedom" (master's thesis, Georgia Southern College, 1977). In the 1950s, Shores represented Autherine Lucy in her unsuccessful attempt to integrate the University of Alabama, and in the 1960s he represented marchers in the 1963 civil rights demonstrations and obtained the court order for integrating Birmingham's public schools.

22. *Birmingham World*, August 20, 1946.

23. Plaintiff's Petition, *Alice P. Allen vs. City of Birmingham*, United States District Court, Northern District of Alabama, Southern Division, August 6, 1946, Civil Docket Number 5840, City of Birmingham Legal Department Papers, box 45, BPLDAM.

24. *Birmingham News*, November 14, 1945.

25. Leavy Oliver, "Zoning Ordinances in Relation to Segregated Negro Housing in Birmingham, Alabama" (master's thesis, Indiana University, 1951), 27–28; *Birmingham World*, January 14, 1947.

26. *Birmingham World*, August 9, 1946.

27. Handwritten notes, *Alice P. Allen v. City of Birmingham* file, City of Birmingham Legal Department Papers, box 45, BPLDAM.

28. Richard Hail Brown, attorney, to J. H. Willis, August 13, 1941, City of Birmingham Legal Department Papers, box 58, BPLDAM.

29. J. H. Willis to Richard Hail Brown, August 20, 1941, City of Birmingham Law Department Papers, box 58, BPLDAM.

30. Exhibit A, Defendant's Motion to Dismiss, *Alice P. Allen vs. City of Birmingham*, United States District Court, Northern District of Alabama, Southern Division, September 30, 1946, Civil Docket Number 5840, City of Birmingham Legal Department Papers, box 45, BPLDAM.

31. Plaintiff's Amendment, *Alice P. Allen vs. City of Birmingham*, United States District Court, Northern District of Alabama, Southern Division, August 28, 1946, Civil Docket Number 4950, City of Birmingham Legal Department Papers, box 45, BPLDAM.

32. Defendant's Defense, *Alice P. Allen vs. City of Birmingham*, United States Dis-

trict Court, Northern District of Alabama, Southern Division, October 26, 1946, Civil Docket Number 5840, City of Birmingham Legal Department Papers, box 45, BPLDAM.

33. Order of Dismissal, *Alice P. Allen vs. City of Birmingham*, United States District Court, Northern District of Alabama, Southern Division, January 9, 1947, Civil Docket Number 5840, City of Birmingham Legal Department Papers, box 45, BPLDAM.

34. Robert Carter to Arthur Shores, October 21, 1946, Papers of the NAACP, pt. 5, "The Campaign against Residential Segregation," Manuscript Division, Library of Congress.

35. Alabama State Bureau of Investigation and Identification Report, September 25, 1947, Statement of William R. Coleman, September 4, 1947, Police Surveillance Papers, Birmingham Police Department, file 7.24, BPLDAM.

36. *Birmingham News*, August 1, 1947; *Birmingham World*, August 5, 1947; *Birmingham News*, August 19, 1947.

37. Plaintiff's Petition, *Samuel and Essie Mae Matthews vs. City of Birmingham*, United States District Court, Northern District of Alabama, Southern Division, October 30, 1946, Civil Docket Number 5903, City of Birmingham Legal Department Papers, box 62, BPLDAM.

38. Ibid.

39. Alabama State Bureau of Investigation and Identification Report, September 25, 1947, Statement of William R. Coleman, September 4, 1947, Police Surveillance Papers, Birmingham Police Department, file 7.24, BPLDAM; *Birmingham World*, August 5, 1947; *Birmingham News*, August 26, 1947.

40. Answer of the Defendant, *Samuel and Essie Mae Matthews vs. City of Birmingham*, United States District Court, Northern District of Alabama, Southern Division, July 31, 1947, Civil Docket Number 5903, City of Birmingham Legal Department Papers, box 62, BPLDAM.

41. Arthur Shores to Thurgood Marshall, August 1, 1947, Papers of the NAACP, pt. 5, "The Campaign against Residential Segregation," Manuscript Division, Library of Congress.

42. Findings of Fact, Conclusions of Law and Decree, *Samuel and Essie Mae Matthews vs. City of Birmingham*, United States District Court, Northern District of Alabama, Southern Division, August 4, 1947, Civil Action Number 6046, City of Birmingham Legal Department Papers, box 62, BPLDAM. In addition, Judge Mullins had dismissed the original suit, Number 5930, on June 10, 1947, agreeing with the city that the plaintiff had sued prematurely because the Matthewses' home had not been completed and therefore was not eligible for a certificate of occupancy until it had passed its final building inspection. Shores contended that since city officials had told the Matthews family that a certificate of occupancy would not be granted, the law does "not require an individual to do a vain and fruitless act before relief from a wrong will be granted." Memorandum in Opposition to Motion to Dismiss, *Samuel and Essie Mae Matthews vs. City of Birmingham*, United States District Court, Northern District of Alabama, Southern Division, January 13, 1947, Civil

Docket Number 5903, City of Birmingham Legal Department Papers, box 62, BPLDAM. When this failed, the Matthews family completed the house, and Shores proceeded with requesting the certificate of occupancy. See Arthur Shores to Marian Wynn Perry, July 17, 1947, Papers of the NAACP, pt. 5, "The Campaign against Residential Segregation," Manuscript Division, Library of Congress.

43. Plaintiff's Petition, *Samuel and Essie Mae Matthews vs. City of Birmingham,* United States District Court, Northern District of Alabama, Southern Division, July 25, 1947, Civil Action Number 6046, City of Birmingham Legal Department Papers, box 62, BPLDAM.

44. Arnold R. Hirsch, *Making the Second Ghetto: Race and Housing in Chicago, 1940–1960* (Cambridge: Cambridge University Press, 1983); Raymond A. Mohl, "The Second Ghetto and the 'Infiltration Theory,'" in *Urban Planning and the African American Community: In the Shadows,* ed. June Manning Thomas and Marsha Ritzdorf (Thousand Oaks, Calif.: Sage, 1997), 62–63; William H. Wilson, *Hamilton Park: A Planned Black Community in Dallas* (Baltimore: Johns Hopkins University Press, 1998), 25–26, 42; A. L. Thompson, HHFA racial relations advisor, to Carlos W. Starr, Field Trip Report—Birmingham, Alabama, May 14–15, 1952, June 3, 1952, record group 207, Race Relations Program, Birmingham, Alabama, file, National Archives II.

45. A. L. Thompson, HHFA racial relations advisor, to Carlos W. Starr, Field Trip Report—Birmingham, Alabama, May 14–15, 1952, June 3, 1952, record group 207, Race Relations Program, Birmingham, Alabama, file, National Archives II.

46. *Birmingham News,* August 19, 1947.

47. Alabama State Bureau of Investigation and Identification Report, September 25, 1947, Police Surveillance Papers, Birmingham Police Department, file 7.24, BPLDAM.

48. *Birmingham Post,* March 24, 1949.

49. *Birmingham News,* March 22, 1949.

50. Statements of John J. Gould, J. E. Monteith, and Sam L. Chesnut, April 7, 1949, April 21, 1949, Police Surveillance Files, Birmingham Police Department, file 6.4(b), BPLDAM.

51. *Birmingham News,* March 22, 1949; *Birmingham Post-Herald,* March 22, 1949; *Birmingham News,* March 25, 1949.

52. *Birmingham News,* March 25, 1949.

53. Statement of Mrs. W. A. Thomas, July 5, 1949, Police Surveillance Files, Birmingham Police Department, file 6.4(b), BPLDAM.

54. Detective P. E. McMahan to Birmingham police chief C. F. Eddins, March 26, 1949, Police Surveillance Files, Birmingham Police Department, file 6.4(b), BPLDAM.

55. *Birmingham News,* May 23, 1949, June 1, 1949.

56. Statement of Robert E. Chambliss, May 23, 1949, Police Surveillance Files, Birmingham Police Department, file 6.4(b), BPLDAM.

57. Frank Sikora, *Until Justice Rolls Down: The Birmingham Church Bombing Case* (Tuscaloosa: University of Alabama Press, 1991), 82–83.

58. Elizabeth H. Cobbs and Petric J. Smith, *Long Time Coming: An Insider's Story of the Birmingham Church Bombing That Rocked the World* (Birmingham: Crane Hill Publishers, 1994), 52; *Birmingham Age-Herald,* May 1, 1950.

59. Cobbs and Smith, *Long Time Coming,* 61, 70.

60. Diane McWhorter, *Carry Me Home, Birmingham, Alabama: The Climactic Battle of the Civil Rights Revolution* (New York: Simon and Schuster, 2001), 73.

61. Sikora, *Until Justice Rolls,* 78.

62. Howell Raines, *My Soul Is Rested: The Story of the Civil Rights Movement in the Deep South* (Harmondsworth, U.K.: Viking Penguin, 1983), 168. Raines uses the pseudonym Robert Matthews, but Allen describes "Matthews" as a former city employee known as "Dynamite Bob," Chambliss's nickname.

63. Sikora, *Until Justice Rolls,* 154. Diane McWhorter contends that Chambliss was "apparently involved" in nearly all of the racial zoning bombings. See McWhorter, *Carry Me Home,* 72–75, 598 n. 75.

64. *Birmingham News,* June 1, 1949; *Birmingham Age-Herald,* June 1, 1949.

65. *Birmingham News,* June 6, 1949.

66. George Byrum Jr. to Jimmy Morgan, July 15, 1949, James Morgan Papers, file 33.19, BPLDAM.

67. Christopher Silver and John V. Moeser, *The Separate City* (Lexington: University of Kentucky Press, 1995), 136–44; Frederick Allen, *Atlanta Rising* (Marietta, Ga.: Longstreet Press, 1996), 92–93.

68. *Birmingham World,* July 19, 1949.

69. Ben F. Ray et al. to James W. Morgan, August 15, 1949, James Morgan Papers, file 33.19, BPLDAM.

70. A. C. Maclin, NAACP president; Emory Jackson, NAACP secretary; J. J. Green, chairman, NAACP Executive Board, to James W. Morgan, June 6, 1949, Papers of the NAACP, pt. 5, "The Campaign against Residential Segregation," Manuscript Division, Library of Congress.

71. *Birmingham World,* July 26, 1949. Editor Jackson was suspicious of the reasons why five blacks, including Arthur Shores, met with the white members of the Morgan committee in a session closed to the public and the press. Jackson wrote, "One day we shall know whether the 'Committee of Five' sold us out behind closed doors." See *Birmingham World,* July 22, 1949. As noted, neither Shores nor the other four black participants signed the Morgan committee's final proposal.

72. *Birmingham World,* August 9, 1949.

73. *Birmingham Age-Herald,* June 2, 1949; *Birmingham News,* June 2, 1949; *Birmingham News,* August 13, 1949.

74. *Birmingham News,* August 9, 1949.

75. James A. Simpson to James H. Willis, city attorney, August 18, 1949, Cooper Green Papers, file 9.24, BPLDAM.

76. James A. Simpson to James H. Willis, August 18, 1949, Cooper Green Papers, box 9, file 24, BPLDAM.

77. Birmingham City Ordinance No. 709-F, adopted August 9, 1949.

78. *Birmingham News,* August 9, 1949.

79. Ibid., August 15, 1949.

80. Birmingham newspaper excerpt attached to Emory Jackson to Thurgood Marshall, August 4, 1949, Papers of the NAACP, pt. 5, "The Campaign against Residential Segregation," Manuscript Division, Library of Congress.

81. *Birmingham News*, August 15, 1949.

82. Ibid.

83. Ibid., August 9, 1949. Two weeks earlier Morgan had noted that only 15 percent of the city's residential areas were zoned for black occupancy. See *Birmingham Age-Herald*, July 24, 1949.

84. *Birmingham Post*, August 9, 1949.

85. *Birmingham World*, August 12, 1949; Birmingham branch NAACP to Cooper Green, president, Birmingham City Commission, August 15, 1949, Cooper Green Papers, file 15.7, BPLDAM.

86. *Birmingham News*, August 18, 1949; *Birmingham World*, August 26, 1949; Resolution, August 17, 1949, Papers of the NAACP, pt. 5, "Campaign against Residential Segregation," Manuscript Division, Library of Congress.

87. *Birmingham World*, August 12, 1949.

88. *Birmingham Post*, September 6, 1949; *Birmingham News*, September 6, 1949. The Graymont–College Hills Civic Association had dropped the idea of the 150-foot-wide commercial buffer when city attorneys succeeded in convincing the association that such a designation could not stand up in court. The city's attorneys had previously stated that the redesignation of a large area of established residential character would be viewed as arbitrary. Assistant city attorney Thomas Huey Jr. to Cooper Green, April 26, 1949, Cooper Green Papers, file 15.7, BPLDAM.

89. *Birmingham News*, September 28, 1949.

90. Statements of Mary Means and Monroe Monk, January 8, 1951, Police Surveillance Files, Birmingham Police Department, file 7.35, BPLDAM; *Birmingham News*, December 22, 1950.

91. *Birmingham News*, December 12, 1949, December 13, 1949.

92. J. R. Gardner Jr., president, Graymont–College Hills Civic Association, November 2, 1949, Cooper Green Papers, file 9.20, BPLDAM.

93. *Birmingham News*, December 13, 1949; Glenn Feldman, *From Demagogue to Dixiecrat: Horace Wilkinson and the Politics of Race* (Lanham, Md.: University Press of America, 1995).

94. *Birmingham News*, December 14, 1949.

95. *Monk et al. v. City of Birmingham, et al.*, 87 F.Supp. 538.

96. *Birmingham News*, April 14, 1950, April 23, 1950.

97. Ibid., December 22, 1950.

98. Brief and arguments of Horace C. Wilkinson, attorney for appellants, *City of Birmingham, et al. Appellants, v. Mary Means Monk, et al., Appellees*, 185 F.2d 859, U.S. Circuit Court of Appeals, Fifth Circuit (1950), 42–46.

99. Ibid., 74.

100. *Monk et al. v. City of Birmingham et al.*, 87 F.Supp.538, 543; *City of Birmingham et al. v. Monk et al.*, 185 F.2d 859, 862.

101. Petition for Writ of Certiorari of Horace C. Wilkinson, attorney for appellants, *City of Birmingham, et al. Petitioner, v. Mary Means Monk, et al., Respondent* (filed in U.S. Supreme Court, October term, 1950).

102. Brief and arguments of Horace C. Wilkinson, attorney for appellants, *City of Birmingham, et al. Appellants, v. Mary Means Monk, et al., Appellees,* 185 F.2d 859, U.S. Circuit Court of Appeals, Fifth Circuit (1950), 54.

103. "Constitutionality of Segregation Ordinances," *Michigan Law Review* 35 (1917–18): 111.

104. Major Gardner, "Race Segregation in Cities," *Kentucky Law Journal* 29 (1940–41): 214, 219. Other contemporary law journal articles that note the inconsistency of *Buchanan v. Warley* with various segregation decisions or with *Euclid v. Ambler* include: Arthur T. Martin, "Segregation of Residence of Negroes," *Michigan Law Review* 32 (1934): 721–42; George D. Hott, "Constitutionally of Municipal Zoning and Segregation Ordinances," *West Virginia Law Quarterly* 33 (1927): 332–49.

105. Petition for Writ of Certiorari of Horace C. Wilkinson, attorney for appellants, *City of Birmingham, et al. Petitioner, v. Mary Means Monk, et al., Respondent* (filed in U.S. Supreme Court, October term, 1950).

106. Quoted in the brief and arguments of Horace C. Wilkinson, attorney for appellants, *City of Birmingham, et al. Appellants, v. Mary Means Monk, et al., Appellees,* 185 F.2d 859, U.S. Circuit Court of Appeals, Fifth Circuit (1950), 129–30.

107. Quoted in the brief and arguments of Horace C. Wilkinson, attorney for appellants, *City of Birmingham, et al. Appellants, v. Mary Means Monk, et al., Appellees,* 185 F.2d 859, U.S. Circuit Court of Appeals, Fifth Circuit (1950), 122–23.

108. Mohl, "The Second Ghetto," 64–71.

109. *City of Birmingham v. Monk,* 185 F.2d 859, 862.

110. *Birmingham News,* May 28, 1951.

111. Eskew, "But for Birmingham," 140–73.

112. These bombings are discussed in more detail in chapter 5.

113. Police Surveillance Files, *Bombings or Attempt* [sic] *Bombings in Birmingham, 1950–1965,* BPLDAM, n.d.

114. Fallin, "A Shelter in the Storm," 249; Howell Raines, *My Soul is Rested,* 154–55.

4. "The Spirit of Racial Zoning"

1. Mel Scott, *American City Planning since 1890* (Berkeley and Los Angeles: University of California Press, 1969), 492–504.

2. Minutes of the Birmingham City Planning Commission (name later changed to Birmingham Planning Board), August 12, 1943, Urban Planning Department Records, box 1135.1.1, BPLDAM.

3. Birmingham Planning Board, *Preliminary Report,* February 8, 1952, 6–8.

4. City of Birmingham, Application for Recertification—1956, Workable Program for Urban Renewal, July 5, 1956, 1–2, Planning and Zoning Papers, uncataloged, BPLDAM.

5. Irving Beiman, "Birmingham: Steel Giant with a Glass Jaw," in *Our Fair City*, ed. Robert S. Allen (New York: Vanguard Press, 1947), 119–20.

6. Lawrence M. Friedman, *Government and Slum Housing: A Century of Frustration* (Chicago: Rand McNally, 1968), 3–24.

7. *Birmingham Age-Herald*, December 25, 1949.

8. Howard L. Holley, "Medical Education in Alabama," *Alabama Review* 7 (1954): 261–62; Development of University of Alabama Medical Center, n.d., Albert Boutwell Papers, box 13, file 37, BPLDAM; Statement of John M. Gallalee, president, University of Alabama, March 30, 1953, Stenographic Report: Public Meeting on the Medical Center, Housing Authority of the Birmingham District (HABD) Papers, uncatlaoged, BPLDAM; Virginia E. Fisher, *Building on a Vision: A Fifty-Year Retrospective of UAB's Academic Health Center* (Birmingham: University of Alabama at Birmingham, 1995), 2.

9. Black physicians at that time were not admitted to the Jefferson County Medical Society and therefore were not permitted to practice in the city's hospitals. Until January 1954, when sixty-bed Holy Family Hospital, run by the Catholic Sisters of Charity in Ensley, was completed, Birmingham had no black hospitals. See Robert Corley, "The Quest for Racial Harmony: Race Relations in Birmingham, Alabama, 1947–1963" (PhD diss., University of Virginia, 1979), 67–68; Negro Hospital Fund Drive, "Who, What, When and Why of the Negro Hospital Fund Drive," January 28, 1950, Cooper Green Papers, box 10, file 9, BPLDAM.

10. Birmingham Planning Board, *Preliminary Report*, February 8, 1952.

11. Mitchell, "Birmingham: Biography of a City" (PhD diss., University of Chicago, 1946), 67; Paul B. Worthman, "Working-Class Mobility in Birmingham, Alabama, 1880–1914," in *Anonymous Americans: Explorations in Nineteenth-Century Social History*, ed. Tamara Hareven, (Englewood Cliffs: Prentice-Hall, 1971), 200–206.

12. W. M. McGrath, "Conservation of Health," *The Survey*, January 6, 1912, 1507, 1509, 1511.

13. J. D. Dowling and F. A. Bean, *Final Statistical Report of Surveys of the Blighted Areas, Birmingham, Alabama, Showing Some Comparative Figures for the Years, 1933 and 1935*, Jefferson County, Alabama Board of Health, 1937.

14. George A. Denison, *Health as an Indication of Housing Needs in Birmingham, Alabama, and Recommendations for Slum Clearance, Redevelopment, and Public Housing*, Jefferson County, Alabama Board of Health, April 12, 1950.

15. Denison, *Health as an Indication*, 10.

16. Housing and Home Finance Agency, *Slum Clearance under the Housing Act of 1949*, Washington, D.C., August 1949, 1–6.

17. Housing Authority of the Birmingham District, *Preliminary Report, Slum Clearance and Redevelopment: Medical Center, Site A*, Birmingham, Alabama, 1952, 30.

18. *Birmingham News*, December 8, 1949.

19. Ibid., January 20, 1960.

20. *Birmingham Age-Herald,* December 25, 1949.

21. *Birmingham News,* December 8, 1949, December 25, 1949.

22. Minutes of the Birmingham Planning Board, April 19, 1950, Urban Planning Department Records, box 1135.1.1, BPLDAM.

23. Minutes of the Birmingham Planning Board, May 31, 1950, Urban Planning Department Records, box 1135.1.1, BPLDAM.

24. Minutes of the Birmingham Planning Board, August 16, 1950, Urban Planning Department Records, box 1135.1.1, BPLDAM.

25. "A Statement of Activities Relative to Title I Redevelopment Program in the Medical Center Area," n.d., James W. Morgan Papers, box 14, file 13, BPLDAM; Samuel R. Gibbons, "Notes Covering Breakfast Meeting in the Steel Room, Tutwiler Hotel, January 13, 1953," January 20, 1953, HABD Papers, uncataloged, BPLDAM; "Participation of and Cooperation with Negro Citizens," HABD Papers, uncataloged, BPLDAM.

26. *Birmingham News,* November 4, 1951.

27. U.S. Bureau of the Census, *Compendium of City Government Finances in 1952* (Washington, D.C.: Government Printing Office, 1953), table 24.

28. Edward S. LaMonte, "Politics and Welfare in Birmingham, 1900–1974" (PhD diss., University of Chicago, 1976), 279–81.

29. J. C. deHoll, HABD District Advisory to Congressman Laurie C. Battle, February 26, 1952, HABD Papers, BPLDAM. Description of Jemison quoted from HABD, untitled listing of members of Birmingham Citizens' Advisory Committee for Redevelopment of the Medical Center, July 28, 1953, James Morgan Papers, box 25, file 19.

30. *Birmingham News,* March 11, 1952, July 9, 1952, August 12, 1952.

31. Housing and Home Finance Agency, *Slum Clearance under the Housing Act of 1949: A Preliminary Explanatory Statement to American Cities,* Washington, D.C., August 1949, 10.

32. Birmingham Planning Board, *Preliminary Report,* February 8, 1952, 7–8.

33. Birmingham Planning Board, *Preliminary Report,* February 8, 1952.

34. Denison, *Health as an Indication,* 8.

35. *Birmingham Post-Herald,* January 14, 1953.

36. *Birmingham News,* June 19, 1952.

37. *Birmingham Post-Herald,* March 31, 1953; Sydney Maslen, relocation–racial relations specialist, to E. Bruce Wedge, HHFA area supervisor, March 19, 1953, HABD Papers, BPLDAM.

38. *Birmingham News,* June 19, 1952, June 20, 1952.

39. Hugh Denman to Cooper Green, June 24, 1952, James Morgan Papers, box 25, file 7, BPLDAM. Denman was vice president of the Mortgage Bankers Association of Birmingham and would later join the Housing Authority as its director of redevelopment. He would be named as executive director of the Housing Authority in 1960 (*Birmingham News,* January 20, 1960).

40. *Birmingham News,* June 25, 1952.

41. Housing and Home Finance Agency, *Slum Clearance under the Housing Act*

of 1949: A Preliminary Explanatory Statement to American Cities, Washington, D.C., August 1949, 11–12.

42. Housing Authority of the Birmingham District, *Preliminary Report, Slum Clearance and Redevelopment, Medical Center, Site A,* 1952, 22.

43. S. R. Gibbons, HABD assistant director for redevelopment, to Colonel Harold Harper, October 22, 1952, in HABD Papers, BPLDAM; Statement of Harold Harper, Public Meeting on the Medical Center, March 30, 1953, HABD Papers, 25, BPLDAM.

44. N. C. Ward to Colonel Harold Harper, "Tabulation of Applications Taken and Processed from January 1952 through October 1952," November 6, 1952, James Morgan Papers, box 14, file 13, BPLDAM. Ward managed the Joseph Loveman Village public housing development.

45. Housing Authority of the Birmingham District, *1952 Annual Report,* Birmingham Public Library.

46. W. C. Patton, president, NAACP Birmingham branch, to Albert M. Cole, administrator, Housing and Home Finance Agency, June 15, 1953, National Archives II, record group 207, Race Relations Program, Birmingham file.

47. "Racial Aspects of Preliminary Title I Planning in Birmingham, Alabama," March 19, 1952, record group 207, Race Relations Program, Birmingham file, National Archives II. Indeed, Loveman was completed in 1952, and the first medical center residents didn't begin to move out until June 1954 (*Birmingham Post-Herald,* June 22, 1954).

48. George Denison to Birmingham City Commission, November 10, 1949, Cooper Green Papers, box 8, file 3, BPLDAM.

49. Housing and Home Finance Agency, *Slum Clearance under the Housing Act of 1949: A Preliminary Explanatory Statement to American Cities,* Washington, D.C., August 1949, 12.

50. S. R. Gibbons, "Notes Covering Meeting in Dean Durrett's Office at 3:00 PM Monday, March 16, 1953," Housing Authority of the Birmingham District files, BPLDAM.

51. Corley, "The Quest for Racial Harmony," 63, 65, 70; S. R. Gibbons, assistant director for redevelopment, Housing Authority of the Birmingham District, "Memorandum of Conversation with Miss Roberta Morgan, Executive Secretary, Jefferson County Coordinating Council of Social Forces, on June 11, 1953," June 11, 1953, HABD Papers, BPLDAM; W. I. Pittman, president, Jefferson County Coordinating Council of Social Forces, to C. A. Wiegand, state director, Federal Housing Administration, June 26, 1953, HABD Papers, BPLDAM; S. R. Gibbons, "Memorandum Regarding Conversation, Washington, June 29, 1953," July 1, 1953, HABD Papers, BPLDAM.

52. Sydney Maslen, relocation–racial relations specialist, to E. Bruce Wedge, HHFA area supervisor, "Birmingham, Medical Center Project Area Relocation Plan," March 19, 1953, HABD Papers, BPLDAM. In addition, there were also seventy-seven single persons, sixty-one of whom were black. Single persons were not eligible for public housing.

53. Sydney Maslen, relocation–racial relations specialist, to E. Bruce Wedge, HHFA area supervisor, "Birmingham, Medical Center Project Area Relocation Plan," March 19, 1953, HABD Papers, BPLDAM. This projection appears to be based on the 1952 turnover rate in black public housing. In the first ten months of 1952, the two black public housing projects, Smithfield Court and Southtown, which together contained 992 dwelling units, experienced a turnover of 151 units, equivalent to 181 turnovers in a twelve-month period, for a 18.3 percent annual turnover rate. N. C. Ward to Colonel Harold Harper, "Tabulation of Applications Taken and Processed from January 1952 through October 1952," November 6, 1952, James Morgan Papers, box 14, file 13, BPLDAM.

54. According to the 1950 census, the percentage of the tract population that was black for each of the three public housing projects was: Smithfield Court (tract 29: 97.4 percent black), Southtown (tract 45: 94.3 percent black), and Joseph Loveman Village (tract 51: 88.6 percent black).

55. Housing Authority of the Birmingham District, July 28, 1953, James W. Morgan Papers, box 25, file 19, BPLDAM.

56. Statement of Colonel Harold Harper, Public Meeting on the Medical Center, March 30, 1953, HABD Papers, 25, BPLDAM.

57. Wilson Fallin Jr., "A Shelter in the Storm: The African American Church in Birmingham, Alabama, 1815–1963" (PhD diss., University of Alabama, 1995), 131, 143, 166; Statement of Reverend John W. Goodgame Jr., Public Meeting on the Medical Center, March 30, 1953, HABD Papers, 61, 63, BPLDAM.

58. Statement of Reverend John W. Goodgame Jr., Public Meeting on the Medical Center, March 30, 1953, HABD Papers, 61–64, BPLDAM.

59. Statement of Oscar W. Adams Jr., Public Meeting on the Medical Center, March 30, 1953, HABD Papers, 93–96, BPLDAM; *Birmingham News*, February 16, 1997.

60. Statement of Reverend J. B. Carter, Public Meeting on the Medical Center, March 30, 1953, HABD Papers, 77–80, BPLDAM; *Birmingham World*, June 2, 1953.

61. *Birmingham News*, March 31, 1953.

62. *Birmingham World*, May 29, 1953.

63. Ibid., June 9, 1953.

64. Housing Authority of the Birmingham District, *Preliminary Report, Slum Clearance and Redevelopment, Medical Center, Site A*, 1952, 10; *Birmingham Post-Herald*, May 26, 1953. The preliminary plan also called for the construction of a white nurses' home to replace an existing facility for white nurses.

65. *Birmingham News*, May 16, 1953.

66. Sydney Maslen, relocation–racial relations specialist, to E. Bruce Wedge, HHFA area supervisor, "Birmingham, Medical Center Project Area Relocation Plan," March 19, 1953, HABD Papers, BPLDAM.

67. *Birmingham World*, June 2, 1953, June 5, 1953. Clarence Mitchell to Albert M. Cole, May 28, 1953, record group 207, HHFA Subject Files, box 75, Racial Relations folder, #350, National Archives II; Ruby Hurley, NAACP regional secretary, Bir-

mingham, to Frank Horne, June 15, 1953, record group 207, Race Relations Program, Birmingham, Alabama, file, National Archives II.

68. *Birmingham World,* October 9, 1953.

69. *Birmingham News,* July 23, 1953.

70. *Birmingham World,* June 12, 1953; J. W. Follin, HHFA director of slum clearance and urban redevelopment, to Albert Cole, September 14, 1953, record group 207, Subject Correspondence files for Albert Cole, box 20, National Archives II; Marjorie Longenecker White, *Downtown Birmingham: Architectural and Historical Walking Tour Guide* (Birmingham: Birmingham Historical Society, 1980), 113.

71. George Nesbitt to N. S. Keith, May 21, 1953, record group 207, Race Relations Program, Birmingham, Alabama, file, National Archives II.

72. Note to files from George S. Nesbitt, Program Committee Review of Medical Center Project and Avondale Project, May 22, 1953, record group 207, Race Relations Program, Birmingham, Alabama, file, National Archives II.

73. Frank Horne, Racial Relations Service, to Albert Cole, June 18, 1953, record group 207, HHFA Subject files, box 75, Racial Relations folder, #350, National Archives II.

74. Albert Cole to Clarence Mitchell, June 19, 1953, record group 207, HHFA Subject files, box 75, Racial Relations folder, #350, National Archives II.

75. Samuel R. Gibbons, "Memorandum, Re: Conversation, Washington, June 29, 1953," July 1, 1953, HABD Papers, BPLDAM.

76. E. Bruce Wedge to Colonel Harold Harper, July 2, 1953, HABD Papers, BPLDAM.

77. Samuel R. Gibbons, "Telephone Conversations with Messrs. Robinson and Maslem, Washington, June 30th, 1953," July 1, 1953, HABD Papers, BPLDAM. Sydney Maslem was a HHFA relocation–racial relations specialist, and R. C. Robinson was assistant to E. Bruce Wedge, area supervisor, Division of Slum Clearance and Urban Redevelopment, HHFA.

78. *Birmingham World,* July 28, 1953.

79. *Birmingham News,* July 23, 1953; *Birmingham World,* July 28, 1953.

80. "Medical Center, Site A," July 14, 1953, HABD Papers, BPLDAM.

81. Samuel R. Gibbons, Memorandum of Conversation with Mr. Robinson, HHFA, Washington, Friday, July 3, 1953, n.d., HABD Paper, BPLDAM. Five years later, the Housing Authority was still attempting to arrange for the purchase of the Republic property. See Hugh Denman, Housing Authority director of urban renewal, to Thomas Patton, president, Republic Steel Corporation, October 23, 1958, James T. Waggoner Papers, box 5, file 14, BPLDAM.

82. Samuel R. Gibbons, assistant director for redevelopment, Housing Authority, Memorandum of Telephone Conversation with Mr. W. I. Pittman, president, Coordinating Council for Social Forces, Friday, July 3, 1953, HABD Papers, BPLDAM.

83. James Andrew Wiese, "Struggle for the Suburban Dream: African American Suburbanization since 1916" (PhD diss., Columbia University, 1993), 194–232.

84. Ibid., 206; Wilson, *Hamilton Park*, 33–53.

85. Corley, "The Quest for Racial Harmony," 70–71.

86. *Birmingham News*, July 24, 1953, July 27, 1953; *Birmingham Post-Herald*, July 23, 1953; *Birmingham World*, July 28, 1953.

87. W. C. Patton to Clarence Mitchell, director, NAACP Washington bureau, July 30, 1953, record group 207, Race Relations Program, Birmingham, Alabama, file, National Archives II.

88. W. C. Patton to Clarence Mitchell, July 30, 1953, record group 207, Race Relations Program, Birmingham, Alabama, file. National Archives II; *Birmingham World*, August 4, 1953; *Birmingham News*, August 18, 1953.

89. *Birmingham World*, July 31, 1953.

90. Ibid., August 14, 1953.

91. Ibid., August 18, 1953.

92. Ibid., October 9, 1953.

93. Ibid., July 31, 1953, August 11, 1953.

94. Ibid., August 28, 1953. James Follin had succeeded Nathaniel Keith as HHFA's slum clearance director.

95. Corley, "The Quest for Racial Harmony," 72.

96. Wiese, "Struggle for the Suburban Dream," 219–20.

97. *Birmingham News*, September 16, 1955.

98. Corley, "The Quest for Racial Harmony," 95; Housing Authority of the Birmingham District, "List of active members of the Citizens' Advisory Committee for Redevelopment of the Medical Center," July 28, 1953, James Morgan Papers, box 25, file 19, BPLDAM.

99. A. Key Foster to Mayor James W. Morgan, August 18, 1953, James Morgan Papers, box 25, file 19, BPLDAM.

100. Corley, "The Quest for Racial Harmony," 110–11.

101. *Birmingham World*, October 9, 1953; *Birmingham Post-Herald*, October 7, 1953.

102. *Birmingham World*, October 9, 1953.

103. Ibid.

104. Samuel R. Gibbons, "Re: Conversation, Washington, June 29, 1953," July 1, 1953, Housing Authority of the Birmingham District Papers, BPLDAM.

105. *Birmingham Post-Herald*, November 14, 1953.

106. James W. Morgan to Val Washington, director of minorities, Republican National Committee, November 9, 1953, James Morgan Papers, box 25, file 20, BPLDAM.

107. *Birmingham World*, September 29, 1953, October 2, 1953, October 9, 1953.

108. Christopher Scribner, "The Quiet Revolution: Federal Funding and Change in Birmingham, Alabama, 1933–1965" (PhD diss., Vanderbilt University, 1996), 189–90.

109. *Birmingham World*, October 16, 1953.

110. Ibid., October 2, 1953.

111. Ibid., November 20, 1953.

112. Housing and Home Finance Agency, "For Immediate Release," November 25, 1953, James Morgan Papers, box 25, file 21, BPLDAM.

113. James W. Follin to Colonel Harold Harper, HABD, November 25, 1953, James W. Morgan Papers, file 25.21, BPLDAM; *Birmingham News,* November 25, 1953.

114. James W. Follin to Colonel Harold Harper, HABD, November 25, 1953, James W. Morgan Papers, box 25, file 21, BPLDAM.

115. J. W. Follin to Albert Cole, September 14, 1953, record group 207, Albert Cole Subject Correspondence files, box 20, National Archives II.

116. Ruby Hurley to James W. Morgan, December 15, 1953, James Morgan Papers, box 25, file 21, BPLDAM.

117. James Morgan to A. R. Hanson, January 21, 1955, James Morgan Papers, box 25, file 9, BPLDAM.

118. Housing and Home Finance Agency, *Relocation from Urban Renewal Project Areas through December 1957,* HHFA Papers, record group 207, box 620, National Archives II. The five projects were Michael Reese Hospital in Chicago; North Allen and Southwest Temple in Philadelphia; Capitol Hill in Nashville; and Redevelopment Project Number 1 in Richmond.

119. Civil Action 7690, Complaint Filed in Clerk's Office, Northern District of Alabama, U.S. District Court, June 7, 1954, James Morgan Papers, box 14, file 14, BPLDAM.

120. U.S. District Court for the Northern District of Alabama, Southern Division, *Rosa Watts, et al., v. Housing Authority of the Birmingham District,* January 28, 1955.

121. *Birmingham World,* May 10, 1955.

122. Ibid.

123. Housing Authority of the Birmingham District, *Annual Report for 1962,* 1962.

124. Corienne Morrow, Racial Relations Branch, to Frank Horne, assistant to the administrator, HHFA, May 7, 1953, record group 207, box 18, National Archives II. For a fuller discussion of the Racial Relations Branch's efforts to address the negative impacts of urban renewal on black housing, see Arnold Hirsch, "Search for a 'Sound Negro Policy': A Racial Agenda for the Housing Acts of 1949 and 1954," *Housing Policy Debate* 11 (2000): 393–442.

5. Urban Renewal and Highways

1. Bernard Frieden and Lynne Sagalyn, *Downtown, Inc.: How America Rebuilds Cities* (Cambridge: MIT Press, 1989), 23.

2. *Birmingham News,* November 28, 1953.

3. U.S. Bureau of the Census, *United States Census of Population, Birmingham, Alabama, Census Tracts* (Washington, D.C.: Government Printing Office, 1952), tables 1 and 3.

4. *Birmingham Post,* July 13, 1926.

5. James C. Ogle Jr., "Avondale, Site C: Planning Studies," Housing Authority of

the Birmingham District, n.d., Housing Authority of the Birmingham District Papers, BPLDAM.

6. Ibid.; *Birmingham News*, August 14, 1955.

7. *Birmingham News*, August 14, 1955.

8. *East End News*, February 7, 1957.

9. *Birmingham News*, August 14, 1955.

10. Birmingham Planning Board, *Preliminary Report*, February 8, 1952, 43.

11. Jeffrey Rush and Abraham Williams, residents of Sloss Quarters, interviews in *Like It Ain't Never Passed: Remembering Life in Sloss Quarters*, ed. Barbara Nunn (Birmingham: Sloss Furnaces National Historic Landmark, 1985), 2, 5.

12. Birmingham Planning Board, *Preliminary Report*, February 8, 1952, 45; Ogle, "Avondale, Site C, Planning Studies."

13. Lewis, *Sloss Furnaces*, 438.

14. *Birmingham Post-Herald*, April 28, 1954; *Birmingham News*, August 18, 1958.

15. Birmingham Chamber of Commerce, *Birmingham—The Industrial City Beautiful* (map), 1952.

16. George S. Nesbitt, Note to Files, Program Committee Review of Medical Center Project and Avondale Project, May 22, 1953, record group 207, Race Relations Program, Birmingham, Alabama, file, National Archives II.

17. George Nesbitt to N. S. Keith, May 21, 1953, record group 207, box 750, National Archives II.

18. Urban Renewal Administration, HHFA, Press Release, March 28, 1956, James Morgan Papers, box 25, file 16, BPLDAM.

19. *Birmingham News*, September 15, 1955, March 28, 1956.

20. Ibid., March 28, 1956.

21. *Birmingham World*, October 9, 1953.

22. Arnold Hirsch, *Making the Second Ghetto*, 2d ed. (Chicago: University of Chicago Press, 1998).

23. Mayer U. Newfield to J. Orlando Ogle, April 13, 1956, James Morgan Papers, box 26, file 17, BPLDAM.

24. Such problems were not unique to Birmingham. Hirsch notes the same phenomenon in Chicago, where the Dearborn Homes public housing project, designated as the relocation site for families displaced from the city's Lake Meadows urban renewal site, displaced black households living in a "densely crowded" neighborhood. See Hirsch, *Making the Second Ghetto*, 123.

25. *Birmingham News*, July 27, 1955, July 28, 1955.

26. *Birmingham Post-Herald*, July 28, 1955.

27. *Birmingham News*, July 28, 1955.

28. Ibid., July 31, 1955.

29. Ibid., August 1, 1955, *Birmingham Post-Herald*, August 3, 1955.

30. *Birmingham Post-Herald*, August 25, 1955, *Birmingham News*, August 30, 1955.

31. *Birmingham News*, August 2, 1955.

32. Leonard Freedman, *Public Housing: The Politics of Poverty* (New York: Holt, Rinehart, and Winston, 1969), 15–57.

33. *Birmingham News,* September 15, 1955.

34. Ibid.

35. *Birmingham Post-Herald,* March 28, 1956.

36. The Section 220 and 221 mortgage insurance programs were enacted in the Housing Act of 1954. Section 220 insured mortgages for rental housing located in urban renewal areas and Section 221 insured mortgages for families displaced by urban renewal and other low- and moderate-income households.

37. Housing and Home Finance Agency, *How Localities Can Develop a Workable Program for Urban Renewal,* October 1, 1954, R-1, 1–4.

38. Bruce Wedge to Hugh Denman, March 25, 1955, James Morgan Papers, box 25, file 9, BPLDAM.

39. In the midst of the Southside Medical Center controversy, the city continued to display the belief that it could affect the racial character of the city's neighborhoods. In late 1953, Mayor James Morgan attempted to assuage black opposition to the project by planning to designate for black occupancy a small area just west of Elmwood Cemetery, located in the southwestern portion of the city. The neighborhood was sparsely settled, containing only a few white households. Hugh Denman, assistant director for redevelopment, Housing Authority of the Birmingham District, to Claude Vardaman, November 18, 1953, James Morgan Papers, box 25, file 21, BPLDAM.

40. *Birmingham Post-Herald,* April 5, 1955.

41. Clarence Arthur Perry, *Housing for the Machine Age* (New York: Russell Sage Foundation, 1939).

42. Birmingham Planning Commission, "Narrative Description of Proposed Future Land Use Map for Northeast Birmingham," adopted November 16, 1955, 1, James Morgan Papers, box 25, file 9, BPLDAM. In August 1955, the Birmingham City Commission reconstituted the Birmingham Planning Board as the Birmingham Planning Commission. Under Alabama planning enabling law, this change permitted the Planning Commission to adopt subdivision regulations and a comprehensive plan (*Birmingham News,* August 4, 1955).

43. Birmingham Planning Commission, "Narrative Description of Proposed Future Land Use Map for Northeast Birmingham," 3.

44. Ibid., 8.

45. Birmingham Planning Commission, *City of Birmingham, Alabama, Future Land Use Plan,* c. 1957, 39, Planning and Zoning Papers, box 668.2.25, BPLDAM.

46. Birmingham Planning Commission, "Narrative Description of Proposed Future Land Use Map for Northeast Birmingham," 12.

47. Ibid., 4.

48. Ibid., 8–9.

49. Ibid., 9–10.

50. Ibid., 10.

51. *Birmingham World,* January 5, 1957.

52. Police Surveillance Files, *Bombings or Attempt* [sic] *Bombings in Birmingham, 1950–1965,* BPLDAM, n.d.

53. Housing and Home Finance Agency, Summary of the Workable Program for the City of Birmingham, Alabama, June 20, 1955, James Morgan Papers, box 25, file 9, BPLDAM.

54. *Birmingham News,* June 28, 1955; *Birmingham Post-Herald,* July 27, 1955, July 28, 1955.

55. *Birmingham Post-Herald,* July 27, 1955.

56. Ibid., December 31, 1955.

57. Birmingham Planning Commission, *City of Birmingham, Alabama, Future Land Use Plan,* c. 1957, Planning and Zoning Papers, file 668.2.25, BPLDAM.

58. Ibid., 14–15.

59. George Foss, technical advisor to Birmingham Planning Commission, to Mayor James W. Morgan, October 27, 1955, James Morgan Papers, box 20, file 31, BPLDAM.

60. Housing and Home Finance Agency, Summary of the Workable Program for the City of Birmingham, Alabama, September 30, 1957, 3, James Morgan Papers, box 25, file 12, BPLDAM.

61. *Birmingham News,* March 18, 1958; E. Bruce Wedge to James W. Morgan, November 6, 1957, James Waggoner Papers, box 5, file 10, BPLDAM.

62. Marjorie Longenecker White, *Downtown Birmingham: Architectural and Historical Walking Tour Guide* (Birmingham: Birmingham Historical Society, 1980), 83.

63. *Birmingham Post-Herald,* November 6, 1957; *Birmingham News,* March 18, 1958, "CBD," special insert in *Birmingham News, Birmingham Post-Herald,* Sunday, August 20, 1961.

64. *Birmingham News,* February 19, 1958.

65. Marjorie Longenecker White, *The Birmingham District: An Industrial History and Guide* (Birmingham: Birmingham Historical Society, 1981), 98–106.

66. Carl V. Harris, *Political Power in Birmingham, 1871–1921* (Knoxville: University of Tennessee Press, 1977), 28–32.

67. *Birmingham Post,* July 13, 1926.

68. Because the Ensley street system had been laid out before the community was annexed into the City of Birmingham in 1910, it has a separate system of names. Hence, Twentieth Street Ensley should not be confused with Twentieth Street in downtown Birmingham.

69. White, *The Birmingham District,* 104; Carolyn Green Satterfield, *Historic Sites of Jefferson County, Alabama* (Birmingham: Jefferson County Historical Commission, 1985), 60.

70. U.S. Bureau of the Census, *United States Census of Population: 1950: Birmingham, Alabama, Census Tract Statistics* (Washington, D.C.: Government Printing Office, 1952), tables 1, 3.

71. *Birmingham Post Herald,* February 13, 1952.

72. Quoted in Ethel Armes, *The Story of Coal and Iron in Alabama* (Birmingham: Chamber of Commerce, 1910), 395.

73. White, *The Birmingham District*, 101.

74. U.S. Bureau of the Census, *United States Census of Population: 1950: Birmingham, Alabama, Census Tract Statistics* (Washington, D.C.: Government Printing Office, 1952), tables 1, 2, and 3.

75. *Birmingham Post*, July 13, 1926.

76. *Birmingham News*, March 21, 1958.

77. De Leuw, Cather and Company, *Ensley–Pratt City Urban Renewal Study*, August, 1958, Chicago, table 2.

78. Ibid., 14.

79. Ibid., 16.

80. Ibid., 15.

81. Ibid., 25.

82. Mark I. Gelfand, *A Nation of Cities* (New York: Oxford University Press, 1975), 227–28.

83. See proposed project map in *Birmingham News*, August 1, 1956.

84. *Birmingham Post-Herald*, March 21, 1958, May 9, 1958.

85. Planning director, to Urban Renewal Committee, March 15, 1960, J. T. Waggoner Papers, box 5, file 19, BPLDAM; J. T. Waggoner, Birmingham commissioner of public works, to A. R. Hanson, director, HHFA Regional Office, August 1, 1957, J. T. Waggoner Papers, box 5, file 10, BPLDAM.

86. De Leuw, Cather and Company, *Ensley–Pratt City*, exhibit 2.

87. *Birmingham Post*, July 13, 1926.

88. De Leuw, Cather and Company, *Ensley–Pratt City*, 3.

89. Mel Scott, *American City Planning since 1890* (Berkeley and Los Angeles: University of California Press, 1969), 501; Gelfand, *A Nation of Cities*, 171–76; U.S. Housing and Home Finance Agency, *How Localities Can Develop a Workable Program for Urban Renewal* (Washington, D.C.: U.S. Government Printing Office, 1954).

90. E. Bruce Wedge, HHFA regional urban renewal director, to James W. Morgan, October 27, 1959, Planning and Zoning Papers, file 668.1.37, BPLDAM.

91. De Leuw, Cather and Company, *Ensley–Pratt City*, table 1, exhibit 15; *Birmingham News*, April 7, 1961; *Birmingham Post-Herald*, December 17, 1963.

92. Birmingham Planning Commission, *Neighborhood Analysis: Ensley Community*, 1978, 3–1, 3–5; Birmingham Planning Commission, *Neighborhood Analysis: Central Park–Five Points West Community*, 1978, 4–1, 4–7.

93. Transcript of Public Hearing on Ensley Number One Urban Renewal Area, February 22, 1961, J. T. Waggoner Papers, box 6, file 2, BPLDAM; *Birmingham News*, November 26, 1961.

94. To Urban Renewal Committee from planning director, March 15, 1960, J. T. Waggoner Papers, box 5, file 19, BPLDAM; *Birmingham News*, November 26, 1961.

95. Housing Authority of the Birmingham District, "Estimated Housing Re-

quirements and Resources for Displaced Families," April 1959, Planning and Zoning Papers, file 668.4.8, BPLDAM.

96. Leslie Williams, *Recommended Location of Interstate and Defense Highways along North and West Sides of Central Business District of City of Birmingham, Alabama*, January 1961, 3, Planning and Zoning Papers, file 668.2.32, BPLDAM.

97. Ibid.

98. Ibid., 4.

99. The black neighborhood lying west of downtown is now identified by the city as part of Smithfield, whereas in 1961 the city identified it as Smith Park. See Birmingham Planning Commission, *The Comprehensive Plan: Birmingham, Alabama*, prepared by Harland Bartholomew and Associates, 1961, plate 37; Birmingham, Alabama, Map of Community Boundaries, 1998, www.bham.lib.al.us/vulcanet/map/map.htm.

100. Police Surveillance Files, *Bombings or Attempt* [sic] *Bombings in Birmingham, 1950–1965*, BPLDAM, n.d.; *Birmingham World*, April 17, 1957, May 4, 1957, October 26, 1957, November 6, 1957, December 11, 1957, July 23, 1958.

101. *Birmingham World*, December 11, 1957.

102. Ibid., October 26, 1957.

103. *Birmingham Post*, July 13, 1926.

104. *Birmingham Post-Herald*, May 9, 1958.

105. Ibid., February 14, 1957.

106. U.S. Department of Commerce, Bureau of Public Roads, *General Location of National System of Interstate Highways*, 1955.

107. *Birmingham News*, July 15, 1956, August 25, 1957.

108. *Birmingham Post-Herald*, March 21, 1958.

109. Harland Bartholomew and Associates, *The Comprehensive Plan, Birmingham, Alabama*, prepared for the Birmingham Planning Commission, December 1961, plate 37.

110. According to the 1998 City of Birmingham Map of Community Boundaries, Interstate 59 remains the boundary between the Ensley Highlands and Tuxedo neighborhoods and the East Thomas and College Hills neighborhoods, while Interstate 65 is still the boundary between Fountain Heights and Enon Ridge and between downtown Birmingham and the Smithfield neighborhood. See www.bham.lib.al.us/vulcanet/map/map.htm. Neighborhood racial change resulted in Fountain Heights becoming predominantly black in the 1960s, College Hills in the 1970s, and Ensley Highlands in the 1980s. See Betty Bock, "An Analysis of the Impact of Racial Transition on the Desirability of Neighborhoods" (master's thesis, University of Alabama at Birmingham, 1976), 71–74; U.S. Bureau of the Census, *1980 Census of Population and Housing, Census Tracts, Birmingham, Alabama Standard Metropolitan Statistical Area*, June 1983; U.S. Bureau of the Census, *1990 Census of Population, Population and Housing Characteristics for Census Tracts and Block Numbering Areas, Birmingham, Alabama MSA*, April 1993.

111. In the 1960 Census, tract 6—through which Interstate 59 was routed—is reported as 92 percent black, while tract 17, which was in direct line of the north-

east-southwest route of Interstate 59, is listed as 62 percent white. Tract 5, which represents portions of the East Birmingham and Woodlawn communities, was 75 percent white in 1960, while tract 3, which contained the heart of the Woodlawn business district, was 96 percent white. See table 5.1.

112. Joe Davis, president, Woodlawn Chamber of Commerce, to Secretary of Commerce Luther Hodges, February 17, 1961, Bureau of Public Roads, General Correspondence, 1960–65, record group 30, box 1664, National Archives II.

113. Undated newspaper clipping, "Many Dissatisfied with Recommended, Freeway Routing"; Mrs. Lala Palmer to Alabama State Highway Department, April 11, 1960; R. D. Jordan to Lala Palmer, April 19, 1960, Bureau of Public Roads Records, General Correspondence, 1912–65, record group 30, box 1665, National Archives II.

114. There were no apparent topographical reasons for replacing the original straight-line route with a curvilinear route. Both routes run through the relatively level Jones Valley, which runs from northeast to southwest parallel to the system of ridges that borders Birmingham's north and south sides.

115. Birmingham Historical Society, *Smithfield: An Historic Birmingham Neighborhood,* 1986.

116. John J. Drew to Congressman George Huddleston Jr., October 15, 1963, Federal Highway Administration Correspondence RE: Federal Aid, record group 406, box 2, National Archives II.

117. Letter of James Hutchinson, November 21, 1963, Federal Highway Administration Correspondence RE: Federal Aid, record group 406, box 2, National Archives II.

118. Eskew, *But for Birmingham,* 206–7; *Birmingham World,* August 31, 1963, September 7, 1963.

119. Rex M. Whitton to John Sparkman, November 20, 1963, Records of the Federal Highway Administration, Correspondence, 1961–78, AL 11–AL 15, record group 406, box 3, National Archives II.

120. H. M. Gousha Company, *Street Map of Birmingham,* 1971.

121. In Chicago, some of the city's white neighborhoods recognized that the city's urban renewal programs in black neighborhoods would relocate blacks who would move into white neighborhoods. See Hirsch, *Making of the Second Ghetto,* 130–32.

6. Civil Rights and City Planning

1. *Birmingham News,* May 9, 1959.

2. U.S. Bureau of the Census, *A Report of the Seventeenth Decennial Census of the United States: Census of Population: 1950,* vol. 2, *Characteristics of the Population,* pt. 2, *Alabama* (Washington, D.C.: Government Printing Office, 1952), 55; U.S. Bureau of the Census, *The Eighteenth Decennial Census of the United States: Census of Population: 1960,* vol. 1, *Characteristics of the Population,* pt. 2, *Alabama* (Washington, D.C.: Government Printing Office, 1963), 167; U.S. Bureau of the Census, *1990 Census of Population and Housing,* CD ROM; Charles Connerly, "Urban Rivalry and the

South: Atlanta and Birmingham," paper presented at 1993 Society for American City and Regional Planning History Conference, Chicago.

3. Hammer, Greene, Siler Associates, *The Economy of Metropolitan Birmingham* (Atlanta, 1966), 75; Glenn T. Eskew, *But for Birmingham: The Local and National Movements in the Civil Rights Struggle* (Chapel Hill: University of North Carolina Press, 1997), 58.

4. U.S. Bureau of the Census, *Sixteenth Census of the United States, 1940 Population*, vol. 2, *Characteristics of the Population*, pt. 1 (Washington, D.C.: Government Printing Office, 1943), 337; U.S. Bureau of the Census, *A Report of the Seventeenth Decennial Census of the United States: Census of Population: 1950*, vol. 2, *Characteristics of the Population*, pt. 2: *Alabama* (Washington, D.C.: Government Printing Office, 1952), 55; U.S. Bureau of the Census, *The Eighteenth Decennial Census of the United States: Census of Population: 1960*, vol. 1, *Characteristics of the Population*, pt. 2, *Alabama* (Washington, D.C.: Government Printing Office, 1963), 167; U.S. Bureau of the Census, *Nineteenth Census of the United States: 1970 Census of Population*, vol. 1, *Characteristics of the Population*, pt. 2, *Alabama* (Washington, D.C.: Government Printing Office, 1973), 233; U.S. Bureau of the Census, *Twentieth Census of the United States: 1980 Census of Population*, vol. 1, *Characteristics of the Population: Detailed Population Characteristics*, pt. 2, *Alabama* (Washington, D.C.: Government Printing Office, 1983), 537–38; Birmingham Chamber of Commerce, *Birmingham Metropolitan Statistical Area Profile*, accessed on July 26, 2000, at www.birminghamchamber.com/bmsap/bmsap.htm.

5. Ann Markusen, *Profit Cycles, Oligopoly, and Regional Development* (Cambridge: MIT Press, 1985), 91–92.

6. Hammer, Greene, Siler, *Economy of Metropolitan Birmingham*, 20.

7. *Birmingham News*, September 28, 1958.

8. Ibid.

9. Ibid.

10. Ibid., August 20, 1961.

11. Harland Bartholomew and Associates, *The Comprehensive Plan: Birmingham, Alabama*, prepared for the Birmingham Planning Commission, 1961, 19.

12. U.S. Bureau of the Census, *A Report of the Seventeenth Decennial Census of the United States: Census of Population: 1950* (Washington, D.C.: Government Printing Office, 1952); *The Eighteenth Decennial Census of the United States: Census of Population: 1960* (Washington, D.C.: Government Printing Office, 1963). About two-thirds of Atlanta's population increase was accounted for by a major suburban annexation accomplished through that city's Plan of Improvement. See Bradley R. Rice, "The Battle of Buckhead: The Plan of Improvement and Atlanta's Last Big Annexation," *Atlanta Historical Journal* 25 (1981): 5–22; Clarence Stone, *Regime Politics: Governing Atlanta, 1946–1988* (Lawrence: University Press of Kansas, 1989), 28–32.

13. U.S. Bureau of the Census, *A Report of the Seventeenth Decennial Census of the United States: Census of Population: 1950*, vol. 2, *Characteristics of the Population*, pt. 2, *Alabama* (Washington, D.C.: Government Printing Office, 1952), 55, *Georgia*, 66;

U.S. Bureau of the Census, *The Eighteenth Decennial Census of the United States: Census of Population: 1960,* vol. 1, *Characteristics of the Population,* pt. 2, *Alabama,* 167, *Georgia,* 236.

14. Ivan Allen Jr., with Paul Hemphill, *Mayor: Notes on the Sixties* (New York: Simon and Schuster, 1971), 103.

15. William P. Engel, "Greater Birmingham and Its Future," November 21, 1950, Birmingham Chamber of Commerce Records, box 1, file 8, BPLDAM.

16. Sheldon Schaffer, "Regional Economic Trends and Their Implications for Birmingham," November 21, 1962, Albert Boutwell Papers, box 41, file 22, BPLDAM. Schaffer made the same speech to several other civic organizations in Birmingham, including the Young Men's Business Club and several Kiwanis Clubs.

17. Carl Abbott, *The New Urban America,* rev. ed. (Chapel Hill: University of North Carolina Press, 1987), 24–35.

18. *Birmingham News,* October 12, 1958.

19. *Birmingham Post-Herald,* January 1, 1962.

20. Eskew, *But for Birmingham,* 10.

21. Quote from Harold H. Martin, "Birmingham," *Saturday Evening Post,* September 6, 1947, 22–23, 54–58.

22. George W. Blanks to Cooper Green, August 21, 1945, Cooper Green Papers, file 8.10, BPLDAM.

23. Cooper Green to Henry Ford II, August 17, 1949, Cooper Green Papers, file 9.19, BPLDAM.

24. D. W. LaRue to Cooper Green, August 25, 1949, Cooper Green Papers, file 3.21, BPLDAM.

25. Charles Morgan Jr., *A Time To Speak* (New York: Harper and Row, 1964), 9.

26. George Patterson, interview by Anthony Underwood, May 23, 1979, Anthony Underwood Papers, BPLDAM.

27. James C. Cobb, *The Selling of the South,* 2d ed. (Urbana: University of Illinois Press, 1993), 36, 46–50.

28. Louis Pizitz to Cooper Green, August 24, 1945, Cooper Green Papers, file 8.10, BPLDAM.

29. Committee of 100, *Birmingham Diary,* c. 1957, James Morgan Papers, box 10, file 19, BPLDAM; *Birmingham News,* February 11, 1951.

30. Alabama Planning and Industrial Board, *Alabama's Plans for Financing Industrial Plants,* January 1960, E. C. Overton Papers, box 1, file 16, BPLDAM; Dan T. Carter, *The Politics of Rage: George Wallace, The Origins of the New Conservatism, and the Transformation of American Politics* (New York: Simon and Schuster, 1995), 77.

31. Minutes of the Meeting of the Industrial Development Committee of the Council of the City of Birmingham, August 21, 1963, Albert Boutwell Papers, box 11, file 42, BPLDAM.

32. Robert Corley, "The Quest for Racial Harmony: Race Relations in Birmingham, Alabama, 1947–1963" (PhD diss., University of Virginia, 1979), 197–205.

33. Southern Institute of Management, *The Birmingham Metropolitan Audit, Preliminary Report No. 2,* "The Personality of Birmingham," 1960, Hill Ferguson Collection, box 18, file 17, BPLDAM, 12, 15.

34. Elton B. Stephens to Albert Boutwell, June 28, 1963, City Council Papers, file 3.32, BPLDAM. Stephens is the founder of EBSCO Subscription Services, which has become a nationally known periodical subscription broker.

35. In the mid-1950s, the Committee of 100's eighteen-member executive committee included such Big Mule executives as the president of TCI–U.S. Steel, Arthur Wiebel; the heads of two of the city's major banks; the heads of the two major utilities, Alabama Gas Co. and Alabama Power Co.; the heads of four other major industrial firms, U.S. Pipe and Foundry, Woodward Iron Co., Avondale Mills, and Alabama By-Products Corporation; and Mervyn Sterne, head of a leading security investment company (Committee of 100, *Birmingham Diary,* 1957, James Morgan Papers, box 10, file 19, BPLDAM).

36. *Birmingham Post-Herald,* August 22, 1963.

37. *Birmingham News,* April 10, 1964.

38. Eskew, *But for Birmingham,* 170.

39. Ibid., 170, 307–8.

40. Ibid., 22; Diane McWhorter, *Carry Me Home, Birmingham, Alabama: The Climactic Battle of the Civil Rights Revolution* (New York: Simon and Schuster, 2001), 107–8; Corley, "The Quest for Racial Harmony," 125; Andrew Manis, *A Fire You Can't Put Out: The Civil Rights Life of Birmingham's Reverend Fred Shuttlesworth* (Tuscaloosa: University of Alabama Press, 1999), 91–95.

41. Eskew, *But for Birmingham,* 125–27.

42. Ibid., 127–28; Glenn T. Eskew, "'The Classes and the Masses': Fred Shuttlesworth's Movement and Birmingham's Black Middle Class," in *Birmingham Revolutionaries: The Reverend Fred Shuttlesworth and the Alabama Christian Movement for Human Rights,* ed. Marjorie L. White and Andrew M. Manis (Macon: Mercer University Press, 2000), 37–38; McWhorter, *Carry Me Home,* 111–12.

43. Eskew, "'The Classes and the Masses,'" 36–37.

44. Aldon D. Morris, *The Origins of the Civil Rights Movement: Black Communities Organizing for Change* (New York: Free Press, 1984), 68–69; Eskew, *But for Birmingham,* 125.

45. Eskew, *But for Birmingham,* 130–32; McWhorter, *Carry Me Home,* 113–15; Corley, "The Quest for Racial Harmony," 141–42.

46. Eskew, *But for Birmingham,* 140–41; McWhorter, *Carry Me Home,* 127–29; Corley, "The Quest for Racial Harmony," 137–38.

47. Eskew, *But for Birmingham,* 153–58; McWhorter, *Carry Me Home,* 200–208; Numan V. Bartley, *The New South: 1945–1980* (Baton Rouge: Louisiana State University Press, 1995), 306–7; Corley, "The Quest for Racial Harmony," 215–18.

48. Eskew, *But for Birmingham,* 160; McWhorter, *Carry Me Home,* 213–14; Corley, "The Quest for Racial Harmony," 218.

49. McWhorter, *Carry Me Home,* 218.

50. Eskew, *But for Birmingham,* 112.

51. McWhorter, *Carry Me Home*, 67.

52. Eskew, *But for Birmingham*, 109–13.

53. Ibid., 171; McWhorter, *Carry Me Home*, 222–23; Corley, "The Quest for Racial Harmony," 219; *Wall Street Journal*, May 26, 1961.

54. Corley, "The Quest for Racial Harmony," 111–14; Eskew, *But for Birmingham*, 175–76.

55. Eskew, *But for Birmingham*, 170–71; McWhorter, *Carry Me Home*, 247–49.

56. David Vann, *Events Leading to the 1963 Change from the Commission to the Mayor-Council Form of Government in Birmingham, Alabama* (Birmingham, 1981), 3–4.

57. Corley, "The Quest for Racial Harmony," 213; *Birmingham News*, February 25, 1962; Eskew, *But for Birmingham*, 180. In 1910, in reaction to the graft of the city's aldermanic form of government, civic reformers persuaded voters to convert to a commission form of government in which voters elected three commissioners, including a mayor, a commissioner of public safety, and a commissioner of public works. See Harris, *Political Power in Birmingham*, 81–82.

58. *Birmingham News*, February 25, 1962.

59. Ibid., December 9, 1961; Eskew, *But for Birmingham*, 178–79; Birmingham Planning Commission, *A Report on Schools and Parks, A Part of the Comprehensive Plan, Birmingham, Alabama*, January 1961, 11; McWhorter, *Carry Me Home*, 247–53.

60. Mel Scott, *American City Planning since 1890* (Berkeley and Los Angeles: University of California Press, 1969), 10–26; Birmingham Planning Commission, *The Comprehensive Plan*, December 1961, 115–31; Daniel Bluestone, *Constructing Chicago* (New Haven: Yale University Press, 1991), 7–35.

61. *Time*, December 22, 1961. Soon after his election as mayor in 1961, Hanes had told a group of businessmen, "Well, before I can promise you anything, I've got to check with Bull" (McWhorter, *Carry Me Home*, 252).

62. Eskew, *But for Birmingham*, 112.

63. Paul Cooper to John Bryan and Emil Hess, May 18, 1956, James Morgan Papers, box 20, file 32, BPLDAM; *Birmingham News*, July 17, 1957. The metropolitan planning commission legislation was not approved by the legislature (*Birmingham News*, August 11, 1957). In 1963, the Alabama legislature created the Birmingham Regional Planning Commission but granted it advisory status only. See Linda Nelson, "Regional Land Use Planning: The Ideal, the Real and the Ruined," February 28, 1980, copy in author's possession.

64. Sidney Smyer to Alex Montgomery, August 22, 1955, James Morgan Papers, box 20, file 31, BPLDAM.

65. Minutes of the Board of Directors of the Birmingham Downtown Improvement Association, November 5, 1957, Robert Jemison Papers, BPLDAM.

66. Corley, "The Quest for Racial Harmony," 223–24; Eskew, *But for Birmingham*, 179.

67. *Birmingham News*, January 10, 1962; Eskew, *But for Birmingham*, 257; McWhorter, *Carry Me Home*, 257–58; Corley, "The Quest for Racial Harmony," 223–24.

68. Birmingham Planning Commission, *The Comprehensive Plan*, December 1961, 129.

69. *Wall Street Journal*, March 12, 1962.

70. *Birmingham News*, December 16, 1961.

71. Eskew, *But for Birmingham*, 180; McWhorter, *Carry Me Home*, 257–58.

72. Corley, "The Quest for Racial Harmony," 225.

73. Vann, *Events Leading to the 1963 Change*, 4–5; Eskew, *But for Birmingham*, 370 n. 51.

74. Vann, *Events Leading to the 1963 Change*, 12; Morgan, *A Time to Speak*, 100–109; McWhorter, *Carry Me Home*, 282–86.

75. Vann, *Events Leading to the 1963 Change*, 12. In Alabama, precincts are called "boxes."

76. Harry Holloway, *The Politics of the Southern Negro* (New York: Random House, 1969), 158–59.

77. McWhorter, *Carry Me Home*, 180–81.

78. Morgan, *A Time to Speak*, 86–91; Eskew, *But for Birmingham*, 167–68.

79. Holloway, *Southern Negro*, 158; Corley, "The Quest for Racial Harmony," 221–22.

80. McWhorter, *Carry Me Home*, 196–97, 202, 243; Corley, "The Quest for Racial Harmony," 222.

81. Eskew, *But for Birmingham*, 366 n. 27.

82. Quoted in Holloway, *Southern Negro*, 159.

83. Vann, *Events Leading to the 1963 Change*, 13–14; Eskew, *But for Birmingham*, 166.

84. Vann, *Events Leading to the 1963 Change*, 14.

85. Ibid., 15–17; Eskew, *But for Birmingham*, 181–82; McWhorter, *Carry Me Home*, 285–86.

86. McWhorter, *Carry Me Home*, 296; Corley, "The Quest for Racial Harmony," 226.

87. Vann, *Events Leading to the 1963 Change*, 20; Corley, "The Quest for Racial Harmony," 226–27.

88. Corley, "The Quest for Racial Harmony," 228–29; Edward LaMonte, *Politics and Welfare in Birmingham: 1900–1975* (Tuscaloosa: University of Alabama Press, 1995), 168; Eskew, *But for Birmingham*, 182.

89. McWhorter, *Carry Me Home*, 299–300; Vann, *Events Leading to the 1963 Change*, 22–23.

90. Corley, "The Quest for Racial Harmony," 229–30; Eskew, *But for Birmingham*, 188.

91. McWhorter, *Carry Me Home*, 300.

92. Eskew, *But for Birmingham*, 189; McWhorter, *Carry Me Home*, 313.

93. Rogers, Ward, Atkins, and Flynt, *Alabama: The History of a Deep South State*, 547–48; Corley, "The Quest for Racial Harmony," 245–46.

94. Eskew, *But for Birmingham*, 190; LaMonte, *Politics and Welfare*, 172; *Birmingham Post-Herald*, February 27, 1963.

95. McWhorter, *Carry Me Home*, 313.

96. Corley, "The Quest for Racial Harmony," 246; Eskew, *But for Birmingham*, 190.

97. Corley, "The Quest for Racial Harmony," 247; Eskew, *But for Birmingham*, 190; McWhorter, *Carry Me Home*, 315.

98. Corley, "The Quest for Racial Harmony," 248; Eskew, *But for Birmingham*, 191; McWhorter, *Carry Me Home*, 320.

99. Corley, "The Quest for Racial Harmony," 248; Eskew, *But for Birmingham*, 191; McWhorter, *Carry Me Home*, 320.

100. LaMonte, *Politics and Welfare*, 173; *Birmingham News*, April 3, 1963; Corley, "The Quest for Racial Harmony," 249; McWhorter, *Carry Me Home*, 320.

101. Corley, "The Quest for Racial Harmony," 251.

102. Eskew, *But for Birmingham*, 193–216.

103. *Birmingham Post-Herald*, November 6, 1957; *Birmingham News*, March 18, 1958.

104. Eskew, *But for Birmingham*, 248–57.

105. Ibid., 259–65; McWhorter, *Carry Me Home*, 366–68.

106. Eskew, *But for Birmingham*, 256–65; Corley, "The Quest for Racial Harmony," 258–59. The children's campaign had been developed and organized by James Bevel and Ike Reynolds.

107. Eskew, *But for Birmingham*, 266–69; Corley, "The Quest for Racial Harmony," 259; McWhorter, *Carry Me Home*, 377–78.

108. Eskew, *But for Birmingham*, 269–70; Corley, "The Quest for Racial Harmony," 261–64; Vann, *Events Leading to the 1963 Change*, 25–26; McWhorter, *Carry Me Home*, 378–85.

109. Eskew, *But for Birmingham*, 269–77; Corley, "The Quest for Racial Harmony," 261–68; Vann, *Events Leading to the 1963 Change*, 26–27; McWhorter, *Carry Me Home*, 389.

110. Vann, *Events Leading to the 1963 Change*, 28.

111. McWhorter, *Carry Me Home*, 287–88, 396; Eskew, *But for Birmingham*, 201–2, 277.

112. McWhorter, *Carry Me Home*, 403–7; Corley, "The Quest for Racial Harmony," 268–69; Eskew, *But for Birmingham*, 279–80.

113. McWhorter, *Carry Me Home*, 407.

114. Eskew, *But for Birmingham*, 283–85; Corley, "The Quest for Racial Harmony," 269–70; McWhorter, *Carry Me Home*, 413.

115. Eskew, *But for Birmingham*, 204–10, 280–95; Vann, *Events Leading to the 1963 Change*, 28–29; McWhorter, *Carry Me Home*, 413–17, 419–20.

116. Eskew, *But for Birmingham*, 299–300.

117. Ibid., 309; McWhorter, *Carry Me Home*, 452; Corley, "The Quest for Racial Harmony," 276.

118. Manis, *A Fire You Can't Put Out*, 386–87; Eskew, *But for Birmingham*, 291–92.

119. Eskew, *But for Birmingham*, 231, 239; *Birmingham News*, September 29, 1963.

120. Eskew, *But for Birmingham*, 194–95; Corley, "The Quest for Racial Harmony," 231–32.

121. Eskew, *But for Birmingham*, 147. Calhoun was an unscrupulous attorney on the *Amos and Andy* television show.

122. Ibid., 127.

123. Ibid., 195, 206–7, 385.

124. Ibid., 286.

125. Manis, *A Fire You Can't Put Out*, 256–61, 281–82.

126. Ibid., 410–13.

127. Ibid., 414.

128. Ibid., 410.

129. Ibid., 412–13.

130. Eskew, *But for Birmingham*, 296–97.

131. Ibid., 300–306; McWhorter, *Carry Me Home*, 427–34.

132. Eskew, *But for Birmingham*, 319–21; *New York Times*, September 16, 1963; McWhorter, *Carry Me Home*, 531–32.

133. Police Surveillance Files, *Bombings or Attempt* [sic] *Bombings in Birmingham, 1950–1965*, BPLDAM, n.d.; *New York Times*, May 2, 2001, May 23, 2002.

134. Corley, "The Quest for Racial Harmony," 277.

135. *Birmingham News*, July 14, 1963, July 17, 1963.

136. Ibid., July 20, 1964.

137. *Birmingham Post-Herald*, October 12, 1963; *Birmingham World*, October 16, 1963.

138. *Birmingham News*, July 20, 1964; Eskew, *But for Birmingham*, 326, 397 n. 52.

139. *Birmingham News*, April 2, 1964; *Birmingham Post-Herald*, April 1, 1964.

140. *Birmingham Post-Herald*, July 20, 1964.

141. Community Affairs Committee Biographical Data, c. 1963, City Council Papers, file 3.10, BPLDAM.

142. Locations of Residences of CAC Members, 1963, E. C. Overton Papers, file 1.114, BPLDAM.

143. *Birmingham Post-Herald*, July 31, 1964, August 13, 1964, August 14, 1964, August 18, 1964. A number of Mountain Brook's well-known leaders, including Alabama Power Company president Walter Bouldin, state senator Larry Dumas, Southern Natural Gas president Pratt Rather, Birmingham Chamber of Commerce president Frank Newton, former governor Frank M. Dixon, Rucker Agee (principal of a leading Birmingham securities firm), Frank Spain (principal of one of the city's leading law firms), Amasa Smith (division manager of Chicago Bridge and Iron), and former Mountain Brook mayor Charles Zukoski Jr., spoke out on behalf of merger during the 1964 campaign. For more on the 1959 campaign and other merger attempts, see Charles E. Connerly, "'One Great City' or Colonial Economy? Explaining Birmingham's Annexation Struggles, 1945–1990," *Journal of Urban History* 26 (1999): 44–73.

144. *Birmingham Post-Herald*, August 10, 1964; June 12, 1964.

145. *Birmingham News*, April 7, 1959; *Birmingham News*, April 17, 1959; Morgan, *A Time to Speak*, 58–60.

146. *Birmingham Post-Herald*, March 27, 1959.

147. Morgan, *A Time to Speak*, 59; *Birmingham News*, April 16, 1959.

148. *Birmingham News*, April 7, 1959 April 12, 1959.

149. Ibid., April 2, 1959.

150. *Birmingham Post-Herald*, May 12, 1959.

151. *Birmingham News*, April 23, 1959.

152. Ibid., April 28, 1959. Motivations for participation in the consolidation campaign varied among the movement's leaders. Some, such as Charles Morgan Jr., had had enough of Bull Connor's reactionary and racist leadership as commissioner of public safety and felt that Homewood and Mountain Brook's leadership was required to establish a more progressive approach to addressing Birmingham's problems. Others, without being very specific, argued that Birmingham faced an economic crisis that required the business elite of the two suburbs to be involved more directly in the governance of Birmingham. In an editorial entitled "Homewood, Mountain Brook, The Birmingham of Us All," the *Birmingham News* maintained that the general economic welfare of Birmingham was at stake and that since Homewood and Mountain Brook residents "work in, have [an] economic interest in, the Birmingham proper area," then these residents need to join in with the City of Birmingham to address its problems. See Morgan, *A Time to Speak*, 56; *Birmingham News*, February 11, 1959.

153. Edward S. LaMonte, "Politics and Welfare in Birmingham, 1900–1974" (PhD diss., University of Chicago, 1976), 316–17.

154. Mayor and City Council of Birmingham, Contract in Trust, c. 1964.

155. Richmond Flowers to Albert Boutwell, July 21, 1964, Albert Boutwell Papers, file 14.26, BPLDAM; *Birmingham Post-Herald*, August 23, 1964 August 10, 1964.

156. *Birmingham Post-Herald*, August 17, 1964, August 22, 1964, August 26, 1964.

157. *Birmingham Post-Herald*, June 3, 1964, June 17, 1964, July 10, 1964, July 21, 1964, August 10, 1964; *Birmingham News*, June 24, 1964. In the August 11, 1964, referendum in Homewood, consolidation at first appeared to be victorious by a vote of 2,423 to 2,417. The election was contested, however, on the basis of several allegations, including the claim that the election lacked the sixty-day notice required under Alabama law. The Alabama Supreme Court ruled on August 25, 1966, that the 1964 election was null and void because of inadequate notice. When a follow-up election was conducted on December 13, 1966, Homewood residents overwhelmingly voted against merger 4,015 to 2,149 (*Birmingham Post-Herald*, August 12, 1964; *Birmingham News*, December 14, 1966).

158. Connerly, "'One Great City,'" 44–46.

159. Ibid., 45–46.

160. Ibid., 57–58.

161. Ibid., 60–65. The One Great City proposal, authored by David Vann, called

for consolidation of city and suburban governments, while leaving schools, zoning, and recreation under local control. Despite the clear attempt to permit suburbs such as Mountain Brook to retain their local school districts, concern about school integration drove opposition to Vann's proposal.

162. Holloway, *Politics of the Southern Negro*, 158.

163. Eskew, *But for Birmingham*, 328.

164. Birmingham Planning Commission, *The Comprehensive Plan: Birmingham, Alabama, 1961*, 106.

165. *Birmingham News*, August 20, 1961.

166. Ibid., February 23, 1962.

167. Marjorie Longenecker White, *Downtown Birmingham: Architectural and Historical Walking Tour Guide* (Birmingham: Birmingham Historical Society, 1980), 83.

168. Birmingham Downtown Improvement Association, *Proceedings of Property Owners Workshop*, December 3, 1963; McWhorter, *Carry Me Home*, 388–89, 391, 396.

169. Charles H. Levine, *Racial Conflict and the American Mayor* (Lexington, Mass.: Lexington Books, 1974), 90, 95, 104 n. 8; McWhorter, *Carry Me Home*, 183. Townsend was officially the assistant to the publisher.

170. *Birmingham News*, December 9, 1963.

171. LaMonte, "Politics and Welfare in Birmingham," 331; *Birmingham News*, January 25, 1965.

172. *Birmingham News*, March 13, 1964; *Birmingham Post-Herald*, March 13, 1964.

173. *Birmingham News*, January 25, 1965.

174. Ibid., June 18, 1965. Gaillard was a general contractor. Community Affairs Committee: Biographical Data, City Council Papers, box 3, file 10, BPLDAM. Williams was an attorney who unsuccessfully ran for city council in 1963 (Eskew, *But for Birmingham*, 260).

175. *Birmingham News*, October 12, 1965.

176. LaMonte, "Politics and Welfare in Birmingham," 332; *Birmingham News*, November 3, 1966.

177. City of Birmingham Annual Review of Progress for Recertification of the City's Workable Program for Community Improvement, February 1, 1966, 6–7, Albert Boutwell Papers, box 25, file 21, BPLDAM.

178. *Birmingham News*, October 19, 1965.

179. LaMonte, "Politics and Welfare in Birmingham"; *Birmingham News*, January 19, 1968.

180. *Birmingham News*, September 24, 1965.

181. Ibid.

182. *Birmingham Post-Herald*, July 17, 1969; White, *Downtown Birmingham*, 129–31.

183. White, *Downtown Birmingham*, 84.

184. *Birmingham News*, June 5, 1968, June 6, 1968.

185. City of Birmingham Review of Progress under the Workable Program for

Community Improvement, December 30, 1968, George Seibels Papers, box 26, file 49, BPLDAM.

186. *Birmingham News,* March 19, 1963.

187. J. F. Volker to Albert Boutwell, July 16, 1963, Albert Boutwell Papers, box 13, file 42, BPLDAM.

188. Virginia E. Fisher, *Building on a Vision: A Fifty-Year Retrospective of UAB's Academic Health Center* (Birmingham: University of Alabama at Birmingham, 1995), 3, 75.

189. J. F. Volker to Albert Boutwell, February 25, 1964, Albert Boutwell Papers, box 14, file 1, BPLDAM.

190. Mayor's Speech, December 24, 1964, Albert Boutwell Papers, box 13, file 37, BPLDAM.

191. Mayor's Committee on the Medical Center, Albert Boutwell Papers, box 13, file 37, BPLDAM. Billingsley, Nixon, and Shores were also among the black leaders that had opposed creation of the ACMHR in 1956. See Eskew, *But for Birmingham,* 127.

192. *Birmingham Post-Herald,* February 24, 1965.

193. *Birmingham News,* December 29, 1964.

194. William Slayton to Albert Boutwell, November 10, 1965, Albert Boutwell Papers, box 14, file 1, BPLDAM.

195. Planning Conference in Connection with Medical Center Expansion Urban Renewal Area, May 19, 1966, Albert Boutwell Papers, box 13, file 41, BPLDAM.

196. Data on Clearance Area, or Clearance Sections, of Project Area, Albert Boutwell Papers, box 14, file 2, BPLDAM.

197. Fact Sheet on College of General Studies, Albert Boutwell Papers, box 24, file 12, BPLDAM.

198. Christopher Scribner, "The Quiet Revolution: Federal Funding and Change in Birmingham, Alabama, 1933–1965" (PhD diss., Vanderbilt University, 1996), 350–58.

199. LaMonte, "Politics and Welfare in Birmingham," 351–52.

200. Ibid., 351–56.

201. Ibid., 357–59.

202. Ibid., 362–64.

203. Ibid., 359, 364, 376–82.

204. Ibid., 367–75.

205. Ibid., 376–78, 397.

206. Levine, *Racial Conflict,* 91.

207. Ibid., 91–98.

208. George Seibels to Earl H. Metzer Jr., HUD, March 4, 1968, George Seibels Papers, file 32.6, BPLDAM.

209. Yale Rabin, "Evaluation of the Application to the Department of Housing and Urban Development by the City of Birmingham, Alabama, for a Grant to Plan a Comprehensive City Demonstration Program." Unpub. rpt., National Archives II, Model Cities Reports 1966–73, box 3, NC3–207–84–2, RG 207.

210. Bernard J. Frieden and Marshall Kaplan, *The Politics of Neglect: Urban Aid from Model Cities to Revenue Sharing* (Cambridge: MIT Press, 1975), 69–72.

211. Judson P. Hodges, City of Birmingham, to John Page, HUD, April 5, 1968, George Seibels Papers, file 32.7, BPLDAM.

212. Marie Jemison to George Seibels, March 22, 1968, George Seibels Papers, file 32.6, BPLDAM.

213. *Birmingham News,* April 6, 1968.

214. Harvey Burg to Robert Weaver, HUD, June 14, 1968, George Seibels Papers, file 32.8, BPLDAM; Rabin, "Evaluation of the Application," 1968.

215. Position Paper of Citizen's Group, Birmingham Model Cities Plan, May 20, 1968, George Seibels Papers, file 32.7, BPLDAM.

216. J. M. Breckenridge, city attorney, to Alan T. Drennen Jr., city council member, May 24, 1968, City Council Papers, file 13.16, BPLDAM; Clarification of the City of Birmingham's Application for Model Cities Planning Grant, May 29, 1968, George Seibels Papers, file 32.7, BPLDAM; Citizen's Proposal to Consolidate Its Position with the City's "Clarification" Proposal of May 29, 1968, May 31, 1968, George Seibels Papers, file 32.8, BPLDAM.

217. Harvey Burg to Robert Weaver, HUD, June 14, 1968, George Seibels Papers, file 32.8, BPLDAM.

218. Edward Baxter, HUD, to George Seibels, November 22, 1968, George Seibels Papers, file 32.8, BPLDAM.

219. *Birmingham News,* May 30, 1968.

220. Harvey Burg to Robert Weaver, HUD, June 14, 1968, George Seibels Papers, file 32.8, BPLDAM.

221. *Birmingham World,* March 23, 1968, April 6, 1968.

7. The African American Planning Tradition in Birmingham

1. Jeffrey M. Berry, Kent E. Portney, and Ken Thomson, *The Rebirth of Urban Democracy* (Washington, D.C.: Brookings Institution, 1993), 301–3. Birmingham's Citizen Participation Plan was selected from over nine hundred nominations as one of five top citizen participation plans in the nation. Selection criteria included equality of opportunity for participation, and ability of the citizen participation process to influence public policy.

2. Information on Birmingham civic leagues was obtained from interviews with twelve individuals directly involved in or knowledgeable about the civic leagues; a survey of the African American newspaper *Birmingham World* for the period 1945–75; and examination of the Emory Jackson files of the Birmingham Public Library. Emory Jackson was editor of the *Birmingham World* from 1943 to 1975 and as such was a central repository for much information on the black community in Birmingham.

3. Alabama State Federation of Colored Civic Leagues, Declaration of Incorporation and By-Laws, January 19, 1933, James Jones Papers, box 4, file 3, BPLDAM. The civic leagues were Enon Ridge, Ensley, Woodlawn, East Thomas, Pratt City, Avondale, Roosevelt, Rosedale, Fairfield, North Birmingham, and Smithfield.

4. Benjamin Greene, interview by the author, June 23, 1995, Birmingham.

5. Benjamin Greene, interview by the author, June 23, 1995, Birmingham; Tommie Lee Houston, Grasselli Heights Civic League, interview by the author, June 23, 1995, Birmingham; Brazelia McCray, Hillman Civic League, interview by the author, June 24, 1995, Birmingham; Calvin Haynes, president, Woodland Park Civic League, interview by the author, May 5, 1995, Birmingham.

6. Constitution of the Woodland Park Civic League, n.d.

7. Benjamin Greene, interview by the author, June 23, 1995, Birmingham; Brazelia McCray, interview by the author, June 24, 1995, Birmingham; John Culpepper, former president, Grasselli Heights Civic League, interview by the author, June 27, 1995, Birmingham; Tommie Lee Houston, interview by the author, June 23, 1995, Birmingham; Constitution of the Woodland Park Civic League, n.d.; *Birmingham World,* July 30, 1966.

8. In 1970, the South Woodlawn Civic League met in the following churches: Metropolitan Community Church, New Community Baptist Church, Saint Bernadette Catholic Church, Morning Star Baptist Church, and Allen Chapel African Methodist Episcopal Church (*Birmingham World,* February 28, 1970, April 4, 1970, May 9, 1970, May 30, 1970, July 4, 1970, July 25, 1970).

9. *Birmingham World,* May 7, 1948, June 15, 1948, February 17, 1950, August 11, 1950. In fact, as late as 1998, the Grasselli community organization, set up under the city's Citizen Participation Program, was still meeting every month at Bryant Chapel.

10. *Birmingham World,* February 26, 1958, January 14, 1961, March 27, 1963.

11. Benjamin Greene, former president, Harriman Park Civic League, interviews by the author, February 24, 1995, June 23, 1995, Birmingham.

12. *Birmingham World,* August 5, 1972. Birmingham Green, completed in 1973, was an effort to beautify downtown by landscaping Twentieth Street, the main north-south street running through the heart of downtown Birmingham. See Philip A. Morris and Marjorie Longenecker White, eds., *Designs on Birmingham: A Landscape History of a Southern City and Its Suburbs* (Birmingham: Birmingham Historical Society, 1989), 64–65.

13. Tommie Lee Houston, interview by the author, June 23, 1995, Birmingham; John Culpepper, interview by the author, June 27, 1995, Birmingham.

14. *Birmingham World,* January 10, 1959, March 7, 1959.

15. Ibid., June 1, 1957. At the time, Mason City was located southwest of the city limits, but it was annexed into the city in 1971 (*Birmingham World,* January 8, 1972).

16. *Birmingham World,* August 16, 1967.

17. Benjamin Greene, interview by the author, June 23, 1995, Birmingham; Program for Dedication of Fountain Heights Park Recreation Center, January 19, 1975, Emory Jackson Papers, BPLDAM; *Birmingham World,* September 26, 1970. In addition, the Brighton Civic League constructed a community center in the 1940s. Brighton is a suburb located just outside of Birmingham. See "Brighton Colored Civic League," n.d., c. 1946, Emory Jackson Papers, BPLDAM.

336 Notes to Pages 223–225

18. Resolution of the Harriman Park Civic League, November 15, 1978; Warranty Deed, November 8, 1972.

19. Fountain Heights, represented by census tract 15, went from 17.0 percent black in 1950, to 30.1 percent black in 1960, to 93.7 percent in 1970. See Betty Bock, "An Analysis of the Impact of Racial Transition on the Desirability of Neighborhoods" (master's thesis, University of Alabama at Birmingham, 1976), 74.

20. *Birmingham World,* January 18, 1975. Tract 16, which corresponds to the Druid Hills and Norwood neighborhoods, located just north of downtown Birmingham, experienced a doubling in the percentage of black residents, going from 9.1 percent in 1960 to 21.9 percent in 1970. See Bock, "An Analysis of the Impact of Racial Transition," 72.

21. *Birmingham World,* February 24, 1973, March 3, 1973.

22. W. L. McAlpine to R. S. Marshall, superintendent, Birmingham Park and Recreation Board, January 8, 1936, James Jones Papers, box 4, file 3, BPLDAM; *Birmingham World,* May 29, 1942.

23. J. J. Ryles, president, Enon Ridge Civic League to James W. Morgan, April 27, 1953, James Morgan Papers, box 19, file 23, BPLDAM; *Birmingham World,* October 3, 1952, May 29, 1956, January 10, 1959, May 2, 1964, May 16, 1964, December 3, 1966.

24. Calvin Haynes, president, Woodland Park Civic League, interview by the author, May 5, 1995, Birmingham.

25. The nursery school was located on the campus of the Carrie Tuggle School, located on Tuggle Hill. See Robert J. Norrell and Otis Dismuke, *The Other Side: The Story of Birmingham's Black Community* (Birmingham: Birmingfind, n.d.); Angela Davis, *Angela Davis: An Autobiography* (New York: International Publishers, 1974), 87–92; Directory of Enon Ridge Civic Day Nursery, Emory Jackson Papers, 1955–56, uncataloged, BPLDAM.

26. *Birmingham World,* February 5, 1952, February 15, 1952, February 29, 1952, March 11, 1952, July 25, 1952, May 1, 1953; Directory of Enon Ridge Civic Day Nursery, 1955–56, Emory Jackson Papers, uncataloged, BPLDAM.

27. John Culpepper, former president, Grasselli Heights Civic League, interview by the author, June 27, 1995, Birmingham.

28. Tommie Lee Houston, interview by the author, June 23, 1995, Birmingham; John Culpepper, interview by the author, June 27, 1995, Birmingham.

29. *Birmingham World,* June 8, 1948.

30. Ibid., July 30, 1954.

31. Ibid., September 30, 1955.

32. Benjamin Greene, former president, Harriman Park Civic League, interview by the author, June 23, 1995, Birmingham.

33. Simmie Lavender, president, Jones Valley Civic League, interview by the author, May 4, 1995, Birmingham.

34. Benjamin Greene, interviews by the author, February 24, 1995; June 23, 1995, Birmingham.

35. The name "Travellick" comes from Richard Trevillick, a lecturer with the

Knights of Labor. Trevillick was built in the 1880s by the Knights after they had built Powderly—named for Knights of Labor leader Terrence V. Powderly—which lies north of the Riley-Travellick neighborhood. See Henry M. McKiven Jr., *Iron and Steel: Class, Race, and Community in Birmingham, Alabama, 1875–1920* (Chapel Hill: University of North Carolina Press, 1995), 60–61. Today, the neighborhood is simply known as Riley.

36. *Birmingham World*, February 4, 1949, February 25, 1949, March 4, 1949, March 12, 1949, April 1, 1949, April 8, 1949, April 26, 1949, May 6, 1949, May 13, 1949, June 3, 1949, October 21, 1949 (quote).

37. *Birmingham World*, May 14, 1948.

38. Birmingham annexed the Riley-Travellick neighborhood in the city's thirteen-square-mile annexation that took place in 1949.

39. *Birmingham World*, April 6, 1957, April 13, 1957, May 25, 1957, June 1, 1957, June 8, 1957, June 22, 1957, July 13, 1957, August 24, 1957 (quote), September 14, 1957, September 21, 1957, October 26, 1957, December 7, 1957.

40. Ibid., February 1, 1952, February 5, 1952, February 12, 1952, October 3, 1952.

41. Ibid., February 27, 1972, March 18, 1972.

42. *Birmingham World*, February 27, 1972, March 18, 1972, April 8, 1972; Charlie Pierce, former president, Druid Hills–Norwood Civic League, interview by the author, June 24, 1995, Birmingham. Jimmie Lewis Franklin, *Back to Birmingham: Richard Arrington Jr. and His Times* (Tuscaloosa: University of Alabama Press, 1989), 57–59.

43. *Birmingham World*, January 30, 1945. Jackson's advocacy of voter registration began in the late 1930s when he supported the Right to Vote Club, headed by Communist Party member Hosea Hudson. See Nell Irvin Painter, *The Narrative of Hosea Hudson* (New York: Norton, 1979), 263.

44. *Birmingham World*, April 8, 1972.

45. For many years, the push for the black vote in Birmingham was seen as a movement to primarily provide the franchise for the limited number of middle-class blacks in Birmingham. This suited the white community, who wished to contain the black vote, but it also suited the black elite, who thought that voting was a privilege associated with education and social position. See Glenn T. Eskew, *But for Birmingham: The Local and National Movements in the Civil Rights Struggle* (Chapel Hill: University of North Carolina Press, 1997), 76–78; Robin D. G. Kelley, *Hammer and Hoe: Alabama Communists during the Great Depression* (Chapel Hill: University of North Carolina Press, Chapel Hill, 1990), 183–84.

46. *Birmingham World*, October 6, 1949.

47. Ibid., March 9, 1960.

48. J. Mason Davis, former member, South Elyton Civic League, interview by the author, June 22, 1995, Birmingham; *Birmingham World*, March 1, 1961.

49. Civic leagues identified as performing some level of voting education outreach include Avondale Community Civic League, Druid Hills–Norwood Civic League. Harriman Park Civic League, Mason City Civic League, North Birmingham Civic League, North Pratt Civic League, Oxmoor Civic League, Pratt City Civic

League, Rose-Mark Progressive Civic League, Rosewood and St. Mark Village Civic League, Riley and Travellick Civic League, and the Sand Ridge Civic League (*Birmingham World*, March 26, 1946, May 29, 1956, May 1, 1957, June 1, 1957, November 8, 1958, March 11, 1961, August 5, 1961, August 14, 1961, August 22, 1964, November 17, 1967).

50. *Birmingham World*, September 28, 1951. Six months later Jackson resigned as secretary of the NAACP Birmingham branch because he believed that the branch's leadership was supporting activities that were in violation of NAACP policy. Among such activities, Jackson cited the branch's effort to get the city to build a golf course for blacks. See Eskew, *But for Birmingham*, 72; Dorothy Autrey, "National Association for the Advancement of Colored People in Alabama, 1913–1952" (PhD diss., University of Notre Dame, 1985), 216–18, 253.

51. *Birmingham World*, February 1, 1952.

52. Ibid., June 13, 1952.

53. John Hope Franklin, *From Slavery to Freedom* (New York: Alfred A. Knopf, 1967).

54. See Autrey, "The NAACP in Alabama," 218, 252–53. In addition to the bombings, Autrey cites the slow progress made by various black voter registration drives and the personal discord among the branch's leaders, including Emory Jackson and William Shortridge, chairman of the branch's executive committee.

55. The CAC should not be confused with the short-lived committee of the same name founded in 1963 during the Boutwell administration (see chapter 6).

56. Jim Murray, "Interracial Communication in Birmingham, Alabama, and the Creation of Operation New Birmingham's Community Affairs Committee," 1990, copy in author's possession, 4–5.

57. Murray, "Interracial Communication in Birmingham," 5–8.

58. Franklin, *Back to Birmingham*, 61.

59. Birmingham Regional Planning Commission, "An Application for Comprehensive Planning Assistance Funds from The Department of Housing and Urban Development," V-1–V-4, May 29, 1970, Operation New Birmingham Records, box 8, file 1, BPLDAM.

60. Ibid.

61. *Birmingham News*, June 3, 1971; Operation New Birmingham, "Neighborhood Planning Grant Project Completion Report, Phase I, August 1970–May 1971," July 9, 1971, 4–5, Operation New Birmingham Papers, box 8, file 3, BPLDAM.

62. Operation New Birmingham, 1971, 6; *Birmingham News*, April 1, 1973.

63. *Birmingham News*, June 3, 1971.

64. George Quiggle, interview by C. Livermore, July 30, 1981; George Quiggle, telephone interview by the author, June 7, 1993; Greater Birmingham Ministries, "Ministry Highlights in Greater Birmingham Ministries' History, 1968–1984," typescript, October 1984.

65. *Birmingham News*, November 8, 1972.

66. Jon Will Pitts to George Seibels, July 6, 1973, George Seibels Papers, box 49, file 34, BPLDAM.

67. City of Birmingham, Annual Review of Progress for Recertification of the City's Workable Program for Community Improvement, February 1, 1966, Albert Boutwell Papers, box 25, file 21, BPLDAM.

68. Jon Will Pitts to William Bondarenko, August 3, 1973, Operation New Birmingham Papers, box 8, file 7, BPLDAM.

69. James R. Land, Birmingham community development director, to William E. Ricker, executive director, Operation New Birmingham, August 10, 1973, George Seibels Papers, box 21, file 15, BPLDAM.

70. Each community consisted of one or more neighborhoods.

71. City of Birmingham, Proposed Citizen Participation Plan, November, 1973, George Seibels Papers, box 18, file 53, BPLDAM.

72. Statement by Mayor George G. Seibels Jr. Concerning New, Comprehensive Citizen Participation Plan, January 15, 1974, George Seibels Papers, box 18, file 53, BPLDAM.

73. *Birmingham News*, February 5, 1974.

74. "Birmingham Citizen Participation Plan: Recommended Procedure for Executing the Field Responsibility of Operation New Birmingham," February 1974, Operation New Birmingham Papers, box 3, file 22, BPLDAM; "Work Report, ONB Staff on Citizen Participation Plan, February 5–28, 1974," February 28, 1974, Operation New Birmingham Papers, box 3, file 22, BPLDAM.

75. *Birmingham Post-Herald*, October 27 (news story and editorial), October 29, 1973, November 27, 1973, November 28, 1973, November 29, 1973; Charles H. Levine, *Racial Conflict and the American Mayor* (Lexington, Mass.: Lexington Books, 1974), 93.

76. Chuck Lewis, interview by the author, February 23, 1995, Birmingham. ONB's connection to this effort was well-publicized in the black newspaper *Birmingham World*, November 3, December 8, 1973.

77. Chuck Lewis, interviews by the author, March 23, 1992, February 23, 1995, Birmingham.

78. George Quiggle, telephone interview by the author, June 7, 1993.

79. Citizen Participation Plan Work Report: Collegeville Nucleus Meeting, February 28, 1974, Operation New Birmingham Papers, box 3, file 22, BPLDAM.

80. Operation New Birmingham, "Neighborhood Planning Grant Project Completion Report, Phase I, August 1970–May 1971," July 9, 1971, p. 8, Operation New Birmingham Papers, box 8, file 3, BPLDAM.

81. Citizen Participation Plan Work Report: Collegeville Nucleus Meeting, February 28, 1974, Operation New Birmingham Papers, box 3, file 22, BPLDAM.

82. Citizen Participation Plan Work Report: Collegeville General Meeting, March 7, 1974, Operation New Birmingham Papers, box 3, file 22, BPLDAM.

83. *Birmingham News*, March 10, 1974.

84. *Birmingham World*, March 30, 1974.

85. Citizen Participation Plan Work Report: Collegeville General Meeting, March 7, 1974, Operation New Birmingham Papers, box 3, file 22, BPLDAM.

86. *Birmingham News*, March 12, 1974.

87. "Let's Put Action Where Our Mouth Is!" handbill, Operation New Birmingham Papers, box 3, file 22, BPLDAM; Citizen Participation Plan Work Report: Collegeville Nucleus Meeting, February 28, 1974, Operation New Birmingham Papers, box 3, file 22, BPLDAM.

88. George Quiggle, interview by C. Livermore, July 30, 1981; George Quiggle, telephone interview by the author, June 7, 1993.

89. *Birmingham News,* March 10, 1974; Citizen Participation Plan Work Report: Collegeville General Meeting, March 7, 1974, Operation New Birmingham Papers, box 3, file 22, BPLDAM. GBM had organized and obtained funding for LEAP, which operated for four years in the mid-1970s. Greater Birmingham Ministries, Ministry Highlights in Greater Birmingham Ministries: History, 1968–1984, October 1984.

90. Benjamin Greene, interview by the author, March 24, 1992, Birmingham; George Quiggle, telephone interview by the author, June 7, 1993.

91. *Birmingham News,* April 2, 1974, April 24, 1974; *Birmingham World,* April 6, 1974; People That Spoke at the Public Hearing, April 1, 1974, Operation New Birmingham Papers, box 3, file 22, BPLDAM.

92. *Birmingham News,* April 2, 1974.

93. Ibid., April 2, 1974; Work Report, Citizen's Participation Plan, March 11–June 14, 1974, Operation New Birmingham Papers, box 3, file 22, BPLDAM.

94. Chuck Lewis, interview by the author, February 23, 1995, Birmingham; *Birmingham News,* April 24, 1974, April 26, 1974; Work Report, Citizen's Participation Plan, March 11–June 14, 1974, Operation New Birmingham Papers, box 3, file 22, BPLDAM.

95. *Birmingham News,* June 27, 1974; City of Birmingham, Citizen Participation Plan, October 1974, George Seibels Papers, box 18, file 53, BPLDAM; Birmingham Department of Community Development, *A Brief History of Citizen Participation in Birmingham, 1972–1988,* 1988, Birmingham.

96. Chuck Lewis, interview by the author, February 23, 1995, Birmingham.

97. *Birmingham News,* November 20, 1974; City of Birmingham, Proposed Citizen Participation Plan, November, 1973, George Seibels Papers, box 18, file 53, BPLDAM.

98. Chuck Lewis, interview by the author, February 23, 1995, Birmingham.

99. Benjamin Greene, interview by the author, March 24, 1992, Birmingham.

100. *Birmingham News,* November 20, 1974. These neighborhoods are: Collegeville, East Thomas, Enon Ridge, Evergreen, Grasselli Heights, Harriman Park, Hillman, Jones Valley, Riley, Tarpley City, West Goldwire, and Woodland Park.

101. Work Report, ONB Staff on Citizen Participation Plan, February 5–28, 1974, February 28, 1974, Operation New Birmingham Papers, box 3, file 22, BPLDAM.

102. Benjamin Greene, Harriman Park Civic League, interview by the author, June 23, 1995, Birmingham; Brazelia McCray, Hillman Civic League, interview by the author, June 24, 1995, Birmingham; Tommie Lee Houston, Grasselli Heights Civic League, interview by the author, June 23, 1995, Birmingham; Calvin Haynes, Woodland Park Civic League, interview by the author, May 5, 1995, Birmingham.

103. City of Birmingham, *Citizen Participation Plan: Neighborhood Associations: The Building Blocks of Birmingham*, 1992.

104. Chuck Lewis, interview by the author, February 23, 1995, Birmingham; *Birmingham News*, September 10, 1974.

105. *Birmingham News*, October 8, 1974.

106. Ibid., November 20, 1974. The list of neighborhood association officers was surveyed for names of individuals who had been identified through interviews, examination of documents, and a survey of the *Birmingham World* for the period 1945–75 as active members of civic leagues.

8. The Evolution of Black Neighborhood Empowerment

1. Homewood's population grew from 7,397 in 1940 to 12,866 in 1950 and 20,289 in 1960. Mountain Brook's population also grew very rapidly to 8,359 in 1950 and 12,680 in 1960. See U.S. Department of Commerce, Bureau of the Census, *A Report of the Seventeenth Decennial Census of the United States*, vol. 2, *Characteristics of the Population*, pt. 2, *Alabama* (Washington, D.C.: Government Printing Office, 1952); U.S. Department of Commerce, Bureau of the Census, *The Eighteenth Decennial Census of the United States*, vol. 1, *Characteristics of the Population*, pt. 2, *Alabama* (Washington, D.C.: Government Printing Office, 1963).

2. Birmingham Planning Board, *Preliminary Report*, February 8, 1952, 19–20.

3. *Birmingham News*, March 6, 1956, April 2, 1956.

4. *Shades Valley Sun*, June 21, 1956.

5. *Birmingham Post-Herald*, March 13, 1958.

6. *Birmingham News*, March 19, 1958.

7. Ibid., March 19, 1958, *Birmingham Post-Herald*, March 20, 1958.

8. *Birmingham News*, May 9, 1958.

9. City of Birmingham, "Recommendations on the South Leg (I-65) of the Interstate and Defense Highway and the Red Mountain Freeway," Planning and Zoning papers, file 668.2.32, June 12, 1961.

10. *Birmingham News*, February 6, 1963.

11. Ibid., April 19, 1962, May 17, 1963; *Birmingham Post-Herald*, May 17, 1963.

12. *Birmingham News*, December 10, 1963; Birmingham *Post-Herald*, February 5, 1964. Stephens, the chief executive of a magazine distribution service, had known Wallace for thirty years, having employed the teenaged Wallace in 1936 as a traveling magazine salesman (Carter, *The Politics of Rage*, 32).

13. *Birmingham Post-Herald*, March 13, 1958, June 12, 1974. Typewritten testimony of Michael A. Dobbins, planning consultant, prepared for *ASTO, et al. v. Ray D. Bass*, n.d., copy in author's possession.

14. Typewritten testimony of Michael A. Dobbins, planning consultant, prepared for *ASTO, et al. v. Ray D. Bass*, n.d., copy in author's possession.

15. Alton McWhorter to Otis Wilson, acting interstate engineer, Alabama Highway Department, August 28, 1969, as quoted in typewritten testimony of Michael A. Dobbins, planning consultant, prepared for *ASTO, et al. v. Ray D. Bass*, n.d., 4–5, copy in author's possession. In 1961, however, city engineer McWhorter had

signed a statement indicating support for extending the expressway north to intersect with Interstate 59. See June 12, 1961, report, J. T. Waggoner Papers, box 6, file 4, BPLDAM.

16. John E. Bryan to Mayor George Seibels and city council members, c. summer 1974, David Vann Papers, box 4, file 5, BPLDAM.

17. *Birmingham Post-Herald*, October 1, 1974.

18. *Birmingham News*, June 12, 1974; *Birmingham Post-Herald*, September 27, 1974.

19. *Birmingham Post-Herald*, July 9, 1974.

20. Typewritten testimony of Michael A. Dobbins, planning consultant, prepared for *ASTO, et al. v. Ray D. Bass*, n.d., copy in author's possession. Complaint of *Alabama State Tenants Organization, et al. v. Ray D. Bass, Alabama Highway Department et al.*, filed December 19, 1974, U.S. District Court, Northern District of Alabama, Southern Division, 15, David Vann Papers, box 4, file 4, BPLDAM.

21. *Birmingham Post-Herald*, July 9, 1974.

22. Ibid.

23. Ibid.; *Birmingham News*, July 10, 1974; Public Notice to All Occupants of Central City, July 17, 1974, David Vann Papers, box 4, file 3, BPLDAM.

24. *Birmingham News*, July 23, 1974.

25. Ibid.

26. *Birmingham Post-Herald*, July 26, 1974.

27. *Birmingham News*, September 26, 1974, November 20, 1974.

28. Ibid., October 1, 1974.

29. *Birmingham Post-Herald*, October 2, 1974.

30. Ibid., October 21, 1974. State highway engineers reportedly believed that rerouting the Red Mountain Expressway would cause "severe geometric problems" (*Birmingham Post-Herald*, December 23, 1974).

31. Hugh Denman, executive director, Birmingham Housing Authority, to Bob Yeager, Operation New Birmingham, May 20, 1974; Commissioners of the Birmingham Housing Authority to mayor and Birmingham City Council, August 20, 1974, David Vann Papers, box 4, file 3, BPLDAM.

32. J. Frank Trucks, chairman, Housing Authority of the Birmingham District, to mayor and Birmingham City Council, December 19, 1974, David Vann Papers, box 4, file 3, BPLDAM; *Birmingham Post-Herald*, December 13, 1974, December 19, 1974; *Birmingham News*, December 19, 1974.

33. *Alabama State Tenants Organization, et al. v. Ray D. Bass, Director of the Highway Department of the State of Alabama, et al.*, Plaintiffs' Brief, Filed in the United States District Court of the Northern District of Alabama, Southern Division, December 19, 1974, item 138; *Birmingham News*, December 25, 1974.

34. *Birmingham Post-Herald*, December 19, 1974, December 23, 1974.

35. *Alabama State Tenants Organization, et al. v. Ray D. Bass, Director of the Highway Department of the State of Alabama, et al.*, Plaintiffs' Brief, Filed in the United States District Court of the Northern District of Alabama, Southern Division, December 19, 1974; *Birmingham News*, December 20, 1974.

36. *Birmingham Post-Herald,* June 20, 1975.

37. *Birmingham News,* June 30, 1975.

38. Statement of Robert Wiggins to the City Council, June 24, 1975, George Seibels Papers, box 43, file 4, BPLDAM.

39. Robert Wiggins to Jon Will Pitts, August 18, 1975; Elton B. Stephens to Mayor George Seibels, September 8, 1975; Jon Will Pitts to Robert Wiggins and Elton B. Stephens, September 17, 1975; Elton B. Stephens to Mayor George Seibels and others, September 22, 1975; George Seibels to Elton B. Stephens, September 23, 1975: all in George Seibels Papers, box 43, file 4, BPLDAM. Pitts, the HUD area office director in Birmingham, was attempting to negotiate an agreement between the parties.

40. *Birmingham Post-Herald,* November 27, 1975.

41. *Alabama State Tenants Organization et al., v. Bass* 549 F.2d 961 (1977).

42. *Birmingham Post-Herald,* June 25, 1977.

43. *Birmingham News,* June 14, 1977.

44. These letters are collected in City Council Papers, Special Correspondence, box 1, files 1–16, BPLDAM.

45. *Birmingham Post-Herald,* June 24, 1977, July 8, 1977, August 9, 1977.

46. *Birmingham News,* August 28, 1977.

47. Ibid., August 9, 1977.

48. Office of the City Council, Inter-Office Communication, September 16, 1977, City Council Papers, box 33, file 24, BPLDAM; *Birmingham News,* November 30, 1977.

49. *Birmingham News,* March 4, 1979, August 22, 1979. The agreement, whose signing was delayed until early 1978, was then sent to HUD, which didn't respond until November 1978. A response to HUD's concerns was not completed until February 1979. Meanwhile, the original engineering consultant employed to prepare the environmental impact study failed to perform its duties, and a new consultant was hired in 1979.

50. *Birmingham News,* August 22, 1979.

51. Ibid., January 17, 1980, February 29, 1980.

52. Ibid., April 10, 1981.

53. *Birmingham Post-Herald,* April 7, 1976, April 8, 1976, April 9, 1976.

54. George Quiggle, interview by C. Livermore, July 30, 1981; George Quiggle, telephone interview by the author, June 7, 1993.

55. *Birmingham News,* September 26, 1974, December 14, 1978.

56. George Quiggle, interview by the author, June 7, 1993; *Birmingham News,* October 30, 1978, December 14, 1978, February 14, 1979; *Birmingham Post-Herald,* February 15, 1979.

57. Center for Governmental Studies, *Neighborhood Decentralization,* March–April 1975, 3.

58. Untitled, typewritten report on Citizen Participation Program, c. 1978, in author's possession; Center for Governmental Studies, *Neighborhood Decentralization,* March–April 1975, 3.

59. Steven H. Haeberle, *Planting the Grassroots: Structuring Citizen Participation* (New York: Praeger, 1989), 105.

60. *Birmingham Post-Herald*, May 2, 1977.

61. Chuck Lewis, interview by the author, March 23, 1992, Birmingham.

62. *Birmingham News*, March 29, 1977.

63. To All Council members from David Rockwell, city council assistant, April 15, 1977, City Council Papers, box 26, file 22, BPLDAM; U.S. Bureau of the Census, Neighborhood Statistics Program, *Narrative Profiles of Neighborhoods in Birmingham and Vicinity, Alabama*, 1984, Birmingham Public Library.

64. Ibid.

65. *Birmingham News*, April 25, 1977.

66. Tommie Lee Houston, interview by the author, June 23, 1995, Birmingham; John Culpepper, interview by the author, June 27, 1995, Birmingham.

67. *Birmingham News*, May 11, 1977.

68. Ibid., May 15, 1977.

69. *Birmingham Post-Herald*, May 14, 1977.

70. Ibid., May 11, 1977.

71. *Birmingham News*, November 14, 1978; "Neighborhood Strategy Areas," n.d., City Council Papers, box 28, file 4, BPLDAM, appendix D.

72. Staff Report, Community Development Block Grant Program, Committee Print, Subcommittee on Housing and Community Development of the House Committee on Banking, Finance, and Urban Affairs, 95th Congress, First session (Washington, D.C.: Government Printing Office, February 1977), 34, cited in Paul Dommel et al., *Targeting Community Development*, U.S. Department of Housing and Urban Development (Washington, D.C.: Government Printing Office, January 1980), 24.

73. Dommel, *Targeting Community Development*, 25–26.

74. Donald B. Rosenthal, *Urban Housing and Neighborhood Revitalization* (Westport: Greenwood Press, 1988), 44.

75. "Triage" is a medical term derived from World War I, during which medics divided the wounded into three groups: soldiers who would recover with a minimum of care; soldiers who would die regardless of what was done for them; and soldiers who could live or die depending upon whether they were given medical care. With battlefield conditions and limited resources, medics were instructed to care for the third group, for which they could make the greatest difference. The triage concept is applied to urban revitalization in Roger Starr, "Making New York Smaller," *New York Times Magazine*, November 14, 1976, and in Conrad Weiler, "Urban Euthanasia for Fun and Profit," in *Neighborhood Policy and Planning*, ed. Philip L. Clay and Robert M. Hollister (Lexington, Mass.: Lexington Books, 1983), 167–75.

76. *Birmingham News*, November 14, 1978.

77. "Neighborhood Strategy Areas," n.d., City Council Papers, box 28, file 4, BPLDAM, appendices B and D.

78. Ibid., 5.

79. Ibid., 6–7.

80. The five recommended neighborhoods had the following black population percentages: North Birmingham (93.6 percent), Woodlawn (40.2 percent), Five Points South (17.3 percent), Bush Hills (60.0 percent), and Jones Valley (85.9 percent).

81. *Birmingham News*, November 21, 1978; Phyllis Kaniss, Cynthia Livermore, and Michael Hindery, "Case Studies of Two Technical Assistance Providers," Community Development Strategies Evaluation, University of Pennsylvania, August 1984, 56–57.

82. "Neighborhood Strategy Areas," appendix A.

83. Carolyn Crawford, Greater Birmingham Ministries, interview by the author, July 8, 1993, Birmingham.

84. Quoted in Greater Birmingham Ministries, *Administrative Performance Case Study, Birmingham, Alabama*, National Citizens Monitoring Project on Community Development Block Grants, May 26, 1980, 4–5, copy in author's possession.

85. Greater Birmingham Ministries, *Administrative Performance Case Study, Birmingham, Alabama*, 7; *Birmingham News*, November 21, 1978, February 19, 1979; Kaniss, Livermore, and Hindery, "Case Studies of Two Technical Assistance Providers," 58.

86. *Birmingham Post-Herald*, February 20, 1979.

87. Ibid.

88. Greater Birmingham Ministries, *Administrative Performance Case Study, Birmingham, Alabama*, 6–7; Kaniss, Livermore, and Hindery, "Case Studies of Two Technical Assistance Providers," 58–59.

89. Ad Hoc Committee on Lower-Income Neighborhood Planning of the Birmingham Citizens Advisory Board, *Committee Report*, June 18, 1979, City Council Papers, box 28, file 1, BPLDAM; untitled, undated history of Neighborhood Services, Inc., copy in author's possession; Greater Birmingham Ministries, *Administrative Performance Case Study, Birmingham, Alabama*, 43; *Birmingham News*, November 12, 1978, November 16, 1978; Kaniss, Livermore, and Hindery, "Case Studies of Two Technical Assistance Providers," 60–61.

90. Citizen Complaint to the Department of Housing and Urban Development Respecting City of Birmingham 1979 Community Development Block Grant Application, May 16, 1979, copy in author's possession.

91. Ibid., 1–2.

92. Ibid., 6.

93. Ibid.

94. Ibid., 16.

95. Ibid., 7.

96. Ibid., 28–29.

97. Dorothy (Lee) Inman-Johnson, interview by the author, May 31, 2000, Tallahasse, Fl., transcript available.

98. Betty Bock, "An Analysis of the Impact of Racial Transition on the Desirability of Neighborhoods" (master's thesis, University of Alabama at Birmingham, 1976), 134–37; *Birmingham News*, August 8, 1979.

99. Cobb/Adams/Benton, Inc., Planning Consultants, *Five Points South Restoration: A Master Plan for the Neighborhood,* 1977; *Birmingham News,* August 8, 1979.

100. Quoted in Greater Birmingham Ministries, *Administrative Performance Case Study, Birmingham, Alabama,* 17–18; Kaniss, Livermore, and Hindery, "Case Studies of Two Technical Assistance Providers," 61–62.

101. *Birmingham News,* June 30, 1979.

102. Ibid.; Kaniss, Livermore, and Hindery, "Case Studies of Two Technical Assistance Providers," 62.

103. Greater Birmingham Ministries, *Administrative Performance Case Study, Birmingham, Alabama;* untitled, undated history of Neighborhood Services, Inc., copy in author's possession.

104. Kaniss, Livermore, and Hindery, "Case Studies of Two Technical Assistance Providers," 63–64.

105. Greater Birmingham Ministries, *Impact of HUD Conditioning of Birmingham's Year VI (FY '80) Community Development Block Grant Application,* 3.

106. Quoted ibid., 3–4.

107. Quoted ibid., 5–6; Kaniss, Livermore, and Hindery, "Case Studies of Two Technical Assistance Providers," 66.

108. Quoted in Greater Birmingham Ministries, *Impact of HUD Conditioning of Birmingham's Year VI (FY '80) Community Development Block Grant Application,* 6.

109. Quoted ibid., 2.

110. Quoted ibid., 21; Kaniss, Livermore, and Hindery, "Case Studies of Two Technical Assistance Providers," 65.

111. Greater Birmingham Ministries, *Impact of HUD Conditioning of Birmingham's Year VI (FY '80) Community Development Block Grant Application,* 23; *Birmingham Post-Herald,* December 24, 1980; *Birmingham News,* December 23, 1980.

112. *Birmingham News,* September 11, 1981.

113. Quoted in Greater Birmingham Ministries, *Impact of HUD Conditioning of Birmingham's Year VI (FY '80) Community Development Block Grant Application,* 29.

114. *Birmingham News,* May 19, 1981, May 31, 1981.

115. Ibid., September 11, 1981.

Epilogue

1. Jimmie Lewis Franklin, *Back to Birmingham: Richard Arrington Jr. and His Times* (Tuscaloosa: University of Alabama Press, 1989), 18–48.

2. Ibid., 59–66. Attorney Arthur Shores was elected in 1969 after having been appointed in June 1968 to fill an unexpired term.

3. Charles H. Levine, *Racial Conflict and the American Mayor* (Lexington, Mass.: Lexington Books, 1974), 97–99. Birmingham did not hire its first black police officer until 1966, well after most southern cities had employed black police. See Glenn T. Eskew, *But for Birmingham: The Local and National Movements in the Civil Rights Struggle* (Chapel Hill: University of North Carolina Press, 1997), 397 n. 52.

4. Franklin, *Back to Birmingham,* 92–133.

5. Ibid., 108–14.

6. Ibid., 116–20.

7. Ibid., 90–91, 120–33.

8. Ibid., 138.

9. Ibid., 134–74; Edward LaMonte, *Politics and Welfare in Birmingham: 1900–1975* (Tuscaloosa: University of Alabama Press, 1995), 240.

10. U.S. Bureau of the Census, *American Housing Survey for the Birmingham Metropolitan Area: 1998,* Current Housing Reports, Series H170/98-43, tables 2-8, 5-7, 5-8.

11. U.S. Bureau of the Census, www.census.gov/statab/ccdb/ccdb312.txt, accessed June 11, 2000.

12. William Julius Wilson, *When Work Disappears: The World of the New Urban Poor* (New York: Alfred A. Knopf, 1996), 6; U.S. Bureau of the Census, *1990 Census of Population and Housing: Population and Housing Characteristics for Census Tracts and Block Numbering Areas, Birmingham, Alabama MSA,* 1993; U.S. Bureau of the Census, *1970 Census of Population and Housing: Census Tracts, Birmingham, Alabama Standard Metropolitan Statistical Area,* 1972.

13. Housing Authority of the Birmingham District Web Site Listing of Public Housing Sites and Census Tracts, accessed on July 25, 2000, at www.rent-a-web.com/habd/habd_dev.html#FREEDOM. Public housing projects located outside of ghetto poverty tracts are Roosevelt City, Tom Brown Village, Benjamin Greene Homes, Collegeville, Ralph Kimbrough Homes, Russell B. Harris Homes, and North Birmingham Homes.

14. U.S. Bureau of the Census, *1990 Census of Population and Housing: Population and Housing Characteristics for Census Tracts and Block Numbering Areas, Birmingham, Alabama MSA,* 1993.

15. See Wilson, *When Work Disappears.*

16. Robert J. Norrell, "Caste in Steel: Jim Crow Careers in Birmingham, Alabama," *Journal of American History* 73 (1986): 669-94.

17. Birmingham Area Chamber of Commerce, *Birmingham Area Profile,* 1988, Section II; Birmingham Office of Economic Development, *Community Profile.*

18. U.S. Bureau of the Census, *A Report of the Seventeenth Decennial Census of the United States: Census of Population: 1950,* vol. 2, *Characteristics of the Population,* pt. 2, *Alabama* (Washington, D.C., 1952), 55; U.S. Bureau of the Census, *1990 Census of Population and Housing,* CD ROM.

19. Birmingham Area Chamber of Commerce, *Birmingham Area Profile,* 1988, II-5.

20. U.S. Bureau of Labor Statistics Data, Birmingham, Alabama, MSA Unemployment Rate at http://146.142.4.24/cgi-bin/SeriesHist?lausm10000003, accessed July 25, 2000; Labor Force Statistics from the Current Population Survey, Unemployment Rate, 1989–2000 at http://stats.bls.gov/wh/cpsbref3.htm, accessed July 25, 2000.

21. U.S. Census Bureau, *Statistical Abstract of the United States: 1999* (Washington, D.C., 2000), 424.

22. U.S. Bureau of the Census, Neighborhood Statistics Program, *Narrative Profiles of Neighborhoods in Birmingham and Vicinity, Alabama,* 1984, Birmingham Public Library.

23. University of Alabama at Birmingham, *Community Outreach Partnership Center Grant Application,* 1995, 4.

24. Ibid., 5, 31. First on the priorities list was a goal that stated that "neighborhoods will be more involved and work together." Since 1995, Tittusville 2000 has received significant funding from HUD and the Fannie Mae Foundation to provide new housing, economic development, education opportunities, youth programs, job training, health care, as well as other community services. See www.circ.uab .edu/cpages/T2000a.htm, accessed June 10, 2000.

25. Charles E. Connerly, "'One Great City' or Colonial Economy? Explaining Birmingham's Annexation Struggles, 1945–1990," *Journal of Urban History* 26 (1999): 50.

26. Ibid., 46, 50.

27. David Vann to Don Newton, September 26, 1974, David Vann Papers, box 1, file 14, BPLDAM.

28. Office of the Clerk-Council, The Effects of Existing Annexation Laws Applicable to Birmingham, Alabama, November 1970, City Council Papers, file 9.35, BPLDAM.

29. Connerly, "'One Great City,'" 52–54.

30. *Birmingham News,* August 4, 1974, August 5, 1974; Paul E. Mayer to David Vann, June 28, 1974, David Vann Papers, file 1.12, BPLDAM; Memo to Birmingham Mayor and Council from David Vann, "An Alternative Approach to Annexation of Unincorporated Areas," n.d., City Council Correspondence, file 18.9, BPLDAM. The latter document also notes that use of tax-exempt annexation became more feasible as the city had shifted by 1974 from its historic dependence upon property taxes to increased reliance on a payroll tax, sales tax, and state and federal revenue sharing, none of which was affected by the tax exemption.

31. Memo to Birmingham Mayor and Council from David Vann, "An Alternative Approach to Annexation of Unincorporated Areas," n.d., City Council Correspondence, file 18.9, BPLDAM.

32. *Birmingham Post-Herald,* March 26, 1975.

33. *Birmingham News,* June 26, 1976.

34. Ibid., April 7, 1975; *Shades Valley Sun,* March 9, 1977; *Birmingham News,* October 12, 1976.

35. *Birmingham News,* July 16, 1985.

36. Ibid., March 10, 1985, March 12, 1985, April 17, 1985, May 10, 1985, May 13, 1985, May 14, 1985, May 5, 1987. Former mayor David Vann, who had become Birmingham's chief attorney for annexations, also was chairman of the Birmingham Water Works Board.

37. *Birmingham News,* August 14, 1985, October 21, 1985, October 3, 1987, March 27, 1988.

38. Connerly, "'One Great City,'" 50.

39. *Birmingham News,* July 11, 1999.

40. Ibid., August 29, 1995, August 31, 1995. The city de-annexed and then re-annexed the land so that the company could enjoy a fifteen-year property-tax exemption.

41. *Birmingham News,* May 7, 1995.

42. *Birmingham Post-Herald,* June 25, 1991.

43. HOH Associates, Inc. *Oxmoor, Phase B, Master Plan Report* (Birmingham, 1990), 17.

44. HOH Associates, *Oxmoor,* 27.

45. *Birmingham News,* August 13, 1995, January 5, 1997; *Birmingham Post-Herald,* December 28, 1996.

46. HOH Associates, *Oxmoor,* 49; *Birmingham News,* May 7, 1995; Janice Johnson, Metropolitan Development Board, Birmingham, telephone interview by the author, January, 1997.

47. *Birmingham News,* April 14, 1997.

48. Franklin, *Back to Birmingham,* 330. Both of Arrington's successors—William Bell, who served as interim mayor after Arrington resigned in July 1999, and Bernard Kincaid, who was elected mayor in November 1999—are black. As of the 1999 election, the Birmingham City Council remained two-thirds black.

49. *Birmingham News,* January 8, 2000.

50. Ibid., April 2, 2000. In 2000, Reverend Porter retired from the pulpit of Sixth Avenue Baptist Church, having served it since 1962 (*Birmingham News,* July 23, 2000). In September 1999, a survey conducted by the *Birmingham News* identified Harris, who is white, as Birmingham's most powerful leader (*Birmingham News,* September 19, 1999).

51. *Birmingham News,* December 14, 2000, May 25, 2001.

52. *Birmingham Post-Herald,* June 10, 2000.

53. *Birmingham News,* April 2, 2000; *Birmingham Post-Herald,* June 13, 2000.

54. Housing Authority of the Birmingham District, *1999 Metropolitan Gardens HOPE VI Grant Application,* 1999. See www.netmart.com/habd/hope1.html, accessed August 19, 2000.

55. Birmingham *Post-Herald,* June 10, 2000.

56. Stone, *Regime Politics;* June Manning Thomas, *Redevelopment and Race: Planning a Finer City in Postwar Detroit* (Baltimore: Johns Hopkins University Press, 1997).

57. Although advocacy planning had been transformed into equity planning, in which planners focused on improving the equity outcomes of the city, it was still clear by the end of the twentieth century that planning's traditional focus on improving business efficiency remained the dominant paradigm in the field. See Norman Krumholz and John Forester, *Making Equity Planning Work* (Chicago: Planners Press, 1990).

58. On the racial impacts of exclusionary zoning, see Joe Feagin, "Arenas of

Conflict: Zoning and Land Use Reform in Critical Political-Economic Perspective,"
in *Zoning and the American Dream*, ed. Charles M. Haar and Jerold S. Kayden, 84–
89; Charles Haar, *Suburbs under Siege: Race, Space, and Audacious Judges* (Princeton: Princeton University Press, 1996), 8–9, 15–16. On the similarities between
HOPE VI and urban renewal, see Larry Keating, "Redeveloping Public Housing:
Relearning Urban Renewal's Immutable Lessons," *Journal of the American Planning Association* 66 (2000): 384–97.

    59. *Birmingham World*, May 26, 1953.

Index